HITLER AT HOME

HITLER AT HOME

DESPINA STRATIGAKOS

Yale University Press   New Haven and London

Published with assistance from the Graham Foundation for Advanced Studies in the Fine Arts.

yalebooks.com/art

Designed and set in Adobe Garamond type by Lindsey Voskowsky.
Printed in the United States of America by Thomson-Shore, Inc., Dexter, Michigan.

Library of Congress Control Number: 2014953548
ISBN 978-0-300-18381-8
A catalogue record for this book is available from the British Library.

This paper meets the requirements of ANSI/NISO Z 39.48–1992 (Permanence of Paper).

10 9 8 7 6 5 4 3 2 1

Jacket illustrations: (front) Eva Braun's room in the Berghof with framed Hitler portrait (detail of fig. 31); (back) detail from cover of Heinrich Hoffmann, *Hitler Away from It All* (*Hitler abseits vom Alltag*) (fig. 42).

To my mother,
who lived it

CONTENTS

ACKNOWLEDGMENTS

Chasing the remnants of Adolf Hitler's domesticity has taken me from Tucson, Arizona, to the Austrian Alps, and along the way I have been met with hospitality and gracious help. Dieter and Margit Umlauf welcomed me into their home and shared their family's history. Charles Turner repeatedly passed along valuable sources. Franz Andrelang gave me access to the sealed personal papers of Gerdy Troost, and Nino Nodia helped me to navigate the immense uncatalogued collection. Richard Reiter offered memories and answered questions about the Obersalzberg. Harald Freundorfer took me through Hitler's Munich apartment building. I thank them all for enabling and enriching my research.

My travels have been generously funded by the Gerda Henkel Foundation, the Graham Foundation for Advanced Studies in the Fine Arts, the German Academic Exchange Service (DAAD), and the Baldy Center for Law and Social Policy of the University at Buffalo. As a fellow at Rice University's Humanities Research Center, I found a home-away-from-home where I could engage with other scholars and undertake research with the thoughtful assistance of the center's staff. The Wolfsonian–FIU Museum in Miami Beach awarded me a fellowship to study its Third Reich collections, aided by its ever-helpful staff. I am deeply grateful to all these institutions for supporting my research. The University at Buffalo has been equally generous in granting me an extended leave that made the research and writing of this book possible, and I am thankful in particular to Robert Shibley, Omar Khan, and William McDonnell for making it happen. I am also indebted to Burcu Dogramaci of the Institute for Art History at the Ludwig Maximilian University of Munich for being the ideal academic host and partner in Germany.

In progressing from the initial idea to the finished manuscript, I have benefited from the sagacity and knowledge of many colleagues, who provided encouragement and feedback at critical junctures. I would like to thank Leora Auslander, Richard Bessel, Joy Calico, James van Dyke, Sean Franzel, Dianne Harris, Hilde Heynen, Keith Holz, Edina Meyer-Maril, Barbara

Miller Lane, Barbara Penner, Leslie Topp, and Rebecca Zorach. David Wellbery's DAAD Interdisciplinary Summer Seminar in German Studies at the University of Chicago inspired me to rethink the role of narrative in my project. At Rice University, I thank in particular Peter Caldwell, Christian Emden, Caroline Levander (then-director of the Humanities Research Center), Uwe Steiner, Sarah Whiting, and Lora Wildenthal. In Munich, Christian Fuhrmeister and Iris Lauterbach of the Central Institute for Art History and Michaela Rammert-Götz of the United Workshops Archive kindly shared their expertise and steered me toward new sources.

On the final leg of revisions and consolidation, help came in doubles. Two expert readers strengthened the manuscript with their insights and immense learning: Karen Fiss of the California College of the Arts and Paul Jaskot of DePaul University. I have been fortunate to work with two wonderful editors: Michelle Komie, whose faith and enthusiasm brought the project to Yale University Press, and Katherine Boller, whose skill and understanding made for smooth sailing to the end. I am also grateful for the keen eyes of Martina Kammer and Laura Hensley, who, from their respective German- and English-language standpoints, identified and subdued the occasional rogue word. Heidi Downey and Mary Mayer deftly guided this book through the production process, and the Graham Foundation once again lent its support with a publication grant.

And, finally, what would a journey be without postcards and shared memories? To my family and friends for keeping the mail, love, and laughter flowing—many times, over and over, thank you.

INTRODUCTION

The Power of Home

As Allied troops moved into Bavaria at the end of World War II in
Europe, soldiers and journalists sought out the places where Adolf Hitler
had lived in an attempt to understand the man who had plagued and ter-
rorized humanity. U.S. Sergeant Harry Sions, writing for *Yank* magazine,
peered into Hitler's bathroom cabinet at the Berghof, the dictator's mountain home, and pondered the bottles of castor oil and mouthwash he found
there. *Vogue* correspondent Lee Miller, staying at Hitler's Munich apartment, rummaged through his closets and noted the monogrammed linen
and silver.[1]

Our domestic spaces and possessions, we believe, reveal our inner
selves, and the deeper the closet or cabinet, the greater the secrets. Hitler's
homes had not only the conventional nooks and crannies but also whole
underground bunkers and passageways, and reporters (and subsequently
tourists) searched them thoroughly for clues. There were rumors of torture
chambers as well as overflowing treasuries, and some went in search more
for buried riches than for hidden truths. But journalists and sightseers were
also drawn to those spaces precisely because Hitler's domesticity had been
so highly visible during the Third Reich. Especially in his mountain home,
where he had often been photographed, Hitler's "private" life had been

carefully orchestrated for public consumption, with the images and stories broadly distributed at home and abroad. Millions of readers felt that they knew "Hitler the man" through this domestic performance, and when Allied soldiers and reporters arrived in Germany, they were drawn to the places where his ghost seemed to linger.

This book follows in the footsteps of these domestic explorers but seeks a different sort of understanding. The first major postwar biography of Hitler, published by Alan Bullock in 1952, dismissed the meaningfulness of the Führer's private life as "meager and uninteresting at the best of times."[2] A wholly different attitude characterized the tell-all books that emerged in subsequent decades, which scoured Hitler's body, family past, and relationships to men and women for anomalies on a personal scale that could somehow explain a cosmic catastrophe. *Hitler at Home* acknowledges the importance of the private realm without seeking to be a biography told through architecture. Instead, I am interested in how Hitler chose to present his domestic self to the public, and in the designers, photographers, and journalists who constructed and conveyed the image to German- and English-language audiences, who were all too eager to consume it.

By the mid-1930s, it was all but impossible to avoid images and stories about the domestic Hitler. The topic was not only covered by the German media with great—indeed, almost obsessive—zeal, but it was also embraced by an English-language press serving a global audience, from London to Sydney, Toronto to Phoenix, and Bombay to Shanghai. In Germany, a market quickly emerged for popular consumer goods bearing images of the Führer's home or of its owner at leisure on the Obersalzberg. One could decorate with a Hitler house–themed porcelain plate or embroidered throw pillow, save pennies in a replica coin bank, play with a toy model, send a postcard showing Hitler feeding deer on his terrace, or buy one of the many photographic albums that documented his life at home, from the dictator entertaining children to hiking with his dog. For a time, Hitler's mountain retreat was arguably the most famous house in the world.

This vast production of images of Hitler at home proved to be enormously seductive and continues to exert its power even today. Its appeal has largely gone unchecked by historians, who have insufficiently exposed and deconstructed the propaganda surrounding Hitler's domesticity. Apart from a small body of articles, books, and catalogues, literature about Hitler's homes tends to be uncritical and, in some cases, reproduces the ideological "charm" of Third Reich publications. Remarkably, given how much has been written about Hitler, the significance of his domestic spaces in the visual imagination of National Socialism has remained underexplored terrain.[3]

Compared to their high visibility during the Third Reich, Hitler's domestic spaces rarely appear in political or architectural histories of the period. Those who have written about the many diplomatic meetings that occurred in these homes have had little to say about the settings, despite Hitler's desire to use them as stage sets to perform his identity as a statesman and man of culture. Studies of the Obersalzberg as an ideological and political center of National Socialism have been more attentive to its structures, but architectural historians themselves have contributed little to this literature. In general, scholars of architecture and fascist aesthetics have focused on monumental building projects and mass spectacle, overlooking the domestic and minute. And yet one could argue that the aesthetics of the mass spectacle at the Nuremberg Rally Grounds or of the gigantic in the New Chancellery, both designed by Albert Speer and associated with the public Führer, correlate with the singular and detailed assemblage of Hitler's private domestic spaces, a choreography of objects and space that enacts the private man. The Hitler who commanded thousands and moved mountains of stone induced awe; the Hitler at home with his dogs and tea inspired empathy. Both images were integral to the Führer's seductive power, and each had its architectural manifestation. Reading the official and monumental together with the domestic and minute allows us to grasp their intended and productive interplay in the representation of the Führer as both beyond and yet of the people.

Hitler himself cared deeply about the production of his domestic spaces, discussing them at length with his interior designer, Gerdy Troost. After the war, she recalled the enthusiastic interest he had shown in even the smallest detail. In his memoirs, Speer admitted that Hitler had devoted a level of personal attention to the design of the Berghof that was unequaled by any of his other building projects.[4] It was Hitler's favorite place to be—about a third of his time in office was spent on the Obersalzberg. In July 1944, Joseph Goebbels confided to his diary that he was relieved that the Führer had decided to transfer his military headquarters from his mountain home to the Wolf's Lair on the eastern front. While Hitler had spent months planning battle strategies from his living room, the Allied armies had pushed ever closer to Germany's borders.[5]

Perhaps if Speer had been involved, historians might have paid more attention to Hitler's domestic spaces. Women architects and designers have only recently begun to receive their due in architectural history books, and little is known about their involvement in the Third Reich. Gerdy Troost has likewise slipped beneath the historian's radar, despite the fact that she was once the tastemaker of choice for Hitler and other prominent National Socialists. This book hopes to raise awareness of a neglected but powerful female figure in the Third Reich, who deserves far greater scholarly attention than she has received. Her work also suggests that we need to consider more generally the role of interior design in the self-representation of the Nazi regime, to which many of its architects, including Speer, eagerly contributed.

Ultimately, the reasons for the neglect of the dictator's homes and their creators may have more to do with scholars having all too readily accepted the propaganda of the Third Reich: namely, that Hitler's domestic spaces existed outside the world of politics and ideology. I believe, to the contrary, that they were profoundly ideological spaces, which demonstrably lay at the heart of some of the most successful propaganda about Hitler produced by his regime. Representations of Hitler's home life played a critical role in the early 1930s, when his public image as a screaming reactionary needed to be softened. The attention and care lavished on Hitler's domesticity by his propagandists also transformed a potential liability—the perceived oddity of a stateless man living without deep connections to family, place, or lovers—into an asset by creating a domestic milieu that grounded and normalized him. Hitler's domestic spaces struck just the right balance with the public of heterosexual masculinity, refined but not ostentatious taste, and German roots. Thus, his publicists and designers killed two birds with one stone, making Hitler seem both warmer and less queer. And all of this was carefully crafted and communicated to German and foreign audiences through a media eager to sell the story and images of the domestic bachelor.

The book is divided into two sections. The first half addresses the physical design and construction of Hitler's three residences: the Old Chancellery in Berlin, his Munich apartment at 16 Prince Regent Square, and his mountain home on the Obersalzberg. Hitler occupied all three places throughout the period of the Third Reich, although he owned only the latter two. Chapter 1 examines Hitler's transition from a prolonged period of marginal domesticity to the setting up of his first independent households in the late 1920s, as he approached his fortieth birthday, and the reasons for his lifestyle change. When Hitler became chancellor in 1933, he insisted on remodeling the official residence before he moved in, and Chapter 2 investigates how this was used to frame a new narrative about a leader with the ability to put his house in order. Having been bitten by the home renovation bug, Hitler then turned to reinventing his private residences. Chapters 3 and 4 chronicle the wholesale renovations of his Munich apartment in 1935 and, as soon as it was completed, the massive expansion of Haus Wachenfeld into the Berghof in 1935–36 by the architect Alois Degano. These projects demonstrate how Hitler used domestic architectural makeovers in the mid-1930s to shed any vestiges of his image as rabble-rouser in order to emphasize his new status as statesman and diplomat. The associated high costs reveal how much Hitler was willing to invest to get it right and also contradict his regime's propaganda, which continued to present the German leader as a simple man unspoiled by fame and power. While Hitler's new domestic facades outwardly proclaimed the leader's maturation and confidence, a cache of unbuilt drawings of the Berghof exposes Hitler's struggle with how to position his domestic self in relation to his public identity. Chapter 4 also briefly considers Eva Braun's photographs of the Berghof and what they suggest about her role as both mistress of the house and its privileged prisoner. Gerdy Troost was central to all three design projects, and Chapter 5 is devoted to her life and work, drawing on her personal papers at the Bavarian State Library in Munich, an astonishingly rich collection that opens officially to scholars in 2019.

The second half of the book explores propaganda about Hitler's homes and their reception, focusing on his Munich and Obersalzberg residences. Chapter 6 begins with the "discovery" of the "private Hitler" by Nazi publicists in 1932 in the midst of a crucial election battle. Chapters 7 and 8, respectively, survey the media's coverage in Germany and abroad of Hitler's homes. In Germany, Hitler's mountain retreat became a site of pilgrimage, and Chapter 7 looks at the hold it exerted on the National Socialist imagination through written accounts and the photography of Heinrich Hoffmann. While one can understand the appeal of journalistic accounts of Hitler at home for German audiences in the 1930s, it is surprising to discover a similar fascination reflected in the pages of foreign newspapers and magazines. Chapter 8 investigates the whitewashing of Hitler's reputation for violence in the English-language press through its depictions of the domestic bachelor as the kind of gentle, cultured man one would be blessed to have as a neighbor. Views of the house-proud Hitler changed from admiration to ridicule when England, and later the United States, entered the war, and Chapter 9 traces the turn in the English-language press's representation of the domestic Hitler from a gentleman-artist to a megalomaniacal house-painter and effeminate dilettante. The close of World War II marked both an ending and a new beginning for Hitler's homes. Chapter 10 chronicles the bombing of the Obersalzberg, the arrival in Bavaria of Allied troops and journalists and their inspections of the Führer's apartment and mountain retreat, and the extensive looting that took place by neighbors and soldiers. Chapter 11 brings the histories of these two residences into the present and explores the headaches that they have created for Bavarian authorities. On the Obersalzberg and in Munich, different strategies have been employed to compel people to stay away from these sites and to encourage forgetting. Yet decades after their owner died in an underground Berlin bunker, these homes continue to exert an unsettling magnetism. Moreover, fragments of Hitler's domestic surroundings—ranging from silverware to bathroom tiles—continue to circulate and fetch astonishingly high prices among collectors of Third Reich memorabilia. Today, bits and pieces of the Führer's domesticity are scattered on bookshelves and coffee tables across the globe, further contributing to the curiously long half-life of this history. The book ends by considering the problem such "relics" create for museum curators, who find them among their own collections, as well as the reluctance of the press in the United States and England to confront its own role in having disarmed its readers in the 1930s with depictions of Hitler at home.

Even as I have set out to analyze and deconstruct the production and power of Hitler's domestic spaces, I remain ever aware of their seductive danger. Today, the vast industry of house decorating magazines and home renovation television shows thrives on the same human attraction to images of handsome interiors, happy children, well-groomed dogs, and stunning landscapes that Hitler's publicists cannily employed to make the Führer seem likable and approachable. When these homes belong to mass-media celebrities—a phenomenon that Hitler's regime helped to forge using new mass communication technologies and marketing techniques—the appeal is even greater. The Nazis knowingly manipulated the interest in Hitler's private life to create a disconnect between the man on the patio feeding deer and the force behind the gas chambers. As Susan Sontag and others have argued, seduction and terror went hand in hand during the Nazi regime.[6] By remaining attentive to broader contexts, both within Germany and abroad, I hope to make clear the political intentions behind the making of Hitler's domestic image and reveal the horrors clinging to the underside of its coziness.

Victims of Hitler's violence still feel keenly the danger of such allures. Over the years, I have spoken about my project with those who bear these personal scars, and I am grateful to all of them for their advice and wisdom. I owe the greatest debt, however, to my mother, who experienced Nazi brutality as a child in occupied Kefalonia and who will never be free of it. When I told her about my plans for this book, she remained silent for a while and then asked me for one thing: "Please do not make Hitler look good." I have kept those words in mind throughout.

PART I

1   HITLER SETS UP HOUSE

A Bachelor's Domestic Turn after 1928

The headline stretched across the front page of the *Regensburger Echo* in inch-high letters: "Suicide in Hitler's Apartment." The story, carried in newspapers across Germany, concerned the death of Adolf Hitler's twenty-three-year-old niece, Geli Raubal, on September 18, 1931. She had been found dead, apparently of a self-inflicted gunshot wound, in the Munich apartment she shared with her bachelor uncle, then the leader of the nation's second-largest political party. For Hitler, the private tragedy threatened to damage him publicly because it struck at a vulnerable spot: his unconventional lifestyle.

In light of the personality cult that later developed around Hitler and that seemed to grip the German nation in a collective state of delusion, many historians have taken for granted that his decision to remain single was an effective strategy for winning female votes. Countless media images from the Third Reich document Hitler's appeal to women as the nation's most eligible bachelor; we see ecstatic throngs of women waving to a smiling Führer or trying to touch his hand. But before he rose to power and silenced his detractors, the advantage of being a middle-aged, single man aspiring to become chancellor was by no means obvious. Voters then, as now, preferred national leaders with outwardly stable personal lives, which for most meant traditional marriage and children.

Following the devastating defeat of the National Socialists in the May 20, 1928, Reichstag election, when they obtained a mere 2.6 percent of the vote, the party set out to broaden its appeal, particularly to the middle classes, by appearing to be more mainstream in both its message and leadership. Indeed, it was in this period that Hitler remodeled his public persona from radical firebrand to bourgeois politician.[1] Among other changes, he appeared to settle down domestically after two decades of transient living. After leaving Linz in 1908, following his mother's death, Hitler had occupied shabbily furnished rooms, slept on park benches, claimed a bed in a men's hostel, and shared army barracks. On May 1, 1920, he sublet a small room (and was allowed the use of a large foyer) from a couple in their thirties, Maria and Ernst Reichert, living at 41 Thiersch Street in Munich, where he remained until 1929, except for a year's absence while interned following the Beer Hall Putsch of November 1923.[2] It was a "poorish" street, the address of an ex-soldier whose army pay had run out.[3] In his memoirs, Ernst Hanfstaengl, who served as Hitler's foreign press chief, suggested that Hitler kept his small room for so long for political reasons:

> He lived there like a down-at-heels clerk. He had one room and the use of a quite large entrance-hall as a sub-tenant of a woman named Reichert. It was all modest in the extreme and he remained there for years, although it became part of an act to show how he identified himself with the workers and have-nots of this world. The room itself was tiny. I doubt if it was nine feet wide. The bed was too wide for its corner and the head of it projected over the single narrow window. The floor was covered with cheap, worn linoleum with a couple of threadbare rugs, and on the wall opposite the bed there was a makeshift bookshelf, apart from a chair and rough table the only other piece of furniture in the room.[4]

Hitler's tax return for 1925, in which he claimed that his only property was a desk and two bookcases along with the books, largely matches Hanfstaengl's description.[5]

On October 15, 1928, Hitler rented a chalet on the Obersalzberg and thereby established his first independent household at the age of thirty-nine (plate 1).[6] He had been coming to this picturesque Alpine retreat since April 1923, when he had visited Dietrich Eckart, an aggressively anti-Semitic writer and early founder of the National Socialist movement, who was then hiding from the authorities at a small Obersalzberg inn after having slandered the German president, Friedrich Ebert, as a tool of world Jewry. (Party legend had it that it was on this trip that plans for the anticipated November Revolution, which would land Hitler in Landsberg Prison, were sealed.) Hitler later claimed to have "fallen in love with the landscape," although the support among local inhabitants for National Socialism (Eckart felt well protected there) also impressed him. The Berchtesgaden group of the National Socialist German Workers' Party (NSDAP) had been founded on February 14, 1922, and events featuring anti-Semitic speakers (including, in the summer of 1923, Hitler) were well attended. Over the years, Hitler stayed at various local hotels. In 1925, following his release from prison, a supporter lent him a log cabin on the Obersalzberg, where he worked on the second volume of his political autobiography, *Mein Kampf*.[7] (After 1933, the cabin was named the Kampfhäusl, or Battle Hut, and became a National Socialist pilgrimage site.) Perhaps the experience awakened a desire for his own home on the mountain; if so, it would be a few more years before he would act on it.

Reminiscing about his early days on the Obersalzberg while at his military headquarters on the eastern front in 1942, Hitler recounted how in 1928, he had learned that a chalet was for rent on the northern slope of the mountain. The vacation home had been constructed in 1916–17 by Otto Winter, a leather goods manufacturer from Buxtehude (near Hamburg), who had given it his wife's maiden name, Wachenfeld. The small, two-story structure had been built in the traditional style of upper Bavarian farmhouses. Hitler recalled that the house was made of poor materials, but had the advantage of a shady location and a spectacular view. From his front balcony, he could see Salzburg in his native Austria as well as the Untersberg, a mountain swathed in medieval legends. Winter's widow, Margarete Winter-Wachenfeld, a National Socialist Party member, rented the house to Hitler's older half-sister, Angela Raubal. Hitler had persuaded his sister to leave Vienna and resettle with her youngest daughter, Friedl, on the Obersalzberg to run his household. This is somewhat surprising, given that the siblings had been estranged for over a decade after Hitler had left Linz. In the 1920s, however, he renewed contact, and, presumably, the relationship deepened. Raubal certainly had ample domestic skills: beyond raising three children and her younger half-sister, Paula, on her own after she was widowed, she was also then managing a kosher kitchen for Jewish students in Vienna.[8] Whether motivated by sentimental or strategic reasons, Hitler's decision to live with his sister helped to soften his image. He acquired a ready-made family, and, in later years, Raubal served as the public female face of his home life.

Hitler's domestic turn after 1928 coincided with a new source of personal income: sales of *Mein Kampf,* the first volume of which was published in the summer of 1925, followed by the second in 1926 (both volumes would eventually be combined into a single book). While the book would only become a best seller after 1933, Hitler's tax statements from 1925 onward indicate considerable royalties. Indeed, he may have rented Haus Wachenfeld under his sister's name in order to avoid paying taxes on a second residence. And yet despite the sales revenue from his book, on his tax returns, Hitler denied being financially solvent, claiming indebtedness and high professional expenses, which the Munich Finance Office disputed. He was often in arrears on his taxes, either out of neglect or an inability to pay. After Hitler became chancellor, royalties from *Mein Kampf* made him a millionaire, and by 1934 he owed an astonishing 405,494 Reichsmarks in overdue tax payments—the equivalent of millions of dollars today. Hitler resolved the problem later that year by making himself exempt from paying taxes altogether.[9]

But having more money did not automatically open every door for Hitler. When, in September 1929, he sought to rent a grand apartment at 16 Prince Regent Square in the Bogenhausen district of Munich, Hugo Bruckmann acted as his legal representative in securing approval of the lease from the Municipal Housing Authority. Although Hitler in the 1920s did have a considerable following in Munich, where the National Socialist movement had begun and which he would later designate its capital, party members made up less than 1 percent of the city's population (and only 0.64 percent in Bogenhausen) before 1930. Moreover, while their social backgrounds were diverse, the National Socialists came primarily from the lower-middle and working classes, groups without great economic or political pull.[10]

Bruckmann, by contrast, was one of the city's social and cultural heavyweights, living in a palatial mansion on Caroline Square, an elegant neoclassical space designed in 1809 by Karl von Fischer. He managed the art publishing firm F. Bruckmann, founded by his father, who had established its reputation by recruiting to his list of authors some of the leading German architects and artists of the nineteenth century, including Gottfried Semper and Wilhelm von Kaulbach. In 1899, seeking to give voice to the formative minds of his own generation, Hugo Bruckmann published *The Foundations of the Nineteenth Century (Die Grundlagen des neunzehnten Jahrhunderts)*, a sweeping anti-Semitic discourse on Aryan culture by Houston Stewart Chamberlain that became an ideological bible for the Nazis. Chamberlain was an honored guest in the celebrated literary salon hosted by Bruckmann's wife, Elsa, born Princess Cantacuzène of Romania. In the early 1920s, both Bruckmanns enthusiastically embraced Hitler's cause, and it was at their home that he was introduced to Munich's cultural luminaries, including the architect Paul Troost, from whom he would commission National Socialism's first monumental buildings. Through the Bruckmanns, Hitler thus gained access to influential new social circles, and when he sought entry into one of the city's most prestigious neighborhoods, he again employed the publisher's social capital. Whereas Bruckmann counted among Munich's social elite, Hitler's associates reminded some observers of its criminal bottom. An international story that ran on September 12, 1929, just as Hitler submitted his lease for approval, linked his name with a ring of "bomb-throwers" who had been terrorizing northern German towns.[11] Bruckmann's support undoubtedly would have had a reassuring effect. Nonetheless, other tenants in the building, who included a lawyer, factory director's widow, and senior government official, must have eyed the newcomer with some trepidation.[12]

On October 1, 1929, Hitler took possession of the new apartment, which occupied the entire third floor of the imposing five-story building designed by the Munich architect Franz Popp in 1907–8. The apartment measured about 4,300 square feet and consisted of a spacious entry hall, nine rooms, two maid's chambers, two bathrooms, and a kitchen (figs. 1, 2). It was reached by climbing an elegant staircase or using an elevator; near the kitchen, a second stairwell led to the basement, where a laundry was located, and to the courtyard in the back. The layout of the rooms was divided into two connected wings that followed the street facades of the corner building. Despite Hitler's protestations to the tax authorities, he was able to afford, either through his own income or gifts, the considerable annual rent of 4,176 Reichsmarks, which was about double the annual salary of a skilled metalworker.[13] To these expenses must be added the cost of equipping the household and the staff to run it. Unlike Haus Wachenfeld, which came furnished, the Prince Regent Square apartment was rented empty. Hitler's few pieces of furniture hardly sufficed to fill its generous spaces, and so he turned to Elsa Bruckmann to make it livable. She willingly took on the task, for the Bruckmanns shared a passion for domestic design. In 1897, Hugo Bruckmann and the art critic Julius Meier-Graefe had founded a new

HITLER SETS UP HOUSE   15

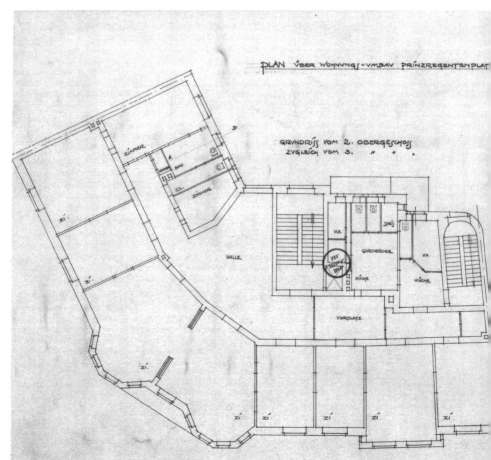

PLAN ÜBER WOHNUNGS-UMBAU PRINZREGENTENPLATZ

GRUNDRISS VOM 2. OBERGESCHOSS
ZUGLEICH VOM 3. " " .

ZIMMER

BAD

CL.

ZIMMER

ZI.

ZI.

HALLE

ZI.

ZI.

ZI. ZI. ZI. ZI. ZI.

KA

SPEIS

GARDEROBE

KA

KÜCHE

KÜCHE

VORPLATZ

Fig. 1. Photograph of 16 Prince Regent Square in Munich, designed 1907–8 by Franz Popp, as it appears today. Hitler's apartment occupied the third story.

Fig. 2. Floor plan of Hitler's Munich apartment at 16 Prince Regent Square. The plan is dated January 1935, shortly before the Atelier Troost began its renovation. To the right is a cross section of the building as well as a site plan, indicating the corner location straddling Prince Regent Square and Grillparzer Street.

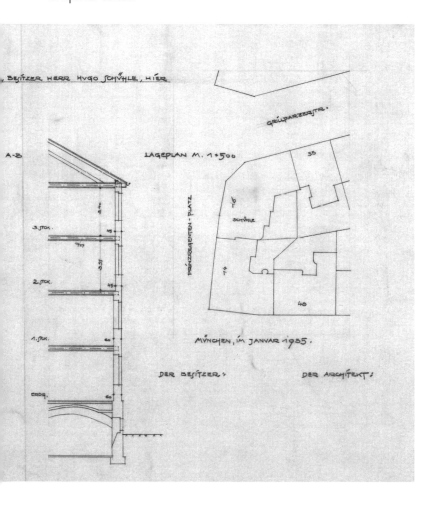

periodical, *Dekorative Kunst* (Decorative Art), devoted to the concept of aesthetic environments that integrated art and life. The Bruckmanns' own home captured this spirit, with its gracious, tall rooms overflowing with paintings, furniture, sculpture, vases, and books, providing an ideal setting for salon discussions about art and literature. In an essay from the 1930s, Elsa Bruckmann wrote that their home had been a revelation to Hitler the first time he had seen it.[14]

Among the furniture purchased by Elsa Bruckmann for Hitler's apartment were items by the Jewish-owned Royal Bavarian Furniture Factory, M. Ballin. The prestigious Munich firm, founded by cabinetmaker Moritz Ballin in the nineteenth century, received commissions from European royal houses and also furnished luxury hotels, villas, businesses, and ocean liners. In the twentieth century, the firm worked with artists, such as Bruno Paul and Paul Troost, who embraced neoclassical styles, which Hitler also favored. Nonetheless, Hitler's patronage of a Jewish firm is inconsistent with the National Socialist stance on boycotting Jewish businesses. It may be explained by the role that Bella Ballin, the wife of the firm's owner and a former nurse, had played in saving Hermann Göring's life after he had been shot by police near the couple's home on November 9, 1923, during the Beer Hall Putsch. Nonetheless, after 1933, restrictions on Jewish businesses drove away customers and, after its bank froze its credit, the firm was appropriated and thus "Aryanized." On November 10, 1938, during Crystal Night, Robert Ballin and his brothers were imprisoned in a concentration camp, as were all adult Jewish men in Germany. Göring's intervention secured their prompt release from Dachau and, in 1942, as the family faced deportation to the death camps, their emigration visas.[15] In recent years, the Ballin furniture created for Hitler has garnered high prices at auctions of Nazi memorabilia.[16]

While the move to a luxury apartment in Bogenhausen signaled Hitler's social respectability to the city's better classes, it also entailed political risk. Even after the National Socialist Party abandoned its electoral focus on working-class voters in 1928, it continued to style Hitler as the people's leader. But two upscale residential moves in rapid succession—to an Alpine resort frequented by prominent and wealthy Germans and to an affluent area of Munich—challenged that image. Indeed, concern about alienating the working classes may have been another reason why Hitler's sister signed the contract for Haus Wachenfeld. When Hitler's move to Prince Regent Square became known, the left-liberal newspaper *Berliner*

Volkszeitung (Berlin People's Paper) was quick to expose what it saw as his hypocrisy. It sarcastically reported that in order to better serve the will of the people, Hitler had taken a stately apartment in "Munich's most feudal neighborhood." His household, it noted, included a valet and two dogs of the same breed, the latter in the manner of Otto von Bismarck, implying that Hitler was now styling himself after the old aristocracy. The *New York Times* picked up the story, suggesting that Hitler's lavish new lifestyle disclosed "material as well as moral" support for "the would-be German Fascisti" among Germany's wealthy industrialists.[17]

Two years later, it was not Hitler's finances but rather the life he led within the apartment that came under press scrutiny when his half-niece Geli Raubal, the eldest daughter of his sister Angela, was found dead of a gunshot wound. The murky circumstances of the young woman's suicide fed speculation that perversity lay beneath the thin veneer of bourgcois respectability with which Hitler had clad himself in his Bogenhausen home. When police were summoned to the apartment on the morning of September 19, 1931, Raubal had already been dead for many hours, and the staff's description of what had happened seemed suspiciously rehearsed. Hitler himself was not present, having spent the night away on a campaign trip. The staff reported that after he had left the previous afternoon, Raubal had seemed agitated and had locked herself in her bedroom. When she did not emerge the following morning or respond to a knock at her door, the staff forced their way in and found her face-down on the floor, dead of a bullet to the chest. The pistol, which belonged to her uncle, lay beside her. There was no suicide note; on her desk was a half-completed letter to a friend in Vienna about an upcoming visit. The staff claimed to have been at a loss to explain the young woman's motive. Nazi publicists later issued a statement that Raubal, who aspired to be a singer, had taken her own life because of anxiety over an upcoming performance, which would have been her first in public.[18] Few journalists believed the official version.

Within days, the story had appeared in newspapers across Germany, and Hitler feared it would damage him politically.[19] Several accounts questioned the nature of the relationship between the twenty-three-year-old girl and her forty-two-year-old uncle. The *Regensburger Echo,* a left-liberal weekly, asserted that it had been a long time since anyone had believed it to be merely one of kinship. Hitler had paraded his beautiful niece in public, taking her to the theater and political events, and even the most servile Nazis, the article claimed, had laughed behind the back of the over-solicitous uncle. But as Hitler's political star ascended, he again and again postponed legitimizing his relationship with the young woman who hoped to become his wife. She found herself reduced to the role of nurse-maid, caring for him after his increasingly common nervous breakdowns. Exhausted by the demands made upon her and disappointed by her feckless uncle, the young woman took her own life.[20] The newspaper thus managed to create a narrative around the suicide that made Hitler look ridiculous, immoral, and weak all at once.

The *Regensburger Echo* reported, as did other newspapers, that Raubal had lived in an apartment adjacent to that of Hitler, although on the same floor. This information seems to have been given to the press to obfuscate the fact that niece and uncle lived in the same dwelling. When Raubal first moved into Hitler's apartment in the fall of 1929, he had her register as a subtenant of Ernst and Maria Reichert, his former landlords from Thiersch Street. They had moved with him to the new apartment, where Maria Reichert served as a housekeeper. This arrangement was undoubtedly intended to make it appear as if the then–twenty-one-year-old was not sharing domestic space with her bachelor uncle. And, indeed, few in the general public knew that Hitler's niece lived with him.[21]

The Social Democratic *Münchener Post* (Munich Post), a newspaper that relentlessly opposed the Nazis before their rise to power, sought to expose the lie of Hitler's domestic respectability. In an article published on September 21 under the headline "A Mysterious Affair: Suicide of Hitler's Niece," it reported that its sources had revealed that Hitler and his niece had "had yet another heated argument" before he left the apartment on Prince Regent Square. The reason was that "the fun-loving, twenty-three-year-old Geli, a music student, wanted to go to Vienna. She wanted to get engaged. Hitler was firmly against it." The paper also reported disturbing details about the body: the nose bone had been shattered, and the corpse bore serious injuries. It thereby implied that Geli had been beaten or even murdered by her jealous uncle, forcing the Munich police department to reopen its investigation of the death.[22]

Hitler moved quickly to contain the damage; his lawyer threatened a libel action if the newspaper did not print a retraction. The *Münchener Post* was thus compelled to publish a statement by Hitler denying the charges, which appeared in the next day's edition. It was not true, he wrote, that he had had a heated argument with his niece. It was not true that he was firmly against his niece going to Vienna. It was not true that she intended to become engaged or that he had anything against an engagement. And so the text continued, rebutting point-by-point the newspaper's allegations.[23]

Ten days later, the anti-fascist Berlin newspaper *Die Fanfare* (The Clarion) repeated the claim of sexual violence. Under the headline "Hitler's Lover Commits Suicide: Bachelors and Homosexuals as Nazi Leaders," it printed a drawing of an overweight SA Stormtrooper distinctly resembling SA chief Ernst Röhm wielding a whip and standing over a prone woman on the ground, her arms protecting her head. The article, drawing on a story in the Berlin *Neue Montagszeitung* (New Monday Gazette), maintained that it was known in Nazi Party circles that Geli Raubal had long been Hitler's lover, and that her suicide had been provoked by disappointment and disgust: "Hitler's private life takes forms that the young woman obviously could not bear." This euphemistic language hinted at the darkest sexual perversities. The article then dropped a second bombshell: Raubal was not Hitler's first female victim. In 1928, the newspaper reported, a young woman in Berchtesgaden had also killed herself because of Hitler. The article was wrong about the actual suicide. Mimi Reiter, unnamed in the article, had attempted to hang herself after being romanced by Hitler, an affair that had begun when she was just sixteen years old. *Fanfare* thus implied that Hitler's female lovers experienced something so awful and demeaning that they were driven to kill themselves. The article then broadened the picture of deviancy among the Nazi leadership by reminding readers of Röhm's homosexuality, which the *Münchener Post* had exposed the previous summer. How much value, it asked, did Hitler's words on the sanctity of the family carry when the party was led by men who preferred the company of boys in the Hitler Youth or drove women to suicide? Rather than protect German families, high-ranking Nazi bachelors and homosexuals, the article concluded, would prey upon them.[24]

As Ron Rosenbaum has written in his investigation of Raubal's suicide, "what's remarkable is how widespread, how public, and how ugly and damning the publicity about Geli Raubal's death was—and not just in Munich. It was as if her death suddenly unleashed or legitimized the expression of the unspoken, the publication of the most vile and virulent whispers about Hitler, embodying the belief, even the wish, by his opponents that he was as much a monster of perversion privately as he was in his politics—a belief, a wish that had already spread beyond the borders of Germany."[25] According to Hans Frank, then the Nazi Party's lawyer, Hitler agonized over the "terrible filth" being spread about him and swore he would not forget.[26] It was

Fig. 3. Cover of Heinrich Hoffmann's *The Hitler Nobody Knows* (*Hitler wie ihn keiner kennt*) (Berlin: Zeitgeschichte, 1932).

HITLER SETS UP HOUSE

a promise that he would keep after he came to power in 1933, when his SA thugs attacked the newspapers and writers who had been involved.[27] More immediately, in the wake of the scandal and spreading rumors, the Nazis, who themselves had never hesitated to attack the private lives of their opponents, realized that they needed to better control the story of Hitler's domesticity.

Six months after Raubal's death, in March 1932, Hitler's photographer and publicist Heinrich Hoffmann published a book, *The Hitler Nobody Knows* (*Hitler wie ihn keiner kennt*), which revealed and celebrated the private man (fig. 3). It marked the beginning of a profound transformation—realized through images, text, and architecture—that shifted Hitler's domestic space from a site of rumored sexual and moral perversity to the anchor, in the public's view, of his humanity and honor. Whereas journalists had once used the bloodshed in Hitler's private life to explain the violence of his politics, in the hands of National Socialist publicists, Hitler's home life became a mirror of their leader's innermost civility, a reflection of a gentle private man that smoothed away the vicious edges of his public rhetoric and actions. It was one of the most remarkable and effective makeovers of his political career. And yet, when one looks at the effort involved in achieving this new domestic image and in maintaining it over the years, it also becomes clear that the process was never entirely finished and that the bachelor Hitler remained vulnerable to suspicions about his unconventional domestic life, which had erupted so publicly after Raubal's death.

After spending much of his adult life seemingly oblivious to his domestic surroundings, Hitler developed in the 1930s an acute sensitivity to the architectural spaces of his homes and to how these reflected upon his identity. While our focus will be on his private residences, the story of this transformation must begin with the Old Chancellery, where he first worked closely with the woman who would become his faithful interior decorator, Gerdy Troost. For when Hitler was appointed chancellor on January 30, 1933, he refused to move into the official residence at 77 Wilhelm Street in Berlin. He took a look around the former eighteenth-century palace and decided it was too shabby for the Führer. Over the course of its renovation in 1934, as the Nazis strangled the democracy out of Germany, Hitler's interior world at the Chancellery grew ever more polished and refined, a denial—in the form of delicate porcelain vases and soft Persian rugs—of the brutality beyond its doors.

2   HOW THE CHANCELLOR LIVES

A New Regime for an Old Palace

In 1939, as Adolf Hitler contemplated the monumental New Chancellery built by Albert Speer, his mind returned to the Old Chancellery that had been placed at his disposal after he became chancellor, and he shuddered at the horror of it. The two-hundred-year-old former palace at 77 Wilhelm Street, located in the heart of Berlin's government district, had undergone numerous "tasteless" renovations, according to Hitler, since it had become, following German unification in 1871, the chancellor's official residence. So-called improvements begun at the end of the nineteenth century, he noted, "steadily disfigured the building with an overwrought grandeur that sought to conceal with its plaster pomposities the lack of honest material and proper proportions." Even the historic hall in which Otto von Bismarck, Germany's first chancellor, had hosted the 1878 Congress of Berlin, a summit of major European powers, had not escaped such "embellishments," which included "awful wall lamps and a gigantic brass chandelier." Hitler also disparaged the poor quality of the items loaned from the Prussian State Art Collections and the "artistically worthless" portraits of the former chancellors that adorned the walls, with the exception of a portrait of Bismarck by Franz von Lenbach.[1]

But it was after the German Revolution of 1918, Hitler claimed, that the old palace truly fell apart. By the time the residence was his to occupy, "not only had whole sections of the roof timbers rotted through, but the floors were also completely dilapidated. In the Congress Hall, where diplomatic receptions ought to have taken place, police limited the number of people allowed in the room to sixty at a time in order to minimize the danger of a collapse." During downpours, Hitler continued, the water penetrated the building from above and below, making it both damp and disgustingly unhygienic. Hitler described how water "gushed" from the street into the ground-floor rooms, where it combined with other "oozing" sources, including the toilets. The smell that filled the house, he recalled, was unbearable.[2]

Hitler laid the blame for this stinking state of affairs on the Weimar Republic's turbulent democracy: "Since my predecessors in general could count upon a term of office of only three to five months, they saw no reason to remove the filth of those who had occupied the house before them nor to see to it that those who came after would have better conditions than they themselves. They had no prestige to maintain toward foreign countries since these in any case took little notice of them. As a result the building was in a state of utter neglect." The extension of the Chancellery with an adjacent office building, located at 78 Wilhelm Street, only made matters worse, in Hitler's view. The modernist design by the Berlin architect Eduard Jobst Siedler, constructed between 1928 and 1930, "gives the impression from the outside of a warehouse or municipal fire station, and from the inside of a sanatorium for consumptives." The new building housed the chancellor's formal office, which Hitler described as "the tasteless room of a sales executive of a mid-sized cigarette and tobacco company." And yet despite these repellent conditions, Hitler resolved to move into the residence and ordered its complete renovation, which, he emphasized, he had paid for out of his own pocket.[3]

This extraordinary narrative appeared in the July 1939 issue of the Nazi art journal *Die Kunst im Dritten Reich* (Art in the Third Reich), which was devoted that month to the New Chancellery. In contrast to the overall celebratory tone of the other contributed essays, a good portion of Hitler's two-page article consisted of a litany of complaints and critical anecdotes about the Old Chancellery; he did not mention Speer's name until well into the second page. Even if we admit that, as patron and inhabitant, his perspective on and memory of the project would differ from those of others, nonetheless, on the cusp of talking his nation into war, why did Hitler feel compelled to write about the aesthetic pain caused by ugly light fixtures?

Hitler's 1939 account of the many renovations and expansions undertaken of the Chancellery demonstrates the ways in which he interwove politics and art. The story he told of putting his house in order was not a parable. For Hitler, rescuing the Old Chancellery from a soulless modernity was an inherently political act, since he believed that the decay of the nation's artistic consciousness (expressed in the abased house) and its racial and social demise grew from the same roots. The sickening of the Chancellery—which he maintained began during the reign of Kaiser Wilhelm II and intensified under the Weimar Republic—was, in his eyes, part of a larger political and cultural degeneration. In Hitler's highly ideological worldview, moldering floor boards and a rotting nation were firmly intertwined.

Historians by and large have accepted Hitler's account of the Old Chancellery, despite Speer having admitted in his memoirs that it was "certainly exaggerated." Speer nonetheless insisted on the residence's poor condition, recalling a dark kitchen and outmoded stoves and the need for more bathrooms with updated fixtures. But mostly he emphasized the "bad taste" with which the house had been decorated: for example, "doors painted to imitate natural wood and marble urns for flowers which were actually only marbleized sheet-metal basins."[4] This hardly amounts to a catastrophic situation, and a close look at earlier records reveals that the rot that Hitler claimed to have found in the old house was, in fact, in his head.

In 1875, the Schulenburg Palace (1738–39)—constructed in the Baroque tradition, with a two-story central structure flanked by two projecting wings surrounding a Court of Honor, which formed the official entrance—was purchased by the nation for the chancellor's official residence. From 1875 to 1878, it underwent an extensive renovation that cost, with furnishings, almost one million Marks. In 1906, the discovery of extensive dry rot and worm damage in the roof construction necessitated replacing almost the entire structure.[5] (Hitler was thus correct about the perilous roof condition, but it had been detected and repaired decades before his arrival—a story that did not serve his purposes to tell.) Dietmar Arnold's myth-busting history of the Chancellery pokes further holes in Hitler's account. He reports that in December 1918, a thorough audit of the building done for the new republican government determined that its overall state was "consistently good." In the summer of 1926, the chancellor's private rooms (then in the northern wing) were thoroughly repaired and modernized. There are no records of former residents having made complaints. For almost a year prior to Hitler's arrival, Paul von Hindenburg had lived at 77 Wilhelm Street while the presidential palace was being renovated. It seems unlikely, Arnold contends, that the German president would have been housed in an unsanitary or unsafe building, where the rain regularly seeped through the roof and the toilets overflowed. Nor did Arnold's search through the building plans commissioned by Hitler turn up critical repairs.[6] In short, there is no proof for the devastating structural damage that Hitler described in his 1939 narrative.

Evidence supporting Hitler's claim to have financed the work himself is similarly lacking. As a multimillionaire who did not pay taxes, he could well have afforded to take on the burden. A letter dated November 28, 1934, from Gerdy Troost to Albert Speer, who acted as building project manager, mentions her willingness to forgo her fee for the part of the renovation not paid for by the state, while accepting a commission for the rest.[7] Troost no doubt made this offer in good faith, believing that Hitler was personally shouldering much of the project's costs and wanting to spare him further expense. (In a 1971 interview with Hitler biographer John Toland, Troost claimed that she had been far wealthier than Hitler, revealing her political naiveté and ignorance of his tremendous fortune.[8]) Nonetheless, the Troost Atelier's own records show that by the end of 1934, of the 172,000 Reichsmarks in invoices submitted for their interior design work, at least 100,000 Reichsmarks had been paid by the Reich Finance Ministry, with indications that this amount was even higher.[9] More than half of the tab was thus picked up by German taxpayers—and this at a time when the country was still suffering from the crippling effects of the Depression, with millions of Germans out of work. By contrast, when faced with the severe economic repercussions of the 1929 Wall Street Crash, the republican government had scaled back its plans for furnishing the new office building at 78 Wilhelm Street in order to spare its citizens unnecessary expenditures.[10] A few years later, this was a sacrifice that Hitler was unwilling to make. But having presented himself to voters as a simple man with few material wants, he would have been well aware that his refusal to move into the Chancellery on aesthetic grounds—based on an aversion to tacky chandeliers or fake wooden doors—would have destroyed that carefully cultivated image. He thereby pledged to pay for the renovations himself as a seemingly generous and heroic gesture to save the house. Rather than acknowledge any privilege, Hitler treated the move to the Chancellery as yet another burden he assumed for the good of the nation.[11]

Despite Hitler's efforts to make it appear otherwise, the renovation of the Old Chancellery thus emerges as a project driven first and foremost by concern for the Führer's domestic image. This was entrusted to Paul Troost, the Munich-based architect whom Hitler had chosen to give National Socialism its built form (see fig. 36). Hitler initially encountered Troost through his furniture, which he began to collect with his first *Mein Kampf* royalty checks (or perhaps with help from Elsa and Hugo Bruckmann). Gerdy Troost later wrote that she and her husband first heard Hitler's name in 1926, when a salesperson from the United Workshops for Art in Handicraft (Vereinigte Werkstätten für Kunst im Handwerk), the Munich firm that produced Paul Troost's designs, called to ask whether Troost would be willing to sell his personal desk, then on display in the firm's showroom, to "a Herr Hitler, a politician, who cannot be convinced that the desk is not for sale." Troost had moved the massive desk to the show-room after he married to make room for the furniture that his bride had brought with her from Bremen. He planned to retrieve it once they had built themselves a house. Gerdy Troost claimed that since neither she nor her husband bothered with politics at the time, the name only faintly rang a bell. Troost refused to sell, but Hitler persisted to haunt the shop, and the calls continued until finally the architect relented, reasoning that he could always make himself another desk and thus please "this dogged, unknown admirer of his work."[12]

But it was not until September 24, 1930, at the Bruckmanns, that Troost and Hitler finally met, at the latter's request. As art historian Timo Nüsslein points out in his biography of the architect, at the time of their meeting, Troost had erected only some dozen buildings, mostly villas, and was primarily known for his designs for luxury ship interiors, commissions that he had undertaken from 1912 to 1930. More than the houses, it was these ship interiors—impressive, grand spaces outfitted with neoclassical furniture and ornament—that fired Hitler's imagination. In them, accord-ing to Gerdy Troost, Hitler perceived an artistic language that synthesized beauty and function and that drew him more than the work of any other German architect.[13] Thus the road to visualizing Nazi architecture began for Hitler from the inside out. Yet Hitler's attention to interior decoration has been little noted in the scholarship on National Socialist architecture, which has primarily focused on Speer's monumental works.

Hitler's first commission to Troost, which was also the first large-scale building project for National Socialism, was the transformation of the nineteenth-century Barlow Palace in Munich into the national headquarters of the Nazi Party, named the Brown House. Beginning in 1930, and in close consultation with Hitler, Troost created and furnished new public rooms for the formerly private residence. These rooms bore the imprint of his earlier designs for the steamship *Europa,* the interiors of which Hitler especially admired.[14] A slew of new party commissions followed rapidly thereafter, culminating in two monumental projects in Munich—the Nazi Party Center at the Königsplatz and the House of German Art—which after 1933 would establish Troost's severe neoclassicism as the look of the new regime.

Sometime in the summer of 1933, Hitler commissioned Troost to remodel and refurnish the Old Chancellery in Berlin. Later that fall, Hitler considered building a new house in the park behind the Chancellery, but realized that occupying the historic structure was symbolically the more powerful move.[15] According to Hans Frank, Hitler had already talked about making changes the night that he was sworn in as chancellor, but the work had to wait until Hindenburg had returned to his presidential palace later that spring.[16] In the meantime, in February 1933, Hitler moved out of his former Berlin headquarters at the Kaiserhof Hotel, located across the street from the Chancellery, and into the spacious, ten-room secretary of state's apartment on the fourth floor of the Siedler office building.[17] Over the next few months, he focused on consolidating his power, issuing the Reichstag Fire Decree, which abolished most civil liberties; passing the Enabling Act, which permitted him to enact laws without parliament; setting up the Gestapo; and abolishing trade unions as well as political parties except for his own.

In the fall of 1933, Troost fell ill and was hospitalized for six weeks. In December, he was released and resumed work, but in January, his health worsened, and he died on January 21, 1934, at the age of fifty-five.[18] His National Socialist projects, many of them barely begun, were left in limbo, and Speer later claimed that Hitler, in a panic, considered taking over the architecture firm himself in order to see them completed.[19] Instead, this responsibility was assumed by the architect's twenty-nine-year-old wife, Gerdy Troost, and his forty-nine-year-old studio assistant, Leonhard Gall. Both had years of experience working alongside Paul Troost, although in different capacities. In the renamed Atelier Troost, which in 1934 had twenty employees, Gall became studio head and employed his architectural and technical skills on building sites and at the drafting board.[20] Gerdy Troost assumed the role of office manager, handling correspondence, finances, publicity, and client relations. She also took on a greater role in the firm's interior design projects. In a postwar interview, she described her responsibilities as choosing colors and materials, consulting with Gall on furniture designs, arranging the rooms, and decorating them with tapestries and other artwork.[21] A 1939 article on the Führer's architects in the lifestyle magazine *die neue linie* (the new line) gave her primary design credit for the interiors of numerous Third Reich projects, including the Old Chancellery.[22]

Because of his illness and the demands of his other building commissions, it is not clear how far Troost had progressed in his designs for the Chancellery before his death. Invoices show that he had received estimates for furniture orders as early as August 1933.[23] A few drawings from his hand survive, including an elevation of the dining room dated December 1933.[24] Whatever work remained in reimagining and remodeling the residence fell to the Atelier Troost and was carried out from January to May 1934. As Hitler described it in his 1939 article, the renovation had two interrelated objectives: concentrating the public living spaces and reception rooms on the ground floor, and arranging the upper story to serve the private and practical needs of the chancellor.[25] Previous chancellors had entertained in the reception rooms on the upper floor, a vestige of the *piano nobile*. The 1934 reorganization created a private apartment for Hitler on the northern side of the main building's second floor (fig. 4). The Congress Hall, which was rarely used, separated this domestic space from offices on the southern side. During the Imperial and Weimar eras, the chancellor's private rooms had been located on the second floor of the projecting northern wing.[26] This area was now reserved for Hitler's adjutants, providing easy access from the chancellor's private apartment. The southern wing contained further offices, service areas, and guest rooms (Speer undertook renovations here as well as in the adjacent Siedler building).[27] The result was an expanded private realm for work and personal life in the upper story that was isolated from the lower public rooms.

But much more than functionality was at stake for Hitler in the redesign. In criticizing the (supposed) deterioration of the Old Chancellery during the Weimar Republic, Hitler had equated the house's shabbiness with the country's loss of foreign prestige. He thus revealed his belief that an impressive house was a political exigency of his new regime. In an August

1938 speech given at the topping-out ceremony for the New Chancellery, he claimed that he had commissioned Speer's building in order to give Germany an image that was as good as or better than that of other nations. He further explained that this desire was divorced from personal vanity, distinguishing between the modesty of the home he occupied as a private citizen in Munich and the representational demands of his seat as chancellor and Führer.[28]

For Hitler, an image worthy of the Führer and the German nation not only required grandeur, but it also needed to be of its own time. In the same 1938 speech, he criticized revolutionary governments that took office in former castles, such as the Kremlin, and insisted that he himself refused to enter them (conveniently forgetting that the Chancellery had once been, if not a castle, at least a palace).[29] This aversion to historical associations not of his own choosing may well have been the primary motivating factor for the renovation of the Old Chancellery. Photographs from 1932 reveal that the building had been furnished in a style that preserved a historical tone. This, more than any structural flaws, may have suggested to Hitler the building's decrepitude. Occupying a former palace was problematic enough, but residing in one that looked old and stuffy threatened the dynamic image that Hitler wished to convey. In the 1932 presidential election, Hitler had taken to the air—a then-unprecedented campaign tactic—to establish his youthful modernity in contrast to the elderly Hindenburg. A comparison of images taken before and after the Chancellery renovation makes clear the effort to modernize its spaces (figs. 5, 6).[30] At the same time, this was decidedly not the modernity of the International Style of the previous decade, which Hitler rejected as worthy only of sanatoriums and fire stations. Thus, for the Atelier Troost, the challenge was to create, within the framework of a former palace, a grand and impressive image of the Führer that recalled neither the pompous regality of dead monarchs nor the "tasteless" newness of the tobacco sales executive.

Ridding the interiors of their dated appearance began with an opening of spaces to light and air. On the ground floor, the largest room facing the garden had been partitioned in the Weimar era to create offices, which were desperately needed as the administration of the Chancellery grew in this period. The construction of the Siedler office building in 1930 freed up this formerly residential space, and the old partitions were removed in the 1934 renovation (fig. 7).[31] Additionally, a load-bearing wall was eliminated to join two rooms, which necessitated the replacement of the Congress Hall's

Fig. 4. Atelier Troost, plan of Hitler's renovated private apartment on the second floor of the Old Chancellery at 77 Wilhelm Street in Berlin, n.d.

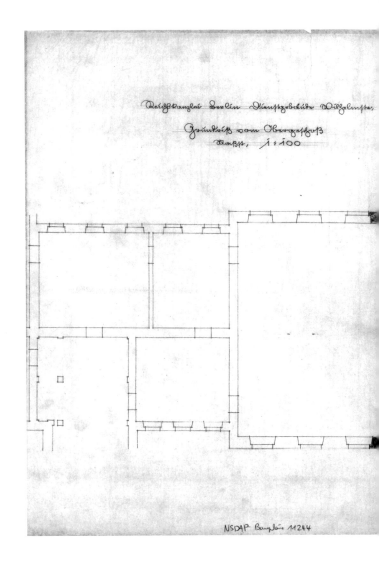

timber floor above with a stronger steel-girder construction.[32] The resulting open, bi-level hall became the main space for receptions (fig. 8).

The length of the hall created a dramatic interior vista, which would become a hallmark of Hitler's spaces at the expanded Berghof and New Chancellery. An oversized Persian-patterned carpet that climbed the stairs emphasized the sweeping expanse of the room while also unifying the two levels. (Hitler liked to tell the story that this luxurious carpet originally had been ordered by the League of Nations for its new Geneva headquarters, but when it was completed, the league was short of funds and could not pay, so he acquired it for his official residence. He thus presented himself, no doubt

HOW THE CHANCELLOR LIVES

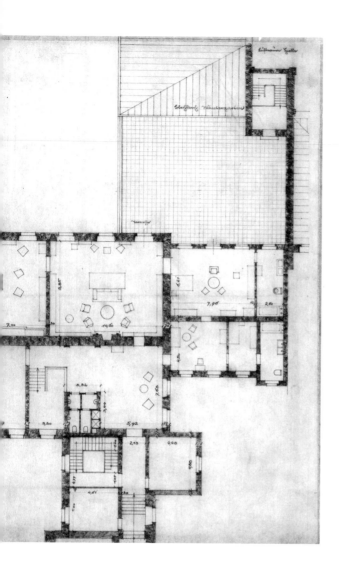

with mocking reference to having withdrawn Germany from the league in October 1933, as literally pulling the carpet out from under them.[33]) The perspectival lines of the carpet led the eye to the large Gobelin tapestry hanging on the far wall. Such tapestries, three of which hung in this room, similarly became distinctive of Hitler's spaces, both domestic and official. Paul Troost had used tapestries in his *Europa* interior, and these would also feature prominently in his National Socialist buildings in Munich. Their richness and scale worked well in large rooms, and Hitler appreciated their narrative qualities; he often chose tapestries with triumphal mythic or historic scenes.[34] While decoration of this sort would seem to counteract the

Fig. 5. Photograph of the library on the second floor of the Old Chancellery in Berlin before the renovation by the Atelier Troost, c. 1932.

desire to update the rooms, other elements, such as the off-white walls, crisp rectilinear forms, and abundant light from the large windows facing the park conveyed a more contemporary feel. British journalist George Ward Price, reporting on the first formal dinner party with invited foreign guests hosted there on December 19, 1934, wrote appreciatively of the modern sensibility.[35] Although not visible, the room also contained state-of-the-art entertainment technology, with a hidden movie projector and screen as well as a radio cabinet. Hitler would often gather here informally with guests in the evenings to watch films, a practice he would continue at the Berghof.[36]

Decluttering the rooms and removing much of the historic ornament also served to update the look of the interiors. In some cases, as in the foyer leading to the Reception Hall, this verged on an emptiness that design historian Sonja Günther argues was meant to intimidate (fig. 9). She characterizes the impression made by the spare furniture and stone floor in the capacious room as cold and museal, despite the presence of a large red carpet. One could argue, however, that the removal of four large Doric columns and the lowering of the ceiling made the space considerably more

HOW THE CHANCELLOR LIVES

Fig. 6. Heinrich Hoffmann, photograph of the library on the second floor of the Old Chancellery in Berlin after the renovation by the Atelier Troost, c. 1934.

hospitable (and less pompous) after its renovation.[37] Whether or not the foyer unnerved its occupants, it certainly held few distractions to divert their attention from the act of waiting. Speer would later pick up and exaggerate these elements in the experience of anxiety and powerlessness that he designed for visitors to the New Chancellery.

In other ground-floor rooms, Günther sees the desire for aristocratic grandeur and the habits of middle-class domesticity warring with one another. She points to the incongruity of rooms with noble proportions and crystal chandeliers decorated with fussy, overstuffed sitting corners meant to convey *Gemütlichkeit* or with mantelpieces and display cabinets filled with porcelain figurines and vases, a showcasing of affluence and taste typical of the nouveau-riche bourgeois home.[38] But what Günther interprets as a fissure in Hitler's decorating psychology equally could be interpreted as confidence that he could occupy both identities at the same time—grand yet homey, a world leader yet an average Joe. The apparent disjointedness at the level of design may not have bothered a client like Hitler, who believed that he himself was the integrating factor.

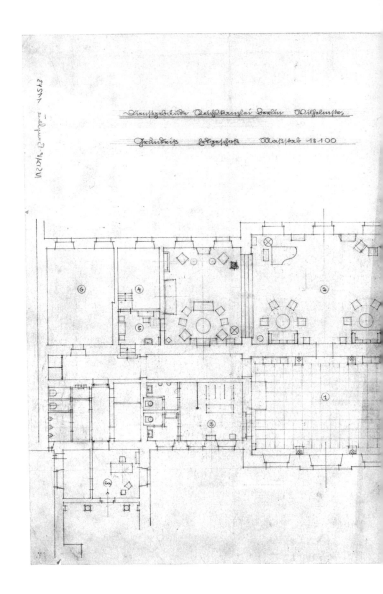

Fig. 7. Atelier Troost, plan of the renovated ground floor of the Old Chancellery in Berlin, c. 1934.

At the same time, and as suggested by his asserted refusal to enter castles, Hitler did not wish to appear to be putting on aristocratic airs. The building at 77 Wilhelm Street was closely associated in the German imagination with Bismarck, who enjoyed cult status among the right. Despite Bismarck's noble ancestry, the soldierly simplicity of his lifestyle, including at the Chancellery, was much admired, especially when weighed against his stature as a statesman. Hitler's criticism of the residence's despoliation around the turn of the twentieth century was directed in large measure at Duke Bernhard von Bülow, who was chancellor from 1900 to 1909. The

HOW THE CHANCELLOR LIVES

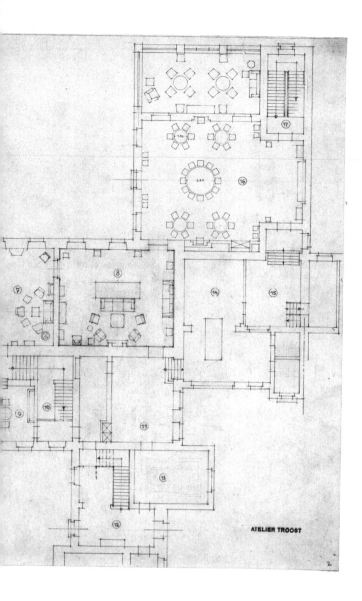

ATELIER TROOST

lavish renovation of the Chancellery undertaken by Bülow and his wife, an Italian princess, sought to evoke courtly associations and led to it being dubbed the Doge's Palace on the Spree. Hitler's commitment to his image as a simple, even poor, man necessitated avoiding the luxuriance with which Bülow had come to be associated. Gerdy Troost claimed that she had designed in the "English style of living," by which she referred to earlier British-inspired design reform movements in Germany that had valued the quality of materials and craftsmanship over showy display. Even so, and despite his criticism, Hitler seemed to appreciate the aristocratic splendor of

Fig. 8. Heinrich Hoffmann, photograph of the Reception Hall on the ground floor of the Old Chancellery in Berlin after the renovation by the Atelier Troost, c. 1934.

some of the Bülow-era decoration. In particular, the striking pine ceilings installed in some rooms by the Bülows in imitation of Italian Renaissance palaces were not only maintained by Hitler but may have inspired the ceiling of the Great Hall of the Berghof (fig. 10 and see plate 4).[39] Thus, the conflicting class associations that Günther detects in the 1934 renovation may also be explained by Hitler being drawn to and yet needing to reject a grandeur that would have hurt his public image.

The dining room designed by Paul Troost similarly reinforced Hitler's vision of himself and his party (fig. 11). Since Hitler found the existing dining room too small, he commissioned a large addition that extended into the park at the back of the house. Speer later described the feeling of this room, with its ivory walls and three glass doors leading on to the park, as one of "openness and brightness." The neoclassical symmetry and ornament, typical of Troost's designs, evoked the ancient Greek heritage that Hitler claimed for his imagined Aryan nation. Standing in niches on marble pedestals, two large bronze statues by Munich sculptor Joseph Wackerle represented *Earth* (female) and *Volk* (male). At the front of the room hung a large classical allegory, *The Triumph of Music*, by Friedrich August von Kaulbach, which had been painted in 1919 for the music room

HOW THE CHANCELLOR LIVES

Fig. 9. Heinrich Hoffmann, photograph of the Waiting Room on the ground floor of the Old Chancellery in Berlin after the renovation by the Atelier Troost, c. 1934.

of a Munich villa. Art historian Birgit Schwarz maintains that the room had been conceived, from the layout facing the garden to the male and female statuary in niches and the central round table, to recall the Marble Hall of Frederick the Great's summer palace at Sanssouci, where the Prussian king, one of Hitler's idols, had hosted a roundtable with diplomats, officers, writers, and philosophers that was famous for its intellectual brilliance and freedom.[40] Yet despite such culturally refined associations, the atmosphere at table was altogether different. Hitler jokingly called the dining room the Merry Chancellor's Restaurant, but Speer found the company, typically consisting of party politicians with little education or worldly experience and too timid to speak their minds, dull beyond measure.[41]

The dining room's seating arrangement buttressed another party legend: a united Volk community. Although Hitler always sat at the large table in the center of the room, its round form suggested equality and the Führer's modesty. "The chairs were all alike," Speer later wrote, "the host's no more elaborate than the rest."[42] But such appearances barely concealed deeply entrenched power hierarchies. To begin, those invited to table were almost all men.[43] And as Reinhard Spitzy, Joachim von Ribbentrop's private secretary, recalled in his memoirs, when the moment came to enter the dining

Fig. 10. Heinrich Hoffmann, photograph of the Smoking Room on the ground floor of the Old Chancellery in Berlin after the renovation by the Atelier Troost, c. 1934. Guests waited here to enter the dining room.

room, electricity passed through the assembled guests as Hitler prepared to announce the selection of his tablemates: "All paladins stood immediately on tiptoe and puffed themselves up as large and wide as possible, so that the prince's eye would chance to fall on them. Hitler visibly enjoyed this situation and took his time. 'Let's see,' he said, 'I would like on my right'—pause—'Dr. Goebbels, please; to my left, Herr von Ribbentrop; the next right, General X, please; and next left, Gauleiter Y. The remaining gentlemen please seat yourselves as you wish.'" As Spitzy asserts, this ritual was highly politicized, establishing the diners' status.[44] Those not among the main table elect sat at smaller tables around the room. Adjacent to the dining room, on its western side, was a sunny, comfortable winter garden where breakfast was served. Günther writes that "the abundance of plants, the large carpet with its profusion of mythical scenes, the armchair upholstery patterned after the Wiener Werkstätte, and the red-lacquered furniture gave this room a certain freshness that was unusual for the Third Reich."[45]

HOW THE CHANCELLOR LIVES

Fig. 11. Heinrich Hoffmann, photograph of the new dining room designed by Paul Troost and completed by the Atelier Troost in the Old Chancellery in Berlin, c. 1934.

Perhaps the excitement felt by guests as they were about to enter the dining room also had to do with the anticipation of finally eating, since Hitler often left them gathered in the comfortable Smoking Room adjacent to the dining room (see fig. 10), waiting for hours as he lingered in his new private apartment on the second floor.[46] This apartment consisted of a private study, library, bedroom, dressing room (later guest room), and large outdoor roof terrace built on top of the dining room (see fig. 4). After dinner, guests were occasionally served coffee and liqueurs on the terrace, from which they enjoyed views of the treetops in the Chancellery park.[47]

Hitler's study was uncluttered and the furniture was arranged for solitary work (fig. 12). The artwork on the walls served more than a decorative function. Near his desk, Hitler hung an engraving of the House of German Art by Paul Troost as well as portraits of Bismarck, Frederick the Great, and Dietrich Eckart, figures with whom he identified politically or intellectually. As Schwarz has demonstrated in her study of Hitler and art, the dictator created carefully controlled narratives about himself through the paintings he displayed in his work and living spaces.[48] Historian Timothy Ryback has found a similar identification process in the books that Hitler collected.[49]

Surprisingly, the latter were not on view in Hitler's library (see fig. 6). This large room, which also functioned as his parlor, contained a fireplace

Fig. 12. Heinrich Hoffmann, photograph of Hitler's private study on the second floor of the Old Chancellery in Berlin after the renovation by the Atelier Troost, c. 1934.

around which a sofa and chairs had been arranged, a timber ceiling, a massive table designed by Paul Troost in 1933 that would become a feature of Hitler's work spaces, and book cabinets with glass doors covered by curtains, which had replaced previously open shelves. Günther speculates that there were no books behind the curtains, and that the obscured shelves suggested learning that the occupant did not possess.[50] Friedelind Wagner, Richard Wagner's granddaughter, who visited Hitler at the Chancellery shortly after the renovation, claimed that Hitler had had curtains installed because the books' different sizes and colors disturbed him.[51] Given the open bookcases in his Obersalzberg and Munich libraries, this seems unlikely. If the book collection belonged to the Chancellery rather than to him, it may be that he did not want to look at or be associated with other chancellors' books. Whatever the case may be, the new cabinets, with their simplified forms, gave the already rich room a visually more restful and uniform appearance. The removal of excess decoration and massive doorframes, along with the substitution of a plain floor covering for the earlier floral carpeting, also gave the library a more contemporary feel.

HOW THE CHANCELLOR LIVES

Fig. 13. Heinrich Hoffmann, photograph of the Cabinet Room (formerly the Congress Hall) on the second floor of the Old Chancellery in Berlin after the renovation by the Atelier Troost, with furniture designed by Paul Troost, photograph c. 1934. On January 30, 1933, Hitler had been sworn in as chancellor by President Hindenburg in this room.

Wagner described Hitler's bedroom, of which there are no known photographs, as exceptionally simple: it "looked more like that of a governess than a dictator." She recalled a cast-iron bed, table, nightstand, and simple wooden chair, all painted white, and nothing else, except for an oil painting of his mother.[52] The floor plan of the room by the Atelier Troost indicates somewhat more furniture than this (see fig. 4). The plainness of Hitler's bedrooms has often been commented on, both then and now, and taken as proof of the unaffectedness and modesty of the private man, the "real" Hitler. The designs for his residences do suggest that he preferred simple bedrooms. However, these must be placed in the larger context of the elaborate residences in which they were found, which speaks no less to Hitler's identity and tastes. Connected to Hitler's bedroom was a sizable dressing room. In a later renovation, he ordered its conversion into a private bedroom, sitting room, and bath for Eva Braun, thus literally keeping her in his closet.[53]

Fig. 14. Heinrich Hoffmann, photograph of Hitler's Ceremonial Office on the second floor of the modernist building annex to the Old Chancellery in Berlin after the renovation of the former Red Room by the Atelier Troost, c. 1935.

Renovations in other parts of the building continued after Hitler moved into his new quarters in May 1934.[54] The Congress Hall, adjacent to Hitler's private study, was transformed into the Cabinet Room, but was little modified apart from the addition of furniture designed by Paul Troost (fig. 13). The eagle and swastika upholstered on the back of the chairs, the swastikas on the table runner, and the massiveness of the walnut table itself, which measured six and a half feet in width by thirty-three feet in length, clearly marked the room as a place of Nazi power.[55] It was an expensive ideological statement, with the embroidered upholstery for the thirty chairs alone costing nearly 10,000 Reichsmarks.[56] The lighting fixtures that Hitler so disparaged in his 1939 speech remained unchanged, reinforcing the purely rhetorical and political nature of those comments. Hitler met collectively with his ministers in the Cabinet Room until 1938, after which he gave up the pretense of any regular government procedure. The furnishings were moved to the New Chancellery in 1939 and the empty space was used to display

HOW THE CHANCELLOR LIVES

Hitler's birthday presents. The room again assumed a political function with the start of the war, serving for Hitler's military briefings with his generals.[57]

In the spring of 1935, the Atelier Troost furnished Hitler's formal office.[58] Having rejected the chancellor's office in the Siedler extension as better suited to a corporate sales executive, Hitler had a large reception hall on the second floor of the same building, formerly known as the Red Room, converted for his use. Located directly adjacent to the Old Chancellery and connected through a suite of rooms, the new office was easily accessible from his private apartment. With gleaming Art Deco features, dating from 1930, the room had the impressive scale and drama that he demanded. This was reinforced by the dimensions of the relatively spare furnishings, such as the length of the inlaid sideboard behind Hitler's desk or the desk itself, which was designed by Paul Troost in 1933 (fig. 14).[59] Despite his complaints about the quality of the state-loaned artwork, Hitler retained the sixteenth-century Italian paintings that had formerly hung in the room, including the large *Enthroned Madonna and Child with Saints* by the Venetian artist Francesco Vecellio, which Günther points out gave the room a sacral air. By moving to this room, Hitler symbolically left behind the Weimar-era office of the chancellor—its smallness evoking "the confinement of bureaucratic rules and regulations"—to enter an expansive space of his own making, a stage that would permit, in his view, an unencumbered performance of his political genius.[60] In the New Chancellery office designed by Speer, these grandiose tendencies, beginning to unfold in the Troost renovation, would reach absurd proportions. Both versions of Hitler's formal office functioned as ceremonial and ideological spaces, and he rarely actually worked in them.[61]

Renovations in the Old Chancellery, including the offices of Hitler's adjutants and the area south of the Cabinet Room, continued through 1935 and into early 1936.[62] This period also witnessed the erection of a large-scale building extension by the Atelier Troost. With the death of President Hindenburg in August 1934, Hitler assumed his powers, becoming not only chancellor, but also president and head of the army. Hitler marked his expanded influence architecturally by commissioning Gall to design a Reception Building where 250 people could dine and diplomatic and state gatherings take place. The structure, completed in the spring of 1936, was built on the grounds of the park (extending into the lot belonging to the adjacent Foreign Office) and was joined to the Chancellery by a new and larger glassed-in Winter Garden that replaced the modest room that had once stood beside the dining room.[63] The interior of the new Reception

Building, a collaboration between Gall and Gerdy Troost, featured massive brown marble columns, a ceiling ornamented with swastika mosaics, and tall bronze wall lamps with eagle and swastika that recalled Roman standards, among other decoration—which, as art historian Angela Schönberger has argued, visually reinforced the unity, following Hindenburg's death, of party and state.[64] The atmosphere was far grander and more formal than the old Reception Hall, which, by comparison, was domestic in scale and look. At the same time that the new Reception Building was built, an air raid shelter was constructed beneath it, which would later be integrated into the larger Führer bunker.[65]

The building of a vast New Chancellery, which Hitler justified as fulfilling the representational and functional needs created by the territorial expansion of the Greater German Reich in 1938 (even though, as historians have pointed out, its planning began years earlier), provided a surplus of new spaces.[66] Nonetheless, Hitler continued to live and work in the Old Chancellery, and his closest staff remained there as well, finding it more convenient to be near him than to relocate to Speer's building, which "proved too far away."[67] In 1944, a bomb fell on the Cabinet Room, but other parts of the residence remained intact and continued to be used. Not long after American bombers destroyed much of the rest on February 3, 1945, including the Merry Chancellor's Restaurant, Hitler moved permanently into the bunker.[68] In her memoirs, Traudl Junge, Hitler's secretary, recalls that by the war's end, the valuable objects in the Old Chancellery had been replaced with less-costly furnishings.[69] If the art and furniture survived the war, their whereabouts today remain unknown.

3 CULTIVATED INTERIORS

The 1935 Renovation of the Prince Regent Square Apartment

Leni Riefenstahl's 1935 film *Triumph of the Will* glorified Adolf Hitler as the titanic leader of a great and unified nation. Whether speaking to rapt audiences from the podium, saluting SA and SS troops in the medieval streets of Nuremberg, or paying tribute to fallen soldiers at a war memorial, Hitler displayed the mastery and gravitas of a statesman. This highly ideological documentary of the Nazi Party's 1934 Nuremberg rally helped to lift the stain of the brutal "Röhm-Putsch" that had occurred just weeks before the event, and that had seemed to confirm in the world's eyes Hitler's blood lust and the chaos of political life in Germany.[1] But with the approach of the 1936 Olympic Games—which the dictator hoped would be an international public relations victory for his regime—and as Hitler prepared to enter a new phase of diplomatic negotiations for expanded territorial claims, the man with a thousand faces determined to remodel his image once more in order to secure his next round of political goals, which required the respect and trust of foreign nations. Architecture would play an important role in this makeover, and not only in its most public and monumental forms, such as in the Nuremberg Rally Grounds designed by Albert Speer. On a diplomatic level, the renovations and expansions of the Old Chancellery spoke of a confident new style in the government district.

And even in the ostensibly private sphere of Hitler's home life, changes signaled a self-possessed maturation.

In 1935, the Atelier Troost renovated and redecorated Hitler's spacious Prince Regent Square apartment in Munich at the extravagant cost of 120,000 Reichsmarks—or more than ten times the average income earned by a doctor in Germany that year.[2] Unlike the Chancellery, Hitler paid for the work personally, from the account his publisher maintained for him, which by then overflowed with royalties from *Mein Kampf*. The high price tag bought him an apartment in which he felt confident to host world leaders such as Neville Chamberlain and Benito Mussolini. The commission to the Atelier Troost testifies to Hitler's satisfaction with their work at the Chancellery and to his trust in their ability to give the right architectural form to his domestic needs and identity. Because this was the most private of his residences, Gerdy Troost and Leonhard Gall could work on a different, more intimate scale than at either the Chancellery or the Berghof. Nonetheless, they found other ways to communicate that this was no ordinary home.

The state of the apartment before the Atelier Troost began their work is not entirely clear. From 1929 until the renovation, the residence appears to have been occupied by a group of adults: Hitler, his niece Geli Raubal (until her death in 1931), and two couples. The first couple, Ernst and Maria Reichert, had been Hitler's landlords for nine years on Thiersch Street, where he had lived with them and their daughter. Antonie Reichert would have been sixteen at the time of her parents' move to Prince Regent Square, but there is no indication that she came with them. Ernst Reichert identified himself as a businessman, although his finances apparently required taking in a lodger.[3] Hitler described the Thiersch Street apartment they had shared as having four to five rooms.[4] Presumably, when the couple moved, they brought their furniture with them.

The other couple, recent newlyweds Georg and Anni Winter, also moved in with Hitler.[5] Georg Winter had worked as a valet for General Franz Ritter von Epp, through whom he had met Hitler. In October 1929, the thirty-three-year-old Winter was hired as a packer at Eher Verlag (Hitler's publisher), and he also helped occasionally in the apartment, including serving at dinner parties. Anni Winter, Georg Winter's twenty-four-year-old bride, became Hitler's cook and house manager.[6] In later testimony before a denazification tribunal, Georg Winter successfully argued that Hitler had asked him to join the SS in 1930 in order to wear the uniform when serving at table or otherwise helping his wife with official functions and thus make a suitable impression on party bigwigs. Although he did not serve in the SS, promotions in rank followed, resulting in an ever-more-imposing appearance. His employer's vanity about livery, Winter claimed, cost him a long and harsh internment at the war's end, which he barely survived.[7]

It is not known whether the Winters brought their own furniture when they moved to 16 Prince Regent Square. Hitler himself seems to have had very little. In a 1948 interview, Anni Winter stated that he had brought only his bedroom furniture from Thiersch Street and then began to add new things. Gerdy Troost later recalled that the apartment had been eclectically furnished, mostly by Hitler's friends. In 1929, Hitler's wealthy admirer Elsa Bruckmann had purchased some furniture for the apartment from the royal cabinetmaker Moritz Ballin. Eyewitnesses later claimed that at this time Hitler also acquired a few cherished pieces by Paul Troost from the United Workshops for Art in Handicraft. On the whole, however, Anni Winter remembers the apartment being sparsely furnished before the 1935 renovation.[8]

How the furniture was arranged and who lived in what rooms cannot be determined, with the possible exception of Geli Raubal's room. After the war, Winter reported that before the 1935 renovation, she, her husband, and Hitler occupied one wing of the apartment, and Raubal and the Reicherts the other. When Raubal died, according to Winter and other witnesses, Hitler closed off her room and preserved it unchanged as a sort of shrine.[9] If this is true, the one room in the apartment conspicuously not renovated in 1935—the room beside the library—can be assumed to have been hers (fig. 15). This is also the room identified as belonging to her by Hitler's secretary, Traudl Junge.[10] Moreover, its location facing Prince Regent Square matches the description given by the police who investigated Raubal's death.[11] Hitler's bedroom after the renovation, with its own private bathroom, was located at the far end of the opposite wing, and it seems likely that he had occupied this same room before 1935. If this is the case, then Hitler and his niece did not live adjacent to one another, as some have speculated, seeing in this presumed spatial proximity evidence of other intimacies. Indeed, the door that directly connected Hitler's room (via the bathroom) to its neighbor and that has contributed to rumors of clandestine encounters did not exist before the renovation. This neighboring room, erroneously identified as belonging to Raubal, had previously been a small maid's chamber and was expanded into a comfortable guest room only in 1935.

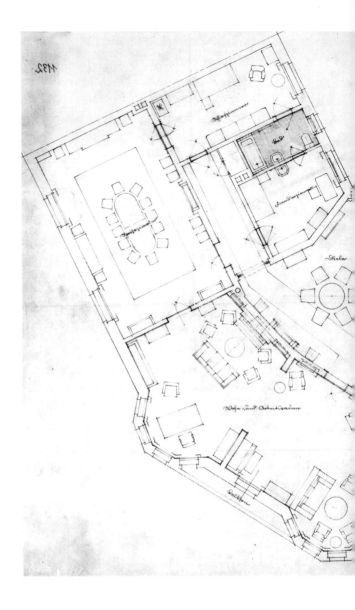

In more general terms, the apartment's appearance prior to the renovation can be reconstructed on the basis of architectural plans and of other
floors in the building whose original interiors have been preserved. When
he designed the building in 1907–8, the architect Franz Popp employed the
Jugendstil forms that were then popular in Munich. Curvilinear, wooden
moldings as well as rounded arches above doorways gave the apartments
an elegant, but also historical feel (fig. 16). Hitler did not like Jugendstil,
according to Gerdy Troost, which he considered "too extreme."[12] In the 1935

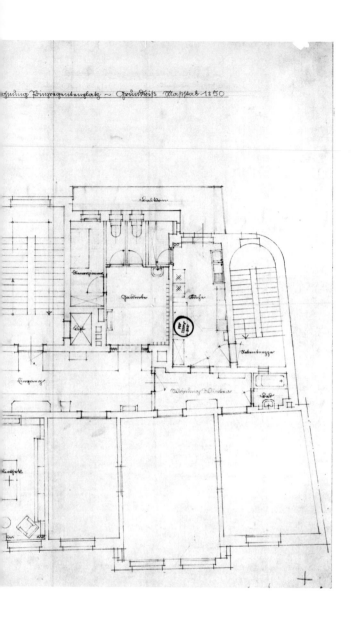

renovation, all such Jugendstil decoration was eliminated from the apartment and replaced with the starkly plain rectilinear forms characteristic of the interiors of Paul Troost's party buildings on the Königsplatz and House of German Art (fig. 17). The removal or reduction of walls also increased the impression of a bright, open interior (see figs. 2, 15). The result, as it is experienced today, is strikingly modern and spare, although the relative emptiness of the apartment, now used for offices, contributes to this effect. When Lee Miller arrived here in the final days of the war and photographed

Fig. 16. A contemporary view of the foyer of the first-floor apartment, 16 Prince Regent Square in Munich, showing the original Jugendstil decoration that had also existed in Hitler's apartment before the renovation.

Fig. 17. Atelier Troost, elevation drawing of the hallway in Hitler's Munich apartment showing the main entrance (left), garderobe (middle), and kitchen (right), c. 1935.

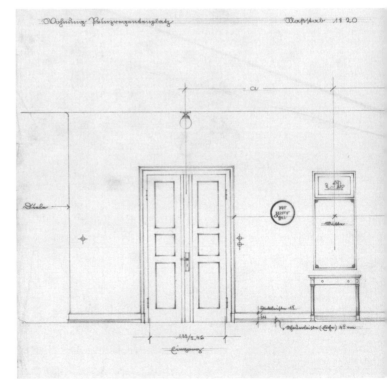

the interiors of Hitler's home, having hours earlier witnessed the starving and dead in the Dachau concentration camp, she avoided conveying any of that sense of light and modernity, which must have seemed impossibly at odds with what she had just experienced. These were not, in any case, glossy photographs for an architecture magazine spread, but images of American soldiers occupying a dictator's lair. Most of the photographs seem to have been taken at night or with the curtains drawn. In some instances, Miller may have rearranged objects to heighten the sense of a claustrophobic jumble (such as in Hitler's bedroom), even though she described the apartment as "quite spacious" and "very simply laid out." The resulting dark, cramped interiors published in the July 1945 issue of *Vogue* (UK) magazine thus do not prepare one for the airy interiors encountered in the apartment today.[13]

Unfortunately, almost no other images exist of the apartment. In 1935, in response to a request by the magazine *die neue linie,* Joseph Goebbels expressly forbade taking pictures of Hitler's domestic spaces in the Old Chancellery (although official and public areas were permissible).[14] Goebbels did not give a reason for his decision, but it reveals that even for

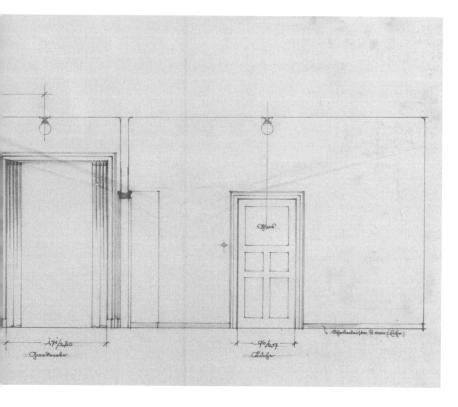

the much-photographed Führer, some spaces were off-limits. Nonetheless, numerous surviving drawings and plans by the Atelier Troost document the transformation. A floor plan of the apartment indicating the proposed changes, signed on behalf of Gall as the architect and dated January 1935, was submitted to local building authorities in early February.[15] Most of the work appears to have been carried out between February and mid-April 1935.[16] Because of the extent of the renovation, the apartment's occupants moved out; when it was completed, only Hitler and the Winters returned. On April 29, Hitler proudly showed off his new home by inviting three influential female admirers—Unity Mitford, the Duchess of Brunswick (the daughter of Emperor Wilhelm II), and Winifred Wagner—to dinner.[17]

Similar to the work undertaken at the Chancellery, although on a smaller scale, the renovation opened up the residence's main living spaces and reorganized its layout to consolidate functions (see figs. 2, 15). Entering the apartment and turning right, one crossed the wedge-shaped foyer and came to what had been a maid's room and separate hall toilet. The toilet was

Fig. 18. Atelier Troost, elevation drawing of the interior walls of Hitler's renovated living room in his 16 Prince Regent Square apartment, showing the new fireplace (across from Hitler's desk) and the double doors leading into the foyer, c. 1935.

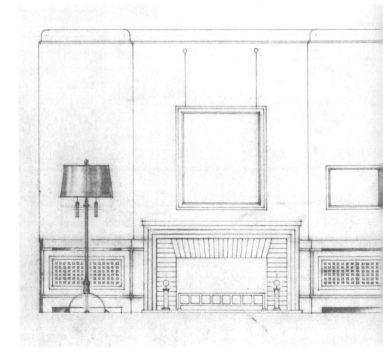

PRINCE REGENT SQUARE APARTMENT

removed in order to expand the small room, which was then connected to a bathroom that was shared with Hitler's bedroom. Eva Braun may have used this room on overnight stays.[18] Across from Hitler's bedroom, on the south-eastern end of the apartment, had been a square room and, adjacent to it, a narrower room. The wall between them was removed to create a large dining room with a marble mantelpiece (which was decorative and covered a radiator) and a table that could seat twelve. From the dining room one entered the largest space of the apartment, with two sets of bay windows. The bay closest to the dining room contained Hitler's study, across from which was a seating area and a newly installed fireplace (fig. 18). The other bay contained a sitting alcove, beside which a wall had been removed to join it to a new library (fig. 19 and see plate 12). Although the space of this living area was more confined than in the Chancellery's Reception Hall, the Atelier Troost nonetheless created a sense of an unfolding interior, with one space flowing into another. In their memoirs, Henriette von Schirach and Traudl Junge recalled the appeal of the apartment's large rooms to Hitler.

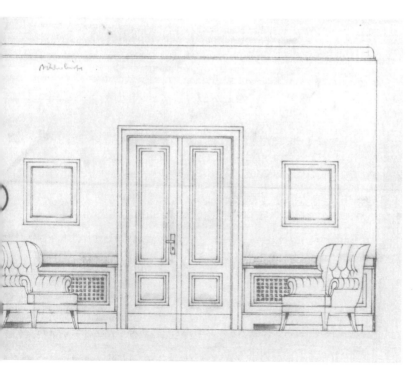

Fig. 19. Heinrich Hoffmann, photograph of Neville Chamberlain, Hitler, and Paul Schmidt (Hitler's interpreter) in Hitler's Munich apartment, sitting in the living room niche near the library. Chamberlain visited on September 30, 1938, after the signing of the Munich Accord. Hitler's book and art collections are prominently displayed in this published photograph, emphasizing how his domestic settings served to convey the image of a man of culture rather than a warmonger.

Hitler told Schirach that people needed room to flourish, a comment that would seem innocuous if it did not come from the man who justified genocide on the same grounds.[19]

This whole section of the apartment was now given over to Hitler, and the western wing, which one entered if one turned left from the foyer, became the service area. The last two rooms in this wing facing the square were made into an apartment for the Winters, consisting of a bedroom, living room, and bathroom. A wall in the hallway directly before their rooms separated their living space from that of Hitler. The kitchen across from their rooms, which served the entire apartment, was expanded and modernized. A maid's room and toilet that had been located beside the pantry in the old kitchen were removed. A preexisting maid's room located within the space of the garderobe (to the left) was slightly expanded.

The Atelier Troost designed much of the apartment's furniture and fittings. The forms tended to be simple, albeit traditional, and minimally ornamented. Numerous elements reappear in the later National Socialist buildings on the Königsplatz and in the House of German Art, the interiors of which Gall and Gerdy Troost also created. For example, the round coffee table with a dark marble top in the nook near the library, where Hitler received his guests, closely resembles those used in the Führerbau, which housed Hitler's office on the Königsplatz (see fig. 19). The combination of colored marbles used for Hitler's living room fireplace—sand for the mantelpiece, and red for the floor in front—recurs in the interior of the Führerbau's grand staircase atrium. Moreover, the grooved linear forms of the mantel (here and in the dining room) resemble the radiator covers in this same atrium and at the House of German Art. The square grid pattern used for the radiator grills in the apartment's living room (see fig. 18) transforms into the railings of the Führerbau's atrium and outdoor balconies, the latter already sketched out by Paul Troost. The distinctive door handles, composed of a cube attached to a cylinder, are also found on the Königsplatz buildings and the House of German Art. The dramatic rectangular opening between the library and the living room, framed in dark wood, resembles the striking treatment of doorframes in the Königsplatz buildings and the House of German Art. The Atelier Troost thus developed a versatile decorative style that encompassed both private and public buildings, and monumental and domestic scales. Within a syntax of spare classicism, the Atelier Troost employed a vocabulary of specific forms, colors, and materials that produced a distinctive visual language of power. Whether private or public, the Atelier Troost interiors were immediately recognizable as the Führer's spaces.

The plans and drawings for the apartment reveal an attention to detail that would also characterize the firm's later work. In addition to new furniture, the cornices, paneling, doors, handles, radiator covers, lighting fixtures, and even bathroom tiling were carefully designed. In the bathrooms and kitchen, there was an emphasis on hygiene and rationalization, which had also characterized modernist architecture in the Weimar era. Unlike the buildings on the Königsplatz or the House of German Art, the design was not as comprehensive as it might have been because of the need to incorporate existing furniture, accommodate the Winters' taste in their own quarters (which appears to have been, from a description on an invoice of "antiqued" furniture, even more traditional), and leave one room (likely that of Geli Raubal) untouched.[20] Hitler did not seem to mind this hybridity in his homes: all three of his residences were renovated or extended structures, representing a newness anchored in the past. Even in Hitler's entirely new state buildings, the past was present in the use of classical forms. In his homes, however, it was tangible in the actual physical traces of older structures. While one can point to practical or symbolic reasons for this approach, it is nonetheless noteworthy that in his lifetime, Hitler never constructed an entirely new home for himself, but instead repeatedly chose to update and improve—and yet also remain attached to—the past. Although plans were drawn up for new residences, none was realized.[21]

A further defining attribute of the Atelier Troost's designs was the quality of the materials used, above all fine German stones and woods, with a good deal of Italian silk. Nonetheless, the effect was not showy. Like Hitler, Speer highly esteemed Gerdy Troost's design talents and largely credited her with determining Hitler's "official tastes." In his memoirs, he described how the materials and colors that Gerdy Troost chose for the Führerbau were "subtle and restrained, actually too understated for Hitler's taste, which inclined toward the gaudy. But he liked what he saw. The balanced bourgeois atmosphere which was then the fashion in wealthy society had about it a muted luxury that obviously appealed to him."[22] These same qualities also characterized the apartment's renovation, but the subdued tone could be misleading. George Ward Price, foreign correspondent for the pro-German *Daily Mail* (with an estimated readership in Britain of 4.5 to 6 million), wrote approvingly of the Führer's apparent modesty: "That Hitler keeps on this unpretentious apartment shows that his modest personal tastes have not been altered by high office. It is the sort of home that a businessman with an income of £1500 a year might have."[23] But no middle-income businessman could have afforded the actual cost of this understated refinement. Take, for example, the museum-quality Persian carpet acquired by Gerdy Troost for Hitler. The dealer described it in detail in a letter he wrote to encourage her to make the purchase. Measuring over twelve by twenty-six feet, it was a Persian reproduction of a famous sixteenth-century royal carpet known as the Paradise Carpet. Employing naturalistic forms, the weaver had represented deer, panthers, lions, and bulls, among other real and imaginary animals, in a landscape with cypress, pomegranate, and flowering apple trees. The dealer noted that the estimated 15.4 million knots in the carpet would have taken a lone weaver working every single day fourteen years to complete. The price of 10,500 Reichsmarks was many times over that of an average businessman's salary.[24]

Thomas Jones, a former senior civil servant and deputy secretary to the cabinet, viewed the apartment with the wealth-discerning eye of a man familiar with the British upper classes when he visited Hitler on May 17, 1936, to discuss Hitler's invitation to Stanley Baldwin, the British prime minister, to visit Germany. In his diary, Jones wrote that he was "shown into a spacious sitting-room with an alcove at one end lined with books, many of them large illustrated quartos. The furnishing was solid and Victorian. There was a small portrait of Wagner, and a half-length of Bismarck by Lenbach. There were also pictures by Feuerbach, Cranach, Schwind, Zügel and Breughel. Nothing modern. We might have been in Park Terrace, Glasgow, in a shipowner's drawing room in 1880." For Jones, this home environment suggested a familiarity and stability that had nothing to do with a dangerous radical. And this was precisely the message that Hitler and his spokesmen sought to transmit. On the day before his trip to Munich, Jones had met with Joachim von Ribbentrop, soon-to-be German ambassador to Britain, who had quoted Hitler saying, "I am the most conservative of Conservatives."[25] Admittedly, Jones was predisposed toward a favorable view. He has been described by historian Gordon Alexander Craig as "one of the most ardent and naïve of those who came to be called appeasers." Nonetheless, the visit further reassured Jones of Hitler's respectability, and he "returned to England," Craig writes, "resolved to persuade Baldwin to accept the invitation."[26]

Although Jones explained that he had visited Hitler in Munich instead of Berlin because the German leader had returned for his chauffeur's funeral, it is no accident that Hitler chose to open his home to him or to Ward Price. Despite the different interpretations of each visitor—Ward Price viewed the apartment as not only more modest, but also decidedly more modern than Jones—both left with overwhelmingly positive impressions. Hitler clearly wished to be seen by a foreign—and, particularly, British—audience in his domestic context. As he no doubt had hoped, the effect was to convey a sense of absolute and even boring normalcy, helping to erase any memory of the lurid rumors of moral degeneracy once associated with his private life. Indeed, it was the apartment's very banality that so unnerved Lee Miller when she encountered it after the war.

For Hitler, convincing British diplomats and journalists that he shared their values was critical in the mid-1930s, as Germany's rapidly expanding rearmament threatened Britain's national interests. While he had no intention of halting his country's militarization, he understood that a well-played diplomatic hand could help him to reach his broader goals by avoiding an arms race with Britain that he was likely to lose. Fearing another war, many in Britain dearly wanted to believe that negotiated accords could create effective arms control and achieve European security. In a major coup for Hitler, the Anglo-German Naval Agreement signed in June 1935 legitimately released Germany from the naval restrictions imposed by the Treaty of Versailles and set the stage for the dictator's desired alliance with Britain against France and Russia. Hitler's self-professed trustworthiness had played a role in persuading the British government to hold the talks. On May 21, 1935, he had made an important "peace" speech in the Reichstag in which he advocated for talks, recognized British naval superiority, and promised his word on whatever was negotiated, provoking "a chorus of relieved comments in Britain."[27] In opening his new-and-improved Munich home to a British audience, Hitler understood how, like words of reassurance, the objects and furniture would speak for him, crafting an image of the occupant in the mind of the onlooker that the latter desperately wanted to see.

The *Daily Telegraph,* preferred by politically conservative middle- and upper-class readers in Britain, painted just such a picture in its pages weeks before Hitler's Reichstag speech. On April 25, 1935, it published an article about the renovation of the Prince Regent Square apartment stating that the Führer was overseeing the work and that "all the furnishings and decorations are being carried out according to Herr Hitler's own designs." Since the source for the article was likely the Nazis' own press office, the erroneous attribution of the creative work to Hitler seems deliberate. The article further reported that "the Fuehrer is a great lover of German 18th-century art," and had recently acquired "six paintings of German 18th-century artists from an American dealer." It also noted his passion for music, telling readers that "the decorations in his flat follow the German heroic colour scheme of blue, gold and white, made famous in Wagner's operas, and the furnishing is all of the same style." (The same article ran in the *New York Times* under the headline "Hitler's Taste Shows Wagnerian Influence.") Through the reinvention of his domestic spaces, Hitler was thus portrayed as an artist and composer in his own right. While the article implied his wealth, it also gave the impression of a man so devoted to art and culture that even the color of his pillows spoke to his idealism. One could argue that there is an undercurrent here of the absurd—the title of the *Telegraph* article was "Baroque," which could refer to Hitler's preferred style (according to the article) or to his elaborate decor. Nonetheless, the picture remained of the cultural refinement of the occupant as revealed through his interior.[28]

Such associations were strongly reinforced by the location of the building itself. Prince Regent Square is a large, dignified plaza that optically terminates Prince Regent Street, one of four royal roads in Munich. The broad avenue was developed beginning in 1891 with an emphasis on the picturesque: setback structures, curves, and green spaces. It commences at the former residence of the Bavarian prime minister, the Prince Carl Palace, and stretches diagonally east for over a mile before reaching Prince Regent Square. (After the square, the road bends southward, narrows, and continues for another three quarters of a mile.) Despite the royal name, the area was associated with the economic and political power of the bourgeoisie in the late nineteenth century—the very audience that Hitler needed to sway to his cause when he took the apartment in 1929.[29]

Less than two hundred yards west from 16 Prince Regent Square stands the Prince Regent Theater, which opened in 1901 as a festival hall for Wagner's operas, designed according to ideas put forth by the composer himself. Tickets to the inaugural opera, *The Mastersingers of Nuremberg* (*Die Meistersinger von Nürnberg*), cost twenty Marks, equivalent to a worker's average weekly wages. It was here that Hitler saw his first Munich performances of Wagner, and he regularly attended the theater's annual Wagner festival, taking to heart the inscription above its entrance: "To German Art." In 1932, the dire economic situation forced the theater to close its doors and dismiss its performers and staff. A few months after Hitler's rise to power, the theater reopened for performances of Wagner's *Parsifal*, and on November 9, 1933, the tenth anniversary of the failed Beer Hall Putsch, the theater's new artistic director marked the new political era with a National Socialist play by Friedrich Forster-Burggraf, *All against One—One for All* (*Alle gegen Einen, Einer für Alle*). The following year, the theater was given to the Nazi organization Strength through Joy, which celebrated it as a "cultural center for the German worker." Although operas continued to be performed at the renamed People's Theater, the programming increasingly turned toward propagandistic works, whose artistic merit was questioned even by critics writing for the National Socialist press. Despite the low price of tickets, which cost only 90 cents, the theater's seats were regularly half empty.[30]

Other connections to Wagner and to German art more generally pervaded the vicinity of Hitler's residence. A massive stone memorial to

Wagner, created by the sculptor Heinrich Waderé and erected in 1913, sits within a small patch of trees to the right of the theater. The marble block for the memorial, which required thirty horses to transport from the quarry to the local train station, comes from Mount Untersberg in Berchtesgaden, across from which Hitler established his mountain retreat.[31] Continuing west along Prince Regent Street, one arrives shortly at the Villa Stuck, the house of the Symbolist artist Franz von Stuck, whose work Hitler prized and collected. Several of Stuck's paintings hung in Hitler's Munich apartment, including a version of the erotic female nude, *Sünde,* or *Sin* (another version is found today in the artist's villa).[32] In May 1936, a colossal bronze statue of an Amazon on horseback, designed by Stuck in 1913, was added to the front of the artist's villa, which opened later that summer as a museum.[33] Stuck's home represents one of the finest architectural examples of the development in the later nineteenth century of the artist's atelier and home as a space of broader social and intellectual discourse, which reached its apogee in Munich and Vienna. As an aspiring young artist in these two cities, Hitler must have dreamed of hosting his own salon. Many of the artists Hitler admired—Hans Makart, Franz von Lenbach, Arnold Böcklin, Franz von Stuck, and Richard Wagner—had been known in their day for the creative brilliance of their salons, and Hitler particularly respected the Viennese Makart for having worked his way up from conditions of poverty to become the reigning artist of his day, with an atelier famous in all of Europe. Some of these artistic settings also became architecturally influential. The lush bohemian interior of Makart's atelier, for example, was widely published and helped to launch a vogue in the later nineteenth century for bourgeois domestic interiors that incorporated romantic notions of artistic informality and disorder.[34]

Leaving the Villa Stuck and proceeding west along Prince Regent Street for less than half a mile, one encounters the impressive neoclassical facade of the Schack Gallery (designed by Max Littmann, architect of the Prince Regent Theater), which houses the painting collection of the diplomat Adolf Friedrich von Schack. Devoted to German painters of the nineteenth century, this collection became one of Hitler's favorite haunts in Munich before World War I, significantly shaping his artistic tastes and later art collecting. Indeed, in 1939, he pursued the possibility of a "Führermuseum" inside the Schack Gallery that would have displayed his own artistic collections.[35] Less than two hundred yards from the Schack Gallery looms the vast Bavarian National Museum, with its rich collections of southern German artwork, ranging chronologically from the middle ages to the early twentieth century. Despite the building's size, the architect Gabriel Seidl arranged its volumes so as to not dwarf the street. In 1929, across from the museum on the southern side of the street, a new building was planned for the New Collection (Neue Sammlung), a branch of the Bavarian National Museum that highlighted modern design work, such as that of the Bauhaus or German Werkbund.[36] Although Hitler overtly rejected the modernist aesthetics of these institutions on ideological grounds, his regime continued to apply many of their goals in the design and production of industrial goods.[37]

Finally, at the point where Prince Regent Street begins, Hitler erected his House of German Art, a commission given to Paul Troost in 1933 and completed by Gerdy Troost and Leonhard Gall in 1937 (fig. 20). The monumental art gallery was to be paired with the House of German Architecture, designed by Gall in 1939, which, if realized, would have stood directly across the street.[38] Adjacent to the House of German Art, the Prince Carl Palace marks the head of the street. The neoclassical mansion, designed by Karl von Fischer in 1803, was renovated in 1937 in order to serve as a guesthouse for distinguished foreign visitors, the first of whom was Mussolini.

Thus, when in 1929 Hitler finally abandoned his bohemian image for the more settled domestic life suitable to a national leader, he chose a location loaded with symbolic significance for his broader political vision. Through his residence on Prince Regent Square and building projects on Prince Regent Street, he created and positioned himself along an axis of specifically German art and culture. At one end lived the Führer, the artist-politician of the New Germany, while at the other end of the axis stood his greatest temple, the House of German Art. Along the length of the axis, one finds many of the leitmotifs—rooted in art, music, and architecture—that Hitler would employ, time and again, to compose the mythic vision of his Aryan superstate.

Violence implicitly and explicitly underlay those ideals, and its presence was visible in the street's transformation during the Third Reich. Hitler let stand the street's most notable monument: the *Angel of Peace,* erected in 1899 on the eastern side of the Luitpold Bridge, which connects Prince Regent Street over the Isar River. Unlike the similar winged monument in Berlin, which commemorated the wars leading to German unification in 1871, the Munich monument celebrated the long period of peace that followed.[39] Incongruous as it may seem, even such a symbol

Fig. 20. Heinrich Hoffmann, photograph of the House of German Art in Munich, designed by Paul Troost and completed by Gerdy Troost and Leonhard Gall, seen here on the Day of German Art, July 1937. The print was included in a stereoscopic-format photographic album by Heinrich Hoffmann and Albert Burckhard Müller entitled *Day of German Art (Tag der Deutschen Kunst)* (Diessen a. Ammersee: Raumbild, 1937). The original caption reads: "Front of stone and front of steel."

could be woven into Hitler's self-mythologizing. Well after he invaded Poland in 1939, Hitler continued to present himself as a man keen to avoid conflict, but provoked to act by aggressive foes. During the Third Reich, the *Angel of Peace* witnessed Prince Regent Street's militarization. On Hermann Göring's orders, an imposing, nearly 250-yard-long regional aviation headquarters (Luftgaukommando VII) was built in 1937–38 across from the Bavarian National Museum (on land once intended for the New Collection). The building was designed by German Bestelmeyer, a conservative architect who supported the Nazis. He placed representations of steel helmets within window gables and decorated gates and grills with swastikas, all of which is still visible today.[40] The Luftgaukommando and the House of German Art imposed an oppressive monumentality on the street that had been assiduously avoided by its original planers and that disrupted the flow of green spaces connecting northern and southern parts of the city. On the stretch of Prince Regent Street between Wilhelm Tell and Bruckner streets, just east of Prince Regent Square and about 150 yards from Hitler's apartment, the regime constructed between 1942 and 1944 a series of model housing blocks that incorporated air raid towers into their design. In one such model, each spacious and comfortable flat had its own private door to a centralized bunker.[41] In the Nazi worldview, home sweet home came with a built-in bomb shelter.

At the end of 1939, Hitler acquired his own bunker at 16 Prince Regent Square, constructed with nearly five tons of steel, in the rear courtyard.[42] It still exists today, with its oak-paneled interior intact. A year previously, on December 27, 1938, Hitler had purchased the entire building for 140,000 Reichsmarks, ending his long phase as a renter.[43] Nonetheless, other tenants continued to reside there. While these neighbors, as Ward Price noted, had been thoroughly vetted by the Gestapo, their presence is surprising, given the elaborate security measures on the Obersalzberg. Ward Price, careful not to criticize the regime, thought that they had the "advantage" of sharing Hitler's security, but one wonders how much their freedom of movement and other liberties were curtailed. Two SS guards patrolled outside the building, another SS man controlled access to the street door, and detectives occupied a flat on the ground floor around the clock.[44] Evidently, Hitler felt sufficiently protected to relax there and even to host dignitaries and world leaders—most prominently, in 1937, Mussolini, and, the following year, Chamberlain.[45]

It was on the occasion of Chamberlain's visit that Hitler consented to have his apartment photographed for publication, the only such instance during the Third Reich (see fig. 19). The image was taken by Heinrich Hoffmann on the morning of September 30, 1938, when Chamberlain had asked for a private meeting with the German leader. The previous day and night, Hitler, Chamberlain, Mussolini, and the French prime minister, Edouard Daladier, had debated and eventually signed the Munich Accord, which had sealed Czechoslovakia's dismemberment. The next morning, Chamberlain went to see Hitler in his apartment to ask him to sign a short joint declaration that the Munich Accord and the Anglo-German Naval

Agreement signed in 1935 were "symbolic of the desire of our two peoples never to go to war with one another again." Chamberlain believed that if Hitler consented and then broke his word, his true character would be revealed to the world. Hitler, who was in a sullen mood, signed the paper but showed little interest in its contents. Chamberlain was delighted, convinced that he had backed Hitler into a corner.[46]

In the picture, Chamberlain, Hitler, and Paul Schmidt, Hitler's interpreter, are shown seated in the living room alcove beside the library. Hitler, who occupies the center of the photograph, is framed by markers of his cultivation: rows of fine books to the left, art objects in the foreground, including what appears to be Richard Wagner's death mask and a bronze bust of a young man (possibly by Renaissance sculptor Luca della Robbia), and behind him a canvas by Eduard von Grützner, a nineteenth-century Munich painter beloved by Hitler.[47] The carefully composed tableau thus identified Hitler as a man of culture, and, more specifically, as a German and Bavarian with classical leanings. During their conversation, Chamberlain had asked that, if Czechoslovakia resisted, there be "no bombardment of Prague or killing of women and children by attacks from the air," to which Hitler had replied that "he hated the thought of little babies being killed by gas bombs."[48] The carefully chosen objects around Hitler seemed to buttress that sentiment, suggesting they were the words of a man steeped in Europe's highest cultural values.

After the 1935 renovation, the Atelier Troost continued to maintain the apartment and to make purchases as needed. On May 19, 1942, six gold-rimmed champagne flutes were ordered for "rush" delivery to 16 Prince Regent Square.[49] What was Hitler planning to celebrate? Perhaps it was the news from his generals. Having abandoned the guise of the Glasgow shipowner for that of the warrior king, Hitler had driven his armies across most of Europe. In the second battle for Kharkov, then under way, the Wehrmacht was crushing Soviet forces. On May 16, in the battle for the Kerch peninsula, the German High Command announced the seizure of the city of Kerch. Within days, the Crimean front had collapsed and 170,000 Soviet prisoners of war, along with legions of tanks and guns, were captured.[50]

If Hitler had planned to toast these victories, then a year later, the champagne flutes were likely in the cupboard gathering dust. In the spring and summer of 1943, Gerdy Troost ordered new suites of furniture, drapes, carpets, and other renovations costing over 24,000 Reichsmarks. The work

began just after the surrender of the German army in Stalingrad and continued through the defeat of Axis forces in North Africa to the Allied invasion of Sicily.[51] This concern with new decor may have been no more
than a mad distraction from the shattering defeats on the battlefield, but
given Hitler's propensity to link politics and design, it is not inconceivable
that something more substantial was at stake. As Germany's military position deteriorated in 1943, Hitler's advisors urged him to negotiate with
Joseph Stalin or Winston Churchill in order to eliminate one of the war
fronts.[52] Despite Goebbels's official declaration of "total war" in February
1943 and Hitler's apparent intransigence on negotiating with his enemies,
the desire to spruce up his apartment—at a time when Allied bombs had
begun to rain down on Munich and the idea of redecorating would have
struck most of its residents as lunacy—raises the possibility that Hitler was,
in fact, preparing for a new round of diplomatic talks. At the very least, he
seems to have been expecting visitors on whom he wanted to make a good
impression.

4 FROM HAUS WACHENFELD TO THE BERGHOF

The Domestic Face of Empire

The chalet in the Alps that the head of a fringe political group had rented in October 1928 had grown too small, four years later, for the leader of Germany's largest parliamentary party. Hitler's rising political fortunes and the increasing number of people who traveled with him taxed the capacities of the house. In the fall of 1932, he commissioned what would be the first of several renovations that, over time, would transform the mountain cottage into a citadel.

The original design, from 1916–17, was a simple two-story structure. The ground floor contained a living room entered through a wooden porch, a kitchen with a pantry, a maid's room, and a toilet; the upper floor held two large bedrooms at the front of the house, two small bedrooms at the back, and a full bathroom. In the spring of 1933, based on drawings completed the previous September, a garage was built on the sloping land just below the house, creating a terrace above it; a conservatory, which projected onto the terrace, replaced the old porch; above the conservatory, the two front bedrooms acquired a larger balcony; a long annex for personnel and guards was constructed to the right of chalet; and the driveway was relocated and enlarged (fig. 21).[1] Although Otto Dietrich, Hitler's press chief, credited his employer with the designs, the plans were signed by Munich architect Josef Neumaier, an early member of the National Socialist Party well known to Hitler.[2]

Already when he had rented Haus Wachenfeld in 1928, Hitler had secured the right of first refusal from its owner, Margarete Winter. The elderly widow, then living in Buxtehude, hesitated to sell the house, but a personal visit from Hitler convinced her. On September 17, 1932, she signed an agreement setting a price of 40,000 Goldmarks (equivalent to about 175,000 Reichsmarks), and on June 26, 1933, nearly five months after becoming chancellor, Hitler bought it with all of its contents. Winter had insisted on guaranteeing the price against a gold value as well as the American dollar and other European currencies to protect against Germany's economic instability in the wake of the Great Depression, which would soon sweep Hitler into power.[3]

Even with these additions, the increasing number of visitors meant that a lack of space and amenities at Haus Wachenfeld continued to be felt. Looking back on conditions that had existed during this period, a *New York Times Magazine* article claimed that "when guests stayed overnight, even such prominent guests as Rudolf Hess, Hitler's deputy party leader, they had to sleep in tents outside or over the garage."[4] In his memoirs, Heinz Linge, Hitler's valet, recalled that the conservatory, "where the meals were served, was so cramped that guests had to stack up the crockery after eating to help the orderlies because of the lack of space."[5]

After Hitler was sworn in as chancellor on January 30, 1933, Angela Raubal endeavored to meet the new demands put on the household. In a thick file of invoices preserved from that spring and summer, we see her expanding the domestic inventory with new dishes, glassware, cooking and serving utensils, bakeware, lamps, and decorative objects. (The numerous dessert-making items attest to Hitler's sweet tooth, including his love of a good bombe.) Curiously, in June, she also purchased five chamber pots, perhaps for the recently completed annex, which had one shared toilet and bath among the five rooms. Purchases of flowers, vines, and shrubs as well as lawn and gardening equipment bespeak a greater attention to landscaping. The receipts thus reveal not only a need to better outfit the house to accommodate the chancellor's new influx of visitors, but also a heightened awareness of his domestic image.[6]

In the summer of 1935, Hitler decided on a radical expansion of Haus Wachenfeld, and after its completion in July 1936, he rechristened his home the Berghof. Albert Speer, recalling its genesis in his memoir, claimed that

Fig. 21. Josef Neumaier, plans for the expansion of Haus Wachenfeld on the Obersalzberg, dated September 8, 1932, and approved by the local building authorities on March 29, 1933. Angela Raubal and Margarete Winter signed as the owners. The relocated driveway is shown at bottom right.

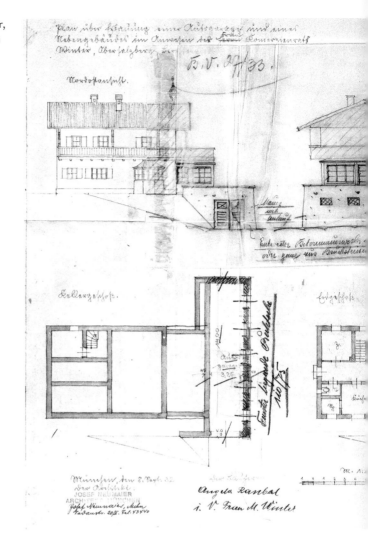

the design was undermined from the outset by the impulsive and over-confident nature of its creator: "Hitler did not just sketch the plans for the Berghof. He borrowed drawing board, T-square, and other implements from me to draw the ground plan, renderings, and cross sections of his building to scale, refusing any help with the matter." Although Speer noted that Hitler lavished great care on the design, he lacked the corrective habits Speer attributed to a trained architect: "Most architects will put a variety of ideas down on paper, and see which lends itself best to further development. It was characteristic of Hitler that he regarded his first inspiration

DOMESTIC FACE OF EMPIRE

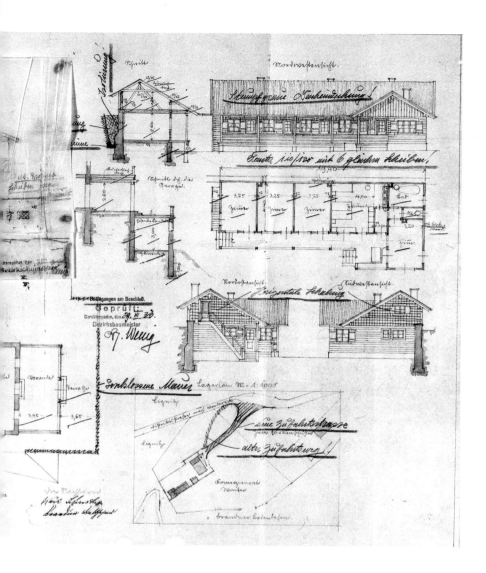

as intuitively right and drew it with little hesitation." Speer described the numerous failings of the "impractical" ground plan, arguing that it "would have been graded D by any professor at an institute of technology. On the other hand, these very clumsinesses gave the Berghof a strongly personal note. The place was still geared to the simple activities of a former weekend cottage, merely expanded to vast proportions."[7]

Speer's account makes no mention of an architect named Alois Degano, but it is his signature that is on the Berghof drawings and plans preserved in state archives (figs. 22–24). Degano, an architect based in the Bavarian

Fig. 22. Alois Degano, elevation drawing of the northwest facade of the expansion of Haus Wachenfeld, dated November 16, 1935, and approved by the local building authorities on January 22, 1936.

town of Gmund am Tegernsee, was known for designing in a modernized Alpine style that rejected the kitschiness that had come to be associated with it. He met Hitler in June 1933, after the chancellor admired the house he had recently built for Franz Xaver Schwarz, the national treasurer of the Nazi Party, in St. Quirin am Tegernsee. Later that year, Degano designed Hermann Göring's home on the Obersalzberg and renovated the nearby Türken Inn (to serve as SS quarters) as well as the Platterhof Hotel. Degano subsequently designed homes for Philipp Bouhler, Heinrich Himmler, and Max Amann as well as the Berchtesgaden branch of the Chancellery and two elite schools: the SS officers' school in Bad Tölz and the Nazi Party cadre school in Feldafing. It seems unlikely that a well-respected architect with a large firm and over two decades of experience would simply sign off on an amateur's designs in order for them to be submitted to the building authorities, even if that amateur were Adolf Hitler.[8] According to contemporary press reports, Hitler had provided the preliminary ideas, on the basis of which Degano elaborated and completed the plans. Still, there is evidence that Hitler was as much designer as client. In September 1936, Adolf Wagner, the *Gauleiter* (regional party leader) for Munich and Upper Bavaria, wrote a letter to Reich Chancellery Chief Hans Lammers

discussing Degano's plans for the Berchtesgaden Chancellery. He warned
that the architect needed closer supervision, describing Hitler's influence on
past designs that he had commissioned from Degano as "decisive." Indeed,
he went so far as to state that "the plans are practically those of the Führer
himself and Degano was more or less only the executor of the Führer's
ideas."[9] The degree of influence is visible in a sketch of the Berghof's new
main section that Speer included in his memoirs and identified as having
been drawn by Hitler. Although it differs in some aspects from the finished
building, it nonetheless captures its proportions and basic features: the retention of the old chalet, incorporated under a long, sloping roofline; the
monumental window on the first floor; three windows and a large balcony
on the second floor; and a loggia under the roof.[10]

The original Haus Wachenfeld stylistically imitated local farmhouses,
and Hitler attempted to continue in this vernacular tradition, despite the
change in scale. With notable exceptions, such as the massive window, the
expansion roughly approximated regional forms or practices. For example,
the low-pitched roof, with its overhanging eaves, is customary in this area
and protects against the rainy Alpine climate (see fig. 22). A balcony on the
upper floor and loggia under the roof are often found in Upper Bavarian

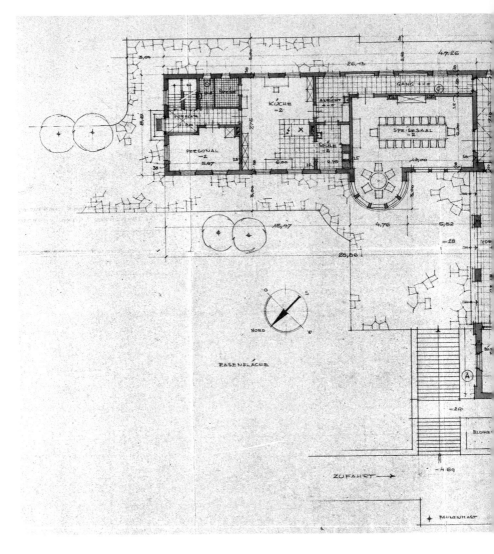

Fig. 23. Alois Degano, ground-floor plan for the expansion of Haus Wachenfeld, dated
November 16, 1935, and approved by the local building authorities on January 22, 1936.

farmhouses. While the extension was built largely of industrial materials,
its exterior cladding evoked traditional timber and plaster construction.
The low wing built to the eastern side of the house also has precedents in
the livestock stalls that were typically attached to a farmer's living quarters.
Moreover, the retention of Haus Wachenfeld recalls the not uncommon
practice in the region of absorbing a smaller structure into an expansion,

DOMESTIC FACE OF EMPIRE

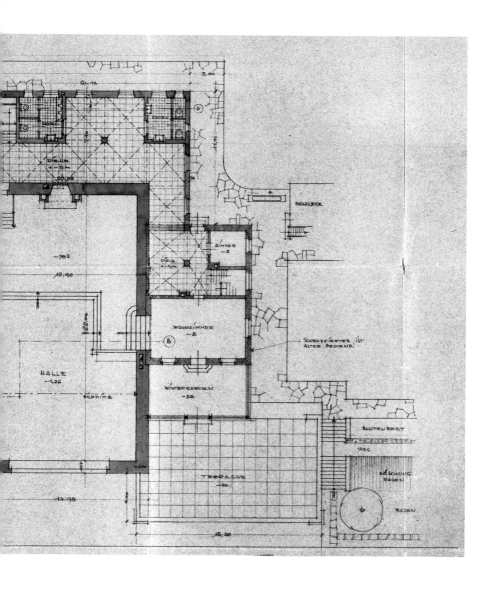

although it is usually done for economic reasons.[11] Presumably, Hitler was fond of the old house and wanted to retain it for sentimental reasons; he did not need to do so financially. But there were also ideological motives for keeping it. By 1935, the house had become iconic and beloved by many Germans, and Hitler wanted to retain its powerful associations and avoid the appearance of having grown distant from his own past.

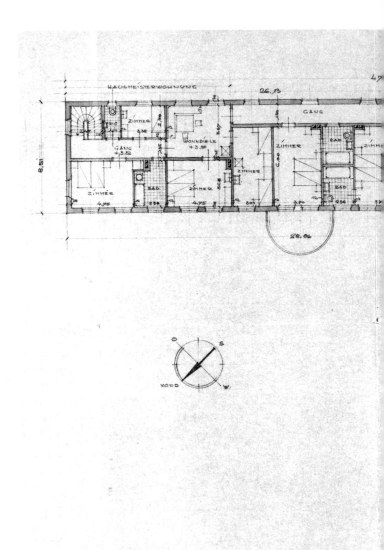

Fig. 24. Alois Degano, second-floor plan for the expansion of Haus Wachenfeld, dated November 16, 1935, and approved by the local building authorities on January 22, 1936.

A file of invoices for book purchases made by Hitler in 1933 and 1934, as he began to renovate Haus Wachenfeld, reveals several works on domestic and vernacular architecture, including a book on German farmhouses, which suggests that he was looking not only at farm buildings in the Berchtesgaden area, but was also reading more generally on the architectural and cultural history of the type.[12] That Hitler renamed his residence the

DOMESTIC FACE OF EMPIRE

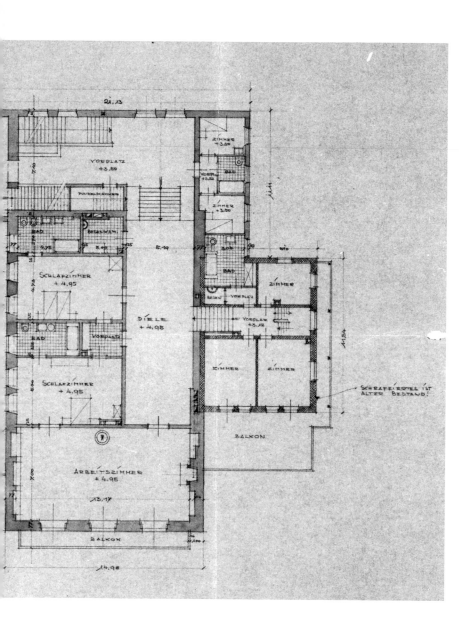

Berghof, meaning "Mountain Farm," also indicates his desire to associate it with agricultural models. Politically, this was a strategic choice, for it suggested humble origins and associations with productivity and German folk ethnicity. In its coverage of the Führer's new house, the contemporary German press took up and propagated the image of "an authentic mountain farm, rooted to the native soil."[13]

Once inside the house, such allusions quickly vanished, although even here, some rooms evoked traditional regional forms or functions. The Atelier Troost, commissioned to decorate the interiors, began their work in the late fall of 1935, when the building was under construction. While Degano concentrated on the structure, the Atelier Troost was responsible for designing complete interiors, from the finishing of ceilings, walls, doors, and floors to lighting, furniture, ceramic ovens, fireplaces, curtains, carpeting, decorative objects, and artwork. Nonetheless, boundaries between the two firms sometimes blurred, and on at least one occasion, Gerdy Troost attempted to intervene in the architectural design itself.

In the original residence, the Atelier Troost confronted a rather gaudy interior, conforming to an industrialist's stereotypical image of a rustic mountain home (plate 2). Onto this layer of kitschiness, Hitler and his followers had added yet another with all sorts of gifts of Nazi paraphernalia from the Führer's admirers. It is striking to see in images of Haus Wachenfeld how much of this stuff lay about the place—a figure of a saluting SA man perched on top of a lamp, swastika-embroidered cushions, even a swastika woven into the sides of a wicker chair. The Atelier Troost discarded these tokens of National Socialism and instead made the entire house a symbol of the new Reich. Convincing Hitler to part with these objects could not have been easy. When Speer visited Haus Wachenfeld and saw the profusion of such items, he noted, "Hitler commented to me with some embarrassment: 'I know these are not beautiful things, but many of them are presents. I shouldn't like to part with them.'"[14] It might have helped, however, that after 1933, Hitler's own government had outlawed the inappropriate use of such "national" symbols, including the swastika. Hitler did not always follow his own laws, but having these objects appear in public images of the house at the same time that National Socialist authorities were campaigning to eradicate Nazi kitsch clearly would have been problematic.

Before-and-after images of the original rustic *Stube,* or living room, in Haus Wachenfeld demonstrate how the Atelier Troost modernized the interiors, while nonetheless evoking a regional tone (see plates 2, 3). The renovation retained the original Bavarian corner nook, but replaced the painted spindly furniture with heavier and simpler straight-edged forms. The traditional dark-green ceramic stove, or *Kachelofen,* with surrounding benches gave way to one in celadon tones with painted relief tiles by the Munich artist Sofie Stork depicting people in traditional regional costumes. The painted wooden door surmounted by a shelf with knickknacks was replaced by a simple windowed door with a rounded arch. The painted wooden moldings were similarly removed and plain, dark wood was substituted. The fussy hanging lamp with the saluting SA soldier disappeared in place of a simpler fixture. The color scheme was reduced to a few strong elements (red, green, cream), and geometric rather than floral patterns dominated. Nonetheless, the room did not lack visual richness and, with its warm oven, made for an inviting space. The room now served as an antechamber, where guests waited to enter the adjacent Great Hall or for the Führer to emerge from within.

The intimate feel and dimensions of the Stube reinforced, in the movement from a compressed to open space, the vastness of the Great Hall, an oversized rectangle of a room with a floor on two levels that presented the Atelier Troost with its greatest design challenge (plate 4 and see fig. 23). It measured over forty-two feet wide by seventy-four feet long and eighteen feet high, the size of a small gymnasium, and was intended as a multifunctional representational space where Hitler would receive foreign and domestic guests, hold meetings with his ministers and generals, host official functions, entertain, and socialize. On the southern end of the room was a grand marble fireplace, and opposite it was a panoramic window measuring over twenty-eight feet long by twelve feet high (plate 5 and fig. 25). Hitler, it has been said, pioneered the work-from-home movement, and the Great Hall was at the center of his intention to rule an empire from the comfort of his living room sofa.[15]

Precedents for such a room can be found in medieval great halls. These multipurpose communal spaces displayed, through design elements such as the length of the room, height of the ceiling, or size of the central hearth, their lord's status. Hitler may have drawn on this domestic model, associated with feudal power, to reinforce his connection to a local legend: folktales about Mount Untersberg, framed by the Great Hall's majestic window, claimed that the court of Emperor Charlemagne (or, sometimes, Barbarossa) slept within the mountain, awaiting the sign that would awaken the king and his knights to fight a cataclysmic battle that would usher in a glorious new Reich. As Hitler told Speer, "You see the Untersberg over there. It is no accident that I have my residence opposite it."[16] The view of the mountain brought the medieval warrior-king's symbolic presence into the room, but perhaps the Great Hall itself was meant to mirror his imagined court buried deep within the mountain. In this context, the name that Hitler gave his house takes on a different significance: the word

Fig. 25. Photograph of the Great Hall at the Berghof with a view toward the fireplace, c. 1936.

"Berghof," although usually understood to refer to a mountain farm, also denotes a mountain court.

At the same time, Hitler may have had another, more modern, architectural precedent in mind for his Great Hall, in keeping with his vision of himself as an artist-politician. Namely, he may have looked to the great artists' ateliers of the later nineteenth and early twentieth centuries: large spaces that encompassed professional, domestic, and social activities. Hitler admired Hans Makart's famous Viennese studio and its accumulated layers of "memories," although he himself sought to instantly fabricate self-mythologizing spaces.[17] A celebrated 1885 painting of Makart's studio before its sale, created by Rudolf von Alt, depicts one of the huge historical canvases at which the artist excelled. Believing that politics was art, Hitler may have conceived the large window in the Great Hall, which pictured "German" nature at its most eternal and invincible, as his own canvas, and beneath it, the fourteen-foot-long Untersberg marble and oak table, where he studied maps with his generals, as his easel.[18] (This piece of furniture also evokes the high table of medieval great halls, at which the lord took his meals, conducted business, and dispensed justice.)

DOMESTIC FACE OF EMPIRE

The difficulties that the Atelier Troost faced in bringing some kind of harmony to the ungainly Great Hall are perhaps best appreciated in images of the room under construction, preserved in the Heinrich Hoffmann photographic collection at the U.S. National Archives. In them, we see how the cavernous room dwarfs the occupants and even the oversized furniture created especially for its spaces, an effect heightened by the scale of the window.[19] Around Christmas 1935, Hitler visited the construction site with his designers (fig. 26). Either then or thereafter Troost attempted to talk Hitler out of the gargantuan window. She later said that she had not seen architectural plans prior to this visit with Hitler, when the building had reached the stage of frame construction. Hitler told Unity Mitford, a fanatical English follower, about the disagreement when she visited him at the Berghof in July 1938. In a letter to her sister Diana, wife of Oswald Mosley, the leader of the British Union of Fascists, Unity described the house in rapturous terms, saving her greatest praise for the huge expanse of window in the Great Hall: "The effect is simply extraordinary. The window—the largest piece of glass ever made—can be wound down like a motor window, as it was yesterday, leaving it quite open. Through it one just sees this huge chain of mountains, and it looks more like an enormous cinema screen than like reality. Needless to say the génial [brilliant] idea was the Führer's own, & he said Frau Troost wanted to insist on having *three* windows."[20] In later years, Gerdy Troost claimed that Hitler usually took her design advice, but in this case, the window remained a single unit rather than being divided into three smaller sections.[21]

Hitler clearly relished having bested his designer, since he was still telling the story years later. The anecdote also reveals their conflicting agendas: whereas Gerdy Troost sought to impress with tasteful reserve, Hitler designed for grandstanding effect. As Mitford's letter revealed, the disappearance of the window contributed just as much as the window itself to the awe experienced by visitors. Thomas Jones, who had been invited to Hitler's Munich apartment in May 1936, accompanied former British Prime Minister David Lloyd George, an admirer of Hitler, on an ostensibly private visit to the Berghof the following September, not long after the renovation had been completed. As Jones reports, the Great Hall made a strong impression, "but what fascinated us all was the vast window at the north end, or rather the absence of it, for it had been wound up or let down out of sight into a groove and there was nothing between us and the open air and sky and mountains and a view of Salzburg in the distance."[22] Indeed, it

Fig. 26. Heinrich Hoffman, photograph of architects and patron visiting the construction site of the Berghof around Christmas 1935. From left to right: Leonhard Gall, Gerdy Troost, Hitler, and Alois Degano (?).

inspired Lloyd George to tear out a wall in the library of his country house at Churt in Surrey and replace it with a similar panoramic window.[23] (A more damaging outcome of the visit was Lloyd George's effusive praise in the British press of Hitler, whom he described as "the George Washington of Germany" and "a born leader of men" who had brought freedom and prosperity to a peace-loving country.[24])

Hitler expected his visitors to be dazzled by this architectural feat of commanding nature, no matter the circumstances. In November 1937, Lord Halifax, then lord president of the council in Neville Chamberlain's administration, visited Hitler at the Berghof to address Anglo-German relations, which had deteriorated as Hitler's hopes for a British alliance faded and Germany's expansionist rumblings pushed the limits of British tolerance for the Nazi regime. Amid the tense discussions, Hitler "insisted" on a performance of his window's vanishing act for the British delegation. Ivone Kirkpatrick, the head of chancery at the British embassy in Berlin, who was present at the talks, later recalled that "a couple of stalwart S.S. men doubled into the room, fixed things like motor-car starting-handles into the sockets and wound violently. The whole structure sank noiselessly into the floor, giving the room the appearance of a covered terrace." Kirkpatrick was

DOMESTIC FACE OF EMPIRE

unmoved and left the Berghof with the memory of Hitler having behaved like a sullen, spoiled child.[25]

Having lost the confrontation with Hitler over the window, Gerdy Troost seems to have embraced the idea of the panorama as the defining experience of the Great Hall. Writer Matthew Stadler has argued that "Hitler loved panoramas" and "his favorite rooms were organized around their panoramic views. . . . Where there was no view out, Hitler organized interior views—the rooms became stage sets for the dramas of the Führer. Their vastness compelled guests to watch rather than touch or feel the closeness of sociality. This spectative logic was the only one Hitler understood." The elevations of the Great Hall interior drawn by the Atelier Troost as well as contemporary photographs suggest how the long walls became their own kind of panoramas (see plates 4, 6). Furniture was arranged along or near the walls so as to create elongated views with nothing to block (or draw) the eye at the center of the room. The intended effect was not a concentration of attention, but its dispersal as the eye roamed over the broad scenes, whether of the mountain peaks seen through the window or the interior vistas of furniture and art. Even some of the furniture specially created for the room could be said to be panoramic, such as the sixteen-and-a-half-foot-long sofa designed by the Atelier Troost and placed in front of the Gobelin tapestry near the window (fig. 27). Stadler contends that Hitler's elongated tables "also served to bring the panorama indoors. Hitler laid his maps on them and stood over, gazing down at the great expanse."[26]

The room's emphasis on visuality, what Stadler describes as a "spectative logic," was also present in its multiplicity of screens and canvases, real or allegorical. The above-mentioned Gobelin, itself a woven canvas, hid the openings of an external projection booth, and on the opposite side of the room, another tapestry concealed the screen. Before the war started, Hitler would watch films here nightly with his guests and house staff, an activity that often must have frustrated the viewers, "for if Hitler did not like a film he used to clap his hands and order it to be replaced by one he did like."[27] The panoramic window could itself be experienced as a movie screen, as captured in Mitford's description of the cinematic unreality of the open-air view. The paintings and sculpture that filled the southern end of the room similarly encouraged a museal gaze in the Führer's "best" room, characterized by an attentive and reverential form of looking.

As is often the case in traditional art museums, the Great Hall's privileging of vision resulted in a lack of attention to the corporeal. Indeed,

Fig. 27. Foto-Technik Kaminski, Munich, photograph illustrating the view into the Berghof's Great Hall from the small living room (Stube), c. 1936.

a number of memoirs comment on the body's unease in its spaces. Jones described how when Hitler received Lloyd George at the Berghof, "Hitler sat on an easy chair and L. G. uncomfortably on a couch which had no back."[28] In fact, the couches in the Great Hall did have backs, but the seats were so deep that guests were forced to perch on their edges. Speer, too, criticized the uncomfortable sofas and the "inept arrangement of the furniture," which discouraged a common conversation and reduced each person to talking "in low voices with his neighbor." He also noted how gasoline fumes blew into the Great Hall when the window, which was situated directly above the garage, was open. While Speer blamed Hitler's poor design skills for assaulting his visitors' noses, it also testifies to the dictator's focus on visual effects.[29] Other public parts of the house displayed a similar

DOMESTIC FACE OF EMPIRE

emphasis, including the external and internal vistas incorporated in the long and narrow dining room (see fig. 30), and the outdoor terrace, on which Hitler installed a telescope.

Comfort in the Great Hall was, in any case, secondary to its main purpose: to impress. In this room, Hitler greeted kings and princes, prime ministers and marshals, religious leaders, secretaries of state, and ambassadors.[30] It was where he negotiated with the powers of Europe that stood between him and his vision of a greater German Reich. Like the renovation itself, the Great Hall was meant to convey the "new" Hitler—not the ex-corporal who roused rebels in beer halls or the dictator who cut down his opponents in cold blood, but rather a powerful, cultivated, and, above all, trustworthy statesman. It was the stage on which he performed this new role and invited others to respond to him accordingly. Jones, describing the meeting between Lloyd George and Hitler, conveyed the intended effect of the room when he noted in his diary how it "made a great impression at once upon the visitors and gave a sense of dignity to the proceedings."[31]

Beyond the Great Hall's impressive proportions and striking panoramic views, its contents also reinforced the image of a man of power, vision, and substance. The increased scale of the furniture in comparison with Hitler's other residences is notable and cannot be attributed solely to the size of the room. Building a vast space did not simply require comparably large furnishings, but also made them possible. On the southern end of the hall, a fireplace almost tall enough for a man to stand inside evoked a luxurious version of a medieval hearth. The mantel was made of red marble from Thuringia and measured seven-and-a-half feet high by eight-and-a-half feet long.[32] On the eastern wall stood a massive cupboard over fifteen feet long and ten feet high designed by Leonhard Gall to hold Hitler's certificates of honorary citizenship—a prominent symbol in the room of the German people's devotion to their leader.[33] How that "devotion" had been won was suggested by the cupboard's most unique feature: five large bronze knobs, sculpted by Eugen Henke, in the shape of heads, representing (from left to right) a Wehrmacht soldier, a girl in the League of German Girls, the Führer himself, a boy in the Hitler Youth, and an SA man (fig. 28). The knob heads embodied the ideal types of Hitler's Aryan nation, with the Führer at their center. Troost compared them to the tradition of Italian Renaissance bronzes, such as the projecting heads by Luca della Robbia on the north sacristy doors of the Florence Cathedral.[34]

Fig. 28. Foto-Technik Kaminski, Munich, photograph of two of the sculptured heads (depicting a boy in the Hitler Youth and an SA man) by Eugen Henke on the large cupboard in the Berghof's Great Hall, c. 1936.

Standing beside the map table near the window was an oversized globe famously parodied in Charlie Chaplin's 1940 film, *The Great Dictator* (plate 7). While Troost had wanted to downsize the Great Hall's window, in the case of the globe, she was responsible for its enlargement, thus assuring its iconic power. Troost had the globe, produced by the Columbus-Erdglobus Company in Berlin, made twice as large as the commercial standard. The base itself was designed by Gall. The globe stood five feet and three inches high, some four inches shorter than Hitler himself (to have been physically dominated by the globe, which Hitler planned to conquer, would have been unacceptable). It was reputedly on this globe that Hitler drew the Arkhangelsk–Astrakhan line as the goal of the military campaign Operation Barbarossa, the name itself inspired by the medieval emperor said to be sleeping in the Untersberg. The globe clearly pleased the Führer, who had similar versions placed in the Nazi buildings on the Königsplatz and in the Chancellery in Berlin.[35]

Hoping paradoxically to achieve both grandness and intimacy in the Great Hall, Hitler ordered it built on two levels in order to create the impression, reinforced by the separate seating areas, of "rooms within rooms."

DOMESTIC FACE OF EMPIRE

The walnut wainscoting installed at a uniform height around the Great Hall served to visually unify these different levels from below, while the walnut ceiling, with its large and deep coffers, did the same from above, also lending further gravitas to the room (see plate 4).[36] Writing about it after the war, Troost took credit for the ceiling, saying she suggested the idea to Hitler because of the dimensions of the room. She had been inspired, she claimed, by her late husband's work (for example, the white-coffered ceiling in the Brown House in Munich).[37] The ceiling, reminiscent of Italian Renaissance palaces, also recalls the pine ceilings in the library and Smoking Room of the Old Chancellery in Berlin, which had been installed in the early twentieth century (see figs. 6, 10). Realized on a smaller scale, these ceilings gave dignity and warmth to the rooms, which were also used to socialize. The size of the Great Hall, however, rendered the vast coffered ceiling more imposing than inviting in its effect.

Gerdy Troost's use of color repetitions and harmonies added a further dimension of visual unity to the Great Hall. As was her habit in rooms with tapestries, she based her color scheme on the two large Flemish Gobelins that hung on either side of the window and that concealed the film equipment. Or rather, she based it on the one that hung above the long sofa, *The March,* which was the only genuinely old tapestry of the two, dating from the seventeenth century. Troost commissioned a specialist to evaluate the tapestries because the garish colors of the one that hung near the piano, *The Battle,* disturbed her. He revealed that it was a modern copy and recommended laying it in the sun to fade its jarring tones.[38]

The colors and fabrics that Gerdy Troost used for the Great Hall, as well as for other rooms in the Berghof, can be studied with unusual immediacy because her fabric sample book survives among her papers in the Bavarian State Library (plate 8).[39] While many are missing, the fabric swatches in the book are well preserved, and their freshness comes as something of a revelation, particularly when compared to the color postcards sold to tourists in Berchtesgaden after the war. In a 1973 letter, Troost complained about the distorted impression these created: "they are not only loud and hideous, but truly have nothing in common with my color scheme at the time."[40]

The velour and brocade used for the Great Hall mixed Tuscan and strawberry reds, terra-cotta, silvery blue, pale and dark moss greens, and gold highlights. The effect was rich, but also formal. The fabrics used in the small living room and guest rooms were simpler and more modern in feel, with stylized botanical or folkish motifs. One color among the samples that is conspicuous by its near absence is brown. It is found only as a subtle element in two of the samples for the Great Hall; otherwise, the closest is a copper tone in the copper-, cream-, and egg yolk–colored fabric used for some of the pillows in the living room. An unpublished postwar interview with Gerdy Troost conducted by the Arizona artist Karen Kuykendall offers an explanation. Asked what kinds of colors Hitler preferred, Troost replied that he liked warm, earthy tones. She then continued, "He was not fond of brown."[41] This astonishing claim—Hitler was, after all, the instigator of the Brown Revolution, builder of the Brown House in Munich, and leader of the Brown Shirts—is supported by color photographs of his interior spaces in Berlin and Munich, in which brown is little in evidence, beyond the woodwork. In his biography of Hitler, John Toland wrote that the brown color of the SA uniform was "purely accidental; a large consignment of brown shirts, originally intended for German troops in East Africa, was available at wholesale."[42] Thus, while Hitler may have led the "brown movement" and identified with the color for symbolic and pragmatic reasons, it does not mean that he actually liked it.

True to their other projects for the Führer, the Atelier Troost used only the finest materials in designing the Berghof interiors. Transposing a Nazi motto intended for the German worker, one historian has stated that when it came to his home, for Hitler, the best was good enough.[43] German design journals writing at the time about the Berghof emphasized the native materials used, such as the red Untersberg and Thuringian marbles, or walnut and oak.[44] In fact, much of the house was constructed of industrial materials, although these were disguised with meticulous natural detailing. This quality came at a price and "cost estimates were exceeded by far." Hitler claimed to have paid for the renovation himself from *Mein Kampf* income, and complained to Speer that it had all but bankrupted him, forcing him to ask his publisher for a large advance on future royalties.[45] But surviving financial records, while admittedly incomplete, contain no evidence of Eher Verlag's involvement (in contrast with the renovation of Hitler's Munich apartment). The private "Adolf Hitler Fund," to which industrialists made "voluntary" contributions, may have paid for some, if not all, of the renovation. From 1933 to 1945, deposits totaled more than 700 million Reichsmarks, equivalent to well over $3 billion today.[46] The assets were administered with a free hand by Martin Bormann, who also oversaw building on the Obersalzberg. Gerdy Troost, who naively believed

Hitler's pleas of poverty and remarked after the war that "he never had spent much money on himself," successfully sought out donors to purchase Berghof furnishings as gifts for the Führer, including a Sung dynasty bowl priced at 600 Reichsmarks—half a year's wages in 1936 for an Autobahn construction worker.[47]

Despite the visual dominance of traditional materials and craftsmanship, Hitler expected his house to have the latest technological comforts and conveniences. The film equipment in the Great Hall was installed by Ufa, the principal film studio in Germany. The eleven-foot-long sideboard beneath the movie screen, adorned with a bust of Richard Wagner, concealed built-in speakers with stereophonic sound, a radio, and Hitler's collection of record albums (see plate 4).[48] Having the latest technologies, however, did not guarantee their smooth functioning. On Degano's recommendation, Hitler ordered the same American-style oil heating system for the Berghof that Degano had installed at Göring's Obersalzberg home. As the architect explained, the system did not produce ash that could settle on the house and was regulated by thermostat, which allowed for an even temperature throughout the house and avoided the overheated rooms that Hitler found so unpleasant. The boiler, however, chronically broke down, and the contractor was slow to respond to repair calls. As winter approached in 1936, a shivering Hitler vented his frustration on his architect, telling him to "rip out the whole damn thing."[49]

Disagreements with designers, cost overruns, and absentee contractors are hardly unusual in a renovation project of this size. They are worth mentioning, however, to dispel the myths of superhuman feats and snag-free productions spread at the time about Hitler's architectural projects—most famously, the claim that the New Chancellery was built in less than a year—that still linger today. Nazi propagandists presented the Führer's buildings as a pure translation of his will, and their seemingly magical construction (no labor disputes, no cost overruns, no shortage of supplies, and no delays) as a manifestation of what was possible when Germans worked together toward that will. Images of mountains dramatically filling the Great Hall's open window or white-gloved SS men arranging the dining room table with minute precision, among others, are still published today with little or no critical commentary in books about the Berghof meant to evoke nostalgia for a bygone era defined by its supposed technological wonders and orderliness rather than its blood.[50]

This aura of perfection also operated at the level of distinguished visitors, unfolding in a careful choreography that brought them from the driveway to the Great Hall. They arrived by car on the northern side of the house, where they were greeted on the stairs by its master. Together, to the accompaniment of a rolling drum, they climbed a broad flight of steps to a terrace (all paved with red marble from Mount Untersberg), where they walked past Hitler's black-uniformed SS honor guard, who presented arms; turned right under a covered walkway; and then entered a vestibule through a heavy oak door (see fig. 23). The low-ceilinged and dimly lit lobby area featured Thuringian red marble columns and vaulted arches that reminded one visitor of "a cathedral crypt."[51] Toilets and coat racks were located here as well. From the garderobe, the Great Hall could be approached in two ways. Continuing to the end of the vestibule, visitors could have turned right, proceeded down a corridor, and come to another small lobby, from which they would have entered the living room. A large rectangular opening covered with a heavy curtain reminiscent of a theater, and foreshadowing the performance of the statesman within, admitted the visitor to the Great Hall (see fig. 27). Alternately, by retracing their steps, they could have entered the Great Hall more directly, through a door immediately to the right as one entered the house. In each case, and as noted above, the progression from low-ceiled, more compact, and darker spaces to the vast, window-lit expanse of the Great Hall made the psychological impact of the room all that much greater.

In inclement weather, tea, if offered, was served in the Great Hall, as it was to Chamberlain on September 15, 1938. The British prime minister had traveled to the Obersalzberg to discuss terms that would diffuse Hitler's threat to invade Czechoslovakia, leading two weeks later to the concessions of the Munich Accord. *Anglo-German Review,* a British journal devoted to fostering "good understanding and co-operation between Great Britain and Germany" and to delivering the message that the Nazi government desired peace, featured the historic refreshments "in the Führer's famous chalet" on the cover of its September 1938 issue, making a choice thereby to emphasize Hitler's hospitality over his bullying tactics, which had forced the sixty-nine-year-old Chamberlain to the Alps in a desperate bid to avoid war (fig. 29).[52]

If invited to join the Führer for lunch, the visitor reentered the vestibule and turned east into the dining room, which was located in the new

DOMESTIC FACE OF EMPIRE

SEPTEMBER 24, 1938

NUREMBERG
PICTURE SUPPLEMENT

ANGLO-GERMAN REVIEW

VOL. II. No. 10   SEPTEMBER 1938   PRICE SIXPENCE

Photo: International Graphic Press

THE MEETING AT BERCHTESGADEN: MR. CHAMBERLAIN WITH THE FÜHRER, HERR von RIBBENTROP, SIR NEVILE HENDERSON AND OTHERS, AT TEA IN THE FÜHRER'S FAMOUS CHALET

NEVILLE CHAMBERLAIN
A BIOGRAPHICAL SKETCH

ALAS, THE PRESS . . .
By ADMIRAL SIR BARRY DOMVILE

★

THE CZECHS IN HISTORY
By PROFESSOR SIR RAYMOND BEAZLEY

THE GERMAN LABOUR SERVICE : By E. K. MILLIKEN

CURRENT OPINION ★ PRESS REVIEW ★ TOPICAL ARTICLES ★ ANGLO-GERMAN NEWS ★ THE LINK ★ BOOKS, Etc.

Fig. 29. Photograph of Neville Chamberlain (left of Hitler) and other guests having tea with Hitler in the Great Hall of the Berghof, as seen on the cover of the September 24, 1938, issue of *Anglo-German Review*. The visit occurred on September 15, 1938, when the British prime minister traveled to the Obersalzberg to discuss the international crisis brewing over Hitler's insistence on invading Czechoslovakia.

wing attached to the main section of the house (fig. 30 and see fig. 23). The long and narrow room, perpendicularly positioned to the Great Hall, could seat eighteen at the main table and six in the semicircular alcove, the latter a cozy spot where early risers could breakfast (Hitler had his breakfast in his study). The room was clad entirely in Swiss pine. Despite the dominance of stone in his public works, Hitler's favorite material, according to Gerdy Troost, was wood. The chairs were covered in terra-cotta–colored leather, continuing the color theme from the Great Hall. Beyond a built-in display cabinet and vase of flowers, there was no decoration, the abundantly knotted wood creating its own strongly graphic effect. Hitler sat in the middle of the table with a view of the Untersberg, and he and his guests were served by SS men in white uniforms, which added to the formal effect. According to Speer, "the dining room was a mixture of artistic rusticity and urban elegance of a sort which was often characteristic of country houses of the wealthy."[53] Meals were prepared in the kitchen located on the eastern end of the new wing, adjacent to the dining room.

Now and then, official visitors would climb the stairs in the lobby to the second floor, walk down an impressive, art-lined corridor that measured seventeen feet in width, and enter Hitler's private study for more confidential discussions (plate 9 and see fig. 24). The spacious room, with three French windows leading onto a balcony and built-in bookshelves on either end, was located directly above the Great Hall. At the center of the room was Hitler's desk, behind which hung oil portraits of his parents (based on photographs). Across from it was a cream-colored tile stove, painted with monochromatic green figures by Sofie Stork. On the western side of the room, a sitting area was arranged in front of a fireplace, over which hung a painting of a young Frederick the Great by Antoine Pesne.[54] The walls were clad in sanded spruce, and Gerdy Troost used what was described as a green-gray base tone for the curtains, carpet, and upholstery, with terra-cotta and beige accents, again picking up elements of the Great Hall's color palette. (Terra-cotta, a dominant color throughout the house, was also a favorite of Paul Troost, establishing continuity with his work. Terra-cotta was central to the color scheme of the *Europa,* the ship interiors that Hitler most admired.[55]) A contemporary German design journal described "the impression of warm domesticity" conveyed by this room, although it must not have felt that way to Kurt Schuschnigg, the Austrian chancellor, who was browbeaten here by his host for hours on February 12, 1938, in an effort to make him agree to violate his own country's sovereignty.[56]

Fig. 30. Foto-Technik Kaminski, Munich, photograph of the Berghof dining room, c. 1936.

Significantly, all three of the public or semipublic spaces in the Berghof used for important visitors—the Great Hall, dining room, and study—were those most closely associated in traditional domestic architecture with masculinity. These were typically the representational spaces of the house, where business was conducted or the owner's wealth and power were displayed. When the Berghof was completed in early July 1936, it had only been two years since the "Röhm-Putsch," or Night of the Long Knives (June 30 to July 2, 1934), when Hitler had political adversaries and old enemies murdered, including many SA leaders and its chief, Ernst Röhm, whom Hitler accused of planning a coup. Röhm's homosexuality was also repeatedly alluded to as a justification, and on June 28, 1935, the first anniversary of the purge, the regime broadened the legal definition of punishable homosexual offenses and intensified its persecutions of so-called sexual degenerates. These actions helped to alleviate suspicions that Hitler shared Röhm's sexual orientation, although whispered rumors persisted.[57] In the rooms that Hitler chose to display himself to those he most wished to impress, he thus communicated not only his power and cultivation, but also his "correct" masculinity, an important part of the appearance of "normality" that he performed in the mid-1930s. In the apparent absence of a flesh-and-blood female companion, sensual representations of women in the Great Hall, placed prominently near the fireplace and often visible in published photographs—such as the reclining nude goddess in *Venus and Cupid* by the Italian Renaissance painter and Titian pupil Paris Bordone, and Anselm Feuerbach's 1862 portrait of his model and muse *Nanna,* said to have been Hitler's favorite painting—further reinforced Hitler's heterosexual bachelor domesticity as well as his cultural sophistication.[58]

Beyond the Great Hall, the best-known area of the Berghof was its outdoor terrace with the spectacular backdrop of the Alps. On the terrace, a less formal space bedecked with tables and parasols in bright colors, Hitler met with party officials, youth groups, members of his inner circle, and others with whom he might wish to have a more casual encounter. Hitler's staff preferred gathering in the informal spaces of the house to the Great Hall. Traudl Junge, Hitler's young secretary, recalled the impression of comfort made by the small living room, with its warm tile stove, the conservatory's inviting flowers and soft armchairs, and the exciting vistas of the terrace, but remembered the Great Hall as "cold, in spite of the thick carpets, the magnificent tapestries and all the precious things adorning the walls and the furnishings."[59] In the evenings, the staff might bowl in the alley built in the basement of the new east wing. Hitler himself "loved bowling," according to his valet, Heinz Linge, who said it was his only form of exercise, "except for the expander under his bed." A photograph of Hitler in Heinrich Hoffmann's albums at the U.S. National Archives captures him in mid-throw.[60]

The second and third floors of the Berghof were used exclusively by residents and guests (see fig. 24). Hitler's bedroom was located beside his office on the second floor. Either for security or privacy (or both), it did not have a doorway opening directly onto the main hallway, but could be accessed only through an adjacent vestibule or from his office. Eva Braun's bedroom was adjacent to his, and their rooms were connected by the vestibule and a balcony. Each room had its own private bathroom. Across from their bedrooms, a flight of stairs led down to the second floor of the old Haus Wachenfeld, which now had three rooms and a shared bathroom. These were used by the on-duty valet and chauffeur.[61] The second floor of the east wing and the third floor of the main building held bedrooms for

DOMESTIC FACE OF EMPIRE

guests and staff, a strict separation not being maintained between the spaces of the two. Speer was critical of the layout, saying that the location of the staircases hampered the freedom of movement of guests on the upper floors when official meetings were taking place downstairs by forcing them to traverse public space.[62]

The offices of the secretaries and adjutants remained in the old wing to the west of the house. The different status of the staff was reflected in their spaces. Junge recalled that the chief adjutant's office was "a charming apartment in the rustic style." By contrast, the secretaries' office was a dark, "plain, ugly room, only sparsely furnished." As she noted, "I never did find out just why this room had been given such perfunctory treatment. Perhaps because Hitler himself had never set foot in it." Beside the secretaries' office was a fully equipped dentist's office, where Professor Hugo Blaschke from Berlin would set up practice with a dental nurse and assistants when needed. (After the war, Blaschke's reconstructed dental records would be used to identify the corpses of the high-profile Nazis he had once treated.) The wing also contained a barber's shop and a dormitory for security personnel.[63]

Beyond being a place to host dignitaries and conduct government business, the Berghof was also a private residence. Due to the widespread publicity about the house, the growth of Hitler tourism in Berchtesgaden, and the presence of high-profile guests, it became necessary to state that not all visitors were welcome. On October 5, 1938, Martin Bormann issued a circular ordering people, in polite terms, to stay away: "The Berghof is the private dwelling and private household of the Führer, where he stays primarily to be able to work undisturbed and in peace. For this reason, the Führer desires that any and all visits be withheld so long as no clearly stated invitation exists from the Führer."[64] It is typical of the regime's propaganda of a self-sacrificing leader that Bormann used work to justify Hitler's need for privacy. The fact that he now shared his home with a woman who was not his sister was kept secret from the German people. Because of Angela Raubal's antipathy to Braun, the latter remained only an infrequent guest on the Obersalzberg until Hitler unceremoniously evicted his sister in 1935, opening the way for Braun to take up residence.[65] The enforced secrecy about Braun during the Third Reich and the destruction of Hitler's private documents at the war's end have left large gaps in our understanding of her life at the Berghof and with Hitler more generally. In his memoirs, Linge recalled how the Berghof staff referred to Braun as the "girl in a gilded cage," but Heike Görtemaker's biography suggests that she was not without power as mistress of the house.[66]

After the war, in response to a comment made by Kuykendall about the Berghof images in Braun's photographic albums, which Kuykendall had seen in the U.S. National Archives, Troost remarked that Braun had never been present when she and the Führer met to discuss work.[67] Nonetheless, in Troost's fabric sample book, on the page facing swatches marked "guest room," she noted in handwriting the initials "E. B.," revealing that she knew for whom the room was intended. The fabrics were printed with stylized animal patterns and colored terra-cotta and cream as well as terra-cotta, cream, and forest green. A black-and-white photograph in one of Braun's albums shows a room with a sofa bed covered in a bird fabric.[68] Above the sofa bed hangs a sensual painting of a female nude. Beneath the photograph, Braun had attached a label stating: "Turkish Room—my room." The name's meaning and whether it was Braun's invention remains a mystery—despite the musings of her biographers, which range from dreams of "harem nights" to the pattern of the room's carpet.[69]

Also mysterious is the appearance in the albums of a different set of rooms marked with the label "Eva's new rooms at the Berghof." The spaces and furnishings of these rooms are notably different from the so-called Turkish Room. Prints and labels identify these rooms as a living room and a bedroom. This matches the memoirs of Julius Schaub, Hitler's chief adjutant, in which he noted that Braun, unlike other guests, had a small apartment consisting of a living room, bedroom, and bath, but did not mention its location.[70] The 1936 plan submitted to the building authorities, however, indicates that there was only one room adjacent to Hitler's bedroom (presumably the one identified in the albums as the Turkish Room). Its accuracy is confirmed by an article that Linge wrote in 1955, in which he described Hitler's study and bedroom as well as the one room that Braun occupied directly beside it. His explanation of the layout of the rooms and the connecting spaces between them conforms exactly to the 1936 plan.[71] It is nonetheless possible that Braun had, in addition to the one room beside Hitler, another suite of rooms elsewhere in the Berghof. On the third floor, immediately above Hitler's office, was a comfortable apartment containing a living room that opened onto the loggia, a bedroom leading to a private bathroom, and a walk-in closet that also doubled as the entrance; perhaps these were Braun's rooms as well. A stairwell near this apartment led to the foyer outside Hitler's bedroom, which would have made movement between the rooms fairly discreet.[72]

In one of the album prints, which Braun labeled as a detail of her living room, we see a chest of drawers over which she placed a framed portrait of Hitler (fig. 31). The image used was from a 1932 campaign poster and showed Hitler's face isolated and hovering on a pitch-black field. He does not smile, and the picture conveys an intense, almost otherworldly power—it may, in fact, have been inspired by images of death masks.[73] In another album print, we see hanging above her desk a small framed photograph of an official portrait of Hitler standing in his SA uniform—the same image that hung in German offices across the country.[74] These official images appear to be the only ones of her lover in the room. Whether she was compelled to maintain the illusion of a platonic relationship even in her private spaces or she actually saw him foremost as the Führer, we cannot know.

Braun photographed the interior and exterior spaces of the completed Berghof, appropriating her new home through the camera lens. Her images suggest both the alienation and intimacy of her domestic experience. For example, a set of photographs depicts an unoccupied, cavernous-looking Great Hall, the low angle of some of the images giving the oversized furniture an intimidating force. These views of the Great Hall, which imitated official publicity photographs, communicated that this was the Führer's domain. In others, however, Hitler is photographed from close-up playing with Braun's dogs or the young children of her friend Herta Schneider, transforming the Great Hall into a family room. Many of the photographs depict outdoor scenes on the terrace, a space that Braun clearly enjoyed. Beyond socializing with friends and sunning herself, it was also the stage on which she filmed Hitler and his cronies. Her color film footage of social gatherings on the terrace, discovered by American soldiers and first shown publicly at Cannes in 1973, has become firmly embedded in the postwar cultural imagination of the Berghof as the perpetually sunny playground of the monstrous.[75]

The convivial side of Berghof life is further depicted in Braun's images of afternoon outings to the teahouse on the Mooslahnerkopf, a hill overlooking the Berchtesgaden valley about a mile from the Berghof. Constructed in 1937 by another of Hitler's favored architects, Roderich Fick, the central round form of the teahouse was simple and severe. The walk to the teahouse with Braun and intimate guests was a regular part of Hitler's daily routine.

Fig. 31. Photograph of Eva Braun's room in the Berghof with a framed Hitler portrait. The print is pasted into one of Eva Braun's photographic albums.

Within this traditionally feminine architectural type, placed at a remove from the main house, Braun presided as mistress. The idea of a teahouse may have been inspired by the mid-eighteenth-century round "Chinese" teahouse that Frederick the Great had erected near his summer palace, Sanssouci, in Potsdam. The dining room designed by Paul Troost in 1933 for Hitler's renovations of the Old Chancellery had drawn on precedents at Sanssouci in its form and imagery. But in this case, the architecture and spirit of the two buildings could not have been more different. The Chinese

DOMESTIC FACE OF EMPIRE

Pavilion at Sanssouci is an architectural fantasy, ornately decorated with a mixture of Orientalizing and Rococo features and with gilded life-size sculptures of eating, music-making, and tea-drinking "Chinese" men and women meant to evoke the geographical source of the tea, and to make the visitor feel that he or she has been transported to the mythical East. Hitler's teahouse inspired no such reveries, although it was a place where he often napped after having finished his cake.

If the terrace and teahouse images captured Braun in her element, her albums also offer glimpses of the restrictions on her domestic life at the Berghof. An arresting set of images from August 1939 depict the Italian foreign minister, Galeazzo Ciano, arriving and being greeted by Hitler on the front steps. As was the case when other official visitors were present, Braun was required to remain hidden upstairs. Linge claimed that Braun admired the stylishness of the handsome Ciano and had wistfully exclaimed, "If only the Führer could be a snappy dresser like Count Ciano." Forbidden to meet him, she rebelled through her camera, capturing the event from a second-floor window (fig. 32). The images explicitly include the frame and muntins of the window itself, emphasizing the constrained position of the photographer, as if she were a prisoner in a tower. A typed label she included below the images defiantly states: ". . . through the window you can see all kinds of things!" She then boldly opened the window and continued to photograph. Ciano noticed, and in one of the images he looks up curiously, to which Braun appended the label: "Up above there is something forbidden to see . . . me!" Hitler sent an SS man to order Braun to stop, which she also noted in a label.[76]

When the Berghof was completed in 1936, it contained more than thirty rooms, at least twenty of which were furnished as bedrooms. When Hitler was in residence, the rooms were occupied by his staff, Braun, occasional guests, and thirty domestic employees, some of whom lived there.[77] Hitler, however, did not seem to think the house was large or impressive enough. In 1939, he commissioned an expansion of the new wing that stretched it farther eastward and added a new bay window as well as a separate driveway and entrance for deliveries.[78] But it appears that originally he had had a far grander scheme in mind, which would have added a second, massive wing to the eastern side of the house. A little-known and largely unpublished portfolio of drawings in the Bavarian Central State Archive in Munich contains unrealized designs for the proposed addition.[79] While these remained

Fig. 32. Page from one of Eva Braun's photographic albums recording Galeazzo Ciano's arrival to the Berghof in August 1939.

paper schemes, they provide important insights into how Hitler imagined his domestic self and how he wished it to be perceived by others.

The collection of unbuilt designs contains numerous elevations, sections, and floor plans representing different versions of the proposed new wing (figs. 33–35). Although unsigned and undated, they were likely created around 1939, when Hitler extended the eastern wing of the house. The quantity and quality of the work reveal that the idea of an expansion on a grand scale was not a mere passing whimsy, but a carefully considered project, with considerable resources expended on its conceptualization and planning. If completed, it would have significantly transformed the architectural form and experience of the house.

Envisioned was a second wing that would have projected eastward from the Berghof's main building, but would have been flush with its facade (see fig. 33). It would have stood parallel to and directly in front of the eastern wing that was completed in 1936, blocking its views of the mountain

DOMESTIC FACE OF EMPIRE

and creating a courtyard, in keeping with the second meaning of the name "Berghof": "Mountain Court." This layout also would have restructured the visitor's experience of arrival by creating a grand new entrance, with a circular roundabout or plaza for cars, at the far eastern end of the wing.[80] In one version, visitors climbed a flight of broad steps to enter a large entrance hall (see fig. 34). Turning right, they passed through a room with an intricately arched ceiling into a cloakroom with adjacent bathrooms. From here, visitors walked the length of the wing before arriving at the Great Hall, which they would have entered through a new door located directly beside the large window. (Although vague on the plan, residents presumably had the option of turning left from the entrance hall to reach the staircase leading to the private second floor, while servants and delivery personnel could easily access the kitchen.) This extended door-to-Führer path, intended perhaps to build suspense, recalls the processional route that Speer created in the New Chancellery, although without the same type of architectural splendor along the way. Instead, visitors would have walked past a long panorama of mountain views, glimpsed through a series of windows, before entering the Great Hall and experiencing the largest panorama of all. Adjacent to the hallway would have been five enfilade rooms (creating another interior panorama), intended for the use of the visitors' entourage. Thus the ground floor of the second wing would have been devoted to visitors, and especially to shaping a more dramatic journey of arrival. It also would have isolated them from the rest of the house, largely resolving the circulation problems noted by Speer.[81]

But the portfolio of unbuilt drawings contains a bigger surprise. Given the attention lavished on the Great Hall in the prewar press about the Berghof, it is astonishing to discover that Hitler had planned a showpiece that might have overshadowed it: namely, a monumental library on the second floor (see fig. 35). As marked on the unbuilt plans, the library would have been a grand chamber—far longer than the Great Hall—on two levels, with a capacity to hold a remarkable sixty-one thousand books, comparable to some public and college libraries. The entrance to the library would have been from the eastern end of Hitler's study. A door would have opened onto the upper level of the library, from which a monumental staircase would have led to the floor below (a smaller staircase was planned for the opposite side of the room as well).[82] The centrality of the library in this conception of domestic identity suggests Richard Wagner's home, Wahnfried, and his prized book collections as a possible model.[83] Typically associated with

Fig. 33. Unsigned
elevation drawing
showing one version
of the proposed
new northwest
facade for the
expanded Berghof,
not built, n.d.

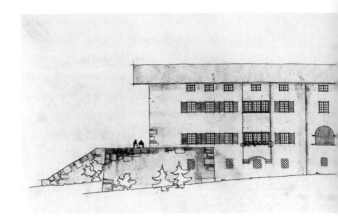

masculine power and creativity, the library would have bolstered Hitler's masculine image. But above all, it would have presented him not only as a powerful leader, but also as a cultivated individual. While this was similarly achieved through the attention to artwork and music in the Great Hall, the inclusion of a major library in the house would have strongly reinforced the image of the Führer as a learned man.

Unfortunately, the portfolio does not contain any conclusive evidence as to why Hitler abandoned the idea of a second eastern wing. The multiple versions drawn of the northern facade reveal the designer struggling to balance the forms and proportions of the extension. One proposed solution would have built a house-like facade and terrace on the eastern end of the wing to mirror those same structures on its western side.[84] Other versions tried to distract from the massiveness of the wing by adding balconies, bay windows, or Bavarian-style painted decoration to the facade.[85] But no matter how many variations were created, it was clearly difficult to avoid a bastion-like effect, and Hitler surely would not have wanted to evoke the nearby Salzburg castle, which represented all too clearly autocratic rule. Looking back in 1942 on the construction of the Berghof, Hitler confessed that when he visited the building site in 1935, "the dimensions of the house made me somewhat afraid it would clash with the landscape. I was very glad to notice that, on the contrary, it fitted it very well. I had already restricted myself for that reason—for, to my taste, it should have been still bigger."[86] Perhaps Hitler later regretted his initial caution, only to again decide, when

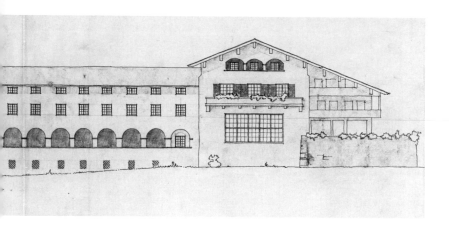

expanding the house in 1939, in favor of a less grandiose option. The slope of the mountainside also may have been a factor in deciding to scrap the plans.[87] In any case, the existence of these unbuilt drawings reveals that, contrary to Speer's story about the genesis of the Berghof, Hitler struggled with how to best present his domestic self to the world.

By the time the war started on September 1, 1939, Hitler's habit of spending long periods of time on the Obersalzberg and away from Berlin was deeply entrenched. In the mid-1930s, he was spending more than a third of the year in the mountains—in 1937, clearly enjoying the fruits of the renovation, it was closer to half. A war did not seem reason enough to give up those comforts, and the Berghof became a military headquarters from which he conducted battles and planned strategy. While his presence on the mountain did decrease during the war years, Hitler was notably absent only for two years—in 1942, as the front was pushed deeper eastward, and in 1945, when it came home.[88] Hitler hated leaving the Berghof. In early 1942, ensconced at the Wolf's Lair, the Führer Headquarters in East Prussia, the man who had driven millions from their homes could not stop talking about his own. "How I'd like to be up there! It will be a glorious moment when we can climb up there again. But how far away it is, terribly far!"[89]

In 1944, Hitler managed to spend over a third of the year at the Berghof; he left for good on July 14, 1944. Before doing so, he seems to have issued a "do not touch my stuff while I am gone" order. On February 4, 1945, Gerda

Fig. 34. Unsigned ground-floor plan for the expanded Berghof, not built, n.d.

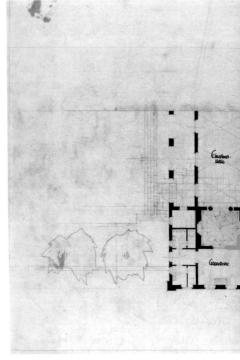

Fig. 35. Unsigned second-floor plan for the expanded Berghof showing the library, not built, n.d.

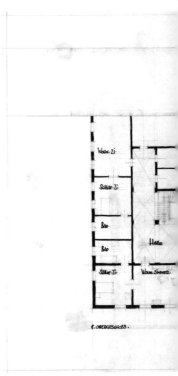

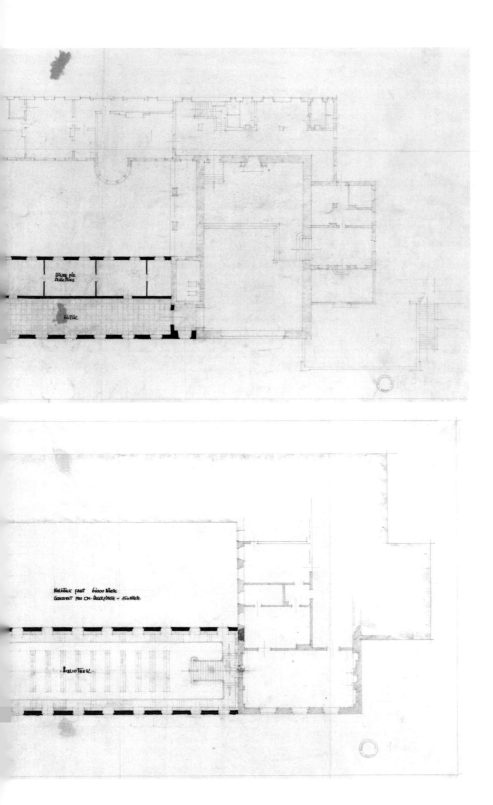

Bormann, Martin Bormann's wife, wrote to her husband in Berlin to report that "Frau Troost rang up yesterday and today; she can go on talking for hours, and everything one answers gives her a fresh theme for conversations! She thinks that the great hall in the Berghof should be repainted in the same colour as that with which time and light have endowed it—otherwise, she says, when the pictures are taken down, it will look frightful. She knew, she said, that the Fuehrer had said that nothing was to be done. But the walls would be spoilt if they were not repainted, and it was only a little job which could be done in a few days, and the Fuehrer probably wouldn't even notice it."[90] (Bormann refused the request.) That Troost could worry about faded paint when half of the nation had been bombed out of their homes is almost beyond belief. But no more so, perhaps, than Hitler's apparent faith that, despite the catastrophe unfolding all around him, he could return to an unchanged house.

5   GERDY TROOST

Hitler's Other Chosen Architect

On May 2, 1945, Germans awoke to the news that their beloved Führer had "fallen" in the war and that they would face their enemies without him. The next day, Gerdy Troost took to her bed and remained there for a week.[1] Troost had been among Hitler's most idealistic and longest-serving artistic collaborators, working with him from 1930 until the end of the war. She was also among his most loyal, refusing to renounce him even when confronted by a postwar denazification tribunal that would punish her not only for her past deeds, but also for her intransigency and pride. And yet in many ways, she was an unlikely partner, not fitting the image of the members of Hitler's inner circle, by virtue of her gender, as well as of her fiercely independent temperament and sometimes contrary beliefs, which she rarely kept to herself.

The woman born in Stuttgart on March 3, 1904, as Sophie Gerhardine Wilhelmine Andresen might never have encountered Hitler if it were not for her relationship with Paul Troost, whom she met in her father's atelier in 1923 (fig. 36). Johannes Andresen, an interior decorator, was the owner and director of the German Woodcraft Studios (Deutsche Holzkunstwerkstätten) in Bremen, which produced Paul Troost's interior designs for the North German Lloyd *Sierra* steamships. Gerdy Andresen worked with her father

Fig. 36. Photograph of Gerdy and Paul Troost, May 1933.

in an unknown capacity after having completed her education at the age of sixteen at a higher girls' school in Düsseldorf. In 1924, she moved to Munich—where Troost lived—ostensibly to study architecture and art history. She did not enroll in the university, for which she (like many other women at the time) did not have the necessary qualifications, but instead audited courses and took drawing lessons.[2] On August 5, 1925, the twenty-one-year-old married Troost, two weeks shy of his forty-seventh birthday, and from this period dated her collaboration with him, first on his ship interiors and later on his National Socialist commissions. The couple made annual study tours within Europe, including to Italy and France, and also traveled to the United States, where North German Lloyd sent Paul Troost in 1926 to familiarize himself with the latest technological and design developments in order to satisfy the demand for greater comfort among its passengers, many of whom were American. The itinerary included hotels and housing developments in Atlantic City, Buffalo, Chicago, Niagara Falls, Philadelphia, and Washington, D.C., the Ford factory in Detroit, and ships at anchor in New York Harbor.[3] After Paul Troost's death, his widow—while fiercely protective of his legacy—nonetheless insisted on their having shared a true artistic partnership from 1925 to 1934. In a letter written as the first

GERDY TROOST

anniversary of his death approached, she recalled, "We had no children, no, but were nonetheless truly life partners. We lived so intensely and consciously together in the realm of architecture, art, and music. And, again, in our common pursuit of a lofty ideal, which in recent years was our whole life. We shared our days from morning until night, starting at 6:00 A.M. with drawing pencil and pad at breakfast and ending evenings with debates about the politics of art. There was hardly a thought of my own that I did not share with him."[4]

The "lofty ideal" to which Gerdy and Paul Troost dedicated their artistic efforts and that brought them together as a couple also united them with their most important patron: Hitler. All three conceived of the arts as a sacred duty and mission. Each revered the classical tradition and rejected the "concrete Zeitgeist" of international modernism, although Gerdy Troost, belonging to a younger generation, was more open than the two men to contemporary design and artistic trends. Hitler believed Paul Troost was the master capable of giving architectural form to the spirit of his nationalist revolution, and Paul Troost believed that he had found a devoted patron who shared his deepest values and ambitions.[5] Thus, the three were joined not only by their common pursuit of an ideal, but also by their recognition that they needed each other for its attainment.

Even so, the partnership among them was not inevitable. In an unpublished postwar reminiscence about the couple's first encounters with Hitler, Gerdy Troost recalled her husband's initial reluctance to accept Elsa Bruckmann's invitation to meet with the politician at her home on September 24, 1930. This hesitancy was rooted less in political differences than in Paul Troost's antipathy to such social events. The couple lived quietly and Troost had little patience for such gatherings, which he considered a waste of time. Bruckmann, however, insisted, and Gerdy Troost, who did not attend the "gentlemen's evening," spent the hours playing Brahms on her piano and reading Cézanne's letters, waiting for her husband to return. (The inclusion of this detail in her narrative reveals that she wanted to be understood as a highly cultivated woman, immersed in the world of music and art. It also mitigated her absence at the meeting, suggesting a connection through their mutual interests.) When he arrived home at 2:00 A.M., he gushed enthusiastically about Hitler, whom he claimed bore little resemblance to the stern image on election posters, but instead proved to be an immensely sympathetic and knowledgeable lover of art and music, eager to recruit Troost for his ambitious architectural plans.[6]

Gerdy Troost reacted to her husband's bedazzlement with skepticism, but was herself enchanted upon meeting Hitler on the afternoon of September 30, when he first visited the couple's apartment. In a November 1930 letter to her mother, she wrote: "Contrary to the unappealing hue and cry and his public persona, Hitler in person and with Paulus behaves like a truly splendid, serious, cultivated, modest chap. Really touching. And with so much feeling and sensitivity for architecture—Paulus says that he has hardly ever met such a person in his life! Here in Munich he is, of course, the hero. Nonetheless, I am not very moved by his politics and views, in that I am first and above all and forever a human being and only then a German—in other words, a pacifist, and that contradicts his doctrine! But work with him is very pleasurable, because he is such an architecturally sensitive person—and so enthused about Paulus."[7] Her unpublished postwar text further reinforces this account of a strong attraction bridled somewhat by unease about Hitler's politics. She recounted how, a short while after this afternoon visit, Hitler came to dinner: "He did not eat, he did not drink, he did not smoke, but he talked and talked." He spoke about his grand architectural plans as well as his political vision for Germany. Near midnight, he left, and the couple stayed up late talking, unable to sleep for excitement, but also for concern about the meaning of "nationalism" in National Socialism, which, she claimed, jarred with their pacifistic and cosmopolitan worldview. Convincing themselves, however, of Hitler's "genius" and his best intentions for Germany, they went to bed in the early morning hours, putting their anxieties to rest as well.[8]

Paul Troost's professional situation at the time undoubtedly motivated the couple to trust in Hitler. After eighteen years of lucrative contracts for North German Lloyd, Troost's commissions for designing ship interiors had come to an end by the summer of 1930. The worsening economic effects of the Depression had put the building of luxury ocean liners on hold indefinitely, giving Troost little hope of new work. He was also aware that the spread of international modernism in Germany had made his designs appear old-fashioned to some of his corporate patrons, perhaps damaging his chances of returning to prominence within the industry. When he met Hitler, Troost was spending his days painting.[9] While his Lloyd contracts had made him wealthy enough to retire comfortably, the fifty-two-year-old architect was no doubt drawn to the possibility that, rather than winding down, his career might be raised by this fanatical admirer to unimagined new heights, encompassing not only monumental building, but also urban planning.

And, indeed, by hitching his talent to Hitler's star, Troost found himself inundated with plum projects, especially after 1933, while other architects joined Germany's long unemployment lines. Following the Brown House interiors, Troost received numerous prestigious commissions from Hitler, including for the Führerbau and NSDAP Administrative Building, House of German Art, redesign of the Königsplatz, and Temples of Honor, all in Munich, as well as for the renovation of the Chancellery in Berlin. He also undertook projects for Julius Streicher, Adolf Wagner, Franz Ritter von Epp, and other prominent figures in the Nazi movement. Troost could hardly keep up with the work, and at the time of his death, in January 1934, most of these projects remained in the planning stages. He might well have remained a footnote in Third Reich history if his widow had not made it her life's mission to complete his buildings and thereby secure his place in the National Socialist pantheon.

Gerdy Troost and Hitler first established a working relationship through her involvement in her husband's projects. This encompassed, from the little we know, consulting on designs, particularly in the selection of colors and fabrics, and helping to manage the office. In his memoirs, Julius Schaub, Hitler's adjutant, claimed that "she inspired her husband in many of his designs" and that her influence extended not only to Paul Troost's ideas, but also to those of Hitler.[10] According to Gerdy Troost, Hitler was a thoroughly engaged client, showing an enthusiastic interest in even the smallest detail. Before and after coming to power, he visited the Troosts regularly, sometimes as often as once a week. Indeed, once he became chancellor, the Troosts' studio was often his first stop upon his return to Munich. Gerdy Troost claimed that, except for the "gentlemen's evening" when Paul Troost had been introduced to Hitler, she had been present at all subsequent meetings, a fact confirmed by Schaub.[11] On April 13, 1933, Gerdy Troost met for the first time alone with Hitler when the two visited the atelier of the sculptor carrying out Paul Troost's design for the memorial to the sixteen Nazis killed in the 1923 Beer Hall Putsch, which Hitler had commissioned for the south side of the Feldherrnhalle, a nineteenth-century military monument on the Odeonsplatz in Munich. Inaugurated on November 9, 1933, with a dramatic re-creation of the putsch march, the memorial would become a sacred site for Nazi followers.

The day after her solo meeting with Hitler, Troost described the experience in a long letter to her friend Alice Hess, thereby revealing how her initial skepticism had by then transformed into utter devotion. Hitler, she said, was "animated, fresh as ever, and enthused about the design." Beaming at the memorial-in-progress, he said, "Yes, indeed, such proportions and such harmony, such internal and external form [Gestaltung], only a Troost is capable of this." Hitler then began to talk about the Parthenon and the Pergamon Museum in Berlin, and Troost listened, spellbound. "And I have to say this again and again, because it grips me so forcefully every time, how these hours of looking and listening enrich and deepen me. This rousing vigor, this spiritedness, this enthralling, glorious warmth of Hitler's. The intensity, power of thought, and compelling, masterful logic with which he always weighs, synthesizes, shapes, and solves a question, thought, theme, or problem, be it in a cultural, economic, political, or other domain. Yet he is never rigid, narrow, dry, or pontificating, like most academics and philosophers."[12] And so the letter continued, a torrent of words of praise for Hitler's knowledge, manner of expression, and vision spilling down the page.

Troost grasped for lofty historical and religious parallels to adequately describe the effect of her encounters with the Führer: "Hours? Moments—eternities. They are filled with richness, profundity, wisdom, and religion. And to me it always seems as if a second Plato were creating a new conception of the world. As if Kant were once more arguing his critique of pure reason. And as if Meister Eckhart and Luther, with strong, devout hearts, once again heard the call of their God, and in defiance of the whole world, and despite all the dangers and demons, followed and served him." Then turning her attention back to her friend, Troost acknowledged that "you are amazed that I repeat here once again what I have already told you so often." Troost asked her to understand "that an overflowing heart does not allow the tongue and the pen to remain still." But even with all that she had said, Troost wanted her friend to realize that it had not been and could never be enough. "One can well love and adore this unique human being, but never do justice to the true measure of his greatness and profundity. Only the future will be able to appreciate it. I am unspeakably happy and gratefully proud to be able to witness the actual hour of birth of the coming Weltanschauung and the coming faith."[13]

Years later, when Troost would be called to testify before a denazification tribunal, her close relationship to Hitler would prompt questions about the dictator's influence over women. On January 21, 1947, the tribunal chairman, a lawyer named Josef Schleifer, asked Troost, "Just what was it about the man that made women run after him, made them so crazy about him—what was it about the man, just tell me that." (The question might have been prompted by a prominent feature in the *Washington Post*, written by Hitler's doctor, Karl Brandt, and published two days earlier, that discussed Troost—described as highly intelligent, but charmless and cruel—as one of Hitler's "legion of ladies" who had profited from as well as bolstered his power.[14]) Troost replied, "I do not know—he was so warm and kindhearted—and, by the way, men fell for him, too. No, I have not been in love with him."[15] But as her letter to Hess shows, Troost was besotted, if not by the man himself, then by the idea of the Great Genius—a Plato, Kant, and Luther, all rolled into one—who would usher in a new golden age for humankind, to which she and her husband would not only be witnesses, but in which they would also play a central role.

Hitler, in turn, revered Paul Troost, whom he considered the greatest architect to grace German soil since Karl Friedrich Schinkel. In claiming to have discovered and thereby rescued Troost's genius late in his career, allowing the architect to realize his masterworks before he died, Hitler elevated himself to a modern-day Ludwig II, and Troost to his Richard Wagner.[16] Like the king and the composer, Hitler saw his legacy intertwined with that of his architect. In a letter to Gerdy Troost, written from his military headquarters and dated January 21, 1944, the tenth anniversary of Troost's death, Hitler stated, "What the professor once meant to me personally cannot be fathomed by someone who does not understand with what concern I awaited the realization of my artistic plans." With the Russians driving the German army out of the Baltic states, and British and American forces fighting in Italy, Hitler perhaps reassured himself when he stated: "If the New Reich is to be more than a passing phenomenon, then, alongside its power politics, it must also have cultural values to leave to posterity. It is only through the art of building, however, that a political order can experience its most beautiful immortalization." He continued, "I have always considered it a great good fortune that providence birthed your husband and allowed me to meet him."[17]

In her postwar denazification testimony, Gerdy Troost stated that after Paul Troost's death, Hitler "transferred his veneration for my husband to me." According to Schaub, Hitler stated that "she is the only person who can continue the work of Professor Troost, because she is deeply rooted within it."[18] The surviving records from the Atelier Troost amply demonstrate Hitler's support for her and her work. Asked in 1973 by Arizona artist Karen Kuykendall whether she had encountered difficulties as a professional woman in the Third Reich, Troost replied that while it "naturally" had not been easy for others in this *"Männerstaat"*—a term Heinrich Himmler had used to denote a manly men's state, in which women and homosexuals would play no part—Hitler's admiration had protected her.[19] High-ranking Nazi officials, including Albert Speer, Joseph Goebbels, and Himmler, knew that Hitler held Troost in high regard and did their best to remain on good terms. When they did go head-to-head with her, they invariably lost.

But Hitler's support, crucial as it was, was not the sole reason for her ability to hold her own in this Männerstaat. Gerdy Troost was not easily intimidated or deterred and had a clear mission to secure and protect her husband's legacy. Schaub maintained that in the Atelier Troost "she set the tone on designs, especially on subtle color compositions, and made Hitler aware in particular of color harmonies."[20] There is evidence to support Schaub's assertion in the business correspondence of the Berlin firm August Wagner, which provided the art glass for Paul Troost's party buildings. Designs hinged on his widow's approval, and when she was absent from a meeting, the decision process stalled. She also appears to have been the partner who was more difficult to please, as suggested by a letter from the Wagner firm to a third party, in which they complained about the "untold effort" it had taken to win her satisfaction.[21]

Rumors that circulated during and after the Third Reich implied a determination on Troost's part to protect her husband's legacy that went far beyond quality control of the design and construction of his projects. In his postwar memoirs, Otto Dietrich, Hitler's press chief, blamed Troost for the demise of the *Frankfurter Zeitung* (Frankfurt Newspaper) in August 1943. At the time, the liberal paper, founded in 1856 and bought out in 1934 by I. G. Farben—the chemical concern that would later produce the deadly gas used in the concentration camps—had, for the sake of public relations abroad, remained protected and enjoyed an unusual degree of freedom. The newspaper reputedly provoked Troost's ire when it printed an article critical of her husband's architecture. She is said to have followed it closely thereafter, keeping a clipping file documenting the newspaper's criticism of National Socialism. According to Dietrich, when Hitler learned about the newspaper's abuse of its freedom from Troost over lunch at the Osteria

Bavaria, one of his favorite Munich haunts, he ordered it shut down, over Goebbels's and Dietrich's protests. But the story is certainly more complicated than Dietrich suggested. The newspaper was already under attack by high-ranking party leaders, and Hitler himself detested it and considered it a Jewish holdout and enemy of the Reich. Moreover, by 1943, with few countries in Europe remaining unoccupied or neutral, the newspaper's foreign propaganda value as an "objective" voice of the Reich was limited. Nonetheless, Troost's protest seems to have catalyzed Hitler into action, prompting the paper's demise.[22]

Troost was also accused of having obstructed or even ruined the careers of her husband's architectural rivals. Speer wrote that she "lashed out" and "violently attacked" Paul Troost's opponents, approaching "the defense of her husband's work with a determination and sometimes a heatedness that made her much feared."[23] Friedelind Wagner, by contrast, suggested that Troost was motivated by jealousy of the newcomers who might replace her husband in Hitler's heart: "This sinister woman," she wrote in her memoirs, "managed to keep his memory green by prejudicing Hitler against everyone else whose work pleased him."[24]

Wagner offered the example of Paul Schultze-Naumburg, an archly conservative architect who had led the fight against modernism in the 1920s. His views were vehemently racist, conflating a "diseased" modernism with mixed-race artists, and arguing for a "healthy" German architecture based on the "blood and soil" of its "northern" people. To his disappointment, when his ideal racist state was founded, Schultze-Naumburg received few government commissions; his political alliances alienated Goebbels, and Hitler did not care for his architecture, which he found provincial. According to Schultze-Naumburg, however, it was Gerdy Troost who caused an irreparable break between the architect and the dictator. In 1934, Hitler had commissioned Schultze-Naumburg to renovate the interior of the Nuremberg Opera House; it would prove to be his first and last project for the Führer. Shortly before the work was completed, Hitler, accompanied by Troost and other architects, toured the building. According to Schultze-Naumburg, the visit was proceeding well, with Hitler expressing delight at the renovation. (Others present disputed this, saying that Hitler was in a foul mood from the start.) But then Troost "began to whisper to him," and when she was finished, Hitler erupted in a tirade of criticism, berating the architect in front of everyone. He ordered Schultze-Naumburg to share oversight of the construction with Troost, at which point the aggrieved architect withdrew from the project. After the humiliating encounter in Nuremberg, Schultze-Naumburg had little further contact with Hitler or the Nazi Party.[25]

In a 1962 letter from Winifred Wagner to her friend Gerdy Troost, Wagner mentioned that Lotte Schultze-Naumburg, the architect's widow, was pressuring her for help and "keeps saying that YOU were responsible back then for her husband being fired!!!!" Schultze-Naumburg, in financial straits and with three children to support, had asked Wagner to confirm her story so that she could transform her husband from perpetrator into victim and thereby claim government entitlements. Troost replied that she had no idea why Frau Schultze-Naumburg would make such an "absurd" accusation and speculated that it was founded on an old grudge nursed by Paul Schultze-Naumburg against her husband's success. Wagner responded that although she had never fully understood the issue, "I can only remember that the couple arrived here utterly devastated when, one summer, USA [Wagner's shorthand for Unser Seliger Adolf, or "Our Blessed Adolf," as she referred to Hitler in her correspondence] had inspected the remodeling or the interior furnishing of the Nuremberg Opera House, in the course of which a fierce disagreement broke out, for which the couple blamed YOU!"[26]

Troost let the matter rest there, but in a 1999 letter to historian Martha Schad, written when Troost was in her mid-nineties, she explained her side of the event. Hitler, she recalled, had requested her presence on the site visit. When he asked her opinion, she stated: "Very well renovated. What I found excessive was that Schultze-Naumburg had installed the swastika in very large—far too large—emblems in front of the box seats." While Troost presented her actions as professional (even if one wonders whether the image of the racist Schultze-Naumburg and his gigantic swastikas has an element of ridicule in it), some historians have ascribed malicious intentions to them, stemming not from jealousy, as Friedelind Wagner suggested, but rather from revenge. In his memoirs, Hans F. K. Günther, a friend of Schultze-Naumburg, recalled that upon learning in 1934 that Troost planned to take over her husband's atelier, Schultze-Naumburg disparaged her abilities by saying, "Oh please, I would not let a surgeon's widow operate on my appendicitis." Günther surmised that Schultze-Naumburg repeated the insult to others, and that the remark found its way to Troost, earning him her enmity.[27]

In the patronage system that Hitler created, resentments, gossip, and paranoia formed a routine part of artistic life, making it difficult to judge, in the absence of contemporary documentation, whether the postwar criticisms about Troost abusing her power represent legitimate grievances or lingering indignation at the power this woman had once exerted. Nonetheless, other sources amply demonstrate how carefully Troost controlled and protected her husband's reputation after his death. In 1938, she published *Building in the New Reich* (*Das Bauen im neuen Reich*), which offered a comprehensive survey of Nazi-approved architecture in the new Germany. The lavishly illustrated volume featured party buildings, memorials, NSDAP schools, youth hostels, administrative and government buildings, barracks, theaters, stadiums, recreation and social facilities, factories and laboratories, highways and bridges, airports, community halls, agricultural buildings, and housing. The accompanying text attempted to unite this impressive range of buildings into a coherent ideological whole by repeating Nazi platitudes about the "organic" connection between buildings and a race's "blood and soil"; the "nomadism" of foreign people in Germany, who were unable to find purchase on its soil; the bond of culture and blood between contemporary Germans and the ancient "Hellenes"; the damage wrought by liberalism, Marxism, Jews, and industrialism; the cultural bolshevism of the New Objectivity (*Neue Sachlichkeit*); the subordination of technology to art; and the importance of architecture as the highest cultural expression of "an awakened, racially aware peoples." Although Schultze-Naumburg was not among the architects represented, the influence of his racial theories is clearly discernible.[28]

The book opens with the work of Paul Troost, who is celebrated as the originating genius of the new German Weltanschauung in built form. The first image is of a Temple of Honor, and the dramatically photographed, stark neoclassical forms, together with the honor guard, graphically convey the sense of a new discipline. The Königsplatz, Führerbau, NSDAP Administrative Building, and House of German Art are also generously illustrated and discussed.[29] The visual attention to Troost's projects and their placement within the book reinforces the narrative of his foundational role for all subsequent National Socialist architecture. Gerdy Troost did not actually write the text herself, although she edited it carefully. She collaborated on the book with Kurt Trampler, an ardent nationalist who had previously published on the Germans' need for and right to Lebensraum.

He approached her about the project, offering to write the text and collect the images. Troost determined the thematic organization of the book, selected the architects who were to be included, chose the illustrations, and corrected the text. According to their agreement, she maintained full control over the text and images.[30] The book that resulted, which appeared only under her name, profoundly shaped the conception of Third Reich architecture. It sold tens of thousands of copies and went through multiple editions (as well as being translated into Dutch after the German occupation of the Netherlands). In 1943, Troost published a second volume largely dedicated to the architecture of war, including military schools, flak towers, air bases, barracks, military hospitals, bomb shelters, and memorials. Two further volumes, on National Socialist interior design and furnishings, were planned but never completed.[31]

Building in the New Reich followed and reinforced Paul Troost's glorification at the inaugural German Architecture and Applied Arts Exhibition, held at the House of German Art from January 28 to April 18, 1938. The architectural section dominated, occupying the ground-floor exhibition halls, while the applied arts displays were limited to the second floor. Each division of the exhibition had its own small jury, and Troost served on both. The architectural jury, which also included Leonhard Gall and Albert Speer, gave pride of place to Paul Troost's work.[32] The visitor entered the exhibition through a room devoted entirely to Paul Troost and featuring large-scale photographs and an architectural model of the party buildings on the Königsplatz. The only work not by Troost was a plaster relief of Pallas Athena by Munich sculptor Richard Klein, the symbol he had created for the House of German Art, which reinforced the classical heritage of Troost's architecture. A huge model of Troost's House of German Art was placed at the center of the second room, which included models and photographs of work by other architects. Dominant among the large-scale photographs were the Munich and Berlin projects of Gall and Gerdy Troost. (Models, plans, drawings, and photographs of Speer's Nazi Party Rally Grounds in Nuremberg filled the first two rooms of the second part of the exhibition, directly across the Honor Court from those of Paul Troost; through this placement, Hitler's "first" architects framed or bracketed the exhibition as a whole.) Thus, in the exhibition, as later in the book, Troost's buildings formed the portal through which National Socialist architecture emerged, shaping the visitor's perception of a direct lineage. Upstairs, among the furniture and decorative arts exhibits, Paul

Troost's designs for tables, cabinets, chairs, lamps, and other interior furnishings were also generously represented.[33]

Although Speer had by then assumed the mantle of the Führer's architect, he understood not to upstage Paul Troost when working with his widow (fig. 37). Speer had early on realized her influence and courted her favor. After the war, Gerdy Troost recalled how Speer had hung around the Chancellery construction site in 1935, trying to ingratiate himself. Although older by only one year, Troost took on the role of a mentor, often inviting Speer to dinner. (She later said that her younger brother's death that year in a motorcycle accident had made her "very soft.") They became friendly, and it was therefore a shock when, two years after they had first met, Troost was introduced to a Mrs. Speer at a reception—in all that time, Speer had never mentioned a wife. Troost found this "unnatural" and a sign of his ambition; he had calculated, she assumed, that she would be more interested in him if she thought he were single. Nonetheless, the two remained cordial throughout the Third Reich. In an August 1944 letter from Speer to Troost, he wrote, "What a pity that we never see each other anymore."[34]

When Speer published his memoirs in 1969, distancing himself from Hitler and National Socialism, Troost developed an obsessive loathing for the man she now considered a liar and a traitor. Among her personal papers in the Bavarian State Library is a thick file dedicated to him. It contains newspaper clippings, notes, and a short text she wrote, "On the Albert Speer Question." Many of the former members of Hitler's inner circle shared her feelings; in fact, their common dislike of Speer seems to have brought them closer together.[35] Troost did not restrict her views on Speer to this group of friends, but openly criticized him in interviews. Troost's 1971 conversation with John Toland is peppered with her rebuttals to Speer's autobiography.[36] Additionally, she told Toland an anecdote about Speer that he included in his book and that also appears in her "Speer Question" manuscript. The latter version is worth repeating here, as it includes revealing details that do not appear in Toland's text:

> During lunch with Adolf Hitler in his Chancellery apartment—this was in the summer of 1935—Dr. Goebbels asked me, "You have known Speer for quite some time now; what do you think of him?" Me: "I can answer that best with a comparison." Turning to Hitler—I was sitting between him and Göring; we were a small group, joined only by the adjutants Schaub and Brückner—"So, you, Herr Hitler"—back then I still called him by his name—"say to my husband, 'Honored Herr

Fig. 37. Heinrich Hoffmann, photograph of Albert Speer (far left), Gerdy Troost, Hitler, and others inspecting the House of German Art construction site on June 29, 1935, on the occasion of the topping-out ceremony.

Professor, I need a building of 100 meters.' My husband replies: 'I must think this over, but I will give you my decision by tomorrow.' The next day he reports: 'For structural and aesthetic reasons, the building can only be 96 meters long.' Then you say to Herr Speer: 'Dear Speer, I need a building of 100 meters.' Speer immediately ejects: 'Jawohl mein Führer—200 meters!' And you clap him on the back and say, 'Speer, you are my man!'" We all laughed a lot at this comparative joke, most of all Hitler. But we did not then sense how horribly its deep, tragic truth would bring catastrophe upon us.[37]

As the last line indicates, for Troost the joke about Speer's character exposed something far darker than his unbridled architectural ego. After the war, confronted by the Nazis' genocidal crimes, Troost refused to reconsider her devotion to Hitler. Rather than hold him accountable for Germany's disgrace, she came to blame Speer. "His ambition, his obsession with power," she told the historian Matthias Schmidt, had encouraged Hitler's worst tendencies and "steered us into disaster."[38] Troost may also have been upset at how Speer's memoirs elevated his own role in National Socialist architecture. Although he paid obeisance to Paul Troost as his mentor, recalling

GERDY TROOST

how he had often visited him in his studio in Munich and thereby developed a close relationship with him—a claim that infuriated Gerdy Troost, who insisted that the two had never met—Speer clearly no longer felt the need to play second fiddle. Nor could she have been happy with how he portrayed her as her dead husband's merciless, aggressive protector.[39]

Yet as important a role as Gerdy Troost did play in upholding her husband's legacy, after his death, as Schaub states, she emerged as a power in her own right. Hitler's growing trust in her abilities led to important new commissions, among them the renovation of the Prince Carl Palace. The neoclassical mansion, designed by Karl von Fischer in 1803, was located at the head of Prince Regent Street in Munich, adjacent to the House of German Art. Since 1924 it had served as the seat of the Bavarian prime minister, but Hitler ordered the resident prime minister, Ludwig Siebert, to vacate it so that it could be converted into a guesthouse for state visitors, the first of whom was to be Benito Mussolini. Hitler, who was desperate to impress the Italian leader, did not skimp on the budget. The structure of the house was remodeled by the state architect Fritz Gablonsky, who demolished a previously added northern wing and built a new extension to the rear (western) side. Troost was responsible for furnishing the interior, down to the china. The project cost 1.3 million Reichsmarks, an enormous sum to spend on a single residence, comparable in price to purchasing multiple luxury apartment buildings in Munich.[40]

Since the Prince Carl Palace was neither one of her husband's commissions nor intended for Hitler, Gerdy Troost was free to design in a manner closer to her own personal style, which blended modern and traditional influences, as seen in her own spacious Munich apartment (fig. 38). For the furniture, she mixed pieces produced by the United Workshops for Art in Handicraft (including designs by Paul Troost) with antiques borrowed from the galleries of the Munich and Würzburg residences. Paintings were loaned from the Bavarian state collections. Troost spent 125,000 Reichsmarks alone on Persian carpets.[41] The new reception room, a large-scale photograph of which was included in the 1938 German Architecture and Applied Arts Exhibition, reveals Troost's awareness of contemporary design trends, particularly in the emphasis on horizontal lines, indirect lighting, rich colors, and sensual materials, such as the red velour upholstery of the sofas and armchairs, which matched the red cloak worn by one of the attacking gods in Peter Paul Rubens's 1618 painting, *The Rape of the Daughters of Leucippus*, hung above the sofa and borrowed from the Alte Pinakothek in Munich (fig.

Fig. 38. Photograph of Gerdy Troost's living room in her Munich apartment at 4 Himmelreich Street, where she moved after her husband's death, photograph c. 1935.

39). The voluptuous materials extended to Mussolini's bathroom, which featured a sunken black marble bathtub surrounded by black marble walls. The house offered every possible comfort and luxury to its honored guest: an order specified that there were to be "fruit in the rooms, Fachingen water, an espresso machine, cognac, vermouth, cigars, cigarettes on a table in the hall." The library contained books that had been specially bound for the visit in leather and gold. On the morning of September 25, 1937, Mussolini stopped at the house for forty minutes, then returned around noon for another ten minutes, and finally spent an hour and forty minutes there in the late afternoon before boarding a train for Berlin. He returned in 1938, but once again did not spend the night. Afterward, the house remained largely unused until 1945.[42]

If money was seldom an issue for Hitler's designers, other resources were. In 1936, Hitler announced his party's Four-Year Plan for economic reform, which limited foreign imports and curtailed the use of materials needed for rearmament, creating shortages that interfered with building

Fig. 39. Heinrich Hoffmann, photograph of the salon designed by Gerdy Troost in the Prince Carl Palace in Munich, 1937.

projects, including those of the Führer. Already by 1935, the production of purely natural fabrics, such as cotton and wool, had ceased and, after 1936, was increasingly replaced by poor-quality synthetic textiles.[43] While imposing severe restrictions on the rest of the nation, Hitler insisted that the best natural materials be made available for his buildings; the Führer would neither sit nor stride on rayon. In December 1936, Hitler told the director of the Raw Materials Allocation Department for the Four-Year Plan that his buildings should be given preferential treatment.[44] When, in 1937, Troost was having trouble securing the Italian silk needed for Hitler's Munich buildings, he ordered his Economics Ministry to make supplying the Atelier Troost a priority.[45] The scale of Hitler's projects further aggravated his designers' inventory problems. As architectural historian Paul Jaskot has shown, Albert Speer, confronted with the massive quantities of building materials required for the proposed rebuilding of Berlin, displayed his "resourcefulness" as Hitler's chief architect by signing contracts with the SS to supply the labor of concentration camp inmates to manufacture bricks and quarry stones.[46]

Once the war began, retaining craftsmen and construction workers became another pressing issue confronting Hitler's architects as more and more young men were drafted to the front. To protect his most highly prized artists and designers as well as his projects, Hitler drew up with Goebbels a list of those to be exempted from military service by virtue of their "God-given" talent (this list also included composers, performers, writers, and filmmakers).[47] This did not, however, alleviate the problem of who would work for them. Beginning in 1940 and continuing for years, Troost found herself battling the military brass over her drafted workers, trying to extricate them from battlefields in order to return them to their atelier desks.[48]

On January 1, 1939, Troost and Gall officially dissolved their partnership, which had all but ended in the fall of 1937, when Paul Troost's buildings were completed. Nonetheless, they continued to share the Troost Atelier premises and name as well as the services of a secretary. Gall retained the architectural staff for his own commissions and, later, for repairing bomb damage to Paul Troost's buildings.[49] In 1937, Gerdy Troost had begun to work in a new area of design: the creation of certificates and presentation folders and boxes for Third Reich awards.[50] After the start of the war, she largely devoted herself to this realm of artistic production, which developed into its own cottage industry. As she herself described it, her role involved developing the design in close collaboration with one or two other artists and overseeing the production.[51] She also discussed the projects with her clients and managed a host of suppliers. The certificates and presentation folders for the more prestigious awards, which were published in Nazi art journals, were costly artifacts, due to the materials and the level of artistry involved in their creation. The certificates were handwritten on parchment with gold leaf, while the containers were sometimes richly worked in gold and bejeweled with diamonds, rubies, and other precious gems, in imitation of medieval reliquaries or treasure bindings.[52] As attested by Troost's correspondence, Hitler took a great interest in, and even contributed ideas for, the documentation and cases created for these awards, which ranged from high military to civilian honors. The nature and number of the awards and certificates mushroomed in the war years as Hitler sought to buy loyalties with decorations and paper laurels. In early November 1940—some two months after the Royal Air Force first bombed Berlin, shocking its residents, who had believed Göring's promise that he would keep them safe—Troost designed a godparent certificate for children born in the New

Chancellery bunker. Hitler acted as honorary godfather, as if the event were an auspicious beginning for the baby rather than a horror.[53]

The German occupation of foreign countries created new sources for materials and labor. For the construction of a communications bunker at the Brown House in Munich, begun in December 1943, Gall used over one hundred *Ostarbeiter,* forced laborers from conquered eastern territories. Troost, who shared offices with him, must have known about the nature of his laborers, especially since two of them were shot.[54] Moreover, among her business correspondence is a copy of a 1944 letter sent by her parchment supplier to the Chancellery regarding his inability to keep up with his orders for the Führer's certificates due to ongoing labor difficulties, including his Ostarbeiter running away. He wrote requesting help with obtaining a permit for building materials to expand a storage shed in his workers' camp so that he could house two Ostarbeiter families, promised to him "on the next transport" as additional labor. The letter was in Troost's files because the Chancellery had sent it to her to ask whether they should intervene.[55] Starting in late 1942, Troost received enormous quantities of diamonds, emeralds, sapphires, and other jewels from occupied France worth millions in today's dollars.[56] After the war, she was accused of having used diamonds stolen from Dutch Jews for her military awards work. The diamonds had been acquired by the Rosenberg Task Force (Einsatzstab Rosenberg), a special Nazi organization dedicated specifically to plundering occupied countries.[57] Although she later claimed, like Hitler's other artistic collaborators, not to have known anything about the nefarious activities of the regime, her business records reveal that it was impossible to carry out the Führer's commissions without operating within the regime's political and economic system and thereby participating in its crimes.

Troost was by no means coerced into such complicity. To the contrary, she eagerly accepted Hitler's commissions and proposed new projects to him (taking over the design of the certificates and presentation cases had been her idea).[58] As her letter to Alice Hess revealed, Troost cherished working with Hitler, and the dictator seems to have reciprocated the feeling. "For Hitler," Schaub wrote, "she was the ideal conversational partner with whom he could talk endlessly about his architectural plans, who understood him, and who gave his ideas practical form in design."[59] In her postwar trial, Troost confirmed that Hitler was "obsessed with architecture and happy to be able to talk with someone about it."[60] Perhaps because of the importance of her relationship to the Führer as well as her own idealism, Troost downplayed the financial dimension of her work. Already in 1934, she had refused to incorporate the Atelier Troost, against her lawyer's advice, because she felt that adding "GmbH" to the name (indicating a limited liability company) left a "peculiar 'Jewish' aftertaste."[61] In her mind, she did not want her "pure" artistic devotion to her husband's legacy to be debased by the soulless commercial motives that Nazi propaganda associated with Jews. After the war, Troost vehemently denied that she had profited financially from the Nazi regime, insisting that her fortune, worth many millions in today's dollars, had been left to her by her husband.[62] Nonetheless, financial records show that the rich widow grew far wealthier during the Third Reich. In addition to the hundreds of thousands of Reichsmarks she earned from her work from 1934 to 1945, she also received three tax-free gifts from Hitler of 100,000 Reichsmarks each in 1940, 1942, and 1943.[63] Hitler was in the habit of making such generous gestures to those whom he wished to reward and bind closer to him: military leaders, government ministers, artists, and others received cash awards.[64] In her trial, forced to account for these funds, Troost explained that Hitler had originally intended the gift (only one of which had been discovered by the prosecutors) as compensation for her unpaid work at the Chancellery and on the Obersalzberg (for which she had not charged him an honorarium). Troost said that she planned to refuse the money and had told Hitler, "I do not want our personal connection to be mixed up with money." They then agreed that the money would be used to establish a Paul Troost archive, which would have been part of a planned contemporary history museum. The judges were not convinced.[65]

Beyond financial gain, Hitler's favored architects enjoyed the high social status of a regime that placed (state-sanctioned) art on a pedestal. Troost not only designed awards—she also received them. On his birthday in April 1937, Hitler bestowed upon her the title of professor. Later that summer, on the occasion of the Day of German Art festival that preceded the inauguration of the House of German Art, the Bavarian Academy of Fine Arts conferred upon Troost its silver medal of honor. In 1943, Hitler awarded her the Golden Honor Badge, a rare distinction given once a year at his discretion to those who had rendered outstanding service to the Nazi Party or state.[66] (The more common Golden Party Badge was a special merit accorded to early members of the Nazi Party with membership numbers below one hundred thousand and faithful service to the party. Gerdy Troost did not receive this version, since she had joined the party on August 1, 1932, with a membership number of 1,274,722.[67]) These honors, and particularly the possession of the badge, would cause her further difficulties with her postwar prosecutors, who saw them as proof of her value and contributions to the regime. Among the evidence presented at her trial was a letter she had written to Hitler the day after the ceremony awarding her the badge, in which she all but confirmed their suspicions:

> Mein Führer, how can I thank you and what should I say to you? I am still completely moved by this deepest and most beautiful of obligations and joys with which you—I do not know, if you can understand me in this, but this is how I see it—have filled me through the bestowal of this holiest of symbols that can be given from your hand.
>
> This proud and honoring bond to what we now consider the symbolic golden age of your early struggle and to the eternally illuminating spirit of your first fellow combatants will ordain my life and my work for you now more than ever, with all my effort and devotion.[68]

Like her late husband, Troost cared little for the lavish parties of the Third Reich elite and declined the social invitations of Hitler, who told her that her constant refusals verged on being a snub. After completing the Berghof interiors in 1936, she avoided the Obersalzberg's social clique, later admitting that "part of his circle was not my cup of tea, and I also needed my time for my work."[69] She did, however, regularly attend his official art openings and other cultural functions. Over the years, she was photographed in the company of Hitler, Göring, Goebbels, Himmler, and other Nazi bigwigs viewing the Great German Art exhibitions, on the review stand of the Day of German Art festivals, at the dedication of Paul Troost's Munich buildings, and at many other public events (plate 10). A tall, slender woman, she cut a distinctive figure and was certainly aware of the impression she made. For these events, she preferred dressing entirely in white, making her stand out prominently from the brown and black uniforms that surrounded her.

Troost's repeated appearances at Hitler's side soon brought her to the attention of the German public and media. A July 1937 newspaper article about her, written by journalist Sophie Rützow and published in the *Münchner Neueste Nachrichten* (Munich Latest News), observed that "thousands of people saw this woman during the festival days and dedication of the House of German Art. In her white lady's suit she sat during the festivities in the front row of the guests of honor, her place near the Führer. For these days of celebration were likewise days of glory for her. It was her work, too, that was being dedicated and delivered to the German people."

While Troost had not been unknown before this, the inauguration of the House of German Art shone a spotlight on the young widow. On opening day, July 18, 1937, the cover of the Berlin illustrated weekly *Welt-Spiegel* (Mirror of the World) featured an image of Troost in the House of German Art gazing with rapt attention at the Führer beside her (fig. 40). A few days earlier, the Nazi Party newspaper, *Völkischer Beobachter* (People's Observer), published an article about Troost that paid tribute to her as the loyal trustee of her late husband's artistic estate. It acknowledged her personal creative contribution only in the decoration of the interiors, particularly in the "feminine" sphere of colors. Rützow's article, by contrast, portrayed Troost more fully as her husband's artistic collaborator, capable of advancing his buildings because she had been immersed in the projects from the start and could draw on her memories of their conversations. Whereas the *Völkischer Beobachter* had Frau Troost managing the office and standing guard as the buildings took form, Rützow placed her in the midst of construction sites and meetings. Rützow also emphasized Troost's considerable impact on the applied arts, thus representing her as an influential artist in her own right.[70]

Over the years, Troost appeared in popular books about Hitler, the illustrated tabloids, newspapers, women's magazines, and design journals. The April 1939 issue of *die neue linie,* an elegant lifestyle magazine, ran a feature on nine of Hitler's favored architects and placed her image and biography first (followed by Leonhard Gall, Albert Speer, and, in fourth place, Paul Troost).[71] Among her papers are numerous requests for press interviews that she did not always have time to give. The attention from the German media was uniformly positive, at least until the end of the war. In the same period, the American press was somewhat cooler, but not yet overtly critical. In a widely published 1938 story on the women around Hitler, Louis Lochner, Berlin correspondent for the Associated Press, drew attention to Troost's influence as a member of "Hitler's inner circle." His description of her physical appearance, with which he began his account, suggested a person of disquieting power. She was, he wrote, "apparently in the late thirties, with deep-set, fanatic dark eyes, a pointed, inquisitive nose, generous mouth and ears, and determined jaw, her dark bobbed hair combed back straight from the forehead." The following year, Sigrid Schultz, Berlin correspondent for the *Chicago Daily Tribune,* who had close connections with the Nazi elite, portrayed Troost as Hitler's design assistant: "[She] carries out Hitler's suggestions for interior decorations and submits sketches for interiors to him. Great efforts are being made to create a new style that

Der Welt-Spiegel

Jahrgang 1937 · Nr. 15   Sonntagsbeilage des „Berliner Tageblatt"   Berlin, 18. Juli

Der Führer im Haus der Deutschen Kunst Neben Adolf Hitler die Witwe des Schöpfers der neuen Heimstätte der Deutschen Kunst, Frau Prof. Troost Aufn. Heinrich Hoffmann

Fig. 40. Cover of *Welt-Spiegel*, July 18, 1937. The caption reads: "The Führer in the House of German Art. Beside Adolf Hitler the widow of the creator of the new home of German Art, Frau Prof. Troost." The photograph is by Heinrich Hoffmann.

in some dim future might rank with Empire, Chippendale, or other styles distinctive to their periods. It is a goal toward which Hitler is striving and the wives of the subleaders are anxiously attempting to emulate him or make new suggestions and thus win Hitler's favor." Schultz, however, misidentified Troost, perhaps not accidentally, as Frau Professor Frost.[72]

In Germany, Troost discovered that the media attention and public recognition brought with it an unwanted role: intercessor. In a nation whose government revolved around the desire and will of a single man, having access to and influence over the Führer made one a very powerful person. The chancellor was shielded by his staff, and even his ministers had trouble obtaining an audience. Troost, by contrast, saw him regularly, usually in her Munich studio. Indeed, senior politicians sometimes asked her to intervene on their behalf, knowing she had the Führer's ear.[73] Among Troost's papers are countless letters, the majority from strangers, requesting her help, offering a microcosmic view of the human misery wrought by the Nazi regime. Their writers included a mixed-race bookstore owner trying to hold on to her business; an imprisoned art historian who had lost his university position and freedom because of his sexuality; a businessman trying to obtain the release of Jewish relatives interned during Crystal Night; and a widow desperate to secure a military exception for her sole surviving son.[74] Many asked Troost to pass on letters to the Führer, knowing that she saw him regularly. Although she did occasionally intervene, in most cases she politely declined the requests, referring them to the Chancellery.

Troost's power to change lives with a well-placed comment is revealed by the case of Ragnar Berg, a Swedish-born biochemist and nutritionist who worked at the Rudolf Hess Hospital in Dresden until his funding dried up in 1936. Troost was avidly interested in the field of nutrition, perhaps because of her own health problems. In her early twenties, Troost had survived a near-fatal automobile accident, the injuries from which continued to plague her; she also suffered from attacks of angina pectoris, aggravated by stress and overwork. In the fall of 1942, Troost experienced a health crisis and spent three months recuperating at the Berchtesgaden sanatorium of Dr. Werner Zabel, who also advised Theodor Morell, Hitler's doctor, on the Führer's vegetarian diet.[75] (Her collapse was likely induced by the mounting pressures to fill Hitler's proliferating orders for military certificates. It was after this illness that Hitler, perhaps worried about losing her as he had lost her husband, awarded her the Golden Honor Badge.) Troost met Berg at the sanatorium, and he confided that his research had come to a standstill.

Troost then had a conversation with Hitler about Berg, and to the latter's astonishment and delight, his funding was promptly restored.[76]

On a number of occasions, Troost intervened to help those persecuted under Nazi Germany's anti-Semitic legislation and policies, usually (although not always) people she knew through her social or professional circles. Among them was Karl Wessely, a world-renowned ophthalmologist and professor in Munich, widely considered to be a great clinician and surgeon. He was also of Jewish descent, and in 1935, following the ratification of the racial Nuremberg Laws, lost his position and was denied his pension. For a few years, Wessely practiced privately in his apartment, but in September 1938, a new law decertified all Jewish doctors. Paul Troost had been treated by Wessely before his death, and his wife had expressed her gratitude at the time for the doctor's help, which had lessened her husband's suffering. Later, she would be able to demonstrate it in more concrete ways. After Wessely's license was revoked, Troost defended him as a man and doctor to Hitler and even showed him a picture of Wessely's children, whose education had been thrown into turmoil because of their Jewish ancestry. Hitler initially resisted her efforts to sway him; the *Völkischer Beobachter* had maligned Wessely already in 1930 when he was named head of the university clinic, and there was a great deal of Nazi antipathy built up against him. Troost, however, persisted, and on another visit gave Hitler a letter from Wessely's wife, which she insisted he read in her presence (rather than pass it off, as usual, to an adjutant). This apparently convinced him, and on Hitler's personal order, Wessely's license was reinstated in 1939, allowing him to continue his private practice. Troost had also helped on an earlier occasion, in November 1937, when the anti-Semitic exhibition *The Eternal Jew* opened at the German Museum in Munich, an institution dedicated to the history of science and technology. In one of the rooms, under a wall text that read "In the guise of science you have poisoned the German people" hung Wessely's portrait. Alerted by a friend of Wessely's wife, Troost complained to Bavarian Gauleiter Adolf Wagner and eventually succeeded in having the photograph removed.[77]

There is no question that Troost acted courageously in such interventions, and in more than one instance, her actions undoubtedly saved lives. At the same time, however, these individual cases do not add up clearly to a larger oppositional stance. In her postwar testimony, Maria Nachtigal, an artist and family friend, stated that Troost's opposition to the Nazi Party's position on Jews had repeatedly cost her "uncomfortable hours," presumably in confronting those who disagreed with her, including Hitler.[78] But at other times, Troost appears to have joined in and even abetted the broader anti-Semitic flow. Historian Wolfram Selig has argued that she lent support to the Aryanization of Wallach Haus, a leading Munich producer of traditional Bavarian costumes and folk art. Also notable is her role as a purchaser of artworks for Hitler's proposed art museum in Linz. Of the seventy paintings she acquired from Munich dealers, the majority came from confiscated Jewish art collections, as she certainly would have known.[79] Troost, moreover, tried to help Julius Streicher, who had hired her husband to renovate his Gauleiter headquarters in Nuremberg and with whom she remained friendly, after he was removed from office because his public attacks on Jews proved to be too excessive even for the Nazi Party. Troost's willingness to defend victims of Hitler's anti-Semitic policies must thus be weighed against her awareness of their persecution by a regime that she chose to support fully—as she said in her letter to Hitler, "with all my effort and devotion."

Troost most faithfully served Hitler and enjoyed the greatest influence in the realm of the fine and applied arts. As a practitioner, she helped to complete her husband's buildings, crafted the look of National Socialist interiors, and left her mark on the elite material culture of the regime, in the form not only of certificates and presentation folders and boxes, but also of utilitarian objects, such as silverware and china for Hitler, as well as of the many gifts that Hitler asked her to design, including the silver frames for his signed portrait that he ordered by the hundreds.[80] Additionally, Troost acted as a kind of cultural arbiter, serving on juries, weighing in on academic appointments, and advancing her own artistic agenda.[81] In her postwar trial, Troost was accused of having "occupied, as Hitler's close friend, a near dictatorial position in artistic life during the Nazi era."[82] While exaggerated, this assessment nonetheless indicates both her real and perceived power. Her role on the House of German Art juries was particularly significant, as this was the state institution that sanctioned the new forms of artistic expression under the Third Reich, from painting to architecture. In her postwar defense, Troost emphasized her resistance to Hitler's exclusion of modern artists, which had famously resulted in what she claimed was their only serious dispute, over what artworks would be included in the inaugural Great German Art Exhibition of 1937.

Troost was among an otherwise all-male jury of twelve artists and heads of art organizations charged with making a preliminary selection from the fifteen thousand paintings, drawings, and sculptures submitted for the first exhibition. German artists (a term that by then explicitly excluded Jews, who had been stripped of their citizenship by the 1935 Nuremberg Laws) were invited to send their "best" work, a directive that gave little guidance as to the qualities sought. Adding to the confusion was the regime's apparent willingness to tolerate within its own ranks proponents of both more radical and conservative directions in art. Hitler's own intolerance for modern art, moreover, was not yet broadly known. The jury's selections included work that Hitler considered subversive and better suited to the *Degenerate Art* show, which opened in a nearby location the day after the official exhibition, and which was meant to serve as a counterexample to the new art fostered by the regime. There is no reason to believe that the jurors, most of whom had come to prominence under National Socialism, wanted to provoke Hitler; Troost said that they had aimed for a representative cross section of the entries, based on the quality of the work.[83]

On June 5, 1937, Hitler arrived with Goebbels from Berlin to review the jury's selection at the House of German Art and to make the final decisions, which he had reserved for himself. The jurors at first accompanied Hitler through the rooms, but as his displeasure became apparent and he began to argue with Troost (since the others, she claimed, kept silent), they slipped away, leaving Troost as the sole defender of their choices. Hitler also challenged the works that had been refused, prompting Troost to ask, "Why do you accept a painter only after he has had his second stroke?" and to protest that "even our grandmothers had rejected those old brown juices." According to Goebbels, Hitler was "furious," and although Troost "fought with the courage of a lion," she could not sway him on behalf of the modern artists. Troost resigned her jury position on the spot; Hitler later dismissed the others and put his photographer, Heinrich Hoffmann, who knew Hitler's sentimental tastes, in charge of the selections. (Troost was nonetheless later asked to serve on future juries, which included only her, Hoffmann, and Karl Kolb, the House of German Art's director.[84])

News of the dispute leaked out and appeared in international newspapers. Paul Westheim, a German art critic writing in exile from Paris, reported that Hitler had told Troost that "she was also infested by cultural bolshevism," whereupon Troost, half fainting, had had to retreat to another room—a version of events that made her bristle.[85] Her own postwar testimony suggests, however, just how heated the exchange became (even if it did not, as she insisted, make her collapse). According to Troost, Hitler said, "Moscow remains neoclassical, and you save Bolshevism in Europe."

She answered, "You can lock me up, but I will always stand by my artistic convictions: this is art, and that is kitsch."[86] The altercation clearly did not affect their relationship. Troost claimed that the next time Hitler visited her studio, she had insisted on going over the issues once again, at length and with the aid of art history books, and that in this private setting, Hitler had been more willing to concede the merits of her argument. In retrospect, what seemed to bother her most of all was the behavior of the other jurors. At her postwar trial, she said that she had urged the art jury members to organize a united protest, but that they had done nothing, only sending her the next day, to her disappointment, "a very large bouquet of red roses and a letter of appreciation." In her desire to avoid blaming Hitler, Troost believed that Germany's "disgrace" might have been avoided if others had had the "personal courage" to stand up to him, and that it was possible to change his mind. Nonetheless, the trial's chairman noted that she had failed to move Hitler about the exhibition, and that such opposition was, in any case, both pointless and dangerous when all the positions of power were occupied by his henchmen.[87]

Recalling the controversial day decades later, Troost said that she had been shocked and dismayed that Goebbels had sided with the Führer. The once-defender of "super modern artists" had made a "180 degree turn," leaving Troost without an ally.[88] Goebbels was likely not unhappy to see Troost thus isolated. While he admired her intelligence and talent, he also found her annoying and threatening. On January 21, 1936, after a lunch with Hitler and Troost, he noted in his diary, "Frau Troost makes cutting remarks. As always. I do not like her."[89] (Recalling Troost's own lunch-time story about her Speer joke, one wonders if Goebbels, who prided himself on his witticisms, resented being upstaged.) According to Troost, their relationship was permanently damaged over the creation of Bavaria Filmkunst in 1938, the Munich film company that Goebbels vehement-ly opposed as a competitor to Universum Film AG (Ufa), which had its studios in Neubabelsberg, outside Berlin. Troost sat on Bavaria Filmkunst's artistic advisory board (to Goebbels's displeasure), and she later stated that it had been her mission to expand its studio complex in Geiselgasteig. Troost claimed that she had donated the initial funds to begin construc-tion and had personally found a wealthy Munich donor to finance the rest.[90] In his diary, Goebbels noted that Troost "intrigued" against him on the board.[91]

On November 21, 1940, Goebbels added a more personal, and pointed, comment about Troost to his diary: "Frau Troost is a clever woman, but bluestocking-ish."[92] Germans used the term *Blaustrumpf,* meaning "bluestocking," to derogatorily refer to an educated woman as mannish, but it also strongly implied that she was a lesbian—in fact, it sometimes was used as a synonym. Goebbels, ever alert to his opponents' vulnerabilities, may have learned that Troost had developed a close relationship with a female photographer and filmmaker named Hanni Umlauf. In the early 1930s, Umlauf established her own film company, Umlauf Films, which her younger brother, Walter, later joined as a partner. Together they made at least thirty-two short instructional films for government or National Socialist organizations, including women's groups. Some were practical in nature, such as how to recycle waste (*Waste Material–Raw Material,* or *Altstoff-Rohstoff,* 1938), while others were intended as propaganda. *Women's War Effort* (*Kriegseinsatz der Frau,* 1940), for example, was produced for the NSDAP Reich Women's Leadership and depicted Nazi women's organizations mobilizing and helping women during the war. The film presented a cheerful, well-functioning home front in which men were almost entirely absent.[93] Umlauf also had considerable success with her color photography, which she took up in 1937. Her photographs of German landscapes and ethnographic portraits were exhibited and won awards as well as appearing in *NS-Frauenwarte* (NS-Women's Watch), the official Nazi magazine for women.[94]

Troost and Umlauf appear to have met in the mid-1930s. A birthday letter Umlauf sent Troost in March 1951 noted that it was the first birthday in fifteen years that they had spent apart. By September 1939, the two women had moved in together in Munich and would continue to live together for the rest of their lives. The exact nature of their relationship remains a mystery; even family members are unsure, although they assume that they were a couple (it was not the kind of question that one could ask an aunt of this generation, nor the kind of information that she would have volunteered).[95] In her letters to her close friend Gerdy Troost, Winifred Wagner referred to the loving relationship between Troost and Umlauf and to their "living together" (*Zusammenleben*). Troost, in turn, referred to Umlauf as "my Hanni."[96] Friends often addressed letters to both of them. Among Gerdy Troost's personal papers in the Bavarian State Library is a small envelope that contains a handicapped identification card issued to her in her late eighties, the kind of thing that one would keep in one's purse. Also in the envelope are six tiny photographs. One is of Paul Troost, taken the winter before they married, showing him standing in a snow-covered field, wearing a sweater and plus fours. Another depicts a landscape of reeds and water with mountains faintly in the background, probably taken at the shore of Chiemsee, a large lake in Bavaria where Troost had built a log cabin in 1936 as a weekend retreat. There are also three photographs of Troost and Umlauf together in a rowboat by the water's edge. They appear to be in their mid-thirties, which makes it likely that the photographs are also from Chiemsee, taken not long after the cabin was built. The day is sunny and the two are in their bathing suits, absorbed in their activity, as if unaware of the photographer. The last picture is of Umlauf on the same day, this time by herself in the boat. One has the impression that at the end of her life, Troost wanted to keep close to her the images of the people and places that she had loved most.

Whether the relationship was romantic or not, Troost and Umlauf clearly shared a deep and meaningful bond. Their domestic life diverged wildly from National Socialist ideals of German womanhood: two young women, pursuing successful professional careers, unencumbered by male spouses or children. Although only twenty-nine years old when widowed, Troost chose not to remarry or, as far as we know, have other relationships with men. She remained, from a public point of view, devoted to the memory of her late husband. Her private life, however, might have raised eyebrows among those who knew about Umlauf. Although the Nazis focused their persecution of homosexuals on men, lesbians also lived in fear of discovery. Female couples living together risked a neighbor or landlord's denunciation and a visit from the Gestapo.[97] Whether Hitler knew about Troost's relationship with Umlauf is not known. Regardless, it is significant that the domestic image of this bachelor was crafted to a large extent by a woman whose private life also did not remotely conform to Nazi ideals.

When war came, Troost was shocked. She later said that she had believed Hitler when he had assured her that there would be no conflict and that he wanted peace. Unconcerned, she had sold a valuable lake property in mid-August 1939, despite the fact that the buyer himself told her that it was unwise to do so with war imminent. But like others who tried to warn her, she ignored him.[98] On September 1, 1939, the German army invaded its neighbor to the east. A week later, Troost bought herself a map of Poland.[99]

The receipt for it, tucked amid other sales slips, is the first sign of her awareness that life as it had once been was about to change.

In late 1944, Troost herself headed eastward. She was one of only two women permitted to visit Hitler at his "Wolf's Lair" Führer Headquarters, located in the woods near the small East Prussian town of Rastenburg (now Poland). When she was asked about this trip in 1999 by Martha Schad, Troost replied that she had gone because she needed Hitler's signature on prepared certificates as well as for "a very personal reason" that she declined to discuss. The true purpose of her visit was Hitler's request to mate their two German shepherds, a breed they both loved. Troost had obtained her dog through Martin Bormann, from whom Hitler had also acquired Blondi.[100] (On neo-Nazi and nationalist websites, the question of surviving descendants of the Hitler-Troost puppies remains an avid topic of discussion.) Troost was disturbed by Hitler's physical condition: "He walked severely hunched over and his right arm shook. On the other hand, his confidence in the victory of German weaponry was rock-solid." Troost said that his unshakable faith reinforced her own. It was the last time she saw him.[101]

On the night of April 24, 1944, a bombing raid damaged the building that had housed the Atelier Troost, and Hitler offered Troost work spaces in the Führerbau. The firm's archive was stored in the bomb-proof basement, which Troost believed to be secure.[102] Troost remained in her Munich apartment until the end of April 1945, fleeing to the town of Chieming just eight days before the arrival of American troops.[103] The Atelier Troost materials in the Führerbau were confiscated by American soldiers and deposited with the Central Collecting Point, next door in the former NSDAP Administration Building. Later, they were sent as captured war documents to Washington, D.C., where they remained for decades.

In Chieming, Troost lived in her one-room cabin with no running water or electricity.[104] As she later told prosecutors, the Atelier Troost closed and her design projects ended on the day the U.S. Army marched into Munich.[105] Instead, she became, by necessity, a farmer. Umlauf had started a small organic farm on the cabin's lakeside property in 1942. Before the currency reform of 1948, in an economy of shortages and bartering, the two women had managed to get by growing and selling produce, although it took a toll on Troost's health. According to Troost's doctor, the manual labor as well as the chilly dampness of the house brought on rheumatism, and the stress of the trial aggravated her angina. She was also malnourished and underweight. A photograph of Troost that appeared in a 1949 news-paper article about her trial shows her looking strained and gaunt.[106] Still, many hungry and homeless Germans in those years would have envied the roof over her head and her garden.

Like all other adult German civilians in the American occupation zone, Troost underwent a denazification process, which involved filling out a questionnaire about one's activities and memberships during the Third Reich, being classified according to one of five categories ranking crimi-nal involvement in the regime (1. major offenders; 2. offenders; 3. lesser offenders; 4. followers; 5. exonerated persons), and, if necessary, testifying before a civilian tribunal and being sanctioned. According to Troost, she was also placed under house arrest, which she resented not only because of the confinement—she was allowed to leave, she later recalled, only to see the dentist or the American military authorities—but also because of the four "*US-Negern*," meaning the African American soldiers, assigned to guard her.[107] Troost's denazification was a drawn-out affair, beginning in the fall of 1946 in Traunstein and ending over three years later, in the spring of 1950, in a Munich courtroom. Delays were caused by the difficulties obtain-ing information from various authorities in the chaotic years after the war (files had burned, witnesses had died or scattered), the change in venue, the discovery of the Atelier Troost archives at the Central Collecting Point in 1949, Troost's absent or alternating lawyers, her deteriorating physical con-dition, and her own attempts to obfuscate the facts, particularly regarding how much she had profited financially from the Nazi regime.

What she could or would not hide, however, was her devotion to the Führer. Those many appearances at his side, captured by the media, now worked against her: people knew she had been a powerful and loyal fol-lower. A July 11, 1945, report from Chieming's mayor on Troost stated that "Her pre-eminent position among Hitler's most intimate friends certainly is sufficiently well known. He often visited her here incognito. Just a short while ago she appeared here at an assembly convened by the Kreisleiter [NSDAP district leader] to testify to Hitler's unbroken power. . . . Naturally, she is and remains a fanatical Nazi follower."[108] Wilhelm Corsten, Troost's financial advisor, who stepped in to represent her in the absence of her first lawyer (Hans Laternser, who was busy defending Luftwaffe General Field Marshal Albert Kesselring), warned her before her initial hearing in Traunstein, held on January 21, 1947, that "it would be regrettable if the chairman were to receive a false impression of you and then no longer be in the position to rectify aberrant perceptions among the associate judges. I suspect that the chairman holds the *entirely wrong opinion,* conveyed to him by others, that even today you champion the ideology of the Third Reich. On the occasion of your meeting, the tribunal chairman can satisfy himself that you do not belong to the thugs of the Nazi regime."[109] Troost did not take the hint. In her first and subsequent court appearances, she spouted Nazi propaganda, defended Hitler, and thoroughly confirmed suspicions of her stubborn, unreconstructed beliefs.

On the stand, Troost described her life in the Third Reich as a peaceful, enclosed orb: she lived, breathed, and thought only about art. Her relationship to Hitler, she averred, had been conducted on an entirely artistic plane. When Schleifer, the tribunal chairman, asked whether she could not have said something to the dictator about "how things looked outside," she insisted that she had not known. "But surely you did not see only the four walls of your studio?" Schleifer asked. "These walls were not blinders, were they?" Troost, in response, waxed poetic about how "when I emerged from the stillness of my studio and entered building sites and workshops, I saw only bright and shining eyes and experienced only the most touching and overwhelming scenes, from little old ladies to young construction workers. And no wonder, for they all had work again and were full of hope after these terrible years of unemployment." Schleifer retorted, "I cannot believe what you say, and even if you recited it on bended knee, I still could not believe you, that you knew nothing, especially you, with your experience of foreign countries, how things looked from abroad." Troost maintained her ignorance: her orb of art had no burning synagogues or Gestapo torture chambers. At her second hearing, held on February 13, 1948, in Munich, Troost went so far as to claim that not a single person in her broad circle of professional and social acquaintances had been sent to a concentration camp. At her final set of hearings, on February 23–24, 1950, in Munich, Troost continued to be confronted with the same questions and doubts and to make the same denials.[110] Yet, throughout these hearings, Troost had built her defense on the backs of those persecuted by the regime. She offered testimonials from dozens of people whom she had helped, representing a broad range of the regime's victims and terrors, which proved that she was well aware of what went on beyond the four walls of her studio.

While Troost did occasionally lie outright—for example, she insisted that she had never used her position in the Third Reich to benefit her family, although private documents confirm that her father's business, which went bankrupt in 1932, recovered and prospered thanks to her mediations—the paradoxes in her testimony are also rooted in the self-denial and cognitive dissonance that was enabled and fostered by Nazi propaganda.[111] "How can a person who can be so kind," she asked Schleifer, "so attached to his dog, who can look at a child with such love, who can stand before a work of art and contemplate it with such feeling, how can such a person be a murderer? How can I accept this? It is inconceivable to me; I cannot put these things together."[112] Troost also flatly refused to believe that Hitler had known about the atrocities carried out in his name, which had fully come to light at the Nuremberg Trials less than two years earlier. Keeping the Führer pure in her mind, recalling him as "warm and kindhearted," was also a self-protective measure: if her good friend were not to blame, then neither was she.

Troost, used to being in charge, provoked the tribunal members with her interruptions, questions, and demands for corrections to the record. At her 1948 hearing in Munich, Troost was asked about her and her husband's meetings with Hitler and whether they had talked about political matters. She maintained that their conversations had been solely about architectural and artistic questions. The chairman, dictating to the secretary transcribing the proceedings, told her to note that the discussions had been about "architectural and other problems that were not in keeping with National Socialist ideology." Troost interjected: "If I may interrupt, I must add here that it is necessary to first clarify what you understand by N. S. ideology. If you mean K. Z. [concentration camp] practices and the things that have filled us all with deep shame, then, of course, neither I nor my husband had anything to do with that. But if N. S. ideology is understood as being a social human being, that is, to feel beholden to one's people as the people of Beethoven and Kant and thus be at the service of humanity, then naturally there were National Socialist ideologies with which we were imbued." The chairman replied, "It is a question here of tyranny, dictatorship, torture, K. Z. and so forth. So," turning to the secretary, "write: N. S. ideology."[113]

Curt von Stackelberg, Troost's second (but not final) lawyer, sought to recast Troost's unreconstructed Nazi beliefs as the romanticized, political cluelessness of the artist. In a written defense submitted to the tribunal, Stackelberg argued that "the artist exists largely outside the political, social, and economic order of the public sphere, leading instead a meditative life of his own in the timeless world of art, in a dream realm. . . . Just as in daily life, so must a different standard apply to the creative person in political life."[114] And yet the National Socialist regime, perhaps more than any other in contemporary history, fused art and politics. It understood the role of the artist as fundamentally ideological in nature and hence carefully controlled artistic activity. Even so, in the postwar period, National Socialist artists, including Troost, commonly asserted that their state projects had had nothing to do with politics. Reporting on Troost's 1950 trial, the *Süddeutsche Zeitung* (South German Newspaper) said that she was "bewildered" by the question of whether building the House of German Art had in some way furthered National Socialist tyranny.[115] Albert Stenzel, chair of the Creative Artists Commission in the Bavarian State Ministry of Education and Culture, prepared an expert report for the denazification trial of Leonhard Gall (who also successfully employed the argument of the apolitical artist), in which he protested the essential dishonesty of this position. Stenzel, however, who was strongly anti-Nazi, was considered unobjective and thus ignored.[116] In subsequent decades, historians would explore the powerful ideological role played by artists, demonstrating how the aesthetic sheen they gave the regime—in posters, films, parades, monuments, and a thousand different objects, from radios to military awards— had helped to disguise its putrid core.[117]

As a holder of the Golden Honor Badge, Troost was automatically classed as a "major offender," the highest of the five categories, the penalties for which included death, imprisonment, and hard labor, among other lesser alternatives. When asked in court how she would rank herself, she replied that she would create a new designation: "decent National Socialists who believed."[118] Clearly, Troost felt that she had done no wrong. In her closing words to the tribunal on February 24, 1950, she stated that "she always acted with human and moral sensitivity and thus even today pleads a clear conscience with regard to her earlier conduct."[119] When the tribunal members issued their verdict on March 2, 1950, they noted that Troost still had not managed to free herself from her bond to Hitler.[120] Insofar as the denazification procedure was intended by the Allies not only to punish, but also to rehabilitate, in the case of Gerdy Troost, it failed miserably.

Troost was ultimately categorized as a "lesser offender," two levels below "major offender," and might have been ranked even lower had it not been for the 100,000-Reichsmarks gift from Hitler. Her punishment consisted of a two-year period of probation (beginning on the date of the verdict) and a fine of 5,000 Deutschmarks. During the probationary period, her earnings were capped at 200 Deutschmarks per month, she lost her enfranchisement and the right to use her professor title, and she was forbidden to have an automobile, among other restrictions. (The latter was no small thing. The cabin was isolated, and after the war, both Troost and Umlauf had had their cars confiscated. For years, they delivered their vegetables and managed their own transportation by bicycle.) Troost was also liable for a small amount (6,500 Deutschmarks, or 5 percent) of the substantial court costs.[121]

By comparison, her collaborator, Leonhard Gall, fared much better. He was tried in 1948 as a "major offender," but was found to be a "follower," the second-lowest category possible, one below that of Troost. His punishment was also far milder. He was fined only 250 Deutschmarks, in addition to having to pay 5 percent (3,250 Deutschmarks) of the court costs. The different outcomes of their trials is striking when one considers that they were partners, and that Gall held many prestigious appointments during the regime, including senator of the Reich Chamber of Culture and honorary vice-president of the Reich Chamber of Fine Arts, as well as being awarded the title of professor in 1935 and the Golden Honor Badge in 1944. Moreover, unlike Troost's involved verdict justification, which included a psychological assessment theorizing that she was particularly susceptible to the power of Hitler's gaze, Gall's short verdict reads like an apologia on behalf of the accused. (Troost clearly represented a conundrum to the tribunal in a way that Gall did not.) In his court appearance and submitted materials, Gall effectively presented himself as a simple, unpretentious man, and he did not challenge or alienate his prosecutors, as Troost had, by debating the meaning of National Socialism or Hitler's merits. Gall's low fine also took into account his having volunteered for sixty days to clean up rubble, which the court took as a sign of responsibility.[122] Gall did not call witnesses or submit anywhere near the number of testimonials of people whom he had helped in comparison to Troost. But Troost's evidence of more serious intervention also spoke to her greater influence with Hitler, and it is ultimately for this and her ideological intransigency that she paid.

Troost (like Gall) successfully petitioned to have her court fines lowered, citing her lost fortune.[123] In 1934, Troost had liquidated her late husband's stock portfolio in Switzerland and transferred the funds to Germany. Her own investment strategies reflected her confidence in and support of the new Reich as well as her waning pacifism. Most of her fortune was placed in government bonds, which she continued to buy as late as 1944, despite the bleak news from the war fronts. She also held the stock of some of Hitler's worst war-machine collaborators, including Dynamit Nobel (manufacturer of munitions for the German army) and I. G. Farben.[124] Many of Troost's investments became worthless after the war, while others were starkly depreciated. Her personal valuables, including her art collection and jewelry, were confiscated or looted. In the end, she largely lost not only what she had gained during the Third Reich, but also what she had inherited from her husband and family. Adding to her financial woes, the Munich Tax Office audited her past returns from the Third Reich and demanded back taxes.[125]

Six months into Troost's two-year sentence, the Bavarian parliament passed a law lifting employment restrictions on lesser Nazi offenders, and Troost immediately returned to interior design, now working as an independent contractor.[126] She partnered regularly with two firms specializing in cabinetwork: her father's former company, German Woodcraft Studios in Bremen, and P. Vogler and Cie in Weinheim, a fine furniture manufacturer. She traveled extensively to meet with potential clients and to carry out commissions, primarily in the Ruhr region. With financial and political stability returning to West Germany, construction soared as its bombed cities turned to rebuilding. By the mid-1950s, Troost and German Woodcraft Studios had numerous joint projects under way, including banks, industrial buildings, hotels, corporate offices, and events facilities.[127] This period also saw Troost developing a new geographical realm of activity: the Middle East. In 1962, she undertook the interior furnishing of a hotel in Amman, Jordan. She was also avidly pursued by a group of Egyptian businessmen, who wanted her to decorate their new six-hundred-room hotel in Cairo.[128]

But while she was busy, Troost struggled to get back on her feet. Her deteriorating health in the early 1960s, which she blamed on the stressful years after the war ended, increasingly prevented her from taking on large design commissions. Her name, moreover, stirred up old "political resentments," putting her at a disadvantage. Troost also encountered a number of serious financial setbacks. Her loyalty to her father's former firm cost her dearly: the firm went bankrupt twice in the 1950s, leaving Troost with crippling debts each time (and forcing her to sell her home on the Chiemsee by the end of the decade). She also discovered that the luxurious style with which she had made her reputation during the Third Reich no longer carried the same prestige. Clients did not want the expense of meticulously handcrafted furniture, and fine wood interiors seemed outdated. Instead, they preferred less costly and more modern industrial materials, such as steel and glass, harking back to the Bauhaus aesthetics that the Nazi elite had spurned for their own representative interiors.[129]

By the late 1960s, Troost's interior design projects had dwindled, although she continued to receive the occasional commission into the late 1970s, when she was in her mid-seventies.[130] These later assignments consisted of small-scale interior design projects for private residences. When not engaged in her own work, Troost helped Umlauf with her increasingly successful commercial photography and lithography business. In 1939, Umlauf had established a small fine arts reproduction press in Munich, specializing in figures of children and landscapes from modern and old masters.[131] In the postwar period, she returned to these activities, publishing a book of color photography in 1952, *Between the Rhine and the Ruhr* (*Zwischen Rhein und Ruhr*), of industrial landscapes and factory interiors.[132] She also produced slides and postcards. The two women traveled extensively on photography trips, mostly within West Germany, but also to France, Austria, and Italy. Writing to Winifred Wagner in 1970, Troost mentioned that Umlauf's work was in demand and that business was prospering.[133]

Troost's correspondence with Wagner provides insights into how the former elite of the Third Reich continued to socialize together and support each other after the war. In a 1962 letter to Troost, Wagner recounted a get-together with Hitler's "scorned aristocrats" and described how "to my intense pleasure, [Tassilo] Fürstenberg told marvelous Jewish jokes in the middle of a public restaurant in a loudly raised voice."[134] When former Nazi artist Adolf Ziegler fell on hard times, Wagner took up a collection, to which Troost contributed (despite having intensely disliked his work).[135]

By the mid 1970s, Troost, too, needed help from her friends. In April 1975, to her distress, she was compelled to accept a loan from Wagner. To pay her back, she decided to sell a bronze sculpture by Eugen Henke, *Girl Tying a Headscarf* (*Kopftuchbindendes Mädchen*), depicting a young nude woman wrapping her hair in a scarf. Hitler had suggested the subject to Henke and liked the finished statue so much that he placed it prominently in the Berghof's Great Hall, where it was often captured in contemporary photographs. As a gift to Troost, who had introduced him to Henke, Hitler had another bronze copy made for her, which she kept in her Munich apartment. Perhaps because it had not been owned by Hitler, the sculpture may have proved difficult to sell. That summer, Wagner wrote to Troost about an idea proposed to her by Lotte Pfeiffer-Bechstein (the daughter of Edwin and Helene Bechstein, whose piano-manufacturing wealth helped to finance the Nazi Party in its early years). At a tea party of old Nazi friends, Pfeiffer-Bechstein had discussed Troost's financial problems, and one of her guests had wondered whether the statue "could be offered to [Idi] Amin, the president of Uganda, who currently wants to erect a Hitler monument in Kampala. Although he is black, he is an ardent admirer of Hitler and it seems to me that one should not have any scruples about selling to a Negro when one is not blessed with worldly goods. . . . We thought it a very good idea and it will not cost anything to try."[136] There is no direct evidence that Troost sold Amin the work, although the file she kept on the sculpture contains the business card of Gerhard Engel, Hitler's former army adjutant and Wehrmacht lieutenant general; Engel was then the head of a company selling German arms abroad, including to Africa, suggesting that she planned to make inquiries through him.[137] Over the years, Troost sold other artifacts she owned from the Third Reich period, including letters from Hitler and Göring.[138]

Women such as Troost, who operated in the highest echelons of the Third Reich, pose a conundrum to historians. Despite being complicit in a regime that was fundamentally elitist, racist, and sexist, could they be considered feminists in any sense?[139] While the Nazi press depicted Troost as the faithful vessel of her husband's work, she openly defied ideal gender norms by running one of the nation's leading architectural firms, holding positions of influence and power, living independently, and having no children. Moreover, Troost often collaborated with female artists and patronized their work through her own design commissions. Yet although Troost contravened gender norms through her work and lifestyle and promoted individual women artists, she did not question the status of women or intervene on their behalf as a whole. This is revealed in a brief but telling exchange of letters in 1939 between Troost and Hanna Löv, a modernist architect who had been prominent in Munich during the Weimar Republic, but who struggled to find work in the Third Reich. "As the Führer's close collaborator," Löv wrote, "you will surely be able to answer a question of principle: Is it in accordance with the Führer's intention and is it really the lot of women in the Third Reich to be permitted always and only to be the subordinate assistants of men who are not their superiors intellectually, artistically, or in their organizational skills, even when these women can prove their abilities at any time? Or, assuming that education, aptitude, and competence are present, can they also assert a claim to a senior position in their field of activity?" Troost answered curtly, "I am surprised at this question and by calling your attention to the fact that the Führer has, indeed, approved women, to the extent that they are suitable, for leading positions (for example, [Gertrud] Scholtz-Klink, Frau Winifried Wagner, Frau Leni Riefenstahl), I believe that any further reply on my part will be superfluous." To which Löv, after a long delay, answered, "Unfortunately, as I have come to discover at every turn, you are almost the only person who admits to having this view on women. This idea has sadly not even remotely begun to penetrate among the *men* in charge of personnel decisions, not even today when one ought to know that an equivalent deployment of a woman could free up a man for the war." Troost did not reply further. Although in the 1970s, as noted earlier, Troost was willing to concede the difficulties professional women had faced in Hitler's Männerstaat, during the Third Reich she firmly denied it.[140]

Today, Troost rarely appears in histories of the Third Reich. Scholars and journalists who interviewed her while she was alive were usually more interested in her husband, Speer, or Hitler than in her own life and work. Unlike Leni Riefenstahl, who in 1940 had invited Troost to visit her on the set of *The Lowlands* (*Tiefland*), Troost did not court press attention. With time, most Germans forgot about the woman in white who had appeared time and again by Hitler's side. When she died on January 30, 2003, her passing went unremarked by the mainstream German media. Instead, her obituary appeared on the right-wing news portal Altermedia Germany, a website popular with German neo-Nazis. It ended with the statement, "Gerdy Troost remained true to her convictions to her death. We bid farewell to an upstanding German and a worthy artist." The obituary was then reposted with an English translation on Stormfront.com, the white-supremacist online forum.[141]

Nor was Troost forgotten by Third Reich memorabilia collectors, who avidly pursue her work. Her military certificates fetch substantially higher prices than the decorations themselves.[142] And despite her reticence about appearing in the public spotlight, Troost clearly wanted to be remembered. Starting in the 1980s, Troost enabled the Bavarian State Library to assemble a vast archival collection documenting the life and work of her husband as well as the activities of the Atelier Troost. The library also acquired Gerdy Troost's postwar professional records and her personal papers, including over seventy years of her correspondence. Some of these materials remain sealed for a period of fifteen years after Troost's death. When the full collection opens officially in early 2019, it will keep historians busy for years to come.

PART   II

6   CAMPAIGN POLITICS AND THE INVENTION
OF THE PRIVATE HITLER

It was in the spring of 1932, in the midst of presidential elections, that the National Socialists discovered the publicity value of Hitler's private life. The electoral campaign pitted Hitler, then the leader of the second-largest political party in the Reich, against Paul von Hindenburg, the elderly incumbent revered by Germans as the war hero of Tannenberg, and the Communist leader Ernst Thälmann. On March 13, German voters returned a strong lead of over seven million votes for Hindenburg, throwing the National Socialists, who had expected Hitler to be swept into the presidency, into despair.[1] Hindenburg's failure to win an absolute majority, however, led to a runoff election the following month, and it was in the period between the two presidential elections that the Nazis seized on a new representational strategy.[2] Although Hitler would lose the next round, the campaign, along with the worsening economic crisis, increased his support among the German people by over two million votes, to a third of the electorate.[3] Having proved its broad appeal, the image of the private Führer would become a staple of National Socialist propaganda for years to come.

The coming out of the Führer's personal life marked a distinct departure from earlier National Socialist publicity, which had focused on Hitler's role as agitator of the masses and leader of a militant political movement. In the 1932 runoff election, the need to cast a wider net pushed Nazi Party propaganda toward a celebration of the personal attributes of their candidate. Hitler's youth and dynamism, epitomized by his much-advertised campaign flights across Germany, became an important selling point. Against the aristocratic honor and dignity that accrued to the remote, eighty-four-year-old Hindenburg, the Nazis offered the modernity and glamor of a candidate who took to the skies to meet face-to-face with the German people. Perhaps most daringly, Nazi publicists brought Hitler's private life into the limelight in order to emphasize his moral and human character and thereby win over the bourgeois voters and women who had overwhelmingly supported Hindenburg on the first ballot.[4]

Given the circumstances of Hitler's private life, this was truly an audacious move. He was a middle-aged bachelor with few family ties and no known romantic relationships. Unsavory rumors about his domestic life and sexuality had flared in September 1931 after his niece Geli Raubal shot herself in her uncle's Munich apartment. Indeed, until the turnabout in 1932, National Socialist publicists had diverted attention away from or suppressed stories about Hitler's personal life. While the Nazis continued to fight reports that could harm Hitler's reputation, they began to construct for public consumption their own version of the private individual. The image of "Hitler as private man" would now be reconfigured into an asset rather than a liability.

The title of Heinrich Hoffmann's photo album, *The Hitler Nobody Knows* (*Hitler wie ihn keiner kennt,* 1932), announced the shift in the Führer's image. The book appeared in mid-March, shortly after the first presidential election. While conceived earlier and perhaps independently, it nonetheless served as an effective tool in the National Socialists' new campaign to appeal to a broader public through the recently discovered "private Hitler."[5] Hoffmann, as Hitler's official photographer, had extensive access to the German leader, and from the thousands of images at his disposal, he selected one hundred to encapsulate the Führer's personal life.

On the cover of the book, Hitler was shown in a Bavarian jacket and floppy-brimmed hat, reclining in the grass in the mountains with one of his dogs by his side (see fig. 3). The image, together with the book's title, signaled to the reader that the camera lens would reveal a different Hitler and thus fulfill, as the dust jacket text stated, the "yearning" of his "countless millions of followers" to know more about his personal life and his "wide-ranging interests and aptitudes." The text also claimed the "documentary truth" of Hoffmann's work, a statement intended not only to instill confidence in his presentation of the private Hitler, but also to refute the less-flattering accounts published by his critics. In fact, and as Germans were to learn after the war, Hoffmann's distorted and highly edited vision of Hitler's personal life bore little resemblance to reality; Eva Braun, for example, would be banished from such portrayals during the Third Reich, despite becoming a fixture of his inner circle by 1936.

The dust jacket text further suggested that the book would serve as a visual complement to Hitler's *Mein Kampf,* and the book did begin biographically, like a family album, with photographs of Hitler as a baby (with a birth announcement "pasted" in the corner), the house where he was born, his parents, his school and army days, and his rise as an orator and politician. In documenting Hitler's contemporary life, Hoffmann included an assortment of photographs that mostly appeared to be candid shots of Hitler engaged in activities either of a private nature or at the peripheries of his political duties—for example, stopping for a quick picnic lunch on the way to give a speech or chatting with a worker who approached his car. Relatively few of the images revealed an urban landscape; instead, Hitler's so-called private life played out mostly on a pastoral stage. A number of the images of Hitler at leisure focused on the Obersalzberg, although Haus Wachenfeld, while described, was not visually depicted. Hitler was shown in the mountains with his dogs, reading outdoors, walking, talking with a neighbor's child, and dressed in casual clothes, including lederhosen. Here, a caption stated, away from the "noise and restlessness of the cities," Hitler could relax and recover from the "stresses and strains" of his political struggle. Yet despite the pretext of being personal, these images of a relaxed and often smiling Hitler were by no means apolitical. Thus, a photograph of Hitler sitting in the grass reading the newspaper and grinning broadly was accompanied by a caption indicating that he was amused by the "fables" printed about him by a hostile press: "champagne feasts, Jewish girlfriends, a luxury villa, French money . . ."[6] The viewer, at whom Hitler gazes, is invited to share in this intimate moment and laugh along with him.

On a deeper level, the book as a whole served a political purpose: to recast Hitler, through the vehicle of his private life, as a "good" man. The foreword by Baldur von Schirach, head of the Hitler Youth organization and Hoffmann's son-in-law, made that intention clear. The German people, Schirach wrote, demanded of their chosen leader the same lofty moral values in his private life as in his public work. Hitler's embodiment of this synthesis, Schirach claimed, put him in the same class as Germany's most revered men, including Goethe and Frederick the Great. "I would like to denote two characteristics that for me are the most striking traits of Adolf Hitler's nature: STRENGTH AND GOODNESS. And it is these very qualities that are apparent in the pictures of this book." Schirach hoped that the images, which offered glimpses of Hitler's "personal experiences," would find an audience far beyond National Socialist circles, and would convey the sentiment felt by those who had worked under Hitler for years "and thereby learned to adore and love him." In pseudo-religious terms, Schirach promised that Hitler's "secret" would be revealed to "whoever reads these images, as confessions, with an open heart"—namely, "here is manifest not only a rousing leader, but also a great and good man."[7]

Germans knew that Hitler was an extreme anti-Semite, convicted traitor, and leader of a paramilitary force of violent street brawlers. How, then, did Schirach and Hoffmann redefine him as a "good man"? In short, they did so by making an appeal to values rather than to ideology. To begin, Hitler was described as a man of Spartan habits and great self-discipline: "It is hardly known that Hitler is a NON-DRINKER, NON-SMOKER, and VEG-ETARIAN," Schirach exclaimed in the foreword. "Without imposing his ways in the slightest on others, including those in his immediate circle, he adheres strictly to his own rules for living."[8] Schirach reinforced this and other messages in the captions he wrote for the book's illustrations. "This is how the 'fat cat' lives!" a caption declared sarcastically under an image of Hitler, looking tired, at the end of a seemingly modest meal. "Marxist liars," it continued, "tell workers that Hitler revels in champagne and beautiful women. In reality, Hitler does not drink a drop of alcohol! (Hitler is also a nonsmoker.)"[9]

Hitler's self-discipline, Schirach further noted, was also evident in his enormous industriousness and capacity for work. Not only was he responsible for leading the party, but he also undertook "the most arduous trips" to speak "today in Königsberg, tomorrow in Berlin, the next day in Munich, all of this with a minimum of sleep, for the Führer usually works until the early hours of the morning."[10] Schirach's words found visual expression in the many photographs showing Hitler on the road, being greeted by supporters, sometimes stopping for a quick rest, and, in one instance, slumped over asleep in the car beside his driver, "exhausted from the efforts of a huge rally."[11] This combination of on-the-road images was undoubtedly meant to provoke both admiration for his work ethic and compassion for its toll on the private individual. And like the campaign by air that was to follow, it reinforced Hitler's personal and direct bond with the German people.

From the topic of work, Schirach turned to Hitler's private hobbies, saying these needed to be discussed because of the gossip and lies spread about them. "His greatest pleasure is his library of about 6,000 volumes, all of which he has not just leafed through, but also read. Architecture and history are the most strongly represented in this library. Hitler is also an unassailable authority in both these domains. Art, and especially music, is for him a life necessity. His statement, 'If the artists could guess what I will do for German art, I would not have an opponent among them,' indicates the depth of his intention to cultural action."[12] A photograph taken at a medieval cloister and titled *Hitler, the Architect* caught the Führer demonstrating his architectural expertise to an attentive audience of SA men.[13] The book also included two images of Hitler's watercolors done as a soldier in World War I, which the caption claimed displayed his "great talent" for architecture. Although he had been unable to pursue professional study, "he became the architect of a new Volk"—the past tense here suggesting it had already happened.[14]

The passage on Hitler's hobbies, with its specific listing of the number of books in his library and the peculiar insistence that he had read all of them, reveals the desire to present him as an educated and cultured man, despite his having left school at the age of sixteen. *Bildung* and self-improvement, together with self-discipline, a strong work ethic, and modesty, formed the core moral values of the German middle classes. The components of the "good" Hitler were thus assembled in part with an eye to appealing to this constituency of voters, who the National Socialists hoped could be persuaded to abandon their allegiance to Hindenburg.

Other qualities ascribed to Hitler in the book were meant to appeal across social and political divides. Commenting on a photograph that showed Hitler at a window overlooking the mountains, Schirach wrote of his "great yearning for nature," which he could fulfill only rarely, for "his life is struggle and work." Associating Hitler with Alpine scenery and activities made him seem vibrant and tapped into the tremendous popularity of nature sports in Germany. Such a stance, moreover, seemed (wrongly) to be as far removed from his controversial ideological platform as one could imagine—while many voters found Hitler's racism distasteful and talk of revolution frightening, it was difficult to be against hiking or nature. Likewise, photographs of Hitler with his dogs conveyed his love of animals, made explicit in the following caption by Schirach: "He loves them almost as much as they love him." ("A subtle distinction," a critic later racily quipped, "that safeguards the distance between master and creature, despite the intimacy."[15]) In an attempt to solicit the reader's compassion, Schirach wrote that "when evil people wanted to hurt him to the quick, they poisoned his favorite dog. That's how the curs fight against a good man."[16] After 1933, Hoffmann would develop the theme of "Hitler as animal lover" into a highly popular motif in the iconography of the private man. The message such images conveyed about the Führer's goodness resided not only in his tender care of animals, but also, and importantly, in the trust the animals placed in him.

Similarly, Hitler's fondness for children, which would also become an iconic theme in Hoffmann's hands, conveyed the Führer's goodness both in his apparent affection and concern for them, as well as in their trust of him. "The young love him," read the caption to an image of Hitler surrounded by young boys. "Everywhere children crowd around him to bring him flowers." Below a photograph of Hitler talking with two members of the Hitler Youth, one of whom was a small boy from the "Pimpf" (cub) division, Schirach's caption claimed that "even the youngest are his fighters."[17] The loyalty of Hitler Youth members, in their innocence as children, suggested that they, like the animals, were drawn instinctively to a trustworthy man. While Hitler was not the first politician to tug on voters' heartstrings by posing with children, together with Hoffmann, he would raise this public relations ploy to a new level of exploitation. Being seen in the company of adoring children was especially useful for a bachelor politician needing to appeal to female voters and to soften the aggressive masculine image of his party.

On April 4, 1932, the first official day of campaigning for the runoff election, Joseph Goebbels published an article in the National Socialist newspaper *Der Angriff* (The Attack) that exemplified the new campaign tactics promoting the private Hitler as a good man. The major points of his argument repeated and reinforced the themes introduced in Hoffmann's illustrated book. The real Hitler, he claimed, was artistically gifted, but had renounced architecture and painting to lead the German people out of their misery. "Adolf Hitler is by nature a good man. It is known that he has a particular fondness for children, to whom he is always a best friend and fatherly comrade." Indeed, Goebbels claimed that the welfare of German children had spurred Hitler to political action, out of his desire to give them a better life than that of their parents. Goebbels also lauded Hitler's comradely bond with and understanding for his colleagues as well as his intellectual tastes, artistic sensitivity, simple lifestyle, modesty, and enormous dedication to work. "This is Adolf Hitler as he really looks. A man who enjoys the highest love and devotion from all those who know him not only as a politician, but also as a person."[18] In Goebbels's testimonial account, then, Hitler's goodness was not only proven by his character, but also by the love of those near him, who knew the "authentic" man.

The left-leaning press countered the personal and sentimental appeal of the National Socialists' campaign with the distancing power of sarcasm. On March 19, 1932, *Vorwärts* (Forward), the central organ of the Social Democratic Party, republished in full the advertisement for Hoffmann's book that had appeared in *Der Angriff* the previous day. As in the book's dust jacket text, the advertisement promised to satisfy the yearnings of "Hitler's countless millions of followers" for a glimpse of his personal life, drawing on the "many thousands of pictures" taken by Hoffmann in the past ten years at Hitler's side. Beneath the original advertisement, *Vorwärts* rewrote the promotional text:

> Listen up, millions, your longing is satisfied! You see the great Adolf of the Morning in pajamas and of the Evening in tails, you see him painting his nails, you see him pomading his side part, you see him eating, drinking, speaking, writing! For the last ten years—that is, since he turned thirty-three—the great Adolf has spent the better part of his life having his picture taken, and so in less than four thousand days "many thousands of pictures" have been produced, thus, evidently, several each day.
> This is how Adolf has worked quietly for his people and satisfied their desire. Though they have not eaten their fill in a long time, they can now glut themselves looking at Adolf Hitler! Heil![19]

It was a biting critique, ripping a hole in the representation of Hitler as a modest, humble man. In his foreword to Hoffmann's book, Schirach had foreseen the criticism and attempted to deflect it with a long statement about how Hitler hated being photographed and did so only for the good of the party—indeed, much of the foreword, ironically, was devoted to framing Hitler as the photographer's unwilling subject.[20] By doing the math, however, *Vorwärts* made a case for Hitler as a vain and self-obsessed man who lived for the camera and offered nothing but its empty illusions to his followers.

Writing at the end of May 1932 in the Berlin weekly *Das Tagebuch* (The Daily Journal), Kurt Reinhold similarly employed sarcasm to critique the contradictions, exaggerations, and dissimulations in Hoffmann's "documentary" book. To Schirach's statement that Hitler's enemies had killed his dog, he responded, "And is it any wonder that National Socialists resort to revolvers, knives, and brass knuckles?" Describing a photograph of Hitler that Schirach had labeled *An Unassuming Man*, Reinhold wrote: "Hitler sits in the countryside, a travel blanket under his bum (or whatever the correct term may be for a Führer), and peels an apple. Hoffmann pleads, 'As modest as possible, please!' and everybody realizes that he doesn't mean the still life, but rather the Kaiserhof bills." (The month before Reinhold's article appeared, the liberal Berlin weekly *Die Welt am Montag* [The World on Monday], had printed Hitler's hotel bill for the Kaiserhof, a luxury hotel that served as his residence and headquarters in Berlin before 1933, which exposed the exorbitant amounts spent on his and his entourage's accommodations and meals.[21]) Reinhold doubted the spontaneity of Hoffmann's candid photography, detecting instead Hitler's "cold-blooded" calculations in procuring images that caught him at just the right moment. Reinhold thus attempted to puncture the book's illusion of transparency and claim to offer a window onto the private man. Reinhold saw here nothing but the same impenetrable "Führer masks," which he believed had only grown thicker with the passage of time.[22]

Despite such criticisms, *The Hitler Nobody Knows* sold and sold: over four hundred thousand copies in multiple printings by 1942. Its success, combined with Hitler's need to solidify his support among the German population in the early years of his rule, ensured that Hoffmann would return to this popular format. After Hitler's rise to power, he published three more books that focused on the Führer's private life: *Youth around Hitler* (*Jugend um Hitler*, 1934), *Hitler in His Mountains* (*Hitler in seinen Bergen*, 1935; fig. 41), and *Hitler Away from It All* (*Hitler abseits vom Alltag*, 1937; fig. 42). Each of these sold over two hundred thousand copies, testifying to the unwavering interest of German audiences.[23] To the books, Hoffmann added a brisk business in Hitler postcards with off-duty motifs, and sold such images to the German and foreign press (fig. 43). In 1937, for example, *Life* magazine published a three-page feature on Hoffmann's photographs

Fig. 41. Cover of Heinrich Hoffmann's *Hitler in His Mountains* (*Hitler in seinen Bergen*) (Berlin: Zeitgeschichte, 1935).

Fig. 42. Cover of Heinrich Hoffmann's *Hitler Away from It All* (*Hitler abseits vom Alltag*) (Berlin: Zeitgeschichte, 1937).

INVENTION OF THE PRIVATE HITLER

DER FÜHRER ALS TIERFREUND

Fig. 43. Heinrich Hoffmann, postcard entitled "The Führer as animal lover."

of Hitler with children, admitting that the images were propaganda, but reproducing them, complete with sentimental captions, nonetheless.[24] As historian Toni McDaniel has argued, the American media's preoccupation before 1938 with maintaining "balanced" coverage of Nazi Germany resulted in a confusing image of Hitler, particularly in the "sugar-coated" stories regularly printed in newspapers and magazines about the private man, a subject that fascinated the American public.[25] But the immense popularity of Hoffmann's images goes beyond editorial choices to suggest how audiences in Germany and abroad wanted to see Hitler in the early years of the regime. A 1934 article in the *Deutsche Presse* (German Press), the journal of the National German Press Association, on national and foreign markets for German photojournalism reported that "photos that depict the Führer as a friend of children or playing with his two German shepherds at Haus Wachenfeld are the most popular." Even American newspapers preferred to buy Hitler pictures with a "human interest" angle, such as the Führer snapped "as he caresses a child."[26] By 1934, then, the most sought-after images of Hitler were not of the new leader giving speeches or reviewing his troops, but rather those that purported to show his softer side. The private Hitler invented for the 1932 presidential elections had become a global celebrity.

While *The Hitler Nobody Knows* established the main characteristics of the Führer's private persona, after 1933, the site of its performance focused predominantly on Haus Wachenfeld on the Obersalzberg. The house in the mountains, as envisioned by Hoffmann and other National Socialist promoters, became a space of projected desires for the good life promised to the German people by the Nazi Party. Here in the expansive Lebensraum and pure air of the mountains, where the sun always seemed to shine and blond children frolicked, the Nazis envisioned and propagated a domestic "utopia" that stood for the nation as a whole. Through officially sanctioned representations on postcards and in magazines, books, and exhibitions, and even in the "spontaneous" pilgrimages to the Obersalzberg tolerated for many years, Germans were encouraged to consume in their imaginations the little house that symbolized the larger reward to come. Not unlike the witch's house in the fairy tale of Hansel and Gretel, it was an alluring and dangerous lie.

7   AN ALPINE SEDUCTION

Propaganda and the Man on the Mountain

When Adolf Hitler became chancellor of Germany in 1933, a book appeared that celebrated the place he had chosen to call home. That place was not Berlin, but the Obersalzberg and nearby Berchtesgaden. In the world imagined by the book, the distance between the capital and the Alps could not have been greater. *Adolf Hitler's Adopted Homeland* (*Adolf Hitlers Wahlheimat*, 1933) featured twenty-two drawings by Karl Schuster-Winkelhof of unspoiled natural landscapes, simple timber houses, villagers in traditional clothing, cozy domestic interiors, and the slow pace of mountain life.[1] The afterword by Walter Schmidkunz, an accomplished mountaineer and author of popular books on climbing and skiing, bolstered the sense of a place beyond time, describing the mountains as the "pedestals of eternity."[2] The artistic quality of the book itself, with its folksy graphic design and thick, cream-colored paper, evoked the craft production for which Berchtesgaden was known. The small rectangular format recalled an artist's sketchbook or souvenir album of postcards. As a type, the book blended travelogue and propaganda, for the centerpiece of the drawings and text was Haus Wachenfeld, the most famous residence of the newly established Third Reich.

In 1933, Germans were still getting to know the man who within a decade had risen from obscurity to become the nation's leader. Heinrich Hoffmann's 1932 book, *The Hitler Nobody Knows,* explored the Führer's personal side in different contexts, including relaxing on the Obersalzberg. Schuster-Winkelhof's book narrowed the focus to the Alpine setting of Hitler's domestic life and offered, in addition to a visual tour of the landscape, an intimate look at Haus Wachenfeld itself. Schuster-Winkelhof was uniquely positioned to offer these perspectives because he was Hitler's neighbor: his father owned the Türken Inn, which was located directly beside Haus Wachenfeld. Hitler had frequented the establishment since his first stay on the Obersalzberg in 1923 and reputedly made speeches to its guests.[3] According to Schmidkunz, Hitler had acted as a kind of mentor to the young Schuster-Winkelhof, who was a passionate climber and painter, and encouraged him to pack his bags and travel eastward.[4] Schuster-Winkelhof's first book, *White Mountains, Black Tents: A Persian Journey* (*Weisse Berge, Schwarze Zelte. Eine Persienfahrt*), was published in 1932.[5] When the young man returned to the Obersalzberg, he pursued the idea of another travelogue, closer to home, and received permission to enter Haus Wachenfeld and sketch its rooms, including the most intimate of its spaces, the chancellor's bedroom.

The book began with vistas of the Berchtesgaden valley and surrounding mountains, which enabled the reader to place the house in its topographical context and to experience what Hitler himself would see. One of the landscapes, for example, depicted the town of Berchtesgaden as glimpsed, the reader learned, along the route taken by the chancellor to a favorite local haunt, the Hochlenzer, a scenic mountain inn about an hour's walk from his home.[6] Similarly, once Schuster-Winkelhof entered Haus Wachenfeld, he framed the views to encourage the impression that the reader, standing in the artist's footsteps, experienced the chancellor's most private visual moments, such as in drawings that captured the views from Hitler's bedroom window and balcony (fig. 44). The sense of intimacy created by the book, then, operated on several levels: the small format of the book, which encouraged holding it in one's hands; the subject of the illustrations, especially those of the interior of the house; and the imagined gaze, which aligned the reader with the chancellor through the artist.

Perhaps because he produced drawings instead of photographs, Schuster-Winkelhof was permitted to reveal the most intimate space of the house: Hitler's bedroom on the upper story. It was the only time that

Fig. 44. Karl Schuster-Winkelhof, drawing of the view from Hitler's bedroom window at Haus Wachenfeld, from *Adolf Hitler's Adopted Homeland* (*Adolf Hitlers Wahlheimat*) (Munich: Münchner, 1933), fig. 10.

German audiences would be granted such a view. The caption said simply, "The bedroom of the people's chancellor." In the drawing, we see a metal-framed single bed, a nightstand with a lamp and vase of flowers, a small woven rug, two framed pictures on the wall, and a glimpse through a glass door to the balcony and mountains beyond (fig. 45). Schmidkunz described the framed pictures as a portrait of the Führer's "beloved mother" and a crucifixion scene by Ludwig von Herterich, a much-honored painter of the Munich School. The selection seems strategic: in the context of Catholic Bavaria, one can hardly think of two more respectable pictures to hang above a bachelor's bed. Although exceptionally simple and modest, the room avoided asceticism through its decorative touches and the comforting appeal of the bed's thick duvets. The bedroom's Spartan qualities, moreover, were balanced by Schuster-Winkelhof's depiction of the ground-floor *Wohnstube* (sitting room), which radiated a warm Bavarian Gemütlichkeit

Fig. 45. Karl Schuster-Winkelhof, "The bedroom of the people's chancellor," drawing of Hitler's bedroom at Haus Wachenfeld, from *Adolf Hitler's Adopted Homeland* (1933), fig. 11.

with its large tiled stove, rustic wooden furniture, houseplants on deep windowsills, and cages of budgies (fig. 46). Schuster-Winkelhof, who seems to have enjoyed drawing animals, devoted two separate pages to Hitler's dogs and birds (fig. 47).

In addition to giving us his own perspective of the house, Schuster-Winkelhof included a page of drawings he labeled, "The neighbors and how they view the house of the 'Great Neighbor'" (fig. 48). Depicted were four men who lived near Haus Wachenfeld: the Türken innkeeper Karl Schuster (Schuster-Winkelhof's father), leaning on a spade and dressed in a vest and long apron; "Bodner Hausl," tenant of the Boden farm, who made a living with his ox transport; the elderly Josef Rasp of the Freiding farm; and the local forester. Except for the forester, who turned his back, the men stood looking directly at the artist (and viewer), who, the title implied, occupied the position of Hitler's house or of Hitler himself. The viewer was thus placed in a conversation of glances with Hitler's neighbors, evoking the bond that existed between the "great" and the common neighbors. The men's portraits, while individualized, offered a typology of the indigenous

Fig. 46. Karl Schuster-Winkelhof, drawing of Hitler's
Wohnstube at Haus Wachenfeld, from *Adolf Hitler's
Adopted Homeland* (1933), fig. 14.

inhabitants living close to the land with whom Hitler had chosen to sur-
round himself, and, in that sense, they reflected back onto the "people's
chancellor" some of their own qualities as a Volk embedded in the soil. In
the afterword, Schmidkunz reinforced the idea of a natural and unalien-
able bond among the neighbors, Hitler, and the land: "Hitler's house has
inserted itself into the chosen homeland and stands with a fraternal sense
of belonging between the old Boden and Freiding estates, so much so that
it is impossible to imagine it not being there, and the neighbors regard the
chancellor as a Salzberger, as one of their own, who like them is inextricably
and forever linked to the free German soil."[7]

The final page of drawings in the book depicted the addition to the
house of a garage and guest quarters carried out from May to June 1933.

Fig. 47. Karl Schuster-Winkelhof, drawing of Hitler's dogs outside Haus Wachenfeld resting by a sign reading "Attack dogs! No entry!" from *Adolf Hitler's Adopted Homeland* (1933), fig. 4.

This might, at first glance, seem a jarring way to end a visual story focused on a traditional way of life. In place of modern building equipment and trucks, however, Schuster-Winkelhof depicted a robust ox and horse pulling wooden-wheeled wagons full of large stones. Around them, masons and laborers yielded pickaxes and shovels and carried pails. There was no sign of the black Mercedes to be housed in the garage or of the Nazi strangers who would occupy the guesthouse. The visual part of the book thus ended on a reassuring note about the continuity and strength of a rural way of life, symbolized in these hardy men and animals. While some change was acknowledged—the expansion to Haus Wachenfeld coincided with Hitler's seizure of power and thus represented the dawn of a new political era—

Fig. 48. Karl Schuster-Winkelhof, drawing labeled "The neighbors and how they view the house of the 'Great Neighbor,'" from *Adolf Hitler's Adopted Homeland* (1933), fig. 13.

life on the Obersalzberg appeared to stand largely outside of time. Indeed, Schmidkunz insisted that, despite the minor alterations to the house, "the spirit who chose and furnished it as home and shelter remains inviolate, like the surrounding mountains, like the meadows and the forest and the soil." In other words, while the face of Haus Wachenfeld grew less recognizable, Hitler and the land remained unchanged.[8]

The book's association of Hitler with the eternal features of the landscape meant that although he was absent in Schuster-Winkelhof's book—the Great Neighbor was not at home when the artist visited—he was, at the same time, present everywhere. Schmidkunz claimed that the special connection between Hitler and the Obersalzberg—"on whose shores his restless heart cast anchor"—had been formed in 1923, when he had first arrived there with Dietrich Eckart, Anton Drexler, and Hermann Esser, "the protagonists and pioneers" of National Socialism. "Those Berchtesgaden days," he wrote, "have intimately bound Adolf Hitler to the mountains and to the land that became his adopted homeland." For Hitler, Schmidkunz explained, the stillness of the land, with its soaring mountains and distant views into Austria, was not an escape from a turbulent world, but rather the ground on which to germinate and ripen his ideas. The land, then, was framed as an active participant, almost like another member of "the protagonists and pioneers" who had helped to forge the path toward the Third Reich.[9]

Further blending Führer and landscape, Schmidkunz implied a connection between the mythologies of the mountains and the coming of the Third Reich. In particular, he focused on two legends that were associated with the Untersberg, whose majestic peaks faced the front of Hitler's house (and would later dominate the view through the window of the Great Hall). The first, as mentioned in Chapter 4, recounted the story of Charlemagne, who by 800 C.E. had conquered and united vast territories in Western and Central Europe, reviving the imperial tradition of the Western Roman emperor. According to the legend, Charlemagne slept enchanted, surrounded by his royal household, deep in the Untersberg. He would awaken when Germany's ancient enemies arrived and the nation stood in desperate need. This would come to pass when the ravens no longer circled the mountain and the king's beard had grown three times around the marble table where he sat asleep. When he awoke, he would unleash the last great battle of humankind, and so much blood would flow that it would fill the warriors' shoes, and the bodies of the dead would form hills. This legend was popular across Germany and was often told with Frederick Barbarossa, the twelfth-century red-bearded Holy Roman emperor, as the sleeping king and the Kyffhäuser Mountain in Thuringia as his resting place (although in some versions, as previously noted, Barbarossa was also identified with the Untersberg). The second legend continues from the first and was also rooted in a natural feature. The war itself would be fought in the shadow of the Untersberg, on a field outside the village of Wals near Salzburg, where the emperor would hang his battle shield on a large, withered ancient pear tree, causing it to sprout leaves. Under the shield's coat of arms, wrote Schmidkunz, "Germans will unite and defeat all enemies, and over the vanquished the bells of German cathedrals will ring in the thousand-year Reich." This last embellished detail demonstrates how such German legends were woven into the rhetoric of National Socialism and Hitler's rise to power portrayed as the fulfillment of folk prophesy.[10]

Haus Wachenfeld stood as the anchoring point in the narratives associating the Führer with the physical and symbolic power of Alpine topography. It was portrayed not only as his home, but also as the place where he absorbed nature's powers, often by looking contemplatively out his windows. In writing about the house, Schmidkunz described the views to be seen from the windows and balcony, reinforcing the reader's identification with the occupant, but also tying the house through sight lines to the majestic natural features around it. At the same time, however, he shifted the focus inward, to the simple comforts of the hearth, leaving sleeping medieval kings and end-of-days battles outdoors. Schmidkunz credited Hitler's sister Angela with the coziness of the home, remarking more than once on her "thick slices of buttered bread," which Hitler and children could not resist. A wholesome domesticity was also implied by Schmidkunz's descriptions of how well Hitler slept in the mountains (as opposed to the capital), the presence of adoring children (whose affection was returned by the Führer), and the comfort of his beloved and loyal dogs. These and other details of Schmidkunz's domestic narrative already seem formulaic by 1933: the vegetarianism and abstinence from drinking and smoking, the cultured mind revealed by the books possessed, the scant leisure time and strong work ethic, the inspiration and strength derived from nature, and the love of children and dogs. Without much variation, these formed the keystones in official descriptions of Hitler's domesticity throughout the 1930s, the main points already having been established by Joseph Goebbels, Baldur von Schirach, and Heinrich Hoffmann in 1932.[11]

For Schmidkunz, what was remarkable about Hitler's domesticity was precisely its lack of remarkability. "Hitler's house," he wrote, "which cynics once tried to falsely transform into an opulent 'palace,' harbors neither secrets nor noteworthy sights." Yet it was precisely this ordinary, everyday quality, according to Schmidkunz, that attracted pilgrims to Hitler's home. Pilgrimages to the Obersalzberg began soon after Hitler became Reich chancellor in January 1933, and the ecstatic joy of the crowds in seeing their Führer and perhaps even shaking his hand was captured by Hoffmann and transformed into yet more lucrative merchandise. These well-known images have obscured the fact, remarked upon by Schmidkunz, that people eagerly came to see the house even when Hitler was not in residence. Haus

Wachenfeld served as an icon of the private Führer, and pilgrims seeking an intimate encounter with the man found it in their physical proximity to his home:

And now they know, this is where he lives and this is where he is a human being; he sleeps behind that southwest window on the upper floor; his desk is over there, on the ground floor, behind the bay window; yes, and those are the three German shepherds that the Reich chancellor loves so much! Muck, the black one, fierce, trained, who guards his master's house as if he knew exactly who he has to protect, Wolf, the funny, playful one, and Blonda, the light-haired female. And the observers, who do not miss a thing, see the burbling fountain with the humorously carved head and see the blossoming flowers in front of the windows and on the balcony and know: from this felicitous vantage point, the Führer comprehends with joyful eyes the magnificence of the mountains. And for some of the onlookers, it may be thoughts such as these that first awaken them to that glory.[12]

Schmidkunz thus asserted that the pilgrimage to Haus Wachenfeld could be spiritually rousing, and that the experience was ultimately not about seeing Hitler, but rather seeing *like* Hitler. Schmidkunz's own narration of Schuster-Winkelhof's drawings similarly guided the reader through this process, suggesting both what to see and what to feel. Through empathetic looking, the pilgrim at Haus Wachenfeld, standing in for the reader, took on the subjectivity of the private Hitler, occupying his domestic spaces, eating his buttered bread, loving his pets, and, while gazing out at the mountains, absorbing their majesty and strength. The reader's encounter with Haus Wachenfeld and its homey aesthetics, captured not just in words and images, but also in the intimate format of the book, represents a very different kind of experience from those analyzed by Susan Sontag in her influential essay "Fascinating Fascism." In particular, she noted how the fascist aesthetics of Leni Riefenstahl's 1935 film *Triumph of the Will*, documenting the Nazi Party rally in Nuremberg, glorified the ecstatic but disciplined masses, who subordinated themselves with an erotic energy to the will of the Führer.[13] By contrast, the experience of Haus Wachenfeld produced in *Adolf Hitler's Adopted Homeland* was a more cerebral and individual one: the projection of the self onto the private Hitler, as embodied and mediated by his house, and, through this identification, a coming into focus of his transcendent vision. In a sense, then, both the onlooker at Haus Wachenfeld and the participant at the Nuremberg rallies came to the same conclusion in terms of the Führer's supremacy, but one arrived there through the feeling of standing in Hitler's shoes, while the other was happily crushed beneath them.

While pilgrims to Haus Wachenfeld may have felt enlightened by their trek, their presence increasingly irritated the resident and his neighbors. The pilgrimage phenomenon brought as many as five thousand people per day to the chancellor's driveway, blocking nearby roads and overwhelming local businesses. If Hitler was in residence, the crowds would wait for hours, chanting, "We want to see our Führer!" In their enthusiasm, some had ripped away the wooden pickets of the Führer's fence to keep as "relics."[14] Seeking to put more distance between himself and the boisterous onlookers and also needing space to house his guards, Hitler asked his neighbor Karl Schuster, the owner of the Türken Inn, to sell him a piece of his adjacent property (see fig. 48). Schuster refused on the grounds of having six children to consider, but offered to let Hitler use the land for free. Despite having supported the National Socialist Party in its early years and been a member since 1930, as well as having known Hitler personally for a decade, Schuster soon learned that old loyalties meant little to the Führer when someone stood in his way.[15]

A month after Schuster refused Hitler's request, he found himself accused of having insulted the drunken SA and SS men who frequented his inn. The incident triggered a boycott by the Berchtesgaden chapter of the NSDAP, whose members blocked the hotel's entrance and forced out guests and staff, leaving only the family within. When they tried to leave, they were hit by rocks and spat upon by the pilgrims waiting near Haus Wachenfeld. Ostensibly because of the threat to his safety, Karl Schuster was taken into "protective custody" and imprisoned for two weeks. Hitler, meanwhile, refused all contact with his neighbor, and as the hotel's finances went into the red, Schuster sought out buyers. Offers evaporated, however, when local officials made clear that the hotel's license would not be renewed. Finally, Angela Raubal, Hitler's bread-baking sister—who was unsympathetic to her neighbor's plight but aggrieved by how it inconvenienced her—notified Martin Bormann, who compelled Schuster to sell him the property and, after the family left in November 1933, transformed the hotel into barracks for Hitler's SS bodyguards. The Schuster family was forbidden to resettle anywhere near the Berchtesgaden region, and its adult members were compelled to sign an agreement not to speak about having been Hitler's neighbor or about their expulsion. When Schuster did confess to his new neighbors, who were suspicious of a man who refused to talk about his past, he was again imprisoned. Around Berchtesgaden, by contrast, talk about the family's treatment was spreading, prompting the town's NSDAP chapter in January 1934 to publish a notice in the local newspaper forbidding any further discussion of "the Schuster case." Those who disobeyed were warned that they would be labeled enemies of the state and sent to the Dachau concentration camp. Karl Schuster, a broken man, blamed himself for his family's ruin and died of a heart attack in 1934, at the age of 58.[16] Eager buyers of *Adolf Hitler's Adopted Homeland* could not have guessed how quickly the book about the "Great Neighbor" had become a tale of misfortune.

The acquisition of the Türken Inn did little to staunch the Nazis' desire for more space on the Obersalzberg to accommodate Hitler's growing entourage as well as to conduct government business and host state visits. As the regime's machinery of oppression churned out masses of victims—some forty-five thousand Germans were held in concentration camps and unofficial torture centers in the first half of 1933 alone—the need to protect Hitler also grew more pressing.[17] In the years following the Schusters' eviction, Bormann directed a radical and violent transformation of the mountain, as its original inhabitants were removed to make way for a heavily guarded enclave of the Nazi elite. If, as Schmidkunz maintained, Hitler's neighbors had thought of him as one of their own, he, clearly, did not return the sentiment. While a few of the villagers departed voluntarily, content with the compensation they had received, many refused to go. Some had businesses that were beginning to flourish with the increased tourism. Others felt the compensation Bormann offered was grossly inadequate. And yet others simply did not want to leave their homes and farms, which had often been in the family for generations. Those who made trouble found themselves on the receiving end of Bormann's brutal tactics. In winter, a favored method to hurry a departure was to remove the roof of a house that was still occupied—the residents tended not to last long in the freezing temperatures and deep snowfalls. In other cases, recalcitrant sellers were threatened with deportation to the Dachau concentration camp. This was no idle threat: a young photographer named Johann Brandner who dared to petition Hitler directly about the loss of his shop was sent to Dachau for two years. By 1937, the majority of the original inhabitants had been removed and their houses demolished to improve Hitler's views or accommodate the needs of the new elite community.[18] Yet throughout the period of seizure and evictions, National Socialist propaganda continued to celebrate a people and way of life on the Obersalzberg that the Nazis were systematically destroying.

In 1935, Hoffmann published a book of photographs celebrating Hitler's mountain life, and revealing, through its title, the Nazis' proprietary mind-set: *Hitler in His Mountains* (see fig. 41). Eighty-six images documented Hitler relaxing or working at home on the Obersalzberg and in other southern Bavarian locations. Schirach provided the foreword, in which he stated that Haus Wachenfeld, now "famous worldwide," had become a "symbol of the Führer's steadfastness." To this very day, he wrote, the same "unaltered gable [of the house] greets the Untersberg as in the time when its occupant stood at the beginning of his path." True, he admitted, there had been some modifications to the house, some workrooms added, but the bewitching power of the Alps remained unchanged and could still be felt when the clacking of the secretaries' typewriters and the ringing of the telephones had ceased: "Then, at night, the mountain house stands under myriads of stars and the Führer stands absorbed in the glowing moonlit landscape, the details of which have been familiar to him for decades."[19] With a strategic deployment of sentimental imagery, and following on Schmidkunz's lead, Schirach thus dismissed and diverted attention from the fact that the house was in constant flux and, after the 1935–36 expansion, more than anything a testament to Hitler's enormous wealth and power.

The pilgrimages to Haus Wachenfeld featured prominently in the book. Hoffmann captured Hitler waving to the crowds assembled outside the fence to his house, shaking hands, and walking through a throng of outstretched arms. Unlike the disciplined crowds depicted by Leni Riefenstahl, the pilgrims swarmed around the Führer, pushing to get closer and trying to touch him. Nor did they resemble the idealized, young, and athletic types favored by Riefenstahl. In one photograph, a stout middle-aged woman salutes the Führer with her upraised arm while firmly clutching her handbag under the other; in another, Hitler shakes the hand of an older woman whose broad smile reveals decayed teeth. (In later images of the pilgrimage, Hoffmann would focus on groups of young blond girls.[20]) Yet what differentiated these masses from those envisioned and filmed by Riefenstahl was, above all, the potential emergence of one from the many: the person whose hand the Führer shook or the child who received special attention. Schirach explained that "every now and then, someone breaks ranks, usually a small boy, who has some worry. Maybe the father is unemployed, the mother ill, and he knows of no other option than to ask the Führer for help. And the

Führer does help. His clear eyes see, behind the lad's fresh face before him, the grave fate that threatens this small, brave family. And so he comforts, as he has done a thousand times before, with deeds and few words, as the father of his faithful and beloved people."[21]

Breaking from the ranks of the pilgrims could, however, also be a joyous occasion. *Youth around Hitler*, Hoffmann's 1934 book devoted to the relationship between Hitler and Germany's young, included an illustrated sequence about a child picked out of the crowd by the Führer. In the foreword, Schirach explained that one summer day in 1933, as Hitler was greeting the throngs of pilgrims in front of his house, a child's voice piped up and announced that it was her birthday. Out of the dense crowd, "the Führer fished up a blond little lass" with "bright blue eyes" and invited her to tea. In fact, the girl's visit had been arranged in advance, but Schirach told the "fairy tale" (his own term) as it was presented in the photographs—as one of the many fortuitous and magical events that could happen to pilgrims at Haus Wachenfeld. The first image depicted a smiling young girl above the caption, "The favored birthday girl." The second image showed Hitler leading her up the driveway, away from the gathered pilgrims, to Haus Wachenfeld (fig. 49). The caption reinforced her privileged position: "Out from the crowd." We then see her indoors eating dessert ("a birthday feast") and standing on the terrace with Hitler, his hands cupped around her face. In the fifth and final image, the girl, standing on her toes, thanked Hitler with "a long kiss."[22]

Nothing remotely like this happens in Riefenstahl's *Triumph of the Will*. Although the camera recorded individual faces and voices in the crowd, there was never a moment in which one person was extricated for special treatment by the Führer. Indeed, the effect of the film on the viewer relied on his or her identification with the unbroken mass that symbolized the newly united nation. The visualization of the mass and its performance required an architecture designed for monumentality and spectacle, such as the site of the Nuremberg rallies, with its large and anonymous marching fields, grandstands, and stadiums. In contrast to Riefenstahl's film viewer, the reader of Hoffmann's book, like that of Schuster-Winkelhof's album, was encouraged to imagine the thrill of the singular—not dissolving into the mass, but exiting from it (at least, temporarily). And it was the architecture of the Führer's domesticity, personalized and intimate in scale, that functioned as the stage set for that other, unique experience. These two imagined encounters with the Führer, as a part of a uniform mass or as an

Fig. 49. Heinrich Hoffmann, photograph of Hitler escorting the "favored birthday girl" to his house on the Obersalzberg, from Heinrich Hoffmann's *Youth around Hitler* (*Jugend um Hitler*) (Berlin: Zeitgeschichte, 1934).

individual, and their two architectural spaces, the monumental and the domestic, complemented each other and opened up different emotional roads to the leader: one, as Sontag argued, through joyful submission and loss of self, the other through the fantasy of recognition and intimacy, however fleeting.

More broadly, Schirach depicted the pilgrimages to Haus Wachenfeld as yet another manifestation of the national unity Hitler had achieved by overthrowing the hated democratic institutions of the Weimar Republic: "This daily encounter between Adolf Hitler and his people is a dazzling revelation of the new German unity. For this mass, which jubilantly greets him, is in itself already an image of the new national community. Here is the industrial worker from the west, whose journey here was made possible by the Strength through Joy association, and beside him boys from East Prussia, farmers from Upper Bavaria, municipal officials, teachers, students, and soldiers. In order to see the Führer, they have set out in the very early morning hours, have stood seven hours or longer in the blazing heat of the Obersalzberg, until in the afternoon the long-awaited hour strikes and they get to look into the eyes of the man who, for some of them, has been the symbol of their struggle for ten years."[23] Here on the Obersalzberg, people and leader came together in a manner more genuine and direct, Schirach implied, than under the former parliamentary system. Recalling the dictum typically attributed to Marie Antoinette, the pilgrimage images published by Hoffmann in this and other books seemed to ask: Who needs democracy when you can have cake with the Führer instead?

Hitler in His Mountains continued to build on the myth, already elaborated before 1933, of the Führer's love of children. In Hoffmann's images, this affection was communicated not just with smiles, but with physical contact as well—Hitler stroked the children's faces, placed a hand on their shoulders, and embraced them tightly. He also indulged them with autographs, sweets, and conversation (fig. 50). As with the pilgrims, Haus Wachenfeld occupied center stage in Hitler's encounters with Germany's children. These took place most often on the terrace rather than in the house, with the Alps providing a spectacular backdrop for Hoffmann's camera.

Historians researching mental illness among Hitler's relatives raise the possibility that he chose not to have children of his own out of fear of passing on (and thereby exposing) his family's genetic defects.[24] Hoffmann's mythologizing lens, however, eliminated such concerns and made Hitler the symbolic progenitor of an idealized Aryan race. "You are blood of

Fig. 50. Heinrich Hoffmann, photograph of Hitler signing an autograph on the terrace of Haus Wachenfeld (a box of Bahlsen cookies in the foreground), from Heinrich Hoffmann's *Hitler in His Mountains* (1935).

our blood, flesh of our flesh, spirit of our spirit," Hitler had declared to the assembled Hitler Youth at the 1933 Nuremberg Party Congress, and Hoffmann's images reiterated that claim.[25] Indeed, *Youth around Hitler* presented a veritable catalogue of perfect specimens: "Many German tribes," the caption for a collage of different girls and boys read, "but only one race." In some cases, Hoffmann heavily touched up images to make the children look even more beautiful. After 1934, he abandoned such interventions, which jarred with the more naturalistic photographic tastes of contemporary audiences, but continued to depict children with Hitler who physically seemed to reflect the regime's racial ideologies. And appearances were everything. In 1933, the blond, blue-eyed birthday girl photographed enjoying dessert at Haus Wachenfeld had been denounced as part-Jewish to the Bavarian Political Police when the images had first been published as postcards. Although the revelation was kept secret, she was no longer permitted to come to the Obersalzberg. Hitler nonetheless sanctioned the continued use of her image in National Socialist propaganda, including in *Youth around Hitler*, which cynically presented her as an object of Hitler's affection and a model Aryan type.[26]

Long before and after Hitler, politicians have seen the advantages of appearing publicly with children or presenting themselves as father to the nation. But the extent to which Hitler and his propagandists worked to cultivate the myth of his special relationship to children was unprecedented. Even in the 1930s, it was viewed—at least by the foreign press—as exceptional.[27] Children were at the heart of National Socialist programs intended to improve the race, from eugenics to health and education.[28] The belief that Hitler truly cared about children helped to instill confidence among parents, who were asked to entrust their children's welfare to the state. In 1936, a Munich newspaper printed a photograph of Hitler chatting with a young girl on the terrace at Haus Wachenfeld and asked, "Is there any better judgment passed on a man than when children acclaim him and give him their trust?"[29] Hitler's unmarried status, and the need to avoid insinuations of the "oddball" bachelor, also made such publicity especially valuable. The fact that images of Hitler with children were among the most popular of all Führer images during the Third Reich suggests how much German audiences enjoyed and cherished this myth.[30]

Indeed, the trope of Hitler's connection to children was so widespread that it continues to be perpetuated in history books, despite our knowledge of the millions of children killed in euthanasia programs, concentration and labor camps, as well as by war and famine under Hitler's regime. Aside from the period's propaganda, however, there is little evidence to support its veracity. Richard Reiter, the nephew of Maria (Mitzi) Reiter, a sixteen-year-old Berchtesgaden girl Hitler pursued romantically in the late 1920s, was among the local children invited regularly to Haus Wachenfeld. In his case, Hitler's adjutant, Julius Schaub, was the instigator of these visits and the person with whom he had a relationship. Asked whether Hitler seemed to genuinely enjoy children, Reiter recalled that, in private, "he behaved rather woodenly and did not quite know what to do with us." In front of the camera, by contrast, "his acting ability made him look as if he adored kids."[31]

Hitler's encounters with his neighbors and other local people, which feature prominently in *Hitler in His Mountains,* were undoubtedly also carefully stage-managed. But what is more striking in this case is how quickly the images Hoffmann published depicting Hitler as a good neighbor became outdated. For example, the book included a photograph of Hitler shaking hands with his neighbor, the farmer Josef Rasp. The caption referred to the Führer's "most tender understanding for the elderly." In 1935, Hitler had bought the 78-year-old's property, but the contract gave designated family members, including Rasp himself, a lifelong right of residence. In the summer of 1937, however, in violation of the contract, Rasp and his family were forcibly removed and their farmhouse was demolished. Rasp died shortly thereafter. And yet well into the 1940s, Hoffmann continued to use the image as a testimonial of Hitler's "tender understanding." Like the myth about Hitler's love for children, the fiction about Hitler's good relations with his neighbors was widely disseminated at the time and continues to be maintained in some history books.[32]

If the house on the mountain represented the place where the Führer communed with his followers, young and old, it was also the setting in National Socialist propaganda for Hitler's confrontation with the powers of nature. *Hitler in His Mountains* portrayed the Führer hiking in the Alpine landscape or absorbed deep in thought in front of a majestic sunset or soaring mountain peaks (fig. 51). Unlike the images of Hitler on the Obersalzberg in Hoffmann's 1932 book, *The Hitler Nobody Knows,* which had depicted the Führer in a happy, relaxed state, the photographs in the 1935 book suggested a more intense and purposeful engagement with nature. In his 1934 book about Hitler's rise to power, Otto Dietrich, Hitler's press chief, presented the mountain as sanctuary and inspiration: "In the tranquility of Obersalzberg, our leader has often designed his most important plans, made his greatest decisions, and perfected the schemes for the most eventful demonstrations."[33] The ability to do his best work on the mountain, a claim Hitler made himself, was about more than getting a good night's sleep.[34] Rather, Hitler was portrayed as tapping into and channeling the primordial energies around him. In the foreword to *Hitler in*

Fig. 51. Heinrich Hoffmann, photograph of Hitler by the Obersee near Berchtesgaden, from Heinrich Hoffmann's *Hitler in His Mountains* (1935).

PROPAGANDA AND THE MAN ON THE MOUNTAIN

His Mountains, Schirach wrote, "Here he dictated the second part of *Mein Kampf,* and it appears that the monumental architecture of the mountain landscape recurs in the structure of the work, which has given support and hope to hundreds of thousands of people."[35] Schirach thus suggested that the Führer was not only in the mountains, but that the mountains were also in him, infusing and shaping the power of his words and actions.

The imagined bond between Hitler and the Obersalzberg mobilized a host of associations with mountains in modern German culture. Romantic artists and writers in the eighteenth century had been the first to explore and define the human encounter with the fearsome, sublime nature of mountains. In his landscapes, German painter Caspar David Friedrich employed the *Rückenfigur*—an anonymous, solitary individual seen from behind—to encourage his audiences to imagine, through identification with this person, the overwhelming feelings evoked by the confrontation with the sublime. Friedrich was one of Hitler's favorite artists, and Hitler's poses in some of Hoffmann's photographs, in which he stands or sits alone framed by and communing with the majesty of the mountain landscape, recall Friedrich's lonely figures.[36] But unlike them, Hitler is never anonymous, and if we are meant to feel the emotional pull of the landscape, it is always through him.

German audiences did not need to draw directly on eighteenth-century imagery to grasp Hitler's message. The fascination with mountains, and particularly the Alps, in the 1920s and 1930s films of Arnold Fanck, Leni Riefenstahl, and Luis Trenker provided well-tilled ground for the positive associations that Hitler's propagandists sought to create for his Alpine identity. These German and Tyrolean directors portrayed the Alps as an antidote to decadent civilization, a place of primal energies, physical vigor, and heroic struggle. Sentimental love plots unfolded amid the breathtaking scenery, which echoed and magnified human emotions. In recording the landscape, the camera appropriated Romantic imagery, including that of Friedrich, to evoke the mystical, overwhelming beauty of the sublime. Mighty and inscrutable, the mountains reigned supreme in the natural order, demanding submission and even death. Siegfried Kracauer, writing in 1947, and, later, Susan Sontag detected in these elements the beginnings of a fascist mindset. While more recent scholarship on mountain films has demonstrated this to be a limited view of the genre, its romantic idealism, sentimental pathos, and preoccupation with transcendent power are defining characteristics of National Socialist propaganda about Hitler at home in the Alps.[37]

In contrast to these earlier traditions, however, National Socialists did not tremble before nature, but rather treated it as one more thing to be brought under their dominion—the Führer, rather than the Alps, is the ultimate power in narratives about Hitler in the mountains. The construction of the Kehlsteinhaus, a pavilion perched defiantly on a remote mountain crag, exemplified this attitude, although it was not a project intended for public consumption. Hitler's much-photographed monumental window in the Berghof's Great Hall, which framed and claimed the Untersberg for his domestic space, was the period's most iconic image of nature contained (see plate 5). Published photographs of the window never included human figures, which would have been dwarfed both by the frame and the mountains beyond.[38] Indeed, and unlike the sometimes tiny human figures found in Romantic landscape paintings, Hoffmann almost always photographed Hitler outdoors on the Obersalzberg from a close angle to seem proportionate to the size of the mountains around him. In *Hitler in His Mountains,* photographs of Hitler and Fritz Todt, the Reich's chief engineer, inspecting road construction in the Alps reinforced the idea of the Führer's will reordering the landscape. These images also portrayed Hitler bringing modernity to the mountains, suggesting technology could serve and enhance, rather than destroy, traditional life. A gentler, non-mechanistic version of Hitler's ability to tame nature was reproduced in the popular images by Hoffmann of Hitler hand-feeding roe deer that appeared in the 1933 book *Germany Awakes* (*Deutschland Erwacht*) and on postcards (see fig. 43).[39] Like the photographs of Hitler with children, these images suggested that innocent creatures instinctively sensed Hitler's innate trustworthiness.

Despite the apparent topographical specificity of Nazi propaganda about Hitler in his Obersalzberg home, Hitler's encounter with the mountains carried a broader message about German space. *Hitler in His Mountains* opens with a stunning photograph of the Berchtesgaden valley seen from a distance, the caption for which reads: "Berchtesgaden, the Führer's destination [*Ziel*] after weeks of hard work."[40] This established for the reader the book's setting, but also introduced the idea of this vast space as a longed-for coming home, a place of rest and reward after struggle—"Ziel" can be translated not just as "destination," but also as "goal," "ambition," or "end." In subsequent images in the book, Hitler is shown looking out over the openness of natural space, including from the balcony and terrace of Haus Wachenfeld (fig. 52). Hitler's domesticity was thus associated with an imagined abundance of space in the Alps, which, in turn, was presented

Fig. 52. Heinrich Hoffmann, photograph of Hitler looking at pilgrims from the balcony of Haus Wachenfeld, from Heinrich Hoffmann's *Hitler in His Mountains* (1935).

as the source of all good things: the renewal of body and spirit, a nurturing domestic life filled with healthy blond children and loyal pets, warm relations with down-to-earth neighbors, and the bounty of nature itself in the hearty food, pure water, and fresh air. In short, National Socialist propaganda situated Hitler's mountain home in the midst of the Nazis' conception of Lebensraum (living space), the racial utopia that in their eyes justified war and genocide. When Germans purchased one of Hoffmann's books or postcards depicting Hitler's domestic bliss within this vast natural space, they were consciously or unconsciously buying into a dream, embodied in Haus Wachenfeld, of a promised land. In this light, the pilgrimages to Haus Wachenfeld can be seen not just as paying homage to the Führer, but also as a desire to travel to the promised land, the place of abundance that Hitler held out as the ultimate reward for sacrifice and suffering. Nestled in the most "German" of landscapes, the Alps, Haus Wachenfeld gave Lebensraum a form and shape, made it seem a tangible and realizable goal.

In helping Germans to frame their desire for Lebensraum, as imagined in a picturesque small house surrounded by nature's bounty, Hitler's domesticity thus had a central role to play in National Socialist propaganda.

Unlike the sarcastic reaction from the left-leaning press that had greeted *The Hitler Nobody Knows,* the Nazis' virulent suppression of the freedom of expression after 1933 leaves us with few contemporary publications to evaluate the responses of German audiences to *Hitler in His Mountains.* Under Goebbels's control, the German press participated in the creation of the Obersalzberg myth. Positive stories about Haus Wachenfeld, often illustrated with Hoffmann's pictures, began to appear soon after Hitler seized power. By the mid-1930s, the foreign press also came to play a significant role in perpetuating and disseminating this Nazi propaganda. Accounts by the German press in exile offered, unsurprisingly, a very different perspective. An article entitled "A Führer behind Barbed Wire," published in April 1937 by *Neuer Vörwarts* (New Forward), the Social Democratic newspaper operating in exile from Czechoslovakia, directly challenged the myth of Hitler's closeness to the German people and their love for him. It pointed to the enormous security measures surrounding the newly renovated Berghof, including the expanded "no entry" zone on the Obersalzberg, the exclusion of civilian traffic, watch towers, barbed wire fences, patrols, and an around-the-clock guard of 150 SS men protecting Hitler. As it noted, the highly idealized stories about Hitler's mountain retreat published by sympathetic reporters had managed to overlook this reality and what it signified.[41]

The exiled German press also brought attention to the massive transformation of the house itself, which Nazi publicists had tried to downplay by emphasizing the eternal nature of the mountains or of Hitler's spirit. In June 1937, an article that appeared in the *Pariser Tageszeitung* (Parisian Daily News), a left-liberal émigré publication, described the Berghof as a "palatial house" that could accommodate "forty or more" guests in "large bedrooms" with "exquisite furniture" comparable to a "luxury hotel." Further stripping away the image of a cozy domesticity, the reporter noted that whereas Hitler's sister had once taken care of his home, it was now in the hands of "skilled hotel staff." The article also commented on the heavy security measures, including air raid defenses on surrounding mountains and bomb and gas shelters deep inside the Obersalzberg itself. Further emphasizing the Führer's isolation, the reporter claimed that children from Berchtesgaden would be brought up to the Berghof to be photographed with Hitler "while he pets their heads," but that he himself never went to the town to see his people. The article concluded by arguing that "Hitler, when ruling Germany from his mountaintop in Bavaria, is as remote and invulnerable as the Dalai Lama on a Himalayan summit."[42]

Despite the lack of objective media reports within Germany, other evidence points to the tremendous popularity among German audiences of Haus Wachenfeld and the idealized domestic Hitler envisioned as its occupant. As noted earlier, Hoffmann's books about the "private" Hitler, including *Hitler in His Mountains,* were enormous commercial successes, selling hundreds of thousands of copies and being reissued multiple times. Additionally, Hoffmann engaged in lucrative business deals with companies interested in marketing their products through his images. The Reemtsma Cigarette Company, for instance, distributed National Socialist collector albums of Hoffmann's images. The albums featured essays by Nazi spokesmen such as Goebbels and Dietrich, and the page layout included designated places to attach photographs, which were obtained through coupons found in Reemtsma cigarette packages.[43] About 2.3 million copies were produced of the 1936 cigarette album *Adolf Hitler: Pictures from the Life of the Führer* (*Adolf Hitler: Bilder aus dem Leben des Führers*), which included a chapter on Haus Wachenfeld.[44] These large albums, bound in rich colors and decorated with images and gilded lettering, "were meant for display in domestic settings, like family or travel albums."[45] The process of the consumer completing the album by submitting the coupons, receiving packets of photographs in the mail, and attaching them to the correct pages also reinforced the personal (albeit systematic) nature of these books. Hoffmann, moreover, sold millions of postcards drawing on the photographs that had been included in his books as well as on the great many more that had been omitted. The Führer's house, both before and after its transformation into the Berghof, appears to have been an especially sought-after image, based on the countless variations published as postcards by Hoffmann and other photographers in the region (see plates 1, 11).

Indeed, the commercial exploitation of Hitler's domesticity and other motifs of Nazi propaganda soon became an issue of concern for the regime. The groundswell of popular support for Hitler that followed the National Socialists' seizure of power in January 1933 tempted many German manufacturers to employ Nazi references to boost their products' appeal. Goebbels moved quickly to regulate the flood of Nazi-themed merchandise and, on May 19, 1933, passed the "Law for the Protection of National Symbols." Local authorities were vested with the power to seize goods and prosecute manufacturers or merchants who sold products that used Nazi symbols in ways that were deemed to "violate" their "dignity."[46] Lists of banned goods, including the names and locations of their producers, were published periodically in the *Deutscher Reichsanzeiger* (German Reich Gazette), the official state newspaper. Over the years, such contraband included Stormtrooper gingerbread, wine bottles and ashtrays ornamented with swastikas, women's brooches with "Heil Hitler" in imitation diamonds, and alarm clocks that played the Nazi anthem, "The Flag on High."[47] What began as a legal measure quickly grew into a broader cultural campaign. A profusion of newspaper and journal articles warned of the damage done to the German people by kitsch, an argument that had already been made by the German Werkbund at the turn of the twentieth century in its design reform campaign.[48] Beginning in 1933, government and cultural authorities, hoping to educate consumers, organized exhibitions of banned Nazi merchandise and similarly "tasteless" products, which attracted tens of thousands of viewers and international attention.[49] Echoing contemporary arguments about German art, critics of kitsch goods medicalized the threat—one Nazi spokesman declared that "kitsch is spiritual cocaine for our nation's soul"—and decried the subservience of culture to market forces.[50]

Because Haus Wachenfeld (and later the Berghof) was so closely identified with the Führer, its commercial use also fell under the broad new legislation. This raises an interesting question regarding what might have threatened the "dignity" of the house. It is easy to understand how kicking a ball decorated with a swastika or wiping one's mouth with a swastika-covered paper napkin—further examples of banned objects—would have been problematic from Goebbels's perspective.[51] In the case of Haus Wachenfeld, by contrast, the quality of the merchandise seems to have been the deciding factor in determining approval or rejection of commercial designs. Thus, porcelain ornamental plates depicting Haus Wachenfeld tended to be approved, while terra-cotta ones were not.[52] Similarly, a design for velvet cushion covers with an image of "our Führer's country home" was rejected as an example of "tasteless products."[53] The concern about the kitschy quality of Nazi merchandise was not limited to Haus Wachenfeld. Guidelines to help interpret the law emphasized the need for high standards in a design's conception and execution—all "artistically inferior" reproductions of National Socialist symbols were to be rejected.[54] Nonetheless, many products did receive approval, since the Nazis realized that such popular consumer goods increased their hold on the public imagination, as consumers brought these loaded symbols into the intimacy of their homes and made them a part of their everyday lives.[55] Thus, children played with toy wooden models of Haus Wachenfeld and saved their pennies in Haus Wachenfeld replica coin banks; framed color prints of Haus Wachenfeld hung on living room walls; Hoffmann's books lay on coffee tables; and the postman delivered postcards of Haus Wachenfeld from friends vacationing in southern Bavaria or just writing to say hello.

In the case of a more upscale clientele, the marketing of Haus Wachenfeld assumed a different role. In February 1938, *Innen-Dekoration* (Interior Decoration), a publication that had been founded in 1890 to promote new directions in interior design, featured the Berghof on its cover and included two articles discussing its creation. In April 1939, the lifestyle magazine *Elegante Welt* (Elegant World, or Smart Set), which offered stories about home decoration, fashion, and leisure, republished the articles in a slightly modified form, adding a remarkable series of color images of the house's interior. Although the audiences for these magazines differed, the Berghof essays targeted a group that overlapped both: educated, urban, middle-class readers with an interest in design and the resources to hire professionals to build or redecorate their homes. Consequently, the articles paid special attention to the relationship between Hitler and his designers, and, in particular, to the work of his interior decorator, Gerdy Troost.[56]

As the client, Hitler stood at the heart of the renovation. His desire, readers learned, to enlarge the old house with "a great hall" that would "retain, despite its impressive spaciousness, an appealing sense of homely comfort" had been the decisive factor in the design. The "challenging and rewarding task" of giving material expression to the "Führer's ideas" fell first to the architect Alois Degano, who skillfully blended old and new through the interlocked structure of the whole. The broad slanting roof, traditional to the region, most obviously united the different parts of the house, but the article also pointed to window and wall surface treatments, repetition of detailing materials, and dynamic balancing of floor and ceiling heights to create a sense of overall coordination. The result was "a powerfully serene building" that "by avoiding anything palatial in nature preserved the character of an authentic, native 'Berghof,'" or mountain farm.[57]

But in fulfilling the Führer's wish for "homely comfort," it was Gerdy Troost who received the most credit. Her stated responsibilities encompassed everything to do with decor, color choice, and fabrics. "With what certainty of taste," marveled the writer for *Innen-Dekoration*, "has she shaped the expression and mood, melody and livability of the rooms." Troost's method of creating color harmonies was described in detail, specifically how she would select an object in a room as the basis for color themes, counterpoints, and variations. In the small living room, that object was a celadon tile stove; in the Great Hall, a seventeenth-century Gobelin tapestry. Colors were repeated among rooms, extending the color harmonies throughout the house. The writer also noted how the essential simplicity of the furniture forms contributed to a visual language that unified the house. Learning how Troost had deftly combined color and form to give the Führer his dream home undoubtedly evoked the reader's admiration for her skills, while also reinforcing the complexity of interior decoration as an endeavor. By thus focusing on how Troost and Degano had overcome the project's considerable architectural and aesthetic challenges, these articles served as an endorsement for hiring a professional for home renovation, while the positive image they conveyed of a collaborative design process inspired trust.[58]

In providing insight into how Degano and Troost worked, the articles also encouraged readers to consider the design qualities most valued at the Berghof. In particular, they commended the livable spaces, honest use of materials, simplicity and clarity of forms, and quality of execution. Also highly desirable was the interweaving of the domestic interior with the natural outdoors through balconies, windows, and terraces—a point that was visually reinforced by the vibrant color photographs included in the *Elegante Welt* article. All of these principles had been advocated by design reform movements since the end of the nineteenth century, including the so-called International Style that arose in the 1920s. Unlike the latter, however, which celebrated modern industrial materials such as concrete and steel, the articles about the Berghof emphasized traditional, homegrown elements, like the red stone from the neighboring Mount Untersberg used for the Führer's outside stairs and terraces. While new technologies and industrial products were employed in the Berghof's construction, the articles ignored this fact and focused instead on natural, "authentic" detailing.[59] Moreover, the attention to the Berghof's complex color schemes, the use of woven textiles and plush fabrics, and the dominance of wood in the interior emphasized the desire for a visually richer and "warmer" domestic environment. These preferences speak, in part, to the reaction in Nazi Germany against the industrial aesthetics and methods of high modernism as exemplified by the Bauhaus. At the same time, however, the design values promoted by the articles reflected broader trends in Europe and the United States toward a commercially more acceptable, "softer" form of modern design. Designers working in this vein were willing to accommodate clients' desires to blend traditional and modern elements, prioritize comfort, and play with decorative features.[60] Thus, the magazines' message to their affluent readers on how to create a "genuine" and tasteful home, as viewed through the lens of the Berghof, cannot be reduced simply to an ideological reaction against high modernism, since it also incorporated continuities with past reform movements and with broader stylistic trends beyond Germany.

Of the various National Socialist efforts to educate the German public on matters of aesthetics and taste, those with the highest profile occurred in the House of German Art in Munich. The annual Great German Art exhibitions, which began in 1937 and featured ideologically correct, state-approved works in sculpture, painting, and drawing, attracted broad media attention and hundreds of thousands of viewers each year. Less well known today are the German Architecture and Applied Arts exhibitions that were held there in winter and meant to complement the summer fine arts shows. The design exhibitions informed the public and professionals about state architectural and urban planning projects as well as sanctioned new directions in the decorative arts and interior design. In addition to display cabinets of individual objects, the crafts section of the show contained entire room ensembles, from living rooms and dining rooms to home offices and children's rooms. The high quality of the work presented, typically created by hand and with expensive materials, meant that it came with a correspondingly high price tag. Nonetheless, the shows were very popular. The first exhibition, from January to April 1938, attracted 260,000 visitors and sold a third of the displayed objects for sale. The second show, from December 1938 to April 1939, attracted even more visitors—295,000. Plans for future exhibitions were put on hold with the start of war and the restrictions placed on nonstrategic building, although the fine arts shows continued through 1944.[61]

Despite the Nazis' violent and highly publicized closure of the Dessau Bauhaus in 1932, modern design by no means disappeared from German homes during the Third Reich. While government housing authorities turned away from the radical modernity of the Weimar period, modernist houses and interiors continued to be commissioned on the private market. Similarly, commercial firms and retailers offered their customers a range of home-decorating options, including modernist styles. Design journals such as *Innen-Dekoration, die neue linie,* and *Das Schöne Heim* (The Beautiful

Home) continued to publish the work of modernist designers, including women, up until the war years. One even finds Bauhaus products in official Third Reich publications.[62] Nonetheless, by the mid-1930s, the image of domestic interiors found in guidebooks and design magazines had undergone a noticeable change. This was due, in part, to the influence of the first National Socialist building projects, designed by Paul Troost, which displayed the regime's preference for a functional classicism. The Nazi ideology of "blood and soil" also resulted in a greater emphasis on Heimat styles, which drew on regional traditions. Additionally, wood emerged as the preferred design material, a shift that was not entirely political. Among nationalists, German wood was hailed as a homegrown "hero" in the fight against the alien industrial materials of international modernism. But metal had also become scarce by 1935–36, as Hitler began to rearm the country for war.[63] It may be that many German consumers would have preferred to purchase the tubular metal furniture that had become so popular in the early thirties. But by 1935–36, the rearmament economy curtailed the materials available to designers and, along with the regime's more clearly defined ideological and aesthetic goals, the look of German homes began to change.

Visitors to the first Architecture and Applied Arts Exhibition at the House of German Art encountered examples of this conservative shift in domestic design on the second floor, where the show's crafts section was housed. Folkish handwoven textiles, rustic pottery, heavy wooden furniture, marquetry, and medievalizing decoration were abundantly on display, although some modern designs inspired by Art Deco also found their way into the show. Additionally, visitors encountered numerous examples of Paul Troost's historicizing classical style. Indeed, despite having been dead for four years, Troost's presence was everywhere in the exhibition. The first and second rooms of the architecture exhibition, on the ground floor, gave pride of place to his National Socialist building projects, reinforcing his primacy in the lineage of National Socialist architects. Upstairs, the crafts exhibits—arranged in open, room-like settings by Gerdy Troost— included several dining and living room ensembles showcasing Paul Troost's furniture and decorative objects.[64] Also on display were examples of his wife's designs, and undoubtedly one of the most attention-grabbing displays of the show represented a marriage of their work: on a dark dining room table by Paul Troost, his widow laid out her design for the Führer's table service (fig. 53).[65]

Here was a tangible piece of the Führer's domesticity, on view to edify the public about good taste in domestic design as defined by two of his

Fig. 53. Heinrich Hoffmann, photograph of Gerdy Troost's design of the Führer's table setting, on display at the 1938 German Architecture and Applied Arts Exhibition in the House of German Art, Munich.

favorite designers and as practiced by the Führer himself. The china was designed by Gerdy Troost and executed by the Nymphenburg Porcelain Manufactory, one of Germany's oldest and most distinguished makers of porcelain. The dishes were decorated with an interwoven pattern, colored "orange with gold," that resembled basketwork. The stylized folkish motif and color choice suggest that the pattern was designed for the Berghof, and a color image by Walter Frentz of a formal table laid out in the dining room confirms this.[66] The silverware, produced by the firm of F. H. Wandinger, bore Hitler's monogram and the national emblem of the eagle clutching a swastika. The glassware was crafted by the Franz Steigerwalds Neffe firm and the Glass School in Zwiesel, and the bobbin lace place mats were woven by the United Workshops for Art in Handicraft.[67] All these producers were located in Munich or Bavaria, in keeping with Troost's preferred patronage of Bavarian artists and firms.

Hitler's tableware was not, of course, one of the items for sale at the exhibition. But even though one could not take it home, it was possible to imagine doing so. If the dining room suite and porcelain service were beyond the means of most exhibition visitors, the intimate setting—only four places were set at the table—made this example of Hitler's domesticity feel familiar. Here, it seemed, was the table not of a prince or ostentatious millionaire, but of a man, as his propagandists repeatedly insisted, "like you and me."[68] Gerdy Troost's simple, beautifully crafted display reinforced the message about the private Hitler as an individual of refined yet modest tastes. If viewers searched these objects for evidence of Hitler's character, they may well have imagined that they had physical proof of the mythic mountain dweller who invited children to tea, cared for his neighbors, and spent his few spare hours reading about art. Surely, this was not the table of a megalomaniacal dictator?

But if the dishes could have spoken, the exhibition's visitors would have heard another story. In 1938, the Nymphenburg Porcelain Manufactory was under the management of the Bäuml brothers, who had taken over from their father, Albert Bäuml, a decade earlier. When Albert Bäuml had originally leased the firm in 1888, it had been in a period of long decline. He revived its high artistic standards and restored the firm's lost prestige. Among the artists with whom he worked was Paul Troost, who maintained a relationship with the firm from 1908 until his death. The directorship of the three brothers—who expanded the manufactory's production into new areas, including an affordable "people's dinnerware"—was also considered highly successful. In 1938, however, life had become very difficult for the Bäuml brothers, whose father had been born Jewish and converted to Catholicism. Beginning already in 1934, the brothers had faced racial denunciations made by opportunists seeking to take over the firm. In a testimonial written for Gerdy Troost's postwar trial, Fritz Bäuml, the eldest brother, recounted how Troost, whom he had known since her marriage to Paul Troost in 1925, had intervened forcefully on his and his brothers' behalf with the Bavarian prime minister, Ludwig Siebert. Another threat came from Heinrich Himmler, who wanted to annex the Nymphenburg Porcelain Manufactory to his SS porcelain factory in Dachau, which used concentration camp labor to create expensive Nazi-themed porcelain objects. Himmler, however, made the mistake of approaching Hitler about the matter while Gerdy Troost was in the room, and, according to Bäuml's testimony, her "energetic intervention" put an end to the idea. Bäuml also noted that even though she knew about their Jewish background, she continued to work with the firm at "considerable risk to herself."[69] One of these commissions, ironically, was for Hitler's table service.

The worst threat the Bäuml brothers faced came in October 1944, when they were notified of their imminent deportation to a Thuringian mine, a satellite of the Buchenwald concentration camp. There the brothers would have served as forced laborers under the harshest conditions; many of the work camp inmates in this region, including those forced to work and live underground in the hellish Mittelbau-Dora, died of exhaustion, disease, and starvation. In his testimony, Fritz Bäuml recounted the futility of appeals made to ministry after ministry and how, "at the last minute," the brothers turned to Gerdy Troost. After a "long discussion," Troost managed to convince Paul Giessler, the acting Gauleiter for Munich and Upper Bavaria, to rescind the order. "And thereby," Bäuml wrote, "Frau Troost saved us from the concentration camp."[70]

As such trial documents reveal, Gerdy Troost did, on several occasions, bravely protect those with whom she and her late husband had working and personal relationships. But countless others in Nazi Germany had no such friends with connections to high places. Seven months after visitors had admired Hitler's beautiful china and crystal in the House of German Art, the streets of the nation were littered with the broken glass of Jewish synagogues, shops, and homes. On the night of November 9, 1938, in coordinated riots, SA Stormtroopers unleashed their hatred on the nation's Jewish residents as they burned synagogues, murdered men and women in their homes and beat them in the streets, imprisoned thirty thousand in concentration camps, and destroyed thousands of Jewish shops and homes. But even after Crystal Night, as the November pogrom came to be known, the aura that Hitler's propagandists had spun around him as a decent and honorable man did not dissipate. Many Germans refused to blame their Führer for the violence in their midst and believed that he would restore order and end the ever-more-brutal persecutions happening before their eyes.[71] One of these people was Gerdy Troost, who even when confronted with her friends' nightmares, never stopped believing in the image of the gracious Hitler that she herself had helped to create.

8   THE SQUIRE OF BERCHTESGADEN

The Making of a Myth in the Foreign Press

For more than thirty years, William George Fitz-Gerald, journalist and novelist, traveled the world and wrote about the political affairs and peoples of the nations he visited. From the creation of new roads in the Peruvian highlands to Haile Selassie's armed forces in Ethiopia and Japan's growing impact on overseas markets, the range of Fitz-Gerald's interests and commentary seemed limitless.[1] Under the pseudonym Ignatius Phayre, Fitz-Gerald delivered eyewitness accounts considered informed and insightful, earning him the trust of editors and readers across the political spectrum.[2] Today he is remembered, if at all, for a series of glowing articles he wrote about a visit to the mountain home of his "personal friend" Adolf Hitler. From 1936 to 1938, Fitz-Gerald sold his Hitler story to at least seven publications with national or international audiences: *Country Life* (1936), *Current History* (1936), *National Home Monthly* (1936), *Saturday Review* (1936), *Windsor Magazine* (1936), *American Kennel Gazette* (1937), and *Homes and Gardens* (1938).[3] It also circulated among Australian newspapers.[4] Whether they were perusing *Homes and Gardens* in Leeds, *Current History* in Boston, *National Home Monthly* in Winnipeg, or the *Sunday Pictorial* in Sydney, English-language readers across the globe eagerly absorbed the details of Fitz-Gerald's home visit with Hitler, whom he dubbed the "Squire of Wachenfeld."

With his international experience and curiosity, Fitz-Gerald seems, at first glance, an unlikely champion of Adolf Hitler. Fitz-Gerald was capable of writing with passion and sympathy for the oppressed. In a 1919 article entitled "Race-Hatred in the United States," for example, he condemned the lynching of African Americans in the United States, documenting the sadistic brutality of the crimes perpetrated on innocent victims. He also reported on the abuse and torture of African American prisoners, the suppression of the black vote, and the arbitrariness of the color line.[5] Some fifteen years later, he raised awareness about the continuing practice of slavery around the world, describing the marketplace auctions of women, children, and men. He argued that the demand for slave labor—"domestic, agrarian, and industrial"—and the profits to be made from human trafficking kept slavery alive. And he criticized the colonial powers that, looking after their own economic self-interest, turned a blind eye to these realities at home and abroad.[6]

A closer look, however, suggests that Fitz-Gerald's global encounters only reinforced his belief in a profoundly divided humanity. Fitz-Gerald was born in 1873 in London to Irish immigrants. His youngest brother, Desmond, a poet and revolutionary, took part in the 1916 Easter Rising in Dublin and was imprisoned by the English. Desmond later rose to prominence in the Irish Free State government, eventually becoming minister of defense—a connection his brother William undoubtedly would have found useful in securing a personal interview with Adolf Hitler.[7] In 1923, following the establishment of the Irish Free State, Fitz-Gerald published an anthology entitled *The Voice of Ireland: A Survey of the Race and Nation from All Angles*.[8] Despite assembling an impressive diversity of contributors, including Dublin's chief rabbi, Fitz-Gerald made clear in the subtitle that Ireland was not a multiracial state.[9] This exclusionary mindset was explicit in other writings, in which Fitz-Gerald claimed that nations with racial and territorial integrity were best able to compete on a global basis. He credited the foreign trading successes of the Japanese, for example, to their being "a clannish people . . . a true 'Family' in Burke's definition of nationhood, and one weaponed for this peculiar fray as no Western polity can ever be."[10] In his 1933 book, *Can America Last?*, he argued that the United States could never establish itself politically "on a secure and enduring basis" because it lacked the unity of "older lands which are true 'nations' of homogenous race and limited boundaries."[11] Significantly, for Fitz-Gerald, strong nationhood rested not only on homogeneity of race, but also on the type of race. The following year, in an odious article on Liberia, he dismissed the very idea of a "Negro 'nation'" as "a contradiction in terms."[12] Hitler's rhetoric on German self-determination thus must have resonated with Fitz-Gerald's own ideas on nation and race.

Moreover, Fitz-Gerald's sentiments were profoundly anti-democratic. Like many others in this period, he hoped for the emergence of "the long-looked for Leader."[13] In the final pages of his 1933 book on America, he wrote that "all classes, from bankers to gangsters, are well aware that Democracy has broken down, and that only the stern τύραννος, or Master, can lift the United States out of its rut of ruin and decay."[14] Traveling in South America, Fitz-Gerald admitted he felt "something like veneration tingeing my admiration" for political strongman Augusto Leguía, Peru's president. He credited Leguía's success in modernizing his nation to his insistence on "public order," but failed to mention the cost to political freedoms.[15] When Fitz-Gerald turned to writing about Hitler in the mid-1930s, he seems to have judged him on similar terms.

The remilitarization of the Rhineland in March 1936 and the Olympic Games in Berlin the following August focused the world's attention on Germany and its leader, and Fitz-Gerald capitalized on the interest by publishing multiple articles that year about his visit to Hitler's mountain home. The personal connection between author and subject was a major selling point: "Holiday *with* Hitler: A Personal Friend Tells of a Personal Visit with Der Führer—with a Minimum of Personal Bias" read the large heading above Fitz-Gerald's article in the July 1936 issue of *Current History.* The frontispiece photograph depicted a smiling Hitler outdoors, wearing a suit but seeming relaxed in the mountain landscape. The caption, "Adolf Hitler: A 'different' pose," summed up the article's intent in a nutshell. Situating his visit in the months following the events in the Rhineland, which had triggered international anxieties about another war, Fitz-Gerald pondered the difference between the dictator whom British Prime Minister Stanley Baldwin claimed had the power to lift the "'black shadow of fear from Europe'" and the man who rushed to greet his plane as it landed on the Obersalzberg. "But was it really such omnipotence as this that hurried towards me with the same springy gait I knew so well, with that hearty smile of welcome, and a chubby hand raised in *the* salute? It seemed incredible."[16]

Seeing his bareheaded host arrive, "the unruly 'browlock' broken loose," Fitz-Gerald remarked that "Hitler might have been a hired gardener. Clad in an old tweed coat, tightly buttoned and too short for him, and shabby trousers that did not match, he was waving a crooked stick wrenched from a cherry tree." Fitz-Gerald did not intend to argue that Hitler did not *look* like an omnipotent dictator who held the fate of Europe in his hands. Rather, he wanted to convince readers that Hitler did not *act* like one either—at least, not on the Obersalzberg, his "one and only 'home.'"[17] Here, Fitz-Gerald suggested, away from the admiring crowds and stresses of the capital, Hitler was able to strike a "different pose" and reveal another self—the "Squire of Wachenfeld."

In the series of articles that he published on Hitler at home, Fitz-Gerald enticed readers away from the frightening and alienating image of a thundering, "messianic" Führer, and offered in its place a portrait of the squire, or country gentleman, a comforting and recognizable figure, especially for British and Commonwealth audiences. The "Squire of Wachenfeld," according to Fitz-Gerald, was a "shy, retiring man" and "a very modest—even a simple, humble soul."[18] As the Führer's "personal friend," Fitz-Gerald claimed to have the insight and access necessary to introduce the reader to this other, private Hitler. Depending on the publication, Fitz-Gerald altered the details of the story to accommodate readers' tastes. Thus, the text for *Homes and Gardens* described the Führer's curtains and the food he served his guests, while that for *Current History* included stories from his formative years in Austria. Despite these minor variations, however, the articles covered largely the same material and developed common themes, with the aim of transforming the image of Hitler in the reader's mind.

There was, to begin, Fitz-Gerald's description of Hitler's clothes. Away from the politics of Berlin and the mass rallies of the Nazi Party, the mountain was a place for civilian attire. As seen in the quotation above, Fitz-Gerald brought the reader's attention to Hitler's old tweeds, suggesting both the unkempt bachelor and the landed gentry.[19] Further emphasizing the English sartorial connection, Fitz-Gerald noted that Hitler's "coarse tweed" suits were "made by a 'London' tailor" in Munich.[20] A certain jaunty tone was also struck by Fitz-Gerald's mention of Hitler hiking in "plus fours," a style of sporting breeches introduced in the 1920s and popularized by the Prince of Wales.[21]

Such clothing befitted the activities of the mountain, which, in addition to leisurely pursuits, encompassed—according to Fitz-Gerald—a working farm. Fitz-Gerald referred to the land Hitler had acquired around Haus Wachenfeld as an "estate."[22] He wrote: "A little farming is done here with well bred stock. The Leader also grows wheat and alfalfa; while his cherry orchards are famous all along the Austro-German frontier."[23] Around the house, noted Fitz-Gerald, "the gardens are laid out simply enough. Lawns at different levels are planted with flowering shrubs, as well as roses and other blooms in due season. The Führer, I may add, has a passion for cut flowers in his home." He also kept in touch with his gardeners' activities, speaking with them "every morning at nine" about the day's work ahead.[24]

Fitz-Gerald further informed the reader that, in addition to his interest in farming and gardening, Hitler bred dogs on his estate. In his essay for *Homes and Gardens,* Fitz-Gerald stated that "all visitors are shown their host's model kennels, where he breeds magnificent Alsatians" (fig. 54). It included a picture of Hitler relaxing on the lawn beside one of his "pedigree pets."[25] While Hitler did not hunt or shoot, Fitz-Gerald managed to allude to the latter through a reference to his dogs, one of whom (Muck) was misidentified as a retriever—a type of gun dog closely associated with the English nobility.[26] Fitz-Gerald, moreover, claimed that Hitler was "never so content as when hobnobbing with the hunters."[27]

Hitler's dog-breeding activities and canine relationships were explored more fully in a feature article, "Hitler Says His Dogs Are Real Friends," published in the *American Kennel Gazette* in January 1937. The magazine, read widely by dog breeders and lovers, occasionally featured stories about "great men" and their canine pets, meaning that Hitler was placed in the august company of, among others, Abraham Lincoln. In this version of his Haus Wachenfeld story, Fitz-Gerald emphasized Hitler's rigorous attention to the purity of his German shepherds. "From all parts of the Reich," Fitz-Gerald noted, "Alsatian-lovers offer Hitler their best strains as an honored gift. But he prefers to follow his fancy and buy his own. Otherwise, Haus Wachenfeld might become an asylum for mongrels, much as the White House gardens were under President Theodore Roosevelt, who was offered dogs by the hundred during his political tours from ocean to ocean."[28] While President Roosevelt had, indeed, enjoyed a particularly pet-filled White House, with a wide assortment of animals and both pure and mixed breeds of dogs, the comparison here carried not-so-subtle racial overtones about the weakness of the United States as a heterogeneous nation.

Farming, gardening, shooting, and dog breeding were typically associated with the activities and interests of the English landed gentry. Moving

HITLER'S
MOUNTAIN
HOME

A Visit to "Haus Wachenfeld,"
in the Bavarian Alps, written and
illustrated by Ignatius Phayre

A closer view of the house, showing the
umbrella-shaded terrace.

I T is over twelve years since Herr Hitler fixed on the site of his one and only home. It *had* to be close to the Austrian border, barely ten miles from Mozart's own mediæval Salzburg. At first no more than a hunter's shack, "Haus Wachenfeld" has grown, until it is to-day quite a handsome Bavarian chalet, 2,000 feet up on the Obersalzburg amid pinewoods and cherry orchards. Here, in the early days, Hitler's widowed sister, Frau Angela Raubal, kept house for him on a "peasant" scale. Then, as his famous book, *Mein Kampf* ("My Struggle") became a best-seller of astonishing power (4,500,000 copies of it have been sold), Hitler began to think of replacing that humble shack by a house and garden of suitable scope. In this matter he has throughout been his own architect.

There is nothing pretentious about the Führer's little estate. It is one that any merchant of Munich or Nuremburg might possess in these lovely hills.

The entrance hall is filled with a curious display of cactus plants in majolica pots. Herr Hitler's study is fitted as a modern office, and leading out of this is a telephone exchange. From here it is possible for the Führer to invite his friends or Ministers to fly over to Berchtesgaden, landing on his own aerodrome just below the chalet lawns.

This view shows the chalet's lovely setting. In the foreground are Hitler (back to camera) with Field-Marshals Göring (left) and von Blomberg (centre).

193

Fig. 54. Title page of Ignatius Phayre's November 1938 article in *Homes and Gardens*.

beyond the active life, Fitz-Gerald also drew parallels between the landed gentry's rooted identity in the land that they owned and worked and Hitler's own deep bonds to his Obersalzberg estate. There was the proximity to Austria, his native homeland, upon which the German leader could gaze (longingly) from the vantage point of his mountain home. Memories of his revolutionary days and of old friends, such as Dietrich Eckart, also tied him to the place. Above all, Hitler felt emotionally connected to this land, Fitz-Gerald claimed, where he could be himself. "You love this place?" Fitz-Gerald asked him, "watching this very 'different' man with surprise, as he jested and told funny yarns to his friends out on the moonlit balcony after dinner." Hitler replied, "I am happy here. . . . High up on these sunny slopes, I feel I can *breathe* and think—and live! The very thought of all that reek and rattle of towns often appalls me as I recall it here. So does all the fuss, all the guarding, and cheering, and flower-pelting with the tedious routine of bureau and official life. Besides, I fancy the folks esteem me. You see, I'm just 'one of them'! They know I can enter into their joys and woes."[29]

Hitler's notion that the mountain brought him closer to "the folks" played into Fitz-Gerald's makeover of the Führer as squire. In National Socialist propaganda, the Obersalzberg had been imagined as the meeting place of leader and nation. Fitz-Gerald took up the idea, but localized it in English terms, evoking the squire and his tenants. In the following passage from *Current History*, Fitz-Gerald described the "squire" setting out to visit his villagers: "A smiling Führer would tap on an open door. Entering—perhaps at meal-time—he would inquire what the brood of babes had to eat (four is the minimum family he likes to see). And of course, he must dilate on the vitamin-values of his own milk soups, cinnamon-rice, potato-pancakes and the rest."[30] Presented as gentle, caring, and mildly eccentric, Hitler was thus transformed in Fitz-Gerald's hands into a nineteenth-century archetype of the kindhearted and charitable squire tending to his people.[31]

Indeed, for his youngest villagers, the squire prepared special delights. At dinner, he announced to Fitz-Gerald that "tomorrow . . . we're going to have a children's party. So we'll hunt the highland villages for guests and then go down Berchtesgaden to complete the list." The next day, "at four o'clock or so, quite a crowd of his little friends came straggling across the upland meadows. Hitler was quite excited; never was there a middle-aged bachelor who so delighted in the company of children."[32] Perhaps to reinforce the wholesomeness of the children's "Fun Fair," Fitz-Gerald noted in the 1938 *Homes and Gardens* article that "Frauen Goebbels and Göring, in dainty Bavarian dress, arrange dances and folk-songs."[33] In the version published in *Country Life*, the duty of female overseer fell to "Frau Scholtz Klink (of the Women's Labour Front)," who "will escort parties of young folk to greet the 'Squire.'"[34]

According to Fitz-Gerald, Hitler was an equally generous and gracious host with his adult guests. *Homes and Gardens* readers, who were used to reading about the culinary tastes of the wealthy, learned that Hitler, although "a life-long vegetarian," was "something of a *gourmet*" and "keeps a generous table for guests of normal tastes. Here *bon viveurs* like Field-Marshals [Hermann] Göring and [Werner] von Blomberg, and Joachim von Ribbentrop will forgather at dinner. Elaborate dishes like *Caneton à la presse* and *truite saumonée à la Monseigneur* will then be served, with fine wines and liqueurs of von Ribbentrop's expert choosing. Cigars and cigarettes are duly lighted at this terrace feast—though Hitler himself never smokes, nor does he take alcohol in any form."[35] Once again, Fitz-Gerald chose his references carefully. The menu of pressed duck and wine-stewed trout testified to the sophisticated tastes and skills of the Führer's household, while the type of food evoked images of the country squire shooting and fishing on his estate's ponds and rivers.[36] The references to liqueurs and cigars added a certain luxurious and masculine aura to the setting of Haus Wachenfeld, perhaps to balance descriptions of "that Nazi amazon, Frau Scholtz Klink" and the children's "Fun Fair."[37]

Beyond the refined pleasures of Hitler's table, Fitz-Gerald reinforced the genteel image of "the squire" with a discussion of his artistic tastes and talents. Fitz-Gerald described Hitler as "his own decorator, designer and furnisher, as well as architect."[38] He credited Hitler with the early expansion of the Haus Wachenfeld, done "in harmony with the simple wooden lines of the original." Fitz-Gerald admired Hitler's "nice taste for eighteenth-century German furniture and pictures."[39] In his own guest room, Fitz-Gerald inspected the "watercolors by der Führer himself" who "still paints at odd hours—chiefly architectural subjects."[40] Given a tour of Hitler's substantial library (Fitz-Gerald estimated the number of volumes at about six thousand), he noted "that quite half the books are on history, painting, architecture and music."[41]

Through these multiple references to Hitler's activities and possessions, the reader absorbed the image of a cultured man, an impression deepened by the company he kept at Haus Wachenfeld: "Hitler delights in the society of brilliant foreigners, especially painters, singers and musicians."[42] In the evenings, music filled the house as Ernst "Putzi" Hanfstaengl, Hitler's Harvard-educated foreign press chief and friend (Fitz-Gerald noted that they were on familiar, *du*, terms), sat down to play the piano enthusiastically, if not with virtuosity, for his host: "Herr Hanfstaengl gave us delicate bits from Mozart, with terrific crashes of Liszt in between. It was a relief when the last Rhapsody was played, and we could listen to the plaintive flutes and strings of a party of guides and hunters who serenaded their Leader from the cherry-orchard close by."[43]

In certain respects, however, Fitz-Gerald was careful to distinguish Hitler from possibly damaging associations with the landed gentry. He emphasized that Hitler was not the beneficiary of a family legacy, but rather a self-made man who had experienced "five years of misery in Vienna."[44] Haus Wachenfeld had not been inherited, but rather bought with the royalties from *Mein Kampf*: "'This place is mine,' he says simply. 'I built it with money that I earned.'"[45] Instead of a grand manor house, Hitler's home was "a cozy but modest *chalet*," with "cactus plants in majolica pots," trilling "Hartz mountain canaries in gilded cages," and presents from admirers—"furniture, china, silver, and rugs"—arranged in a bachelor's clumsy manner.[46] Not one of Fitz-Gerald's articles mentions the massive expansion of Hitler's mountain home between November 1935 and July 1936, which resulted in the Berghof. The 1938 *Homes and Gardens* article noted that Hitler was "constantly enlarging the place, building on new guest annexes" and included one photograph of the new interiors (Hitler's study), but otherwise all the photographs and descriptions in this and the other publications were of the older Haus Wachenfeld, as it existed before the 1935–36 renovation.[47]

Fitz-Gerald's retellings of his overnight stay with Hitler did not ignore political activities at the house, but framed these in ways palatable with the gentler image of the squire he wanted to construct. Thus, he wrote of Hitler leaving the house "soon after dawn, clad in plus fours, and with his retriever Muck, or else his trained Alsatian Blonda, trotting at his heels. One or the other of these will be carrying on his back a little hamper containing tomato sandwiches and fruit, with a couple of bottles of mineral water. Then amid the pines, or on some commanding knoll beside a cross and wayside shrine, Herr Hitler will sit down to ponder his problems and speeches."[48] Politics were thus reduced to abstractions and submerged into narrative

MAKING OF A MYTH

distractions, leading readers' attention away from the substance of those "problems and speeches" to the contents of a picnic basket. Fitz-Gerald had spent decades probing the actions of politicians and diplomats, but that analytic mindset is wholly absent in his account of the goings-on at Haus Wachenfeld, which reduced men such as Goebbels to a droll raconteur, Ribbentrop to a wine connoisseur, and Hanfstaengl to a piano player.[49] In Fitz-Gerald's hands, the noise and fuss of politics that Hitler claimed to dislike was left as far behind for the reader as it was for the Führer himself, both of whom were left in Fitz-Gerald's narrative to enjoy the beauties and solitude of the mountain.

Thus, with care and craft, Fitz-Gerald transformed the dictator into the squire, creating a seductive, comforting image that soothed rather than inflamed his readers' fears. Reassuring as it may have seemed, however, the story Fitz-Gerald told was riddled with inaccuracies. Some of these can be attributed to artistic license. Wanting to add a dash of modernity to the traditional portrait he drew, Fitz-Gerald gave Hitler an imaginary landing strip on his estate, which, he claimed, the Führer used to commute between Berlin and the Obersalzberg.[50] Along more conservative lines, while Hitler favored Alsatian (or German shepherd) dogs, he did not breed or promote them in the manner of the English landed gentry, as Fitz-Gerald suggests. Perhaps to suggest a soft spot for Anglo-German royalty, Fitz-Gerald sometimes renamed Hitler's dogs after German and English monarchs: Otto, Fritz, and Victoria.[51] (The dogs' actual names were far less illustrious: Muck, Wolf, and Blonda.) Similarly, Fitz-Gerald's description of Hitler's cherry orchards and wheat and alfalfa crops may have made him seem more like a proper squire, but the land was too poor and at too high an altitude to sustain such agriculture.[52] And as invigorating as hikes at dawn or early morning chats with the gardeners may have seemed, Hitler's routine in the mountains, where his days typically began around noon, did not accommodate either one. These are but a few of the many instances where poetic license trumped the facts.

Some of the more glaring errors, however, raise concerns that are harder to ignore. Most obviously, and as mentioned previously, Haus Wachenfeld had been swallowed by the construction of the Berghof beginning in November 1935. By the time that Fitz-Gerald's articles appeared, the place that he so lovingly described no longer existed. Moreover, the massive fortification of the Obersalzberg and the forced removal of its inhabitants at about this same time meant there were few neighbors left for the "squire" to visit.[53] The notion that Hitler might leave his heavily guarded compound to knock on villagers' doors and discuss the vitamins in milk soup was hardly plausible in 1936, if ever. Hanfstaengl, furthermore, far from being on *du* terms with Hitler, had fallen out of favor in the fall of 1934 and never met with him again, at Haus Wachenfeld or anywhere else.[54] Indeed, by the time the *Homes and Gardens* issue appeared in 1938 and its readers learned of Hanfstaengl's piano serenades of the Führer on the Obersalzberg, Hanfstaengl was living in England, having fled Germany the previous year in fear for his life. Hanfstaengl's fall from grace was known outside Germany before Fitz-Gerald began to publish his stories in 1936, and newspapers reported on his exile in England in 1937 following the attempt on his life.[55] In other words, despite what was widely known, Fitz-Gerald insisted on an older, more charming story—like a fairy tale that transcends time. Most damning of all these inaccuracies, however, is Fitz-Gerald's claim in *Current History* to have visited Haus Wachenfeld in the spring of 1936, when the house was a large and thoroughly unlivable construction site and Hitler was not in residence. Fitz-Gerald, in short, could not have possibly visited Hitler or been his houseguest on the Obersalzberg when he claimed to have been there.

Digging deeper, it becomes apparent that many of the narrative details are copied—sometimes verbatim—from other sources. Fitz-Gerald records an anecdote that he says Hitler recounted over dinner at Haus Wachenfeld in 1936, supposedly based on an event that happened earlier that day; in fact, Fitz-Gerald took the story from two *Time* magazine articles published in 1934.[56] His brief description of Hitler's Munich apartment, which he claimed to have visited, is based on a 1935 article in the *Daily Telegraph*.[57] But the most troubling appropriations are from Heinrich Hoffmann's propagandistic works on Hitler, particularly his 1935 illustrated book, *Hitler in His Mountains*.[58] While these books targeted German audiences, they were also known abroad. *Hitler in His Mountains* even received a positive review in the *Observer*, which noted that the book "gives a picture of the Nazi leader as a simple country gentleman"—a remark that may have inspired Fitz-Gerald to take up his pen.[59]

Fitz-Gerald mined Hoffmann's books as a source for anecdotes, picking up details or references and elaborating them into stories. As a result, reading Hoffmann and Fitz-Gerald together produces a strange echo effect in the reader's mind, as the images of one are returned in the words of the other. For example, in *Hitler in His Mountains* Hoffmann included a photograph of a girl, about six years old, standing beside a seated Hitler (see fig. 50). In one hand, he holds a pen, and in the other a card, which she is in the process of giving to or taking from him. The caption reads, "And again: 'Please, please, an autograph!'"[60] Compare this to an anecdote told by Fitz-Gerald about the children's party he claims to have attended at Haus Wachenfeld. He begins by describing how somber and uncomfortable Hitler had seemed when Fitz-Gerald had seen him at work in Berlin:

> But here in his hill-perched eyrie, Hitler is wholly changed and calmed. He can laugh heartily as he grabs up a tiny tot to show her all the fun that is going on in the aerodrome. Or again, some rustic maid of six or eight plucks up courage to creep up and pipe, "*Eine Autogramme, Mein Fuhrer!*" Out flashes that golden pen, and in a moment Hitler's name is scrawled in a way to defy the handwriting expert. They say his autograph is negotiable anywhere in the Reich for ten marks or so. It is certain that scraps of paper with "A. Hitler" on them have already built orphan homes and hospitals from here to the far marches of East Prussia.[61]

The reader assumes Fitz-Gerald witnessed the exchange between Hitler and the girl and is here personally testifying to the Führer's kindness. Our narrator then spins the alleged event further, transforming Hitler's scrawled signature into a network of charitable institutions. Fitz-Gerald thus managed to outdo even the Führer's propagandist.

Fitz-Gerald illustrated his Hitler articles almost exclusively with photographs taken from Hoffmann's 1935 book. Relying on Hoffmann's work was not unusual for journalists at the time, since he had a virtual monopoly on photographing the Führer. However, *Country Life* and *Homes and Gardens* credited Fitz-Gerald with the images, further lending credibility to his role as intimate observer. Fitz-Gerald sometimes altered the original captions in a misleading manner to support his narrative. For example, to illustrate the "squire's" friendly relations with the local villagers, Fitz-Gerald employed a photograph identified by Hoffmann as Hitler greeting General Karl Litzmann (on a visit to the Obersalzberg) and changed the caption to: "Neighbors: Hitler Says 'Hello.'"[62] The unreliability of Fitz-Gerald as a narrator recalls a criticism made in a *Times Literary Supplement* review of his 1933 book, *Can America Last?*: "Mr. Phayre has a free and easy way with names, quotations and dates."[63]

Even allowing for the artistic license so abundantly taken in these articles, the extent and scale of the inaccuracies and plagiarisms in Fitz-Gerald's accounts of his visit to the Obersalzberg make the question of authenticity unavoidable. Could it be that Fitz-Gerald, who had begun his career as a novelist, was never Hitler's guest at Haus Wachenfeld? Indeed, could the entire account be an elaborate fabrication? Former Irish Prime Minister Garret FitzGerald, writing about his uncle William George, stated that "the latter part of his life was spent as an invalid in London, where he died in 1942."[64] Perhaps Fitz-Gerald had been well enough in the mid-1930s to travel to Germany, or perhaps he fantasized the story about his country holiday with Hitler from a sickbed in London. Whatever the case may be, the fact remains that Fitz-Gerald plagiarized sources, including Nazi propaganda, for his reports and passed it off as his own firsthand experience. The editors of highly trusted and respected publications then passed on these lies to tens of thousands of readers as serious journalism.

How could so many reputable journals and newspapers have missed the warning signs? Even if the editors had failed to recognize the inaccuracies and plagiarism, some of the ludicrously flattering anecdotes about Hitler should have set off alarm bells. By the mid-1930s, the pathological violence of the National Socialist regime was well known, and it is hard to believe that editors did not notice the whitewash in Fitz-Gerald's pen. Indeed, the article's subtitle in *Current History* acknowledged the story's "personal bias," but ascribed it to the author's friendship with Hitler, as if this made it acceptable. Fitz-Gerald's thirty-year career in journalism may have played a role in alleviating doubts as to the slant or veracity of his story. As noted above, his political reporting was often admired for its insights. Nonetheless, his reputation was not without its holes. According to Garret FitzGerald, his uncle "edited the magazine *Wide World,* which was supposed to publish only true stories of travel but which strained its readers' credulity with a story of an intrepid explorer crossing the Pacific on the back of a dolphin, as a result of which *Punch* published a cartoon showing my uncle, shipwrecked on a raft, spying a vessel in the distance and crying 'A sale! a sale!'"[65]

In certain cases, the politics of the editor publishing Fitz-Gerald's story may have come into play. Under the guidance of the archly conservative Lady Houston, for example, *Saturday Review* became a voice for the extreme right and lent its support to fascism. The accuracy of Fitz-Gerald's pro-Hitler story was unlikely to be questioned by a journal that proclaimed the need for a dictator in England.[66] But not all the editors who published Fitz-Gerald's work shared his politics. Perhaps most importantly, Fitz-Gerald had a highly marketable commodity—an insider's peek at the home life of the dictator casting the "black shadow of fear" over Europe, a man who both alarmed and fascinated people outside Germany. If editors had their doubts, they were willing to put them aside to publish Fitz-Gerald's "scoop."[67]

Alternately, we may ask why English-speaking readers would have been interested in Fitz-Gerald's stories about the "Squire of Wachenfeld." Many, no doubt, were anxious for the comfort that Fitz-Gerald offered: the hope that the seemingly peaceful Hitler on the mountain would be able to control the warmongering Führer in the Reich Chancellery. This hope was shared by people both within and beyond Germany's borders. Not a few foreign readers, moreover, were sympathetic to Hitler and must have been content to have their positive views reinforced by Fitz-Gerald's portrait. Indeed, 1936, when the majority of Fitz-Gerald's accounts were published, marked the high point of Hitler's popularity in Britain.[68] On the whole, however, very significant differences—cultural, political, and historical—existed between audiences in Germany and elsewhere. National Socialist propagandists drew on existing national myths or created new ones in order to foster powerful associations between Hitler and the mountains for German audiences. But the legend of the sleeping King Barbarossa or the unity of Führer and Volk, among others, held little appeal for a broader global audience. Why, then, would our reader in Leeds, Boston, Winnipeg, or Sydney have been interested in hearing about Fitz-Gerald's holiday with Hitler?

Fitz-Gerald owed his success in selling the story in part to the growth of celebrity culture in the 1920s and 1930s. The advent of new technologies in broadcasting, recording, and film brought entertainers and politicians into the everyday lives of people. Celebrities were both larger-than-life and a part of the family, creating a voracious market for information on the lives of these intimate strangers.[69] In the mid-1930s, Hitler may have been the dictator casting the "black shadow of fear" over Europe, but he was also a celebrity. His image-makers, including Leni Riefenstahl, adeptly used the machinery of celebrity culture to increase the popularity and exposure of their "star."

English-speaking audiences were keenly interested in Hitler's private life. When Angela Raubal, Hitler's sister, remarried in February 1936, it made the front page of the *Daily Express*. The gossipy story, which covered details of the wedding and honeymoon, noted that "Herr Hitler has lost the sister . . . who for years has mothered him, 'bossed' him, cooked his meals, and darned his socks at Haus Wachenfeld, his Alpine retreat. He has lost her to tall, dark, handsome Professor [Martin] Hammitzsch of Dresden. . . . Haus Wachenfeld . . . is today very empty. Blonda, the dictator's faithful favorite will be there to greet him. Blonda is an Alsatian sheep-dog."[70] Other stories sought to associate the bachelor with glamorous women, even if they were other men's wives. Milton Bronner, for example, London correspondent for the Newspaper Enterprise Association, wrote an admiring article on the close and trusting relationship between the "good-looking Frau Goebbels" and the "confirmed bachelor" Hitler.[71]

Curiosity about celebrities' homes dominated the public's desire to see beyond the mask of fame to the "real" person within. Since the nineteenth century, American and European middle-class cultures had come to focus on the domestic milieu as the site of the authentic self.[72] Hollywood fan magazines and newspaper gossip columns gushed about what the famous did at home—"what they ate, what their beauty secrets were, what pets they pampered, what cars they drove, what they wore."[73] Articles on movie stars' houses typically blended details about the architecture and interior decoration with details about the occupant's personality, thrilling readers who believed they were getting to know the actor on more intimate terms.[74] Beyond fan magazines and gossip columns, the mainstream media also embraced the popularity of celebrity homes. In the 1930s, for example, *Architectural Digest* began to run a regular feature on the homes of Hollywood movie stars and directors.

The publication of photographs of celebrities' homes responded to and stimulated the desire to visualize their private lives. In Germany, such images had become an integral part of the political effort to broaden Hitler's appeal starting in 1932. By 1935, the English-language press had also begun to offer "candid" and sympathetic images of Hitler's home life to its audience. In March 1935, *Newsweek* claimed to have "secured first publication rights in America for these exclusive candid camera shots of Adolf Hitler. They constitute the only informal record of the Reich Leader in private life."[75] In the two-page feature, Hitler was shown at Haus Wachenfeld, hiking in the snow, playing with his dog Muck, reading in the solarium, and sharing "a bowl of stew with neighbors," among other "candid" shots. Most of the images, created by Hoffmann, also appeared in *Hitler in His Mountains,* published that same year for German audiences. By 1936, in part due to the self-promoting efforts of Fitz-Gerald, a broad spectrum of English-language

MAKING OF A MYTH

publications had familiarized their readers with Hitler's home life through such ostensibly informal, behind-the-scenes images.

The growing interest in visualizing the domestic spaces of the rich and famous also had a physical dimension. Specifically, the 1920s and 1930s witnessed a dramatic rise in the popularity of house museums, where one could experience firsthand the homes of history's "great men."[76] In a 1932 essay, Virginia Woolf noted that "London, happily, is becoming full of great men's houses, bought for the nation and preserved entire with the chairs they sat on and the cups they drank from, their umbrellas and their chests of drawers." The owners of these houses, she continued, may have had little artistic taste when it came to decorating, "but they seem always to possess a much rarer and more interesting gift—a faculty for housing themselves appropriately, for making the table, the chair, the curtain, the carpet into their own image." Here, amid their possessions, Woolf contended, one could get to know the great men of history far better than from any biography.[77]

In August 1936, the American edition of *Vogue* magazine took its readers, attuned to the worlds of fashion and style, on a virtual tour of the houses of three "makers of foreign policies": Adolf Hitler, Benito Mussolini, and British Foreign Secretary Anthony Eden (fig. 55). "All of these rooms are obviously characteristic of man and country—Anthony Eden's London house, British and reticent, impersonal as British diplomacy; Hitler's chalet, German, jumbled, and *gemütlich;* and Mussolini's villa, decoratively violent, magnificently proportioned, the home for a nation's impressive pride." Going beyond Woolf's belief that individuals mirrored themselves in their home environment, *Vogue* suggested that one could also read the psychology of nations in the domestic decor of its "great men."[78]

The article illustrated the interiors of the three men's houses with photographs and simple captions tying the occupant to a function appropriate to the room: "Where Hitler dines," "Where Mussolini plays his violin," "Where Eden sleeps," and so forth. Hitler's domestic space was represented by the dining nook in the ground-floor Stube at Haus Wachenfeld, pictured as it existed before the 1935–36 renovation. "On the side of a mountain, the chalet has a suburban neatness, with a sun porch and canaries, and its rooms, like this one, a cozy podge of clocks, dwarfs, and swastika cushions." True to the description, the accompanying photograph (by Hoffmann) reveals dwarf figures lurking in the corner, a grandfather clock, and a prominently placed swastika cushion. One wonders what Jewish

MUSSOLINI, HITLER, AND EDEN – IN RETREAT

When these makers of foreign policies go home, they go mildly to
these places. All of these rooms are obviously characteristic of
man and country—Anthony Eden's London house, British and
reticent, impersonal as British diplomacy; Hitler's chalet, German,
jumbled, and *gemütlich*; and Mussolini's villa, decoratively violent,
magnificently proportioned, the home for a nation's impressive pride.

Just below is a corner of Hitler's dining-room at Haus Wachenfeld, his hiding spot at little Berchtesgaden in southern Bavaria.

Where Hitler dines

Where Mussolini dines;

On the side of a mountain, the chalet has a suburban neatness, with a
sun porch and canaries, and its rooms, like this one, a cozy podge
of clocks, dwarfs, and swastika cushions. Nothing at Wachenfeld
suggests the "agitated simplicity" of his Berlin home, the constant
exercise of his power as governmental art dictator. (He is the author
of the classic comment: "There exists no art except Nordic-Grecian.")

Quite different are the flamboyant rooms of Mussolini at his
Villa Torlonia. There, for instance, he has this enormous oval dining-
room, of such elaborate proportions that it holds, like a drop in the
bucket, this scanty dining-table. (He never entertains there.) In the
niches stand his famous collection of Roman statues. Perhaps because
of his rumoured claustrophobia, Mussolini prefers his bedroom on a
grand terminal scale, all curves and the splendour of gold.

Unlike the imperial floridity of Mussolini's rooms are those of
Eden. With a hotel's bleakness and a shorn good taste, they show
none of the charming unorthodoxies of Britain's Foreign Secretary.
(He reads Persian, refuses to shoot stags, and is a pacifist.) They reveal with their bright chintzes, their careful translations of the eighteenth century, only an oddly expressionless, but aristocratic good taste.

Fig. 55. *Vogue* (U.S.) magazine's August 15, 1936, feature on the homes of Hitler,
Mussolini, and Eden.

VERA AND HUMPHREY JOEL

Where Eden sleeps

Where Mussolini sleeps

Home, sweet home—the exceedingly reticent refuges of three men involved in Europe's public policies

Where Mussolini plays his violin

Where Eden entertains

readers might have thought of Vogue's insistence that this interior, with its swastika-accented decor, "is obviously characteristic of man and country," thus rendering as alien and "uncharacteristic" Germans who stood outside this racially coded definition of home.[79]

In contrast to the "gemütlichkeit" of the German leader's home, Mussolini's "flamboyant rooms" in the Villa Torlonia embodied for Vogue an "imperial floridity." The magazine illustrated Mussolini's "enormous oval dining room," with its "famous collection of Roman statues," and his bedroom, executed "on a grand terminal scale, all curves and the splendour of gold." Eden's rooms, possessing "a hotel's bleakness and a shorn good taste," provided yet a third way in domesticity, different from the coziness of Hitler and the augustness of Mussolini. According to Vogue, they "reveal with their bright chintzes, their careful translations of the eighteenth century, only an oddly expressionless, but aristocratic good taste." Accompanying photographs depicted Eden's parlor and bedroom. Taken as a whole, the illustrations for the article seem to have been chosen with an eye to reinforcing stereotypes about national character. Thus, Hitler's bedroom, characterized by a simplicity that would have been difficult to present as "jumbled" or "gemütlich," was not illustrated alongside those of Mussolini and Eden (although it is also possible that the magazine failed to obtain an image).[80]

Vogue thus justified the voyeuristic pleasures of peering into the hidden lives of these famous men with its stylistic analysis of the national character of these "makers of foreign policies." Compared to Fitz-Gerald's wildly romantic and barely disguised pieces of propaganda, Vogue's treatment of politicians' domestic spaces seems relatively innocuous. But even here, the magazine trod a dangerous line. In August 1936, when Vogue published the article, the Olympic Games took place in Berlin, despite the threat of an international boycott. The Nazi regime, sensitive to its international image and eager to secure the foreign currency of tourists, countered allegations of racial discrimination by allowing one Jewish athlete to participate on the German team and by temporarily removing anti-Semitic materials from the capital's streets and public spaces.[81] Vogue's article, with its comparative approach, aided in this normalizing effort by placing two fascist dictators and an elected member of Parliament on the same footing, blurring the political differences among them and shifting the reader's attention instead to issues of interior design. Here differences among rival nations in Europe were grounded in national stylistic temperaments, rather than in the more immediately relevant conflicts over political ideology. Furthermore, the focus on comfort and beauty distracted from the extreme brutality of Mussolini's and Hitler's regimes. At the end of the war, when *Vogue* would carry Lee Miller's photographs of the concentration camps, the magazine was prepared to expose its readers fully to the consequences of those ideologies. But in 1936, for *Vogue,* swastikas remained pillow decorations.

From 1935 to 1941, the *New York Times Magazine* grappled repeatedly with how to present Hitler's domesticity. Time and again, it returned to the subject of his mountain home, publishing four articles that probed his domestic life and spaces through the eyes of different reporters. It began in October 1935 with a short but admiring article, "Hitler His Own Architect: He Practices His Art on a Simple Chalet." Noting that Hitler had once wanted to be an architect, the article credited him with the renovations to the house (still minor at that point), which it lauded for its modesty and tastefulness: "Haus Wachenfeld . . . differs in no way from thousands of other Bavarian chalets except for the enlargements and the fact that it is furnished more simply and in rather better taste than the average home of the Bavarian peasant." Readers learned of the green color scheme chosen for the interior and the "tasteful" furnishings as well as the exotic gifts given to him by admirers. "In Hitler's bedroom there is a portrait of his mother, who died when he was 18, along with a jeweled hunting horn presented to him by some unknown follower and a magnificent rug of silver fox skins sent him by some friend in the Argentine." The article also commented evocatively on the beauty of the natural surroundings and explained the history of the Nazis' relationship to the mountain. Thus, in its first detailed report on Hitler's home, the *New York Times* left its readers with an unequivocally positive and even poetic impression.[82]

On May 30, 1937, the cover of the *New York Times Magazine* featured a large and stunning photograph of the town of Berchtesgaden above the words: "Where Hitler Dreams and Plans" (fig. 56). Otto Tolischus, the newspaper's Berlin correspondent, contributed the three-page illustrated feature. His report began with a clear-eyed assessment of the significance of Hitler's mountain residence:

> Germany is administered from Berlin, capital of the Third Reich. It
> is inspired and spurred onward from Munich, capital of the National
> Socialist movement. But it is ruled from a mountain top—the mountain
> on which Fuehrer and Reich Chancellor Adolf Hitler has built himself
> a lofty country residence where he spends the larger part of his time and

The New York Times
Magazine

MAY 30
1 9 3 7

Section
8

Copyright, 1937, by The New York Times Company

WHERE HITLER DREAMS AND PLANS

At the Berghof on a Bavarian Peak He Lives Simply, Yet His Retreat Is Closely Guarded

"Here, amid gorgeous mountain scenery, not in set conferences but in informal walks and talks, Hitler mulls over new ideas for the application of his ideology."

The photograph at top shows Berchtesgaden. Times Wide World and Neswith.

By OTTO D. TOLISCHUS

BERLIN.

GERMANY is administered from Berlin, capital of the Third Reich. It is inspired and spurred onward from Munich, capital of the National Socialist movement. But it is ruled from a mountain top—the mountain on which Fuehrer and Reich Chancellor Adolf Hitler has built himself a lofty country residence where he spends the larger part of his time and to which he always retires to ponder events and to make those fateful decisions that so often startle the world.

Der Berghof, as this residence is now called, is rapidly becoming a place of German destiny. Here, more than 3,000 feet above sea level and 1,400 feet above Berchtesgaden, in the southeasternmost tip of Bavaria and only two miles away from his native Austria, Hitler takes refuge from the clamor of Berlin that irritates him and from the daily grist of routine paper work that stifles him. Here, amid the most gorgeous mountain scenery to be found in Germany, not in set conferences, but in informal walks and talks with his closest collaborators and with chosen representatives from all walks of

German life, he mulls over new ideas for the practical application of his National Socialist ideology that later find expression in pontifical speeches and pronouncements at National Socialist festivals or party gatherings.

And here, in the solemn solitude of a higher region, where frozen mountain peaks symbolize the eternal pattern of this world that yet changes in appearance with the constant change of atmospheric moods, and where the little things of everyday life below seem to drop away to let the essentials come out in all the clearer relief, the man who has assumed sole responsibility for a nation of 67,000,000 finds the strength to continue on his self-imposed mission.

However, the presence of the head of a mighty nation is already transforming the rustic and unsophisticated simplicity of the place and is giving it—more sensed than seen—a formidable and a martial air.

BERCHTESGADEN — which means mansion of the Goddess Berchta—was once a little-known spa of less than 4,000 inhabitants. Because of its beauty it was always patronized by the Bavarian royal family and Hitler likewise selected it as a place of recreation while still a struggling party leader. With a company of friends to which belonged his early mentor, the poet, Dietrich Eckart; his erstwhile foreign press chief, Dr. Ernst Hanfstaengl, and Max Amann, his publisher and now head of the Reich Press Chamber, Hitler used to spend many pleasant

hours in Berchtesgaden, especially in the Platterhof Inn which has now been absorbed as part of the Berghof estate; and the time had by all was so pleasant that some of his more puritanical followers protested. But here also he wrote the second and more substantial part of his book, "Mein Kampf," following his release from imprisonment after the Munich putsch.

Now Berchtesgaden is rapidly turning into a miniature national capital. A speedy motor road has been built to it from Munich and a private airport is being constructed on the Rossfeld, near Hitler's residence. A special building has been erected to house a branch of the Reich Chancellery, because, as State Secretary Dr. Hans Heinrich Lammers explained at its dedication early this year, "the Fuehrer is always on duty, even when on vacation." New homes are being built for the staff of officials and new barracks have gone up for the guarding garrison. This garrison, incidentally, consists not of army troops but of Hitler's own body guard, recruited from the "SS," from which is also recruited the Gestapo, or secret State police. Despite efforts of the army generals to abolish the body guard as a semi-independent military unit, Hitler insists on keeping it.

IN the same way the Berghof has grown from a little mountain chalet into a stately manor house on a large estate. Originally it was little more than a mountain cottage, furnished in the rustic but

Fig. 56. May 30, 1937, cover of the *New York Times Magazine*.

to which he always retires to ponder events and to make those fateful decisions that so often startle the world.

Der Berghof, as this residence is now called, is rapidly becoming a place of German destiny.

Going on to describe the changes that had transformed Haus Wachenfeld into the Berghof, Tolischus suggested that this destiny might not be a happy one.[83]

Picturesque little Berchtesgaden, Tolischus informed the reader, "is rapidly turning into a miniature national capital." Improved transportation systems provided rapid access by automobile and air, and new buildings accommodated growing government functions, including a Berchtesgaden branch of the Reich Chancellery. Such a branch was needed, head of the Reich Chancellery Hans Lammers claimed at its dedication, because "the Fuehrer is always on duty, even when on vacation." Alongside the construction, the atmosphere was changing as well. "The presence of the head of a mighty nation," Tolischus noted, "is already transforming the rustic and unsophisticated simplicity of the place and is giving it—more sensed than seen—a formidable and a martial air."[84]

On the Obersalzberg, these changes were visible in the creation of new barracks for the SS men who guarded Hitler. They were also evident in the measures taken to protect Hitler's residence, which had transformed from rustic cottage into "an impregnable fort." Mystery surrounded the Berghof: "Nobody is authorized to talk about it; no publication about it is permitted except for a few official photographs and some lyric but vague explanations of them; even the workers who constructed it have been pledged to silence." Rumors circulated that the Berghof was now equipped with gas-proof bomb shelters and was "girded by anti-aircraft guns" that could bring down a "fleet of planes long before they had any chance of doing damage." Around the wooded estate, "little turrets which look quite romantic" were, in fact, guard posts, and the "entire mountain side, covering several square miles" had been enclosed with a high barbed-wire fence. The Nazi elite had homes within the protected perimeter, "but everything else, including a children's sanatorium and a score of peasant homes, has been removed from it." Berchtesgaden itself was "reported to have been cleansed of all 'unreliable' elements," and tourists were required to answer a battery of police questions. All of these precautions were "so elaborate . . . as to convince the native populace that Berchtesgaden is destined to become the real national capital in case of war."[85]

With surprising accuracy, given the shortage of information, Tolischus thus became one of the first reporters to alert English-language audiences to the transformations occurring in and around Berchtesgaden. He also described the expansion of Hitler's residence "from a little mountain chalet into a stately manner house." Tolischus did not particularly warm to the design, calling it "a modernistic mansion of indefinable architecture." But he displayed a chatty enthusiasm in describing the details, including the "thrill for the guest in the automatic self-connecting house telephone which has one button labeled 'Der Fuehrer.' The guest may luxuriate in the feeling that all one has to do in order to talk to his host is to press the button. But, of course, he doesn't."[86]

On the whole, Tolischus did not offer readers a comforting or traditional image of Hitler's domesticity—framed, as it was, in the context of modern transportation systems, military defenses, and communications technology—until, that is, he began to write about the host. The change in tone began with the following sentence, which came toward the end of the second page, after lengthy descriptions of the newly militarized Obersalzberg region: "With safety and privacy thus assured, Hitler is able to relax, and to his visitors he shows himself here from his most charming side." In exploring this side of Hitler, revealed only at home, the article took a turn and drew closer to the narrative and tone familiar from Fitz-Gerald's stories. Like other writers, and despite the evidence he offered to the contrary in his description of developments in Berchtesgaden, Tolischus maintained that, as much as possible, Hitler liked to minimize "the work and cares of office" at home. Accordingly, readers learned about his mostly nonpolitical daily routine, the "Bohemian" nature of which was more accurately portrayed than it had been by Fitz-Gerald. A leisurely breakfast of "milk, bread, oatmeal, honey and cheese" was followed by a walk in the mountains. Only then did the official workday begin, which ended again by lunch. Like Fitz-Gerald, Tolischus paid attention to the Führer's vegetarian habits; he also introduced readers to his sweet tooth, particularly his love of chocolate. After lunch, he told readers, Hitler retreated to a "special studio built at the Berghof," where he indulged in "his favorite hobby—architecture." Evenings were spent "around the fireplace in the big hall in the company of his guests" and might include a musical performance or, more often, an informal discussion about current events. The latter helped Hitler to gauge the public mood in making his decisions.[87]

In exploring the Führer's "charming" domestic side, Tolischus was keenly interested in how it affected those who encountered him at the Berghof. "Even those who come with a certain reserve," he noted, "are captivated by the Fuehrer's complete naturalness in these surroundings." Tolischus quoted at length from the published testimonial of a Czech critic who had had a change of heart after meeting his down-to-earth and "comradely" host: "He sat among us. It seemed to me as if I had spent at least two years with him in the trenches. He repudiated the word 'dictator' for himself." While Tolischus admitted that most visitors to the Berghof did not experience such a dramatic turnabout, he insisted that encountering Hitler at home rather than at the Reich Chancellery in Berlin left a very different impression.[88]

Returning to the dreams referred to in the title, Tolischus ended the article with the following anecdote:

> While Hitler and [Max] Amann [his publisher] were climbing about in these mountains early in their careers, before they always knew where their next meal was coming from, the latter jestingly remarked: "When we get rich, we'll build our homes here."
> Hitler is said to have replied: "I shall never get rich, but some day, perhaps, my people will build a house here for me."
> That dream, like so many others that Hitler dreamed, has come true to a degree surpassing dreams.[89]

On this narrative tour of the Berghof, then, the reader is led away from a disquieting fortress being prepared for war to a gentler place of gifts and dreams. The shift in how we view Hitler at home enacts the very process of seduction Tolischus described, resulting in a mixed and confusing message. Tolischus offers two polar views of Hitler's domesticity: from outside, we see the fortress, with its repressed freedoms and military secrets; from within, we see the home, with its "comradely" warmth and fireside chats. Are we supposed to fear the fortress or hope for an invitation to the home? Tolischus leaves unreconciled the dissonance between the inner and outer worlds of the Berghof, which ultimately reflects the confusions engendered by Hitler's inhumane politics in the public realm and the sympathetic image he could project at home.

Mixed as it may have been in its messages, Tolischus's article nonetheless had begun to steer the *New York Times*'s coverage of Hitler's domestic spaces away from the uncritical stance it had initially adopted in 1935. It comes as a surprise, then, to witness a complete reversal in the third article on Hitler's home to appear in the *New York Times Magazine*. "Herr Hitler at Home in the Clouds" appeared on August 20, 1939, and was authored by Hedwig Mauer Simpson, reporting from Munich.[90]

The article began with a brief history of Hitler's mountain house, acknowledging that its transformation from Haus Wachenfeld to the Berghof reflected the Führer's "consolidated" powers and an accommodation of governmental and diplomatic functions, making the residence "less private" in nature. "Yet this does not mean that Hitler has given up the privilege of retiring when he likes," Simpson contended. And as if following the Führer's lead, Simpson then shifted her attention away from the outside world to the spaces and routine of "ordinary life" at the Berghof.[91]

The author admired the interiors of the house, which had been "furnished harmoniously, according to the best of German traditions" and boasted "beautiful common rooms," including "a sitting room facing west and overlooking the deep bowl amid Alpine heights in which the quaint old market town of Berchtesgaden is situated." In this setting, the Führer's daily routine played itself out, a narrative by now familiar to readers of the Sunday magazine—the late breakfast, walks in the mountain, and vegetarian meals. What Simpson's account lacked in originality, she made up for in the details, such as the quality of the tomatoes on Hitler's table or his love of not only chocolate, but also gooseberry pie. Similarly, she offered a glimpse into some of his official work duties—attending to private petitions from the "widows and orphans of party martyrs." Such business took "about two or three hours" in the morning, after which Hitler received callers. Then host and guests gathered for a "leisurely" lunch, and after taking a nap, Hitler might invite guests to go for a walk to the nearby teahouse. In the afternoon, the gates of the house might be opened up to the pilgrims who came to see their leader. Simpson described a typical scene at these encounters between Führer and Volk: "a particularly pretty child with a mop of fair curls attracts his attention, and then Heinrich Hoffmann takes those photographs of the Fuehrer bending over a little child which touch Nazi hearts."[92] (In fact, the "walk by" had been discontinued years before.)

An elegant dinner, with the ladies in evening dress and Hitler in a "dark lounge suit," was followed by coffee "in front of a blazing log fire." Hitler's guests came "from all kinds of German circles, as well as from foreign countries." As coffee was passed around, Hitler used this time to collect impressions. "Hitler can be a good listener and seems to gather a good deal by letting American solo dancers or German film stars talk to him. Non-political-minded persons will often tell him inadvertently, or by implication, things which his trained staff usually keep from him." And on this image of Hitler by the fireside, conversing with dancers and movie stars, Simpson concluded her article.[93]

This idyll about Berghof life was far removed, to put it mildly, from the world captured on the front page of the *New York Times* on August 20, 1939, the day Simpson's article appeared in the Sunday magazine. A third of the stories described the growing unrest in Europe. About one hundred thousand German troops had massed on the Polish border as the Slovak army, which had pledged its cooperation to Hitler, began its own mobilization. "Squads of police" had been sent to Bratislava's Jewish ghetto to protect the inhabitants from repeated beatings and vandalism by the German minority. A front-page editorial in the Bratislava German-language newspaper *Grenzbote* (Frontier Courier) called for "the Jews [to] be quickly and thoroughly punished this time for their evil provocations." Pope Pius XII, speaking to pilgrims in Italy, made a "fervent plea for peace" and expressed hope that Europe's statesmen would succeed in avoiding war. Lord Halifax, then the British foreign secretary, cut short his vacation and returned to work at the Foreign Office in London, increasing apprehension among the British people. Switzerland began to strengthen the garrisons along its German and Italian borders.[94]

It is difficult to imagine what readers thought as they paged through the newspaper and arrived at Simpson's article in the magazine. Nothing in her happy and harmonious fable reflected the realities of the front page. The article was accompanied by recycled photographs of the Berghof and Hitler hiking as well as by an editorial cartoon drawn by the London-based artist David Low. The latter depicted Hitler, looking pensive, seated at a table at the Berghof between the lovely female figure of Peace and an ominous, shroud-covered figure of War. While the cartoon, probably added by an editor, made sense in relation to the front page, it bore no relationship to Simpson's story.

Without knowing anything about Simpson's identity, we can only guess at her intentions in writing a highly misleading account of Hitler and "ordinary life" on the Obersalzberg. This article appears to have been her only contribution under that name to the *New York Times* or any other publication. But it is not only the writer's identity or intentions that raise questions. One also has to wonder about the *New York Times*'s decision to publish at this highly fraught moment what amounted to an ode to life at the Berghof. Portraying Hitler as a lover of orphans and gooseberry pie made it perhaps just a little easier to hope that the stories on the front page were exaggerated. Twelve days later, when German forces invaded Poland, *New York Times* readers, along with the rest of the world, discovered that they were not.

9 WAR AND THE ENGLISH-LANGUAGE MEDIA'S REAPPRAISAL OF THE DOMESTIC HITLER

At the end of October 1939, as the American people nervously followed the German defeat of Poland and the spread of conflicts in Europe, readers of *Life* magazine opened their weekly issue to discover a lush color feature on Adolf Hitler's paintings and mountain home (fig. 57). The October 30 issue offered the usual *Life* mixture of political reporting and more lighthearted human-interest stories, spanning the U-boat sinking of the British battleship *Royal Oak* to the athletic feats of glamorous Texan cowgirls. The article entitled "Paintings by Adolf Hitler: The Statesman Longs to Be an Artist and Helps Design His Mountain Home" sat awkwardly between these two journalistic approaches. Although Hitler continued to have his champions in the United States, a sympathetic portrait of the dictator who, a few weeks earlier, had threatened Europe with a devastating secret weapon would not have been well received by the majority of the magazine's readers.[1] The editors handled the tricky situation of writing about a warmonger's love of art and interior decoration with a new weapon of their own: sarcasm.[2]

The article began with a remark made by Hitler to British Ambassador to Germany Sir Nevile Henderson about his desire to one day give up politics and return to his youthful pursuit of art. If he were to do so, *Life*'s

PAINTINGS BY ADOLF HITLER

The artist who turned statesman wants to pick up his brush again

The last important conqueror in Europe to be greatly interested in art was Napoleon. His interest was largely acquisitive. It consisted of swiping Italy's art treasures and putting them in the Louvre. Adolf Hitler has a deeper personal interest in art. He himself was a painter whose struggles with art brought him no success and little satisfaction. But Hitler has never stopped wanting to be a painter. In his famous pre-War conversations with Sir Nevile Henderson, published in the Blue Book, he told the British Ambassador: "I am an artist and not a politician. Once the Polish question is settled, I want to end my life as an artist."

If Hitler were really to give up public life for art, which Sir Nevile Henderson doubts, the world would lose a very shrewd politician and gain a very poor painter. Hitler's ambition to be an artist was never dimmed by his lack of talent. When he was a jobless youth in Vienna, he was denied admission to the Vienna Art Institute because his work "showed more talent for architecture than for painting." Later the young Austrian, who tinted postcards and painted houses for a living, used to hang wistfully around the artists' cafes in Munich, trying to get established artists to look at the paintings he carried in his portfolio. If the artists had encouraged him instead of ignoring him, Adolf Hitler might never have become the bitter frustrated leader of a bitter frustrated nation.

Hitler probably completed hundreds of paintings. Most of them have by now been gathered in, supposedly by the Führer. The ones on the following pages, smuggled out of Germany and here published

for the first time, are reputed to be his very early work. They are the crude daubs any amateur produces when he first puts brush to canvas. These paintings show Hitler's preoccupation with architecture and with empty, desolate places. Hitler rarely put people in his paintings, perhaps because he found them too difficult to do. As he practiced Hitler grew in skill, and his later work, like the farmhouse sketched at left, reveals a fair amount of adroitness. Through much of the War, Hitler carried his painter's kit, did water colors of War-ruined buildings.

Today Hitler's artistic impulse has a grandiose outlet. As the defender of German art, he has purged it of modernism, handed it over to the academics. On the walls of his "Berghof" near Berchtesgaden, he hangs classic paintings, some taken from German museums. He owns a large collection of works of Vienna artists, is supposed to have bought the famous Vermeer self-portrait for $200,000. Every spring, he personally opens and approves the most important art exhibit in Germany, "The Day of German Art."

But most of Hitler's artistic urge is released through architecture. At night when the rest of his work is done, Hitler sits in one of his rooms at the Berghof (below) and works furiously over architects' designs. Plans for all important German public buildings and monuments must be personally approved by Hitler, whose suggestions are religiously followed. As a result, most German public buildings are being frozen into the decent but uninspired modernized-classic architecture that Hitler insists on.

Fig. 57. Title page of *Life* magazine's October 30, 1939, feature on Hitler as an artist and designer. The magazine's content page bears a somewhat different article title: "Paintings by Adolf Hitler: The Statesman Longs to Be an Artist and Helps Design His Mountain Home."

editors suggested, "the world would lose a very shrewd politician and gain a very poor painter." Despite Hitler's rejection from art school, his "ambition to be an artist was never dimmed by his lack of talent." The young Austrian "tinted postcards and painted houses for a living," haunting Munich's cafés in the hope of being noticed by established artists. Demonstrating why they ignored him, the article turned to examples of Hitler's early paintings, reproduced on two full color pages, that it claimed had been smuggled out of Germany and were being published for the first time. The strengths and faults—mostly faults—of Hitler's work were assessed for readers, such as the crudeness of the technique and the obsession with "empty, desolate spaces." A painting entitled *Battleship Wien,* an Austrian ship torpedoed in 1917, prompted the criticism that Hitler had hidden the "stern of [the] ship in [a] smudge of smoke" because he was "too tired or lazy to finish details."[3]

Having largely dismissed the German leader's own artistic skills, the article then addressed his impact on the nation's artistic production. "As the defender of German art," it stated, "he has purged it of modernism, handed it over to the academics." The article featured two photographs of Hitler in the company of Gerdy Troost (who was not identified) and high-ranking Nazi officials visiting the Great German Art Exhibition earlier that month. The article also noted that the Nazis enjoyed nudes that were "literal and very explicit," a claim accompanied by a photograph of Adolf Ziegler's *The Four Elements,* which had become infamous when first displayed at the Great German Art Exhibition of 1937 for its attention to Aryan pubic hair.[4] The article thus undercut the Nazis' claim to protect the purity of German art with a reference to the salaciousness of its defenders.

When the article turned to Hitler's involvement with architecture, both as patron and creator, the biting tone of the article began to subside. Hitler's artistic impulses, it stated, were now mostly channeled into architecture, and he stayed up nights in his mountain home "furiously" poring over architects' designs. He personally approved all important public buildings, which "are being frozen into the decent but uninspired modernized-classic architecture that Hitler insists on."[5]

Less ambivalent words of praise were reserved for the Berghof, "a huge mountain mansion" designed, readers were told, with Hitler's help.[6] Two full pages of color photographs, the first color images of the interior most Americans had ever seen, revealed the rooms with prismatic intensity. Burgundy and jade green hues predominated, with the eye being drawn to the richness of the red marble banister in the entrance hall or the warmth of the polished wood in Hitler's study. To contemporary readers, who had heard much about Hitler's simple and "soldierly" tastes, the vividness and complexity of the color scheme must have come as a surprise.[7]

Beginning with the architecture itself, the article described the "combination of modern and Bavarian chalet" styles as "awkward but interesting." The interiors, "designed and decorated with Hitler's active collaboration, are the comfortable kind of rooms a man likes, furnished in simple, semi-modern, sometimes dramatic style. The furnishings are in very good taste, fashioned of rich materials and fine woods by the best craftsmen in the Reich." The ingenuity of repeating the colors of the Gobelin tapestry hanging in the Great Hall in the room's furnishings was also carefully noted. The main stairway leading up from the ground floor was particularly commended for being "a striking bit of modern architecture." This admiring assessment of design ability was balanced by a jibe at the type of paintings hung on the walls: "Like other Nazi leaders, Hitler likes pictures of nudes and ruins." Nonetheless, the article concluded that the success of the design indicated that "in a more settled Germany, Adolf Hitler might have done quite well as an interior decorator."[8] With their backhanded compliment, the editors thus insinuated that the man reordering the map of Europe had missed his true calling of rearranging furniture.

Not all of *Life*'s readers were amused. In the November 20 issue, a number of letters to the editors defended Hitler's artistic tastes. A group of readers in Canton, Ohio, took the magazine to task for its snobbishness: "Let's not confuse personal opinion with art criticism!" Referring to the comment that Hitler had been "too tired or lazy" to finish the stern of the *Battleship Wien,* they countered that the rest of the painting was done well enough and that the "smudge of smoke" critiqued by the article "shows a fair amount of thought and work." A Mrs. Seefried, writing from Pontiac, Michigan, wrote: "Adolf certainly scores one up on the Roosevelt family when it comes to decorating a home. Maybe there are too many women in the Roosevelt household." Mrs. Seefried's suggestion that the White House had been spoiled by a domineering female presence (a comment directed at the president's outspoken wife, Eleanor, and his mother, Sara) would surely have pleased the bachelor Adolf. Finally, a reader in Chicago complained: "A preference for nudes plus ruins indicates a normal, male romanticism. . . . Architectural preferences, be they for the elaborate or the simple, indicate nothing beyond a normal inclination to create, cause, impress, possess."

In that reader's eyes, the magazine's efforts to psychoanalyze Hitler through his artistic or decorative tastes amounted to a blasé, "So what?"⁹

Other readers, however, took the magazine's analysis a step further. Examining Hitler's paintings closely, several readers observed that "all the lines in his pictures slant definitely to the right," thus implying a link between his ideology and his brushwork. A reader in Portland, Oregon, believed that on the basis of the Berghof, Freud might diagnose "not only claustrophobia but a Hitler aversion to any close physical contact with others, expressed even to the point of separating the chummiest grouping of chairs by an intervening table." Several other readers inadvertently revealed the anxieties taking root in the country when they believed that they recognized the Statue of Liberty in a tiny, blurry detail of the *Battleship Wien,* thus seeing in the painting, presumably completed decades earlier, an ominous portent of Hitler's plans to invade New York Harbor.¹⁰ Their fears were likely not quelled by the photograph of Hitler's study. In the caption, the editors brought the reader's attention to the world atlas placed prominently on his desk, with a magnifying lens lying on top for ready consultation.¹¹

By introducing critical and even sinister tones in its reporting on Hitler's domestic spaces, *Life* magazine began the shift away from the positive assessments that had appeared in the mainstream English-language press since the mid-1930s, and that had culminated in the fawning portrayals in *Homes and Gardens* and the *New York Times* just months earlier. While such admiring accounts had seen in Hitler's artistic endeavors the charm and abilities of the gentleman-amateur, those same activities now evoked the embarrassing foibles of an untalented and pompous dilettante—a person tinting postcards and house-painting while imagining himself a Vermeer. Yet the change in tone did not entirely displace feelings of appreciation, even if these were now expressed more grudgingly and with defensive wit. And since *Life's* readers were particularly attuned to its photographs, which were at the core of the magazine's journalism, the publication of such appealing color images of Hitler's home must also be seen as contributing to a favorable presentation. The text may have poked fun at the (absent) occupant, but the elegant interiors stood as a substitute for the man, proclaiming his taste and sophistication.

While *Life* gently mocked Hitler's artistic ambitions and taste, the *New York Times* adopted a more neutral tone. In mid-March 1941, it published a two-page illustrated feature in its Sunday magazine that attempted to give readers a behind-the-scenes account of Hitler's Berghof. Written by its correspondent C. Brooks Peters, the article "In Hitler's Chalet" promised to explain the workings of a new hybrid: a residence that also served as a workplace—and, in this case, a military center. Peters thus picked up on the lead developed by Otto Tolischus in 1937, but subsequently abandoned by the newspaper.[12] Whereas most earlier accounts represented the Berghof as a retreat for Hitler from the hustle and bustle of political life, Peters alerted *New York Times* readers to a quiet, but profound, change: "for, in a chalet on a mountain slope near this once slumbering Bavarian village, meetings both publicized and secret take place which may have the most profound importance for the future political alignment of Europe and the world."[13]

Peters seemed concerned that his contemporaries, used to democratic and open forms of political discourse, might miss the significance of what was happening at the secluded mountain chalet. "But the historian of the future, in chronicling the events of this time, will no doubt examine the comings and goings at Berchtesgaden, the Obersalzberg and the Berghof, the Fuehrer's private and personal domain, where, at a distance from the war fronts and the diplomatic bustle of the Reich's capital, he strolls with his three sheep dogs along majestic mountain trails or sits before an open fire with his closest advisers, discussing events far into the night."[14] Peters was thus one of the first to bring political activity squarely into the picture of the house itself, and not simply treat it as something that the Führer dealt with before lunch.

Yet having begun the article with this tantalizing thread—the double life of the Berghof, a place where dogs and generals were a routine part of daily life—Peters then dropped it for a more conventional narrative of the house. He began with a brief history of Haus Wachenfeld, drawing on the 1934 account of Otto Dietrich, Hitler's press secretary.[15] He then discussed the renovations, credited to Hitler's designs, and described the interiors of the expanded Berghof. From the spaces of the house, Peters shifted to writing about its occupants—although, interestingly, not about Hitler himself. Instead, we learned about the young male adjutants and young female secretaries whom Hitler liked to have around him. We were also introduced to Arthur Kannenberg, Hitler's majordomo and a bon vivant who ran the household and amused the Führer in the evenings with his accordion playing and singing. The article closed with a list of the Berghof's regular guests, including Heinrich Hoffmann, Hitler's court photographer; Albert Speer; and the Führer's doctors, Theodor Morell and Karl Brandt. The essay ended without conclusions, but the reader could draw his or her own about the lack of a "real" domestic life, with Hitler's house being filled with his pets, officers, and employees.[16]

Peters's account was not particularly vivid and divulged little that had not already been reported by others.[17] The flattering photographs of Hitler and his home, too, had been recycled. Already in 1937, Tolischus, writing in the *New York Times Magazine,* had exposed the secrecy surrounding the Berghof; in 1941, the situation could only have been worse. The blandness of Peters's reporting, however, suggests less a lack of information (which, after all, hardly impinged on the purple prose of William George Fitz-Gerald's earlier accounts) than a desire to avoid overtly praising or criticizing Hitler, and the house itself was described in pleasant but measured terms. Writing about the people around the Führer rather than about the owner of the house himself may have been another strategy to achieve a sense of neutrality—and to avoid the dangers of seduction evident in Tolischus's writing. The resulting tone is considerably more respectful than that of *Life* magazine, but also far less colorful (and, in 1941, less objectionable) than the glowing report published in the *New York Times Magazine* two years earlier by Hedwig Mauer Simpson.[18] Whether Peters was concerned about offending the newspaper's readers or the German leader is not clear. The article alluded to the Nazis' censorship of dispatches sent by foreign correspondents, who risked reprisals for offending the regime.[19] But Peters gave an inkling of his true feelings in the caption for a photograph of the Berghof nestled in the hillside: "Peaceful birthplace of Blitzkrieg."[20]

Both the mild sarcasm of *Life* magazine and the restrained neutrality of the *New York Times* reveal that the press knew it was dealing with a volatile subject when addressing Hitler's domesticity after the outbreak of war in 1939. The continuation of such stories in the American press, albeit far fewer than before, indicates that editors believed that glimpses into Hitler's home life still interested readers. But they were less sure of the responses that they would provoke—the range of which was readily apparent in the readers' letters published in *Life* magazine. In particular, the press was now wary, in a way that it had not been before, of humanizing the dictator or normalizing his war machine through sympathetic stories of his home life.

A third approach to the subject adopted a more open-ended method of writing that allowed the perceptive reader to construe an underlying criticism. In December 1940 and January 1941, the *Washington Post* published a four-part series presenting an "intimate, first-hand picture of the opposing war leaders," Winston Churchill and Adolf Hitler. The series described a day in the life of each leader, while also exploring little-known details about his personality and domestic habits. It began with two reports filed by Hugh Wagnon, London war correspondent for the Associated Press, on Churchill, who had been British prime minister for only seven months. The headline of the first story, "Churchill Devotes 17 Hours a Day to His Only Hobby—War," set the tone for the series. Wagnon described how the "vigorous 66-year-old Prime Minister" devoted his "prodigious energy" and long days solely to the war effort, keeping a close eye on all developments: "he likes to know everything that is going on." Although "a voracious reader in peacetime," he now limited himself to news and reports. He had "little time for ordinary family life, but he sees Mrs. Churchill every day and the rest of the family 'as much as possible.' There are frequent family dinners." His exercise consisted of "striding about Whitehall or walking tirelessly on tours of inspection of fighting commands, defense areas and bombed sectors." Even his cigar smoking had to be reduced due to work, although he still consumed "six long Havanas a day." In the evening, he enjoyed "the roast beef of Old England" or "a thick steak, rare."[21]

Having established the powerful physical masculinity of the British leader, the second article turned to his matching masculine mindset. Readers learned, for example, that Churchill had been attacked twice by "irate suffragettes armed with dogwhips" because of his fierce opposition to women's emancipation. While insisting on the traditional order of the sexes, he appeared appreciative of women who knew their place, claiming that his "most brilliant achievement" had been persuading his wife to marry him. Returning once more to the physical, the article informed readers that the prime minister enjoyed "big cigars which he holds fondly in full hand." With his "stout, thick-set figure," "heavy shoulders hunched," and "large head bent forward, he walks like a charging football player." Shifting metaphors, the article claimed that when Churchill "clamps his jaw in determination," he resembled the British bulldog. In London, the prime minister liked to dress "in rumpled formality, cocky bow tie askew." But he knew his way around clothes and had designed some of his own beloved hats. If this evoked any doubts about the grit of Churchill's masculinity, readers also learned that "in the country, where he now is seldom seen, he is likely to don overalls for a stint of bricklaying." His bulldog toughness was further emphasized by his humor, which was "of the political, crushing club variety." In a report to the House of Commons a few weeks earlier, he had quipped that "he didn't like to compare Adolf Hitler with Napoleon because 'I don't like to insult the dead.'"[22]

Preston Grover, Berlin war correspondent for the Associated Press, contributed the two articles on Hitler that followed. The headline of the first story declared, "Hitler Leads Life of Wakeful Spartan." The German leader's days were "a mass of hard work," although Hitler, an "unregimented Bavarian," disliked Prussian discipline. Amid the riches of the palatial New Reich Chancellery, Hitler lived in private quarters of "unadorned simplicity," sleeping four to six hours a night on an "army-styled bed." His mornings began with a quick read of the newspapers, "not overlooking the sports or theatrical columns." At his mountain retreat, by contrast, Hitler "lets himself go, if he is not pressed with emergencies, and sleeps himself out." While not a fussy eater, Hitler did not consume meat or alcohol. He liked small animals and hated to see them killed, putting a halt to vivisection when he came to power. Grover informed readers that Hitler, contrary to hearsay, was "an extremely good listener and possesses a phenomenal memory." At night, he studied texts and maps of battles reaching back a thousand years. He enjoyed opera and movies, but played no sports, and his exercise was limited to walking and burning up energy on the job. Grover reported that Hitler's associates insisted that he liked children, although he had never married. "Nevertheless, his poses with children as disclosed in 'publicity pictures' show him stiff, uncomfortable."[23]

The second article began with a truly eye-catching headline: "Warlord Hitler Designs Table Silver in Spare Time." It was hard to reconcile the image of "the man who is giving Europe a painful face-lifting operation," Preston admitted, with his time-consuming devotion to designing silverware. Indeed, even the dictator's intimates, whom Preston claimed as his source, were surprised that "Adolf Hitler, in leisure moments, will quietly sit down at a table and test the weight and balance of knives, forks and spoons he is planning to give away as wedding presents." Preston also credited him with designing the silverware for the Berghof and the New Reich Chancellery in Berlin. And yet despite Hitler's fastidious attention to the details of design, readers were told that he did not care much about minor daily matters and was irritated by the "Prussian punctuality" of his "underlings" at the Reich Chancellery.[24]

The article then described at some length Hitler's official and private residences, including his long-held apartment in Munich, as well as the luxurious accommodations set aside for him in hotels. Readers learned about the Munich locations of his *Stammtisch,* a reserved table for regulars. Hitler's "intimates" claimed that he was "a good mixer" and "tells a good story well." But while Hitler could be charming company, he often preferred that of his cronies. Hitler's associates also spoke of the "acts of kindness" and generosity that characterized his private life, "which so many find hard to associate with a man who is able to order destruction of an entire city in order to further military operations." Grover ended by referring to an early war speech by Hitler in which "he said it was his capacity to act over people like a huge magnet and draw from them their greatest efforts."[25]

At first glance, there is nothing overtly demeaning in this "intimate" account of Hitler—to the contrary, it seems remarkably generous, as if written to please Goebbels's censors. By the time of the series' publication, German forces had invaded half of Europe, bombed its cities, and left hundreds of thousands dead or displaced in their wake. To write of Hitler's "acts of kindness" or his entertainments, even if Grover was careful to attribute this information to his associates, must have struck some readers as taking journalistic objectivity a step too far.

Read against the stories about Churchill, however, and with an eye to the gendered nuances of the references, a subtext emerges. Whereas the reader was encouraged to imagine Churchill in his overalls laying bricks, perhaps while puffing on a Cuban cigar, Hitler was evoked in the splendor of the Reich Chancellery delicately testing the weight of a silver fork. This is not to say that the details were inaccurate, but rather to question what information was chosen for inclusion in the articles. Both Hitler and Churchill were amateur painters, for example, but the series avoided suggesting similarities between them. Instead, readers were given the contrasts of the raw steak eater and the vegetarian who cared about small animals; the cigar-loving smoker and the abstainer; the indefatigable Brit and the unregimented Bavarian; the dedicated family man and the awkward bachelor. Seemingly balanced in their reporting, a between-the-lines reading of the articles suggests how Hitler was positioned as somewhat odd and effeminate in relation to Churchill. The comparative approach of the series encouraged readers to evaluate the opposing leaders in this way, and to search for clues as to which one would prove to have the "right stuff" to emerge victorious. Would it be the bulldog or the Spartan?

If we are to judge from these newspaper stories, American audiences, divided in their desire to commit to another European war, were not yet entirely willing to divest themselves of the reassuring image of a German leader who appreciated domestic elegance, as if a taste for good design somehow militated against barbarity. And if such tastes were perceived as distracting Hitler from the war effort, so much the better. Among the British, by contrast, there was no need to write coyly or between the lines after 1939, even though the British press had been just as guilty of whitewashing Hitler through his domestic image before the war as their American counterparts. With German war planes dropping bombs on them, the British quickly lost interest in how Herr Hitler took his tea. Stories in the British press admiring Hitler's gentlemanly domestic tastes and pursuits evaporated with the start of hostilities. Yet the attention to Hitler and interior decoration did not disappear entirely. The Führer as the creator of elegant country estates now resurfaced in political cartoons as his poorer cousin, "Hitler the housepainter" and "Hitler the paperhanger."

On April 10, 1940, the satirical English magazine *Punch* published a cartoon by Ernest Howard Shepard with the caption, "The White Paper Hanger" (fig. 58).[26] It depicted Hitler wearing a smock and hanging white wallpaper inscribed with the words "American Plot" and "Poland" over a broken wall surface on which were scrawled the words "Gestapo barbarism," "German atrocities," "murders," and "Nazi brutalities." Bloodied handprints on the wall are also visible. Goebbels is shown assisting Hitler, applying the glue to the wallpaper. The cartoon referred to the publication of a number of White Books or White Papers published by the Germans after the invasion of Poland, which laid the blame for the war on Poland, France, and England. At the end of March 1940, the Nazis broadened their allegations of warmongering to include American ambassadors to Great Britain (Joseph P. Kennedy) and to France (William C. Bullitt)—the "American plot" to which the cartoon refers.[27] The British and American governments condemned these White Papers as Goebbels's handiwork and an attempt to conceal or paper over the crimes committed by the Nazis in Poland, a criticism cleverly translated into visual terms by the cartoonist through the image of "Hitler the paperhanger."

On August 6, 1941, George Butterworth, cartoonist for the *Daily Dispatch* in Manchester, England, published a drawing that depicted Hitler sitting in an Art Deco–style armchair critically assessing the "work" around him: on walls representing the nations that his regime had brutally subjected to Nazi rule, swastika-covered wallpaper had been applied hastily and violently with "new order paste" and "gestapo glue" (fig. 59).[28] The title,

©Punc

'The White Paper Hanger'

Fig. 58. Ernest Howard Shepard, "The White Paper Hanger," editorial cartoon, *Punch*, April 10, 1940, 391.

"Inferior Decoration," implied that the house that Hitler had built would not stand because, unlike an architect, who proceeds from the ground up, the paperhanger's work was applied and only surface-deep.

The earliest press descriptions of Hitler, dating back to his days as a beer hall agitator in Munich, described his former occupation variously as sign painter, mason, architectural draftsman, machinist, paperhanger, and housepainter—and sometimes a combination of these.[29] In his autobiographical *Mein Kampf,* published in 1925, Hitler kept things vague. Of his time as a young man and aspiring architect in Vienna, he wrote that he had supported himself as an unskilled worker on construction sites, an assertion

MEDIA'S REAPPRAISAL OF THE DOMESTIC HITLER

Fig. 59. George Butterworth, "Inferior Decoration," editorial cartoon, *Daily Dispatch*, August 6, 1941.

that historians have dismissed for lack of evidence.[30] Whether true of not, the image of Hitler as an honest laborer served the purposes of National Socialist propagandists who, wishing to depict him as a man of the people, further propagated the story.

In the early 1930s, as Hitler began his political ascent to the Chancellery, his opponents revived the image of the uppity tradesman to stir the social prejudices of Germany's intellectual and ruling classes. On April 8, 1932, the left-liberal *Wiener Sonn-und Montags-Zeitung* (Vienna Sunday and Monday Times) published a sensational exposé about Hitler's past that received international coverage, including on the front page of the *New*

York Times. The paper reported that "a correspondent sent to Braunau-on-the-Inn in Upper Austria, the birthplace of Adolf Hitler, had ascertained from parish registers that Herr Hitler's followers would be shouting 'Heil Schuecklgruber [*sic*]!' today had not his father, who was a customs official, changed his name to obtain an inheritance." The article also revealed that "Herr Hitler, after an undistinguished school career at Braunau, worked in Vienna as a paperhanger and painter, and that when he was called to the colors in February, 1914, he was rejected as 'too weak and unfit to bear arms.'"[31] The humiliating story appeared just two days before Hitler faced national presidential elections in Germany, in a bid to tarnish the Nazi Party's newly minted image of the "private" Hitler.

References to Hitler as a paperhanger or housepainter and other belittling monikers appeared less frequently in the foreign mainstream press as Hitler's stature as a statesman grew in the mid-1930s. Nonetheless, exiled German writers, such as Bertolt Brecht, and Hitler's foreign critics still resorted to such appellations.[32] In 1937, Cardinal Mundelein, Roman Catholic archbishop of Chicago, incensed the National Socialist regime and worsened Nazi-Vatican relations when in a speech to five hundred prelates and priests he denounced the "malicious" propaganda and actions undertaken by the Nazis against the Catholic Church in Germany, calling Hitler "an Austrian paperhanger, and a poor one at that."[33] While the National Socialist regime protested the "insult" to the Führer, the Brotherhood of Painters, Decorators, and Paperhangers of America protested the insult to their trade: "That egotistical, anti-labor dictator might have hung paper at one time, but that does not qualify him for the honorable title 'paperhanger.' . . . The only thing Hitler has hung in the past ten years is the liberty of the German people."[34]

Following the international controversy sparked by Mundelein's words, American cartoonists found a variety of ways to incorporate "Hitler the paperhanger" into their critiques of current events. In early March 1938, for example, as Austrian Chancellor Kurt von Schuschnigg desperately fought off Nazi encroachment, a cartoon published in the *Los Angeles Times* under the caption "The Paper Hanger Returns" depicted Hitler in overalls papering over a wall identified as Austria with swastikas.[35] When the number of German casualties soared after the June 1941 invasion of the Soviet Union, some America cartoonists imagined Hitler as a macabre paperhanger, adorning the walls of his empire with long casualty lists.[36] In February 1942, a widely circulated news story provided fresh inspiration to cartoonists.

Benny Nussbaum, an émigré and paperhanger in New York, claimed that he knew Hitler when he "was known as plain Schicklgruber, the paperhanger." Nussbaum commented, "He was not only a crack-pot . . . but he couldn't put paper up straight. His work was terrible. With one arm I could do a better job than that guy. No wonder he gave it up."[37] Later that year, New Yorkers expressed their feelings about Nussbaum's alleged former colleague by hanging a "Hitlerian grotesquerie in paperhanger's costume, with paste smeared on its face, bits of wallpaper stuck to the clothes and an American flag stuck in the right hand" from a lamppost in Yorkville, a Manhattan borough with a high number of German, Central European, and Jewish immigrants.[38]

Perhaps not coincidentally, Nussbaum spoke up when the military tide had begun to turn against Hitler. At the end of 1941, the German army's attacks on the Soviet Union began to fail because of harsh weather conditions, for which the Germans were not prepared; on December 11, Hitler further extended the conflict by declaring war on the United States. The image of the inept paperhanger suggested by Nussbaum was ripe for humoristic exploitation. In 1942, a spate of cartoons appeared in American newspapers depicting the harried Hitler running from one front to the other, attempting to hold up his paper empire as it unfurled and collapsed around him (fig. 60). Following the disastrous siege of Stalingrad, in 1943 a new crop of American cartoons imagined a desperate Führer trying to get his old paperhanging job back. In January 1944, with German forces in rapid retreat on the eastern front, the Allies sensed a demoralized enemy nation. William Shirer reported that the German people blamed Hitler for the catastrophe in the Soviet Union, and that signs of pessimism could be detected among the Nazis' highest echelons. Even Goebbels, according to Shirer, seemed to be "slipping."[39] A cartoon published a few weeks later depicted Goebbels, standing beneath a portrait of Hitler, whispering to Göring, "Confidentially, Hermann—I'm Beginning To Wonder If He's Even Any Good At Paperhanging."[40]

As the war front drew nearer to Germany, the Berghof itself began to appear in American and English editorial cartoons. When Hitler had first become chancellor, thousands of Germans had flocked to the Berghof in pilgrimage. With the intensity of Allied bombing increasing, people again began to stream to Berchtesgaden, but now as refugees from devastated German cities, prompting the Nazi regime to issue a decree prohibiting people from approaching the area.[41] Referring to the ban, an August 27,

"THE EVER-BUSY PAPER HANGER"

SECOND FRONT

HOME FRONT

RUSSIAN FRONT

May '42

Fig. 60. Vaughn Shoemaker, "The Ever-Busy Paper Hanger," editorial cartoon, *Chicago Daily News*, reprinted in the *New York Times*, May 10, 1942.

1943, cartoon by the London-based David Low depicted Hitler, with reports about the bombed cities at his feet, looking out worriedly at the faces of the dispossessed peering at him through the world's most famous window (fig. 61). A 1943 cartoon by Reg Manning in the *Arizona Republic* showed a sinister castle with the face of Hitler on a remote mountain peak surrounded by ghostly figures (fig. 62). The title put it simply: "The Most Haunted House."[42]

In its extreme and isolated location—in close proximity to the ghosts of Hitler's victims, but not to the German people—Manning's cartoon house visually captured the English-language press's new focus on estrangement in its coverage of Hitler's mountain residence. This shift in perspective in the final years of the war marked a sharp, if tardy, departure from the official German story about the Berghof. In part because Hitler spent so much

Fig. 61. David Low, "Faces at the Window. (It is strictly verboten for refugees from bombed areas to go near Berchtesgaden—German news.)," editorial cartoon, published August 27, 1943.

time on the Obersalzberg, National Socialist propagandists had worked hard to militate against possible associations of the mountains with isolation. Instead, in their hands and drawing on past Romantic traditions, the mountains became a symbol of the German nation and German consciousness. When Hitler "retreated" to the Alps, the propagandists maintained, he actually drew nearer to the *Volksgeist*, the spirit of the people. The idea of Hitler's immediacy while in the mountains was reinforced by the pilgrimage of admirers to the house, a phenomenon at first encouraged and exploited by the regime's propagandists as proof of Hitler's accessibility. Hitler's mountain retreat was thus constructed as the site of mediation between the German leader and his people, suggesting a more "authentic" form of communication between the two than offered by the democratic institutions of the previous Weimar Republic.

For much of the 1930s, the mainstream English-language press was complicit in perpetuating the myth of the Berghof as a place that united folk and Führer. When Fitz-Gerald mythologized Hitler as a country squire living among his tenants, he was rewriting the Nazi story in terms familiar to English audiences. After the war began, however, and especially in the last years of the conflict, narratives about the house flipped from emphasizing

The Most Haunted House By Reg Man: Arizona Republic Staff

Fig. 62. Reg Manning, "The Most Haunted House,"
editorial cartoon, *Arizona Republic*, 1943.

the proximity between the occupant and his fellow citizens to the distance
that separated them—in keeping with what German writers in exile had
been saying all along. In a 1942 *New York Times Magazine* assessment of
Hitler's personality and political fortunes, Walter Brown, a Washington
news correspondent, directed readers' attention to the "nouveau riche"
grandeur of Hitler's private lifestyle and his preference for dwelling in "surroundings of ostentatious, often almost morbid, splendor." He compared
Hitler's "lavish tastes in architecture and decoration" to Versailles—a pointed reference to a "decadent" and doomed regime. A drawing accompanying
the article depicted Hitler in front of the Berghof's great window gripping
a globe with bloody paws, while outside, a ragged crowd of his victims
approached.[43] Beyond the divide of riches, Hitler's mountain home was
increasingly described in terms that suggested the emotional and physical

removal of Hitler from the German people as well as his desire to hide, both from his countrymen and his Allied enemies. Words such as "hideaway," "fortress palace," "castle," and "mountain fastness" became common in descriptions of the home.[44] Once touted as the site of rapprochement, the Berghof was now reimagined as a place of alienation and reckoning.

More than the Berghof, however, it was the Kehlsteinhaus that, after the start of war, came to represent for foreign observers the architectural evidence of the dictator's folly. The pavilion, located a few miles from the Berghof on the neighboring Kehlstein peak, was commissioned by Martin Bormann and designed by Roderich Fick as a showpiece for the National Socialist Party and, reputedly, a fiftieth birthday present to the Führer. The costly interiors, decorated with stone and wood, consisted of a spacious octagonal reception hall with an Italian marble fireplace (said to be a birthday gift from Benito Mussolini), a dining room for thirty people, a smaller lounge with retractable panorama windows, a study for Hitler, and a kitchen and guard room. There was also an outdoor terrace for sunning and strolling. The construction, directed by some of Germany's and Austria's best engineers, took thousands of men laboring around the clock and in all weather conditions just over a year to complete. It also necessitated the building of a dangerous mountain road with multiple tunnels and the excavation of several hundred feet of solid rock for the creation of an elevator shaft that climbed directly to the building, which perched on an outcrop more than six thousand feet above sea level. The project, which vaunted the mastery of the National Socialist regime over nature at its most rugged, cost an immense fortune and ten workers their lives to complete. Hitler, as far as we know, used the pavilion only fourteen times and did not return after a final visit in 1940 with Crown Princess Marie José of Italy.[45] The extravagant architectural project, constructed at a time of material shortages and economic belt-tightening, was not publicized or widely known within Germany. By January 1939, however, articles about it began to appear in the non-German press based on the reports of a few foreigners who had been invited by Hitler to the Kehlsteinhaus in the fall of 1938.

The prewar reports in the English and American presses admired—indeed, appeared mesmerized by—the pavilion they dubbed "the Eagle's Nest." Ralph Barnes, writing for the *Washington Post* in January 1939, compared it to something out of German mythology or the Arabian nights. Hitler, Barnes wrote, "sits there for hours at a time, gazing over the magnificent vista of snow-swept summits or down into his Austrian valley."[46]

Without photographs to rely on, some of the details journalists provided were inaccurate—for example, the house was described as being constructed of steel and glass when, in fact, it was a more traditional brick structure faced with granite. And yet perhaps because no images were available, the awestruck descriptions of a crystalline retreat high above the clouds where the sun shone every day, huge bronze doors opened onto a cavern deep inside the mountain, and an elevator glided through rock evoked all the more vividly in the reader's imagination a sense of an impossible, magical place.[47]

After Germany invaded Poland, the fairly-tale qualities ascribed to the Kehlsteinhaus took a dark turn. In December 1939, the French government issued a Yellow Book, which contained diplomatic documents chronicling its relations with Germany in the period from the Munich Accord to the start of the war. Among them were reports filed by André François-Poncet during his time as the French ambassador to Germany, including a lengthy description of his visit to the Kehlsteinhaus on October 18, 1938, where Hitler had invited him to discuss the outcome of the Munich Accord before François-Poncet left for a new diplomatic post in Rome. In high literary style, François-Poncet analyzed the architectural project as part of the riddle that was Hitler:

> The visitor is not quite sure that he is not dreaming. He has to pinch himself to make sure that it is not a hallucination.
>
> Is it the Castle of Monsalvat, where the Knights of the Holy Grail lived; or a Mount Athos built for the meditations of a Cenobite or the Palace of Antinea rising in the heart of the Atlas? Is it the realization of these fantastic drawings with which Victor Hugo adorned the margins of the manuscript of Burgrave's "The Fantasy of a Millionaire," or merely the den where brigands take their rest and accumulate treasures? Is it the work of a normal spirit or that of a man tormented by the folly of grandeur, by a haunting desire for domination and solitude, or simply a prey to fear?[48]

An Associated Press article summarized François-Poncet's impressions in less eloquent but more succinct terms: the envoy's visit to Hitler's Eagle's Nest "definitely gave him the creeps."[49] If Hitler read François-Poncet's report, he perhaps regretted his earlier hospitality. But more likely he would have been pleased to see how his desires and actions continued to confuse his adversaries.

A few years later, foreign journalists no longer entertained doubts as to what the Kehlsteinhaus represented. In a 1942 article for the *New York*

MEDIA'S REAPPRAISAL OF THE DOMESTIC HITLER

Times, Frederick Oechsner labeled Hitler "the most dangerous and one of the shrewdest political gangsters in existence." Oechsner was in a position to know: the former chief of the United Press Berlin bureau, he had just returned to the United States after a six-month internment in Germany. In Oechsner's view, the so-called Eagle's Nest embodied Hitler's "tremendous egoism" and "fantastic whims." He wrote: "In that lofty retreat have occurred councils of historic importance, quarrels that have made history, a romantic suicide and an occasional Hitler revel that makes the place roughly the equivalent of a tired business man's seat in the first row of a burlesque show." Oechsner's lurid (and highly exaggerated) account of events at the Kehlsteinhaus emphasized it as a place of degeneracy—the lair of moral monsters. It was also, he further revealed, a dangerous place, a fortress equipped with "a powerful radio transmitter and receiver" and a vault to protect the "innermost Nazi secrets" as well as "dynamite chambers" that, if discharged, would make it impossible to access the top of the mountain. It was from the Kehlsteinhaus, Oechsner warned, that the "evil genius" Hitler had conceived and was now putting into action his plans to subjugate the world to his "master race."[50] An article in the *Daily Mail* that appeared in June 1944 reinforced the idea of the Kehlsteinhaus as a last-ditch stronghold, citing reports of the arrival of "huge trucks laden with supplies," enough "to keep Hitler for years."[51] Beyond fueling fear about the ability of the Nazis to hold out, rumors such as these also bred confusion about the relationship of the Berghof to the Kehlsteinhaus, which seemed to merge into one fantastical creation (indeed, the Manning cartoon discussed previously suggests just such an amalgam, although the drawing was clearly meant to be more of a symbolic than accurate depiction of the Führer's house).[52]

By 1944, the Kehlsteinhaus had transformed in press descriptions from an "Eagle's Nest" to what the *New York Times* now called an "ogre's nest," a place in "a monstrous fairy tale" from which Hitler could "see neither the charred ruins nor the mounds of dead he has scattered over Europe." This man, more a Grimm fairy-tale figure than real person, "puts himself on a mountain top, above the world, above humanity, above the laws and codes and limits which make peace possible either within nations or between nations." The article, written in the weeks leading up to D-Day, consciously positioned the Kehlsteinhaus for American readers in relation to the tremendous task that lay ahead of liberating the European continent from Hitler's grip: "In this tense moment before the grand assault on his stronghold, it is well to place this symbol of the evil we fight against the dangers we brave to destroy it." The Kehlsteinhaus had become the symbol for the war as a whole, for the final battle approaching between good and evil.[53]

In Germany, the start of war also brought changes to Hitler's image. While Hoffmann continued to reissue books, such as *Hitler in His Mountains,* that presented Hitler enjoying nature and relaxing at home with neighbors and friends in his earlier days as chancellor, new publicity about the Führer focused on his role as the nation's military leader.[54] At a time when German soldiers were off fighting an unpopular war and those on the home front were shouldering ever-greater burdens, images of Hitler surrounded by domestic comforts would have sent the wrong message about the Führer's own willingness to make sacrifices. Nor could Hitler have been eager to emphasize how much time he was spending on the Obersalzberg and away from the German capital.

Perhaps to alleviate such concerns, Hitler was filmed several times at the Berghof in the 1940s for *German Newsreel* (*Deutsche Wochenschau*), rare instances in which his Alpine home was filmed for public consumption. The black-and-white weekly newsreels, produced by the Ufa film company between 1940 and 1945, were widely distributed wartime propaganda that public theaters in Germany were obliged to show before every film screening. In the Berghof footage, typically lasting from one to two minutes in the newsreels, a uniformed Hitler is captured at work: conferring with Göring, accepting the papers of Japanese Ambassador Hiroshi Ōshima, examining maps with his generals, and meeting with friendly heads of state, including the Croat fascist Ante Pavelić and Mussolini. The spaces of the Berghof that viewers see are the outdoor main entrance, where visitors arrive and are sometimes greeted by Hitler, and inside the Great Hall, where he holds his meetings. Dramatic intensity is created by the arrival of large black Mercedes; the honor guard standing at attention; the soundtrack of triumphal music or the drumroll heard as the visitors and the Führer enter and exit the house; the power of uniforms and medals; and the figures silhouetted in the light of the Great Hall's vast window, with its majestic Alpine panorama. The terrace at the back of the house appears only once, when Pavelić presents Hitler with a flag that Frederick the Great had used in the Seven Years' War as well as Frederick the Great's chess set (both taken from the former Croatian National Museum at Zagreb)—gifts with obvious allusions to military strategy and victory.[55] Thus, in these wartime films, the Berghof is depicted as a sober yet vibrant place of diplomacy and government work, a notably different representation from Hoffmann's early books about Hitler in his mountain home.

But while the Nazis no longer found it strategic to emphasize the "gentler," homey side of Hitler to German audiences, they had not lost faith in its propagandistic power over others. The publication in 1941 of *A Leader and His People: A Man among Others* (*Un Chef et son Peuple: Un Homme parmi les Autres*) testifies to the ability of the National Socialist regime and its supporters to delude themselves about the limitations of Hitler's charisma. The creators of the book, intended for French audiences and almost certainly funded by the Germans, believed that they could persuade a subjugated people to appreciate and admire their conqueror. After all, in the years before the war, efforts at rapprochement between Germany and France as well as direct German interventions in the French press—which, in any case, already leaned heavily toward the right—had laid a foundation for sympathetic portrayals of Hitler and National Socialist culture. To zealous collaborators, Germany's invasion of France in 1940 did not repudiate the Nazis' benevolent intentions or negate the possibility of a positive relationship between the two nations. By continuing to promote the "good" Hitler, much like Goebbels and Hoffmann had done in Germany, they believed that they could convince their fellow citizens that the German occupation would benefit France.[56]

The foreword to *A Leader and His People,* written by the fervently pro-Nazi French author Alphonse de Châteaubriant, explained that the album was meant to "bring to life before the eyes of the French the personality of the Führer Adolf Hitler in moments of intimate contact with his people." It was also meant, he continued, as a corrective to the hateful, "distorting slander" directed at Hitler by his opponents, including the uncomprehending former ruling classes, jealous adversaries he had defeated, and foreign nations that cowered before his mounting achievements. The images, according to Châteaubriant, had been chosen with care to evoke "interest, understanding, and intelligent sympathy." Châteaubriant, who idolized Hitler as the "prototype" of a new kind of leader, the significance of which extended beyond the German people, already used the pages of *La Gerbe* (The Sheaf), the weekly French pro-Nazi newspaper that he directed, to trumpet collaboration with the occupiers. When he was asked, he said, to contribute a foreword for *A Leader and His People,* an album compiled specially for the French people, he "naturally" agreed.[57]

The images so "carefully" chosen for French eyes were a rewarmed hash of photographs that Hoffmann had been peddling to German and foreign audiences for years. But it is precisely their lack of originality that is of significance here, revealing that the book's creators believed that the propaganda that had worked so effectively in peacetime could work just as well in war. The majority of the photographs depicted Hitler interacting with Germans within Germany, although he was also shown as the welcome "liberator" of the ethnic Germans in Czechoslovakia and of the Austrian people. Only a handful of photographs showed Hitler in France, and these were contextualized with quotes in which he praised the valor of the French people. Châteaubriant claimed that the book's images manifest the new type of leadership embodied by Hitler. Thus, nationality was less important than the nature of the relationship between people and leader captured in these documents, and it was with an eye to this dynamic that Châteaubriant encouraged French readers to study the images.[58]

The Berghof took pride of place in this visual exploration of a new kind of leader who shared an intimate, spiritual bond with his followers. The first pages of photographs were devoted to different views of the house seen from the exterior and interior, including an image of the "thousands who arrive each day at the Berghof to greet the man who is for his people more than the head of state."[59] In subsequent pages, Hitler was depicted chatting with his Obersalzberg neighbors, interacting with children at the Berghof, and deep in thought in the mountainous landscape—in other words, the very same tropes that had been used so effectively to seduce German and foreign audiences in the prewar period. Even in a nation torn apart by the German occupation, Hitler's propagandists believed that they could win hearts and minds with these images of the man from Berchtesgaden.

PLATES

Plate 1. Postcard of Adolf Hitler's home on the Obersalzberg, c. 1934.

Plate 2. Heinrich Hoffmann, postcard of the original rustic *Stube* or living room in Haus Wachenfeld, c. 1934.

Plate 3. Heinrich Hoffmann, postcard of the Stube or living room after the Atelier
Troost renovation, c. 1936.

Plate 4. Heinrich Hoffmann, postcard of the Great Hall, c. 1936.

Plate 5. Heinrich Hoffmann, view of the window in the Great Hall, c. 1936.

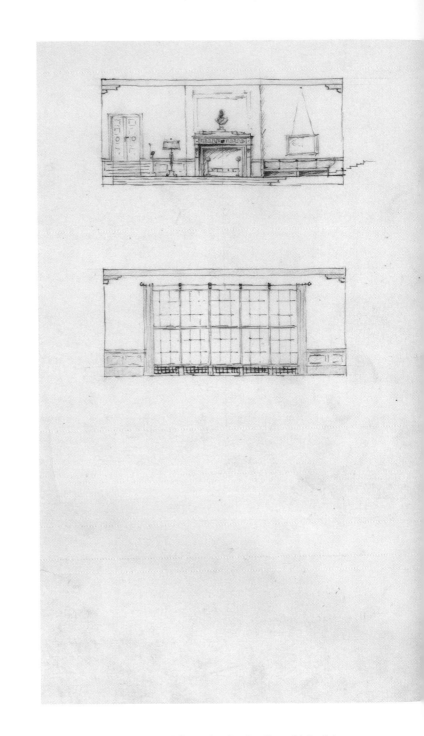

Plate 6. Atelier Troost, sketched elevation and floor plan for the Great Hall of the Berghof, c. 1935.

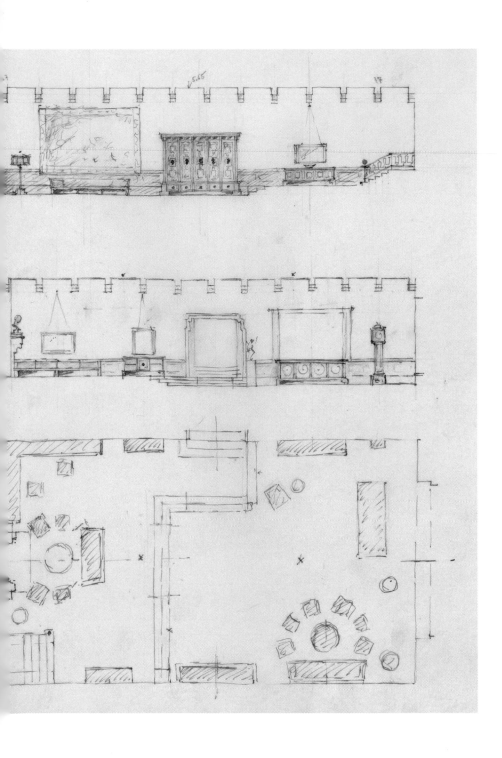

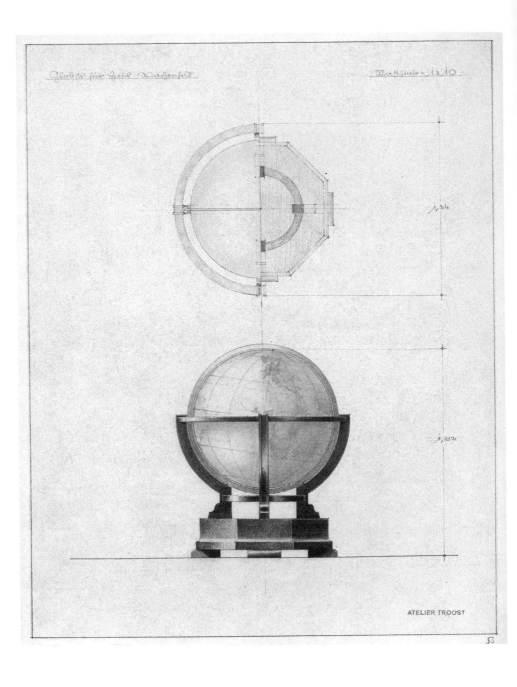

ATELIER TROOST

Plate 7. Atelier Troost, drawing of globe for the Great Hall of the Berghof, c. 1936.

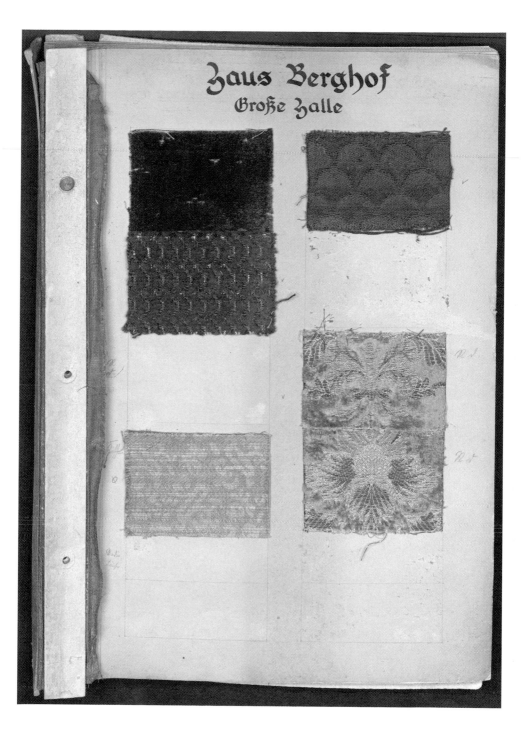

Plate 8. Gerdy Troost's Berghof fabric book, showing the first page of samples for the Great Hall. Subsequent pages contain more samples for the Great Hall, living room, guest rooms, and the adjutant and caretaker's rooms.

Plate 9. Heinrich Hoffmann, postcard of Hitler's study on the second floor of the Berghof, c. 1936.

Plate 10. Gerdy Troost speaking with Hitler and surrounded by a crowd of Nazi bigwigs at the House of German Art on the Day of German Art, July 16, 1939. Photograph by Heinrich Hoffmann.

Plate 11. Heinrich Hoffmann, postcard of the Berghof, c. 1936.

Plate 12. Chief Superintendent Manfred Albert in Hitler's former library, the shelves now occupied by the trophies won by the police soccer team, the Bogenhauser Cops. Photograph from 2007.

Plate 13. Sergeant Ursula Lechner in Hitler's former bedroom, now used as a locker room for the police officers who work in the building. A poster of the actress Milla Jovovich hangs on a locker. Photograph from 2007.

10   SECRETS IN THE CELLAR

Bombing, Looting, and the Reinvention of
Hitler's Domesticity

By mid-April 1945, it appeared that the Obersalzberg might survive
the war without being touched by Allied bombs or ground fighting. With
German resistance collapsing, American and French forces were advancing rapidly southward toward Berchtesgaden. On April 16, Allied air forces
smashed what little remained of Hermann Göring's Luftwaffe: the majority
of the nine hundred planes they hit had been on the ground, unable to fly
because they lacked both fuel and pilots. That evening, General Carl Spaatz,
commander of the U.S. Strategic Air Forces in Europe, announced that the
strategic air war against Germany had been won. American and British
heavy bombers would now focus on tactical support to the ground forces
in order "to secure the ultimate objective—complete defeat of Germany."[1]
The aerial attack on the Berghof on April 25, in the final days of the war,
thus came as a surprise to many, raising questions as to how its destruction
contributed to Germany's "complete defeat."

On several prior occasions, beginning in the spring of 1944, the Allied
air forces had devised plans to bomb the Obersalzberg, but in each case the
raids were vetoed or canceled. The main argument in favor of bombing
was the chance to kill Hitler and thereby hasten the unraveling of Nazi
Germany and the end of the war. But because of the Obersalzberg's strong

defenses, it seemed probable that Hitler would survive such an attack, causing the German people to rally. Some also questioned the wisdom of killing
Hitler at this point in the war, when his inept military leadership seemed
to be aiding the Allies. In his diary on June 20, 1944, Henry "Hap" Arnold,
commanding general of the U.S. Army Air Forces, wrote: "The general
impression among the higher officers in the Allied Air Forces is that . . .
'Our secret weapon is Hitler, hence do not bomb his castle. Do not let him
get hurt, we want him to continue making mistakes.'"[2] Nor, for that matter,
could the Allies be certain that Hitler would be at the Berghof when they
attacked. In his absence, the house counted little as a military target, and
the danger of flying in mountains frequently covered in clouds along with
the expectation of encountering heavy anti-aircraft fire made it difficult to
justify the attack as a symbolic gesture.[3]

Still, Allied servicemen and -women as well as civilians on the home
fronts, weary from the years of terror and hardship that Hitler had imposed
on them, longed to see it happen. On February 21, 1945, a team of U.S.
Air Force Thunderbolts, unable to complete a mission in Italy, diverted to
Berchtesgaden, bombing the rail yards. The flight leader, who initially did
not realize the planes were passing over Hitler's home, later reported that
they had dropped their empty gasoline tanks in the vicinity, giving rise to
press speculation that the Berghof had been hit. The day after the story
broke, the *New York Times* described the reaction as a "tremendous political
shout that has been heard around the world."[4] When it emerged that the
Berghof remained unscathed, the response from the public was something
more than disappointment. In a letter to the editor published on March 1
in the *Washington Post,* a reader wondered why "the Allies [have] continued
to show such great delicacy in avoiding the bombing of Hitler's retreat at
Obersalzberg." The writer reasoned, "Certainly, within the many months
that our and British planes have been flying from Italy to bomb certain
localities in Austria, there must have been some occasions when it would
have been convenient to leave a calling card at Hitler's place, of which he
appears to be so fond and where so many plans have been hatched to make
it difficult for the Allies. I don't recall that back in that fateful September, the
Luftwaffe hesitated to bomb some of London's public buildings, or private
ones either. So, why do the Allies so studiously avoid wrecking the Hitler
layout at Berchtesgaden?"[5] Even Hitler seemed to think it was overdue. In
a proclamation made on February 24, three days after the bombing of the
Berchtesgaden rail yards, he stated, "I read in British papers that there is a

plan to destroy my Berghof. I almost regret that this has not yet happened." For, he explained, he "would be happy" to shoulder every burden that others must bear, thus alluding to the millions of Germans made homeless by the war.[6] No doubt many of them wholeheartedly shared the Führer's regret. When the Berghof did go up in flames, Johanna Stangassinger, a young woman watching the fire from across the valley with her family and still feeling the pain of forcibly losing her own home on the Obersalzberg to Martin Bormann eight years earlier, turned to her father and said, "This is the most beautiful sight of my life, Hitler's house burning, just as our houses have burned."[7]

When the attack finally came on April 25, 1945, the Allies made up for the delay with a spectacular display of firepower. With aerial strikes in Europe focused on a reduced number of tactical targets, a large number of bomber aircraft were available for the raid. On a clear morning, in ideal flying conditions, a Royal Air Force (RAF) fleet of 359 Lancaster and 16 Mosquito bombers, escorted by 88 P-51 Mustang fighters of the U.S. Air Force, flew over the Obersalzberg in two waves. According to RAF operations record books, the first sweep occurred from 9:51 to 10:11 A.M. and the second from 10:42 to 11:00 A.M., with the heaviest bombing occurring around ten o'clock and again from 10:48 to 10:58 A.M. (local time).[8] Through sometimes heavy flak, the squadrons dropped 1,232 tons of bombs on the buildings and surrounding landscape, including the last of the twelve-thousand-pound Tall Boys, "earthquake" bombs designed to explode underground against reinforced concrete targets. This bomb tonnage was enormous—enough to level a small city. Allied intelligence had discovered the construction of a massive underground bunker system, and the size and type of bombs had been chosen with the goal of penetrating and destroying those structures as well as targets above ground. Nonetheless, the bunkers held up well: about three thousand people safely sheltered underground. While the reported number of deaths was low, given the scale of the attack, it included children who had been caught in the open.[9]

The next day, in newspapers around the world, banner headlines trumpeted the obliteration of "Hitler's lair" by "vengeful RAF Lancasters." A British flight sergeant recalled seeing "one terrific flash right on Hitler's house," which was described as having been "wiped off the face of the earth." The "Kehlstein fortress," or Eagle's Nest, one of the main targets, was believed to have been hit, although it was unclear if the pavilion itself had been damaged. The SS barracks had been "smashed" during the first and second rounds of bombing.[10] Two Lancasters were reported missing, and it would later be learned that both planes had been hit by anti-aircraft fire; four crewmen died and the survivors were taken prisoner, soon to be liberated by the advancing Allied troops.[11] The Obersalzberg raid would be the last major attack by the RAF against Germany. A returning navigator told reporters, "This was the mission we have been waiting for all through the war."[12]

The view from the ground suggests the raid was less successful than portrayed by British air command. The snow covering the buildings and surrounding area made targets difficult to distinguish, and the mountains blocked radio signals that could have helped to pinpoint bombing locations.[13] Some crews reported that the high mountains and the direction from which they had been ordered to approach prevented them from seeing their targets until it was too late.[14] Despite claims by the British Air Ministry that all targets had been successfully identified, the operations record book of 617 Squadron reveals that of its sixteen Lancaster crews, ten could not find their primary targets and aborted the mission or released their bombs elsewhere. Many of the badly damaged buildings—Martin Bormann's and Hermann Göring's houses, the camp for Czech workers, and a settlement for evacuated children, among others—seem to have been secondary or accidental targets. The SS barracks, a primary target that was clearly visible because of its size and square shape, received the most accurate drop of Tallboys, reducing the compound to smithereens. The Kehlsteinhaus was untouched, although the land around it was seeded with bombs. The small size of the building, estimated at seventeen square yards, militated against a direct hit. In the case of the Berghof, another primary target, snow made the house difficult to see, and one Lancaster crew observed that "bombing was very scattered."[15] British and German reports, aerial photographs, and firsthand accounts indicate that three smaller bombs hit their target. An eyewitness arriving at the Berghof shortly after the raid ended saw the east and west wings smoldering where they had been hit by high explosive bombs, and the roof of the main house (the section containing the Great Hall and Hitler's quarters) in flames, possibly from incendiary bombs.[16] Christa Schroeder, Hitler's secretary, recalled that the old part of the house—the original Haus Wachenfeld—had "burst open" when a bomb had landed beside it, and that inside the new section, "the floor was thickly covered with debris and much of the furniture had been demolished."[17] Although thus damaged, the house was far from obliterated, as claimed by the press, and considerable sections remained standing, including much of the east wing and the Great Hall (despite damage to the roof and third story; the great window lay in shards on the ground).[18] On May 4, before departing, SS guards doused the Berghof with gasoline and set it alight, gutting much of the interior and adding to the structural damage caused by the air raid (figs. 63, 64).[19]

Such a large-scale bombing attack on the Obersalzberg entailed heavy risks and costs, especially coming at a time when Germany's defeat seemed imminent. While the press accounts that followed celebrated the news, they seemed unable to offer definitive reasons for the raid. Charles Chamberlain, reporting from London for the Associated Press, described the raid as "an apparent attempt on the fuehrer's life." At the same time, however, he admitted that Hitler's location was unknown: "German radio propagandists insisted that Hitler was inside encircled Berlin, directing its wild defense, but reports from many parts of Europe lent support to the story he had taken refuge at the Berchtesgaden retreat to which for years he had summoned the heads of states who were his selected dupes to hear his bidding." But if the mission's goal had been assassination, it did not explain why "such a shining target had never been bombed before," a question, Chamberlain noted, that "remained officially without explanation."[20]

In his pursuit of an answer, Chamberlain shifted the focus away from a personal attack on Hitler. Since 1944, stories had circulated that the Nazis were preparing a "National Redoubt" in the southern Alps as a last-ditch stronghold for Hitler's most fanatical followers. The Obersalzberg and Kehlstein, rumored to have vast underground networks of facilities and bunkers, seemed a likely hub of this mountain bastion. Although the National Redoubt would eventually prove to have been a myth, as Berlin collapsed, western Allied leaders, including General Dwight D. Eisenhower, grew anxious that the Nazis fleeing southward would entrench themselves in the Alps and engage in prolonged guerilla warfare.[21] Chamberlain stated that "an RAF staff officer said unofficially today, 'with the fall of Berlin near, Berchtesgaden is looked upon as a sort of Nazi capital—the last spot over which the swastika will fly. Thus the bombing at this time has a psychological effect, and it also can be assumed that the Germans are gathering there for a last stand. Thus it becomes a military target of more importance than before.'" Unofficially, then, the attack was explained as an attempt to take the fight out of die-hard Nazis by eliminating their hope or basis for a last stand in the Alps.[22] A correspondent for the *Christian Science Monitor*,

Fig. 63. Lee Miller, "End of a Myth," photograph of the Berghof in flames, published in the July 1945 issue of *Vogue* (UK).

reporting from Supreme Headquarters, similarly reasoned that only expectation of fierce resistance from a mountain redoubt and the desire to decisively eliminate the threat could explain the scale of the attack: "It is hardly conceivable that otherwise would there have been such a concentration yesterday of heavy bombers upon this small area even though it happens to be Hitler's headquarters."[23]

Looking back in 1968 on the Obersalzberg attack, John W. Snyder, who in 1945 had served as director of the U.S. Office of War Mobilization and Reconversion, blamed British eccentricity for the raid, forgetting the contribution of American air forces: "The British for some strange reason, after the war was over, came over and bombed that area pretty badly for no

Fig. 64. Photo Marburg, photograph of the bombed and burned Berghof at the end of October 1946, with a view of the main stairs and eastern wing (in the distance to the left is the Türken Inn).

apparent reason; the war was finished, but they came over anyway and took pleasure in bombing out Hitler's retreat." Snyder offered these comments as a former government official who had toured Germany in September 1945 to assess surplus property disposal for President Harry S. Truman, and who, while supporting the goals of strategic bombing, had been sickened by the scale of destruction he encountered on his travels.[24] While he thus may have been predisposed to take a negative view of the Obersalzberg attack, it is surprising to discover that even some of the participating crewmen shared his opinion. As the operations record books reveal and as recalled in later years by the crewmen, the mission's poor planning had created chaos in the air, with planes orbiting in all directions and nearly colliding with or bombing each other. This situation, together with the loss of two Lancasters so late in the war, angered some crews who viewed the mission as a public-relations ploy. Even so, "on the way home and back at base there was a mood of celebration."[25]

With the advantage of hindsight, some historians have similarly questioned the tactical value of the raid. Nonetheless, the rationale provided

SECRETS IN THE CELLAR

to Charles Chamberlain by the RAF officer on the day of the bombing supports U.S. Commander Spaatz's assertion, made nine days earlier, that future air attacks would focus on bringing about Germany's "complete defeat." That defeat, as conceived by the Allies, was not just material, but also psychological, and in raiding the Obersalzberg, the intended impact went beyond the fanatical Nazis imagined to be digging themselves into the mountains. As the Allies well knew, the Berghof had tremendous symbolic significance. Through Heinrich Hoffmann's images and other Nazi propaganda, the house had come to be intimately associated in the minds of the German people with Hitler himself, acting as a proxy for the leader. Destroying the Berghof allowed the Allies to ritually kill Hitler while he remained in hiding and thus reinforce the end of his regime. The psychological effect of the bombing was thus potentially vast, capable of sending a message beyond the Alps to the German nation as a whole—as the RAF officer himself seemed to imply.

Moreover, the victors, who desired not just to end the war, but to end it decisively and triumphantly, also derived a psychological boost from the bombing. For General Eisenhower, the Obersalzberg represented the "symbol of Nazi arrogance" and seeing the images of how "our bombers had reduced the place to a shambles" gave the Allied command "a gleeful and understandable satisfaction."[26] Following criticism voiced in the United States and England of the "terror bombing" of German cities in February 1945, it has also been proposed that Arthur "Bomber" Harris, head of RAF Bomber Command, wanted one last heroic mission to remind politicians and public alike of the decisive role of the air war in defeating the Third Reich.[27] Charles Chamberlain's article, however, suggests a more broadly held unease among the victors at the war's close, which may have contributed to their desire to bomb the Obersalzberg into oblivion. Former British Prime Minister David Lloyd George, Lord Halifax, the British press magnate Lord Rothermere, Prime Minister Neville Chamberlain, British Ambassador Sir Nevile Henderson, the Duke and Duchess of Windsor, French Ambassador André François-Poncet, and former U.S. Ambassador to Belgium John Cudahy were among the "selected dupes" who had visited Hitler at the Berghof and thereby served to legitimize his claims to being a respectable world statesman. The memory of Chamberlain's 1938 meeting with Hitler at the Berghof to negotiate the partition of Czechoslovakia, which had bolstered Hitler's belief that Europe's strongest powers would not oppose his plans of empire, especially stung. Reporters covering the

Obersalzberg bombing referred to the visit and to Chamberlain's tragically mistaken confidence that he had achieved "peace in our time."[28] By 1945, then, the Berghof stood as a humiliating reminder of how Allied nations had contributed to the European catastrophe through denial and appeasement, and the sheer force with which RAF bombers set out to annihilate the place suggests a desire to wipe from memory the stain of that capitulation.

If the Allied air forces had hoped to eradicate the Berghof's physical traces, the epic looting that followed the bombing worked against them, preserving the physical remnants of Hitler's house and dispersing them to the far reaches of the globe where, in collections stored in basements, living rooms, and attics, the presence of the house lives on. Lee Miller, *Vogue's* war correspondent, arrived at the Berghof as it was still burning on the night of May 4 (see fig. 63). "In the morning," she noted, "the fire was nearly out and so were the looters, in force."[29] French and American soldiers, having competed—and nearly come to blows—in the race to be the first to claim the prize of Hitler's mountain retreat, were now united in their search for souvenirs.[30] Observing the "very wild party" of drinking and trophy hunting in the crumbling ruin, Miller commented sardonically that "there isn't even a piece left for a museum on the great war criminal, and scattered over the breadth of the world people are forever going to be shown a napkin ring or a pickle fork, supposedly used by Hitler."[31] As it turns out, she was right.

The bombing of the Obersalzberg revealed a Nazi landscape of luxury that verged on the surreal. On the morning of April 25, Richard Reiter, a seventeen-year-old SS courier who as a child had visited Hitler's home and played with his dogs, was called to his battalion's temporary headquarters outside Piding, a Bavarian village north of Berchtesgaden; he was ordered to deliver a courier case that had arrived from the Reich Chancellery in Berlin to Bernhard Frank, commander of the SS detachment on the Obersalzberg, who then had Göring under house arrest. Reiter had been assigned the task because he knew the area well and could take back roads to avoid enemy forces, then less than ninety miles from Berchtesgaden. He had just handed over the case to the commander when the air raid sirens began to wail. Frank pointed Reiter to a one-man bomb shelter beside Göring's pool and disappeared into the house. When the bombing ended and Reiter emerged, he saw that Göring's house, like a pirate's cave, had literally exploded with treasure. Unaware of the extensive underground bunkers, Reiter assumed that everyone in the demolished house was dead. He picked up an exquisite silver Persian plate and a bejeweled Persian hunting knife lying in the

SECRETS IN THE CELLAR

debris, tucked them into his jacket, and sped off on his motorcycle toward the Berghof. Stopping briefly on the driveway, he saw that a number of art portfolios had blown free of Hitler's home and lay charred on the nearby ground. He took one that seemed only slightly scorched, put it in his saddlebag, and drove on to rejoin his battalion. Later, he discovered that it contained reproduction prints of six figures painted by Michelangelo on the Sistine Chapel ceiling, including the Old Testament prophet Jeremiah, whom the artist depicted lamenting the destruction of Jerusalem.[32]

With the collapse of the Third Reich, the homes of the Nazi elite on the Obersalzberg and the riches they contained became fair game in the eyes of soldiers and civilians. After Hitler's death, the first to plunder the Berghof were those who had once been his most faithful followers: Hitler's personal SS bodyguards, the Reich Security Service.[33] Berghof employees brought trucks and emptied out the rooms.[34] Next came area residents, who gazed in amazement at "things that had long disappeared from the rest of the Reich": in the bunkers, storerooms overflowed with sugar, butter, flour, honey, and coffee beans—unimaginable luxuries after years of rationing and barely digestible substitutes. Rooms were stocked with clothes, soap, shoes, dishes, and furniture. Near Bormann's bunker, the ever-more-astonished looters "stumbled upon large quantities of French Champagne, wine, and cognac." Utter havoc broke out, and with wheelbarrows, carts, bicycles, and horse-drawn wagons, local residents carried away all that they could manage before the arrival of the Allied troops.[35]

When French and American soldiers reached the Berghof in early May, yet another round of frenzied looting began. David Kenyon Webster, a private with Easy Company in the 506th Parachute Infantry Regiment, who later became a reporter, recounted how he came to drink "Hitler's champagne" in the *Saturday Evening Post* (fig. 65). He began by describing the long, roundabout journey to reach Berchtesgaden, which took the soldiers through "sweet and warm" country landscapes as well as German cities that stank of the dead. As the Bavarian Alps approached, the men's anxiety mounted: "We had all heard a little too much about the so-called National Redoubt, where Hitler was supposed to have ordered a final hearty SS stand—one of those fight-to-the-last-man things he was always ordering— and we did not look forward to cleaning out the Alps just when the war was almost over. As we rode the Munich-Salzburg *Autobahn* and looked up at the huge, dark sharks'-teeth mountains on our right, we wondered if they held the last fanatics." While the Allies met with no organized resistance, a pocket of SS men in the mountains attacked the Third Battalion, and "several men who had been with the regiment since its start died in this last tragic ambush."[36]

Webster's battalion, the Second, was luckier, and once they entered Berchtesgaden on May 5, they relaxed and enjoyed its comforts. They identified a small suburban development just north of town that had been "lovingly built for the local SS police and their families," and giving the occupants half an hour to pack their bags, "leased our building with M-1's." Inside the "very modern Alpine style dwellings," Webster and his squad ate well, "drank what liquor remained in the apartment and after spells in the bathtub lay in Oriental splendor on beds with sheets and listened to the radio." Later, they encountered soldiers with cases of champagne from Hitler's house and, deciding it was "too good to miss," made their way up the Obersalzberg. On the way, they discovered that "everybody else in town apparently had the same idea we had. Recon cars, half-tracks, 6-by-6's, DUKW's, *Volkswagens, Schwimmwagens*—all were winding uphill in a desperate drive to the treasure trove." When they reached the house, they encountered "a frantic scene that I shall never forget: the midnight looting of Hitler's home. . . . The front yard was an ugly mass of timbers, broken glass, mortar and brick, over which thirsty soldiers milled about frantically in the rainy darkness."[37]

As G. I.'s drank and toasted their dead host ("Heil Hitler, the bastard"), Sergeant Harry Sions, correspondent for *Yank* magazine, went in search of other prey, exploring the house for traces of its former inhabitants. The Great Hall, where Hitler had once entertained foreign leaders "after he completed the business of sealing a country's doom . . . is an empty, charred room smelling of spilled wine and burned wood, and great timbers hang from the ceiling at sharp angles" (fig. 66). On the second floor, in Hitler's former office, nothing but a safe remained containing "only a few autographed copies of *Mein Kampf.*"[38] Sions then arrived at Hitler's bedroom and bath, which had "been sacked, but there was enough left to indicate they had been simply furnished, although his combination bed and day-couch was burned and the rest of the furniture was gone. The bathroom was a simple affair, like those in less-expensive apartments in New York City. The sit-down toilet, washstand and tub were plain white porcelain. There was no shower; sometimes the *Fuehrer* used a rubber shower attachment fastened to the tub faucet, similar to those which used to sell for $1.98 at any cut-rate drug store in the States. Inside the medicine chest were a bottle of castor

Fig. 65. "Third Division men drink liberated wine at the Berghof, Hitler's halfway house on the mountain above Berchtesgaden, in May, 1945." This caption and image were published in David Kenyon Webster's 1952 memoir essay, "We Drank Hitler's Champagne," for the *Saturday Evening Post*, May 3, 1952, 25.

oil, a bottle of liniment for rheumatism and a sample bottle of mouthwash marked in German: 'Not to be sold in the trade.'"[39] In these most private of spaces, Sions thus evoked a strange mixture of intimacy, banality, and loss. The portrait of the modest man that emerged was eerily reminiscent of earlier Nazi propaganda, the influence of which may have colored visitors' experiences as they combed through the ruins searching for traces of the Führer. One can almost imagine Baldur von Schirach's obsequious, overexcited commentary: "Look, Hitler is just like us: he likes free samples, too!" But unlike Schirach, who drew on the quotidian to praise Hitler as a man of the people, Sions undoubtedly meant to use the references to castor oil and rheumatism to deflate the image of the Führer as it had appeared to many outside Germany: a fearsome, nearly invincible force. For Lee Miller, this deflation was in itself terrifying.

About one hundred miles away and a few days earlier, Miller had conducted her own interrogation of Hitler's domestic spaces in Munich. She was staying in his apartment at 16 Prince Regent Square with soldiers from

Fig. 66. L. Ammon, postcard of the Berghof's Great Hall window with a view of Mount Untersberg, as the hall looked after the Allied bombing.

the 179th Regiment of the 45th Division, having arrived there after seeing and photographing the heaps of skeletal dead and the walking corpses in the Dachau concentration camp, which had been liberated on April 29. The apartment building had not been touched by the war and the apartment's contents were largely intact, giving Miller the impression of having walked into a home that had just been vacated—which, in fact, it had, Hitler's housekeeper, Anni Winter, having left just hours earlier.[40] Miller's sense of horror only increased when she came to Munich and encountered Hitler on more intimate terms: "He'd never really been alive for me until today. He'd been an evil machine-monster all these years, until I visited the places he made famous, talked to people who knew him, dug into backstairs gossip and ate and slept in his house. He became less fabulous and therefore more terrible, along with a little evidence of his having some almost human habits; like an ape who embarrasses and humbles you with his gestures, mirroring yourself in caricature. 'There, but for the grace of God walk I.'"[41]

Having tracked down and entered the monster's lair, Miller was unnerved to discover the familiar and the commonplace at the end of the road from Dachau. "Superficially," she wrote in the July 1945 issue of British

SECRETS IN THE CELLAR

Vogue, "almost anyone with a medium income and no heirlooms could have been the proprietor of this flat. It lacked grace and charm, it lacked intimacy, but it was not grand. It wasn't empty enough to be 'sub-let' as it stood, but a quarter of an hour's clearing cupboards (especially the medicine chests) would have made it ready for any new tenant who didn't mind linen and silver marked A.H." Miller did not glamorize these signs of the Führer—the monogrammed crystal and china—but framed them in the larger context of his prosaic tastes and domesticity. Nothing seemed either remarkably good or remarkably bad: the "mediocre" art, the chintz fabric in his bedroom (fig. 67), the out-of-tune Bechstein piano, even the rubber tree plant in the hallway. Historic events similarly slipped into the vortex of banality in these domestic spaces. The *Vogue* article included a photograph taken by Miller of a beer mug in the shape of the head of King George VI sitting on a desk. Miller explained that the mug, which played "God Save the King" when it was lifted, had been given to Hitler by Chamberlain in 1938 when he visited the Führer's apartment to negotiate the Munich Accord, and that Hitler had ordered it to be brought down to the bomb shelter during alerts.[42] Through such details, Miller revealed the "almost human habits" she found so disconcerting—here, however, tinged with humor, as the reader was left to imagine the mug playing "God Save the King" all the way down the stairs to Hitler's bomb shelter.

For Miller, it was all intolerably ordinary and familiar—a seductive coziness that both fascinated and repelled her. This uncomfortable tension between banality and evil infused Miller's reporting from Germany and culminated in the now famous image, published in the same *Vogue* article, of Miller in Hitler's bathtub, taken by David Scherman, a photographer for *Life* magazine and Miller's lover (fig. 68).[43] The image shows a naked Miller posing modestly, her arm lifted to soap her shoulder, surrounded by the Führer's attributes: a framed portrait of a stern Hitler in uniform and a sculpture of an idealized female torso indicative of his classical tastes, both items placed there by Miller. On the once-clean mat in front of the tub, Miller has left her boots, covered with the mud of Dachau, as if she has just stepped out of them and into the water. Given that there was another full bath in the apartment, at the other end used by the servants, Miller clearly chose to enact this ritual of cleansing, made poignant by the impossibility of washing away what she had witnessed, on Hitler's turf.

In a letter to Audrey Withers, her *Vogue* editor, Miller stated that no other reporters had yet been to Hitler's Munich apartment and "it is an

Fig. 67. Lee Miller, photograph of Sergeant Arthur Peters reading *Mein Kampf* on Hitler's bed in his Munich apartment bedroom, 1945. The photograph was published in the July 1945 issue of *Vogue* (UK).

absolutely exclusive story."[44] As much as that must have pleased Withers, she may have been even more excited to hear of another exclusive: a visit to Eva Braun's villa, a short distance away at 12 Wasserburger Street. Hitler's propagandists had kept Braun a secret from the German public, and it was only after his death that they discovered that their Führer had not married the German nation, as he had long insisted, but rather a real, flesh-and-blood woman. Reporters arriving in southern Bavaria with the Allied forces and with access to Hitler's and Braun's domestic spaces were the first outsiders to investigate this secret life and the woman for whom Hitler had jilted his nation-bride. Both Sions on the Obersalzberg and Miller in Munich sought

Fig. 68. Lee Miller with David E. Scherman, photograph of Lee Miller in Hitler's bathtub in his Munich apartment, 1945. The photograph was published in the July 1945 issue of *Vogue* (UK).

to capture something of Braun's essence by sifting through her domestic remains. Their discoveries helped to shift the narrative of Hitler's domesticity away from official portrayals of the Führer's lonely celibacy toward an interest in his sexual life—a topic that had been silenced in Germany since the fall of the Weimar Republic and the imposition of strict press controls. But Sions's and Miller's house searches suggested a rather ordinary and banal intimate life, an outlook that would quickly be supplanted by journalists' hunt for a more sensationalistic story.

When Miller arrived at Braun's house, she found it in good repair, although sacked and a mess. The looters seem to have been looking primarily for food and alcohol, and furniture and some personal items remained. Unlike Sions, who maintained an observer's distance, Miller put her body at the service of pursuing her subject. In Hitler's apartment, she had sat naked in his bath; at Braun's house, she lay down on her bed and took a nap. By engaging these most intimate spaces with her own body, Miller reenacted Hitler's and Braun's moments of vulnerability (in the bath, asleep), as if she wanted to test a shared humanity or to steel herself against it. Of the experience, she wrote in *Vogue* that "it was comfortable, but it was macabre . . . to doze on the pillow of a girl and man who were dead, and to be glad they were dead." Miller avoided a sensationalist tone in describing these intimate infringements and did not glamorize Braun's home. While providing glimpses of luxury, such as the "self-striped ice blue satin" sheets on Braun's bed (the "self-striped" contrasting here with the stripes enforced on the Dachau inmates), Miller emphasized the ordinariness of its "department-store" furniture and of the odds and ends left behind by the occupant, such as the remnants in her bedroom cupboard ("a few belts, a tweed beret and a douche bag"), or the items on her dressing table ("tweezers, Elizabeth Arden lipstick refills") and on her bedroom desk (stationery, clips, pencils, an unfinished letter about "a deal for some eggs in the country"). Turning to the bathroom, Miller declared it "supernormal" except for the two medicine chests full of drugs and preparations, which seemed to suggest a hypochondriac.[45] Through this accumulation of mundane details, and despite (or perhaps, because of) the matter-of-fact tone, Miller nonetheless blurred the line between the "supernormal" and the surreal. It was profoundly disturbing to imagine the "almost human" domesticity of the monster and his mate, a feeling that Miller both chased after and pushed away.

In Braun's rooms at the Berghof, Sergeant Sions found a contrast to Hitler's puritanically tinged asceticism, his castor oil and $1.98 bathroom hose, but as in Miller's description of her Munich home, a sense of banality remained, despite the flashes of glamour. "Her bedroom measured about 18 by 27 feet. It had a fireplace and simple maple furniture, most of which had been wrecked and looted. Scattered on the floor was some of Eva Braun's stationery, light blue, unscented, with EB in the corners; there were some of her calling cards, a couple of booklets on amateur movie photography, and a tailor's bill dated June 8, 1940, for a dress. The dress cost Hitler 500 marks, or about $125." Sions then peeked into an even more intimate interior space: "Inside a closet were hundreds of clothes hangers and shoe trees, and a November 1942 copy of *La Femme Chic,* a Paris fashion magazine." In a corner of her sitting room, Sions found "an envelope with a last-minute shopping list scribbled on the back." Finally, entering the most intimate domestic space of all, Sions was surprised that "Eva Braun's bathroom was simple and nothing like the Hollywood conception of the bathroom of a dictator's mistress. The wash basin, douche bowl and bathtub were plain white porcelain. Inside her medicine cabinet, above the wash basin, were a jar of Ardena skin cream, made by Elizabeth Arden of Berlin and New York, and a bottle of a disinfectant used for athlete's foot." While Sions's account left no doubt that Braun had enjoyed privileges beyond the means of most Germans—a 500-Mark dress was more than a month's wages for a skilled worker—the references to a scribbled grocery list, plain bathroom fixtures, and athlete's foot made her appear less alien and remote.[46] As was true for Miller, Sions's reader was left with an overall impression of Hitler's and Braun's domesticity that was underwhelming rather than overwhelming. And as the full horror of what had happened in Europe became known, this perspective was deeply troubling to those who wanted to put more distance between themselves and the perpetrators. Before the war, Germans and non-German audiences alike had been drawn to the seeming similarity between their modest lives and that of the Führer, as depicted by his propagandists. Once he had been exposed as a mass murderer, the familiar became a threat rather than a comfort.

The G. I. looters described by Private Webster did not much share this interest in interrogating the spaces of the Berghof in search of the psychic interiors of Hitler and Braun. Instead, they wanted booze and treasure. And in pursuing their desires, they constructed an alternative narrative of domesticity that diverted from and sometimes conflicted with that of Sions and Miller. Arriving in the dark at the Berghof, Webster and his fellow paratroopers made their way over debris down to a large, bomb-proof wine cellar, which was intact and "filled to the ceiling" with bottle racks holding wine of "every brand and blend in the world, or so it seemed—and the victors were making merry with the spoils. Small desperate groups of warriors drank with one hand and filled boxes with the other in the uncertain flicker of matches, candles and flashlights. Bottles were breaking on the floor; men were cursing and clutching; lights flared and faded; and everybody was having one hell of a time."[47] In their joyful immoderation, the G. I.'s told a story not just about "making merry with the spoils," but also about the spoils themselves. Just as British bombers had exploded Hitler's house, the widely reported stories of the après-war party at the Berghof detonated the myth of the Führer's modest, self-sacrificing domestic lifestyle that Nazi propagandists had expounded for years. Here was definitive proof that while his people had suffered, Hitler had surrounded himself with every luxury. In place of a National Redoubt, the Allies discovered the world's best-stocked wine cellars. "It looks to me," an infantry colonel told Harry Sions, "like they were expecting to defend the place with wine bottles."[48]

As Webster and his squad mates prepared to leave with their haul of Hitler's champagne, "we noticed a curious thing. The French weren't putting any liquor in their trucks. A practical people, they were carting off more durable souvenirs. They had discovered a tunnel into the hillside across the road that contained most of Adolf's household furnishings. We saw them with Hitler's silver and Hitler's linen and Hitler's furniture, but reluctantly decided not to help them dispose of the remainder of the estate." Other G. I.'s, however, did join in the plundering and shipped home a wide array of "liberated" objects from Hitler's homes. Unlike their French counterparts, who returned to a country deeply troubled by its relationship to the Third Reich and who largely kept their war spoils out of sight, many American soldiers happily announced their acquisitions to friends, family, and the press. They felt comfortable doing so despite the military's insistence that looting was illegal—a stance weakened, however, by the fact that some of the worst offenders were high-ranking officers.[49] In August 1945, for example, an Associated Press story reported that "one of the postwar social events planned by Lieut. Col. and Mrs. Willard White of Austin" in Texas was a dinner party featuring Adolf Hitler's table linens and over a hundred pieces of his crested silverware, which White, commander of the 1269th Engineer Combat Battalion, and among the first to reach Berchtesgaden, had collected as "trophies."[50] (The story did not mention that this was only a small part of what White had amassed. He has been called "a strong candidate for top souvenir collector at Berchtesgaden" for the "fortune in spoils" that he acquired, the sale of which allowed him to live in "grand style" upon returning to the States.[51]) Earlier that summer, newspapers had carried photographs of Mrs. Eileen Doran Morris, the wife of Major Frank Morris and the recipient in Springfield, Illinois, of silverware, tablecloths, and plates taken by the major from Hitler's apartment in Munich. In the photograph, Mrs. Morris posed with her young daughter, Margaret, beside a table displaying the items, above which hung another of the major's spoils: a large Nazi flag.[52]

Texans had a chance to gaze at the relics of the Führer's domesticity at the end of 1945, when a Victory Loan train made its way through the state. In a five-hundred-city tour to show what war bonds had bought and to promote new purchases, six trains laden with artifacts from the war traveled through forty states in November and December 1945.[53] The exhibits, manned by decorated combat veterans, varied from train to train, but included German and Japanese surrender documents, American war weaponry, and various "trophies," such as captured Japanese and German weapons and uniforms. Crowds of thousands greeted the trains at each stop. On the train heading to Atlanta, "possibly the biggest attraction of all will be the fabulous jewel-studded marshal's baton taken from Nazi no. 2 Hermann Goering."[54] The train arriving in Texas had another "star" relic on board: Hitler's silverware from his house in Munich.[55] In Texarkana, a small group of reporters was invited to have a meal on the train using Hitler's silverware. Guards carefully laid out the silverware on a handsomely appointed table, to which a chef then brought a large plate of steaks. "Then the photographers came in. For 20 minutes they snapped pictures of us looking at that silverware. The steaks got cold. So did the coffee." Then the steaks, uneaten, were taken away, as was the silverware. Associated Press correspondent William Bernard, describing the strange event, insisted on being able to use a coffee spoon to stir his coffee, and after some hesitation from the guards, he "managed to get one spoon in a cup of cold coffee before it was snatched away from me, carefully polished, and put back under lock and key."[56]

Long before the Victory Loan trains rolled across the American landscape, the spectacle of the King Midas riches of the Nazis, lurid and moral in its fascination, had played out on the front pages of the world's newspapers. Since 1940, stories had appeared warning that the Nazis were looting gold, art, and other valuables in the countries they occupied. An article in the *Manchester (UK) Guardian* from March 2, 1940, for example, revealed that Poles had been forced to hand over "all articles of value which date from before 1850." These included "oil-paintings, etchings, drawings, furniture, glassware, woodcuts, all articles of silver and gold, historical autographs, manuscripts, miniatures, frames, coins, medals, and rings. No compensation will be paid for any of these, which are to be taken to Germany. Even museums are not exempt from the order, and heavy fines and imprisonment up to fifteen years are provided for those who do not comply with the Nazi order." Only German nationals in Poland were exempted, leading to a frenzied rush among the Germans to buy what they could from their Polish neighbors.[57]

Nonetheless, in the spring of 1945, as the Allies advanced into the heart of Germany, the scale of the plundering they uncovered defied all expectations. On April 4, the Thuringian village of Merkers fell to units of the Ninetieth Infantry Division of General George Patton's Third Army, leading a few days later to a startling and widely reported discovery. In a local mine, army engineers blasted a false wall to reveal a large room, about seventy-five feet wide and one hundred and fifty feet long, filled with one hundred tons of gold bullion and gold coins, silver and platinum bars, and vast hoards of foreign currency, including $2 million.[58] The division had stumbled upon the gold reserves of the Reichsbank, much of it stolen by the Nazis from central banks in Europe as well as from SS victims.

The American occupation of Berchtesgaden in early May brought with it a slew of new discoveries documenting the unimaginable riches and luxuries enjoyed by the Nazi elite. The treasures, liquid and other, that soldiers had found in the still-smoldering ruins of the Berghof were only the beginning. Louis Lochner, who had written about the Kehlsteinhaus in 1939, when it was inaccessible to all but a tiny group of Nazi elite, headed to the mysterious Eagle's Nest to see it for himself a few days after the Allied forces arrived in Berchtesgaden. Since the elevator was not functioning, he and two other correspondents in the company of a group of soldiers made the difficult hike up the steep, snow-covered mountain. Arriving at the pavilion, which Lochner likened to a "lavish castle," they were "amazed" by the "palatial dimensions of Hitler's aerie" and its "expensive appointments." Lochner carefully described each room, marveling, for example, at the massive "mauve colored sandstone" walls in the main hall, which reminded him of a medieval fortress, with its heavy oak furniture, including a round table "twelve feet in diameter," and its "huge fireplace of chocolate marble streaked with white," decorated on the inside with "figures of medieval knights on horseback." The reporter noted the costly Meissen china used in the dining room, bearing a red "Chinese dragon motif," and the fine linens and glassware, which "all bore the monogram 'A.H.'" Beyond the splendor of the rooms themselves, Lochner reported on the "immense wine and liquor cellars stocked with the finest of beverages, including cognacs dating back to 1832 and the rarest of French champagnes. There were also vast stocks of food." In reporting these discoveries, Lochner sought to "expose the myth of the fuehrer's simplicity."[59] But he also went one step further: in making analogies to castles and medieval fortresses, Lochner presented his readers with a more satisfying or comforting version of Hitler's domesticity than that offered by Miller and Sions, endowing the evil overlord with a suitably fantastical and imperious architecture. The article thus not only exposed the deceit of National Socialist propaganda, but also encouraged the reader to think, "You see, Hitler is *not* like us." On a more personal level, it allowed Lochner to revise his earlier, more positive account of the Eagle's Nest, written in March 1939, under the watchful eyes of German press censors.[60]

Lochner, who wrote several articles about Hitler's domestic spaces in 1945, was one of the few reporters writing on the topic who had known Hitler personally, having served as Berlin correspondent for the Associated Press since 1924. Indeed, he had visited the Obersalzberg in August 1932, where he had interviewed Hitler. Well versed in earlier National Socialist propaganda that claimed Hitler derived his best ideas at his mountain home, Lochner asserted that the Berghof was now "symbolic of the Fuehrer's entire work—it is totally wrecked." Like Miller and Sions, but with a focus on the extraordinary rather than the ordinary, Lochner evoked what had once been: "gone is the celebrated 30 by 20 foot window of the huge parlor which Hitler used to look across the deep valley at Bavaria's most famous mountain, the Watzmann. Gone is the spacious dining room in which he entertained European bigwigs. Gone are the reception halls and private apartments for visiting friends. Gone also are those costly paintings and sculptures which made Haus Wachenfeld a veritable art museum." Lochner speculated that the art objects "may be hidden somewhere in the mountain recesses behind Hitler's estate." He also interviewed a local resident who claimed that two days before the arrival of the Allies, the SS had "sealed with thick stones many caches in the mountains which, on opening, may yield surprises." The Berghof that Lochner evoked was thus a memory of past splendors as well as a promise of future treasures. In other words, the great riches of Hitler's domestic spaces were slipping (or being pushed) into the realm of the legendary.[61]

Following in Miller's footsteps, Lochner then visited Hitler's Munich apartment, but his description of a "sumptuous" residence bore little resemblance to hers. Lochner noted the "costly furnishings, large rooms, modern gadgets and expensive paintings." He also explored the bunker that had been built for Hitler once the war began, describing it as "one of the most modern and replete bombproof cellars in all of Germany." The ceiling of the shelter was made of "seven inch steel plates, embedded in four foot thick concrete," and "every room was separated from the next by steel doors. There was a modern little electric kitchen, a small but comfortable bedroom and several small underground living rooms." For Lochner, unlike Miller, these domestic spaces distanced Hitler from common people, rather than demonstrating the similarities between them. "The more one studies Hitler's various hide-outs," he wrote, "the more one realizes how deceitfully official propaganda built him up as a simple man of the people, whose personal wants were the most modest and whose every hour was so concentrated upon Germany's welfare that he had no time for private life."[62]

Admitting that he himself had been fooled, Lochner advised readers to reassess what had been written about Hitler's celibacy. But unlike Miller, who evoked a more-or-less conventional private life, Lochner pointed toward a different form of deviancy. A painting and bust of Hitler's niece, Geli Raubal, prompted Lochner to note that "she was reported to have committed suicide in her bedroom in this dwelling soon after Hitler's ascension to power because she was jilted by her uncle. However, the story that Hitler strangled her in a fit of passion never died." Hitler's bedroom, which Miller found unremarkable, struck Lochner "as effeminate, except that the couch-like bed was exceptionally hard. The upholstery of the couch and chairs had delicate, light colors." But in Braun's house, Lochner came closest to Miller in perceiving something almost ordinary, "some sort of bond between the Fuehrer and the former photographer's assistant." He deduced this entirely from Braun's book collection, which suggested shared interests in art and architecture and contained personal gifts from Hitler and his friends. Braun herself, however, remained an abstraction for Lochner. Based on her oil portrait, he described her as "a blue-eyed, blond, Gretchen type of Teutonic maiden."[63]

Articles such as these and, later, the Victory Loan trains served to readjust the picture of the private lives of the men who had claimed to lead Germany toward a new morality. In mid-May, a much-publicized exhibition opened in Berchtesgaden that put on display Göring's private collection of art treasures, further exposing the rapaciousness of the Nazi elite. While it was also an opportunity for those who had liberated the art to enjoy it, the exhibition's presentation and the press surrounding the show encouraged viewers and readers alike to appreciate the art more as loot than for its aesthetics. As was broadly reported, the collection contained paintings, sculpture, tapestries, rugs, and objects made of silver and gold and was valued in 1945 at $200 million—an astronomical sum when one considers, for example, that a fourteen-story apartment building with penthouse on Park Avenue in New York City could be had at the time for well below $1 million.[64] The objects had been acquired for Göring from collections throughout Europe that had either been looted or sold at "holdup" prices and had been found in or near Berchtesgaden on railcars, in a house, and in bunkers.[65] In "one of the strangest art exhibitions in history," the recovered treasures were put on display at the former Bavarian Hotel, "a rustic three-story inn" in the small town of Unterstein, on the southern edge of Berchtesgaden.[66] Although the exhibition was proudly guarded by the American 101st Airborne Division, which claimed the discoveries, security was insufficient and some of the smaller pictures on display disappeared, exemplifying the growing problem of more serious looting by American soldiers.[67]

Among the artists represented in this makeshift gallery of "tiny, pine-walled rooms" were Rembrandt, Cranach, Rubens, Boucher, Fragonard, Memling, Holbein, van der Weyden, Brueghel, van Dyke, Bellini, Andrea del Sarto, and Renoir. The quality and quantity of the artworks stunned viewers: "In one room alone are two Rembrandts—one of them a hitherto unknown portrait—the Memling Madonna, valued at $240,000, and three Cranachs." In total, there were about a thousand paintings on display, all of which, a reporter noted, were "originally intended to wind up on the walls of Goering's mansions." Richard J. H. Johnston, reporting from Berchtesgaden for the *New York Times,* said that the exhibition "proved that Hermann Goering is either one of the wealthiest men in the world or one of the most discriminating thieves in history."[68]

The show proved to be something of a blockbuster: "Scores of tourist American soldiers and officers threaded their way through the art objects and the maze of 'positively no smoking' signs." Captain Harry Anderson, an art historian serving with the 101st Airborne, who had been put in charge of locating and securing the safety of the Göring collection, had conceived the idea for the show. Despite the cramped conditions and security problems, the exhibition was not without its professional touches, including a guide who "patiently lectured to those interested in learning what they were looking at. He was Walter Andreas Hofer, Goering's chief curator." Hofer, who had also been Göring's chief purchasing agent, and was thus deeply involved in the ransacking of European collections, insisted that everything had been properly purchased and that he was not a Nazi, a claim that prompted knowing smirks from the G. I.'s listening to his tour. In remarks that were widely reported by the press, Hofer boasted of having successfully competed against Hitler's art agents in the race to acquire the most desirable masterpieces, thus implicating the Führer in the looting. Moreover, "damning evidence of [art] larceny on a stupendous scale" involving Göring and Hitler had been found in the Bavarian Neuschwanstein Castle in mid-May 1945, and further evidence of Hitler's involvement had turned up among his personal effects at the Berghof: twelve albums of looted artworks with indications that "he had been thumbing through the volumes, perhaps to select some for his mountain hide-out." As one reporter sarcastically commented on the voracious art collecting activities of the top Nazis, "They were all gentlemen of culture."[69]

The sensational discoveries of Nazi hordes of art, gold, and other treasures came so quickly in the first weeks of the Allied advance into Germany that there was barely time to absorb the news of one fantastical stash before another would surface. In June 1945, the press announced the discovery by American troops of a Nazi treasure hoard that eclipsed the one found in Merkers and that was valued at $5 billion. It consisted primarily of foreign and domestic securities that represented the main national wealth of Austria and Bavaria as well as stolen jewelry, gold bullion, and church objects, such as a solid gold tabernacle from a church in Prague. For most people, $5 billion was a surreal, almost imaginary, figure, like so many of the values being attached to the finds of Nazi plunder. A story from May 29, 1945, in the *Chicago Daily Tribune* about U. S. Army Sergeant George Murphy, who set the blast that revealed Hitler's gold in the Merkers mine, helps give a more human perspective on these numbers. A preliminary inventory of the gold, silver, and currency found there valued the find at over $520 million; Murphy, on an emergency furlough to visit his seriously ill mother, arrived home in Seattle, Washington, with "15 cents in his pocket."[70]

In July 1945, the press reported that the Allies had brought all the looted wealth they had discovered to the Reichsbank building in Frankfurt am Main in order to inventory the accumulated caches. The task was Herculean. An article in the *Chicago Daily Tribune* described paper currency "stacked in canvas bags from floor to ceiling," bullion "stacked like cordwood," and barrels brimming with pearls, rubies, and sapphires. Judy Barden, a reporter allowed to see the vaults, wrote that "Ali Baba and his 40 thieves had nothing on Adolf Hitler and his band of robbers and murderers."[71] If such fictional metaphors seemed to best capture the immensity of the riches, the crimes they represented were all too real. Among the recovered SS loot were wooden cases filled with "gold and silver fillings from the teeth of tens of thousands of murdered Jews." In another stash, "thousands of wedding rings stripped from the fingers of women victims of the Nazis in Germany, Greece, Poland, and other occupied countries were strung on ropes like country sausages."[72] To speak of Hitler's modest way of life or the self-sacrifice of his elites in the face of such colossally criminal greed was, in a word, obscene.

But with the death of one myth arose another that would exert its own profound and long-lasting fascination. In his famous images, Heinrich Hoffmann had presented the Berghof as all surface: the countless scenes he recorded of Hitler on the terrace, in the midst of friends, children, and dogs, enjoying the sunshine and fresh air, were meant to suggest to the German people a goodness and wholesomeness that was aboveboard and visible—what you see is what you get. The discoveries that followed in the wake of the Allies' arrival transformed the Obersalzberg into a place of subterranean mysteries, secret caverns, and buried treasure. Indeed, Hitler's former residence came to resemble the folk legends about the neighboring Untersberg, which imagined kings and their courts hidden inside the mountain. The surface life of the Obersalzberg now seemed deceptive, and attention turned to what lay beneath, to the porous mountain the Nazis had created and where, some believed, their treasures still lay buried.

Within weeks of the Allied capture of Hitler's homes, then, a very different image of the private Führer began to emerge. Secrecy, luxury, and crime replaced accessibility, modesty, and morality. In the process, the question of what had been at stake in the careful construction of the earlier image of the Führer's domesticity and why it had exerted such enormous appeal both within and beyond Germany's borders began to be lost. The revelations of the magnitude of the Nazis' deception could be used to conveniently excuse German and non-German audiences alike for having previously been taken in by Hitler's publicists. Rather than contemplate the disturbing possibility of complicity in having once enjoyed and willingly accepted the earlier images of the Führer as a modest man and kindly neighbor, despite ample evidence to the contrary, it was easier to see oneself as yet another of his "selected dupes."

11 "ADOLF DOESN'T LIVE HERE ANYMORE"

The Troublesome Afterlife of Hitler's Homes

At the war's end, it was clear that the Obersalzberg would never be the same again. During their reign, the Nazis had violently uprooted the people and structures that had grown up over centuries on the mountain side, replacing them with a military compound of barracks, underground bunkers, defense installations, and luxury buildings for the political elite. The Allies' cataclysmic air-raid attack on April 25, 1945, had transformed the landscape itself, ripping trees to shreds, pushing up new hills, and hollowing out vast craters. It also left behind shattered and burned heaps of architecture and twisted, impassable roads. In its ruined state, this Alpine resort would hardly seem to have been the type of place to attract the tourists who had flocked to its natural charms earlier in the century. And yet, when a journalist for the *Christian Science Monitor* toured the Obersalzberg in the summer of 1945, he noted that "What used to be Hitler's closely guarded mountain retreat here is now a sort of Coney Island sideshow with free admission, patrons approach the 100,000 mark and autographs from all the states of the Union are written on the walls. Or rather what is left of the walls."[1] Instead of staying away, then, tourists had come back to the Obersalzberg in force, but the attractions were no longer just the clean air and scenic mountain views. Hitler's connection to the place was a considerable part of the draw, creating both an economic opportunity for local inhabitants and a political headache for government authorities, a tension that never quite went away.

The occupation of Berchtesgaden that began in May 1945 established a U.S. Army presence that would continue for the next fifty years. That summer, the United States Forces European Theater Special Services, concerned about the morale of U.S. troops remaining in Europe, who were no longer fighting but not yet permitted to return home, set up recreation programs and areas for military personnel.[2] One of the most popular destinations was Berchtesgaden, and in the summer of 1945, there came a "steady stream of sightseers, mainly G.I.'s and nurses. But there have been senators, congressmen, generals, and other 'distinguished visitors' as well."[3] To Ronald Stead, writing for the *Christian Science Monitor,* the atmosphere in Berchtesgaden could not have been more different from that of the wrecked and depressed German cities he had traveled through on his tour of the defeated nation.[4] "The fairground touch first became noticeable," he wrote, when he drove into town "and saw a billboard bearing the words 'Hitler's Home' and an arrow indicating the route to it."[5] Thus began the victors' triumphal parade to the Berghof, inverting the pilgrimage that had taken place in the 1930s, when Germans had come by the thousands to pay their respect to their almighty Führer. The victors relished the destruction of Hitler's domestic haven, while also being impressed by its remains.

Stopping at a hotel that had once housed Hitler's guests, Stead noted a corporal in the 101st American Airborne Division at the reception desk handing out maps and advice about the area's attractions, including the Eagle's Nest, which he warned Stead not to visit in the heavy rain and mist, when "it would be too easy to launch a jeep into space at one of the hairpin curves with a precipitous drop over the side." The next day, after an arduous climb, Stead finally made it to the pavilion atop the Kehlstein and marveled at the views: "Especially at sundown on a clear day when the jagged Bavarian peaks take on a deepening lavender hue touched off with crimson splashes and jet-black shadows. In the words of one GI, 'It's a straight Walt Disney.'"[6] Beyond the spectacular scenery, the Eagle's Nest also drew sightseers because of its pristine condition—with "no scar of war" showing, it was almost as it had been in its Nazi heyday. "The only difference," noted an officer, "is that Adolf doesn't live here anymore."[7]

The subterranean world of the Berghof's bunkers provided a similar, although more covert, thrill. By then, the tunnels were off-limits to the public and guarded by soldiers. Despite the rounds of looting that had taken place after the bombing, the underground rooms still contained a good deal of furniture and objects, which gave them the uncanny feel of a living relic. Price Day, foreign correspondent for the *Baltimore Sun,* was permitted to tour the tunnels alone in June 1945. Compared to the crowd milling about in the Berghof overhead, Day noted that he was "absolutely and eerily alone" in the dark tunnels and soon lost his way. The tunnels were in excellent condition; as he observed, their "plaster and cabinets look as though they had been put in last week." Many of the cupboards were still stocked, including with SS glassware and china, but what caught Day's eye were the "books by the thousands in new, pine bookcases ranging from leather-bound, fifteen volume histories of architecture to pamphlets on how to bake a cake."[8] Ronald Stead, who was also given access to the tunnels, commented on Hitler's simply decorated bedroom, where he tried the bed and found it uncomfortable.[9] Like the Eagle's Nest, the bunkers revealed the bizarre mindset of the Nazi elite, which combined a familiar domesticity with delusions of god-like power and preparations for an end-times battle. It was as if one had encountered a demonic Zeus on Mount Olympus reading a cookbook in a cozy armchair and sipping tea from fine china, while his thunderbolts hung on the wall in preparation for war with the Giants. And it was this mixture of the familiar and the fantastical that made such spaces utterly irresistible to visitors—a real-world Coney Island of haunted mazes and horror houses that had threatened to colonize the world.

Reemerging aboveground, Stead ended his explorations with the Berghof's kitchen, then the best-preserved of its rooms.[10] But most visitors came to see the famous large window in the Great Hall and to stand where Hitler had stood and look out over the scenery that had inspired his plans for world domination. The Great Hall was a shambles, according to Day: "The big main room is burnt down to its concrete foundations. Nothing is left except remarkably few pieces of charred wood, the blackened frames . . . that once were on the ceiling but are now on the floor, some dozens of chair and couch springs and some American chewing-gum wrappers."[11] The window glass had been shattered in the Allied attack, leaving an open rectangle framing the scenery. Richard Reiter, who served as a guide and interpreter for the Special Services in Berchtesgaden from 1946 to 1948 and gave hundreds of tours to G. I.'s and officials, reports that there were two must-sees on the list of most visitors: the Berghof's great window and the Eagle's Nest. The window had become iconic during the Third Reich, while rumors of the magnificence of the Kehlsteinhaus had not been confirmed until the war's end. Both sites were defined by their spectacular natural views, and by appropriating Hitler's vistas, people seemed to believe that they gained some insight into his psyche and the formidable will and power that had almost brought the world to its knees.[12] They thus unwittingly replicated propaganda from the Third Reich that had similarly encouraged Germans to empathetically share the masterful gaze of the Führer in nature, as experienced through his mountain home.[13]

Having seen like Hitler, tourists to the Berghof also wanted to be seen, to inscribe their presence on a house that itself was lodged in the minds of millions. According to Day's report in the *Baltimore Sun,* the house "now has become the three-dimensional roster of a good part of the United States Army, whose names, ratings, home towns and sometimes serial numbers are scratched on every square foot of the blackened walls. Only strips near the ceilings are unmarked."[14] For the soldiers signing their names, it was a personal, self-made memorial to the long and bitter struggle to defeat the homeowner. Stead interpreted the ruins more broadly, as "a symbolic monument to the collapse and destruction in a wider sense of the house that Hitler built."[15] In similar terms, Philip Hamburger, writing in the *New Yorker* in June 1945, called the site "a grotesque and instructive heap of rubbish."[16] A year later, an article in the *Christian Science Monitor* reported that Hitler's home would "not be rebuilt, but left in ruins as a symbol for future generations of the condition in which he left all Germany." But "even in this state," the article continued, "visitors will be able to get some idea of the sumptuousness of what Nazi propaganda described as 'his simple home.'"[17] Thus, the ruined Berghof would serve to expose the Nazi lies about the private Hitler that it had once served to generate. Similarly, for Day, the house—along with the surrounding service buildings, such as the SS barracks, greenhouse, offices, and workers' camp—revealed the enormity of the cult around Hitler, or as the G. I. on duty guarding "Hitler's door" put it, "it seems like a lot of trouble for just one man."[18] Missing from these projections onto the wreckage was a more direct connection between the perpetrators and their crimes. The propensity to frame the ruins' meaning in generalized or abstract terms suggests the lingering influence of Nazi propaganda, which, while acknowledging Hitler's mountain retreat as an inspirational wellspring for his mission and plans, had also insisted on its status as a place apart from work and government business—despite all evidence to the contrary. Local residents of Berchtesgaden, for their part, had little interest in reinforcing the connection between the Nazis on the hill and the catastrophe in Europe.

Perhaps the utter physical devastation of the Obersalzberg and its emptiness also played a role in this dissociation. Unlike the concentration and work camps, the very essence of which spoke to the Nazis' crimes, or the ruined German cities populated by a resentful, defeated enemy, evil seemed, to some visitors, to have left the Obersalzberg when its former residents had fled or died. Henry Taylor, writing for the *Los Angeles Times* in May 1945, soon bored of touring Hitler's house: "You can poke around the ruins of Hitler's valley house, as dead and uninteresting as a bashed-in derby hat, only so long." He found Hitler's "hide-out" on the Kehlstein much more attractive a place to visit, partly because, as noted previously, it still seemed to retain some presence of its former owner.[19] A few weeks later, *Baltimore Sun* correspondent Day, emerging from his tour of the bunkers, summed up his visit to the Berghof as follows:

> The place isn't interesting anymore. It isn't even evil now, and if there is a lesson in it, it is merely the old lesson of vanity. This place is now almost intolerably dull.
>
> You glance at a shelf filled with Christmas-tree decorations, including candle holders with old wax at the bottom, and go back up the 67 steps and out into the clean air and down the mountain.[20]

For many of Day's readers, the pronouncement of the Berghof as dead and boring must have come as a relief. The fortress of evil that had held the world prisoner was now reduced to the contents of an interesting garage sale. Its very dullness and the ability to walk away from someone else's secondhand junk must have seemed like liberty itself.

For others, however, just being there and experiencing Hitler's banal domesticity was deeply meaningful. Gertrude Stein and Alice B. Toklas were among those who visited the Berghof in the summer of 1945. Despite her literary radicalism, Stein held political views that were conservative, even reactionary, and she admired strongmen such as General Francisco Franco and Marshal Philippe Pétain.[21] Stein had remained in France throughout the Nazi occupation, living with her lesbian lover under highly dangerous conditions. The Gestapo visited her Paris apartment during the war, Stein reported, and, not finding her at home, "stole linen and dresses and shoes and kitchen utensils and dishes and bed covers and pillows," although not, significantly, her highly valuable collection of modern art.[22] As Janet Malcolm asks in her biography of the two women, "How had the pair of elderly Jewish lesbians escaped the Nazis?" She and other critics have suggested that Stein's friend, Bernard Faÿ, a Vichy official and Gestapo agent, protected her and Toklas, as did Stein's endorsement of Pétain and his pro-Hitler regime.[23] Others, however, have argued that her collaborationist activities have been exaggerated, and that Stein and Toklas were also protected by their neighbors.[24] In 1944, she and Toklas were photographed for *Life* magazine by Carl Mydans (who was traveling with a U.S. Seventh Army unit) in front of their village house in eastern France. Stein suggested the title for the article: "The Liberation of Gertrude Stein."[25] Now, at the war's end and at the insistence, Stein wrote, of her friends in the U.S. 441st Troop Carrier Group, "off we went to visit Hitler."[26]

Stein chronicled her German trip for *Life* magazine, a journey that—apart from some stray luggage problems—she seemed to enjoy thoroughly, especially the stay in Berchtesgaden. The story appeared in August 1945, almost six years after the magazine had published a largely admiring feature on the Berghof. Whereas in October 1939, *Life* readers had gazed at lush color images of the interiors of Hitler's home, described as being furnished "in very good taste" and "the comfortable kind of rooms a man likes," they now were presented with Stein and a group of American soldiers standing on the ruined terrace, the charred frame of the great window behind them, and striking "Hitler's pose," an audacious gesture made to look like (although not quite) the Nazi salute (fig. 69).[27] This act of mockery through mimicry fit with the tone of the article, which expressed the buoyant good cheer of the victor.

The group stopped first to see Göring's art collection, which Stein appreciated, despite being a collector of distinctly more modern tastes. She gave Göring, however, little credit, ascribing its merits to his having had "excellent advice, apparently." The tone of the article then became almost giddy as the time arrived for their Berghof tour:

> And then we all climbed into our transport, that is our cars and off we went to Hitler. That was exciting. It was exciting to be there, the other houses were bombed but Hitler's was not it was burned but not down and there we were in that big window where Hitler dominated the world a bunch of GIs just gay and happy. It really was the first time I saw our boys really gay and careless, really forgetting their burdens and just being foolish kids, climbing up and around and on top, while Miss Toklas and

I sat comfortably and at home on garden chairs on Hitler's balcony. It was funny it was completely funny, it was more than funny it was absurd and yet so natural.[28]

Although it was left to the reader to decide exactly what Stein meant by "absurd and yet so natural," she clearly delighted in the existence of the ordinary—horseplay, sunning oneself in garden chairs—in this apocalyptic wasteland.[29] And in her euphoria, one hears not only the triumphal voice of the victor but also, beneath it, a survivor's relief. Stein's life and work were deeply rooted in and dependent on a familiar domestic routine with Toklas, and when the war came, she feared the unmooring of her center of gravity.[30] Indeed, despite pleas from friends and American officials, she refused to leave her adopted nation for the safety of a neutral or Allied country.[31] While Stein did not overtly identify as Jewish or, it seems, feel specifically threatened by Nazi persecution, her decision to stay appears to have been driven above all by the need for the comforts and sustenance of home. Later, when France was liberated, she felt belatedly the terror of what might have been lost.[32] The encounter with Hitler's domesticity in its ruined state was no doubt joyous in that it confirmed the security of her own.

As Stein and Toklas sat on the terrace, the soldiers explored the ruins. "And then they began to hunt souvenirs, they found photographs and some X-ray photographs that they were convinced were taken of Hitler's arm after the attempt on his life. What I wanted was a radiator, Hitler did have splendid radiators, and there was one all alone which nobody seemed to notice, but a radiator a large radiator, what could I do with it, they asked, put it on a terrace and grow flowers over it, I said, but our courage was not equal to the weight of it and we sadly left it behind us." This desire to appropriate and reformulate Hitler's domesticity tamed the dictator through a kind of Dadaist reinvention. Hitler's lingering presence was transformed into something harmless and absurd—the much-feared despot reduced to a radiator converted into a trellis. It also rebalanced the score: the Gestapo had taken Stein's linen, so she would take Hitler's radiator. But even if she had to leave it behind (taking instead the X-ray of Hitler's injured arm), Stein departed happy: "After we had played around till it was late off we went, down the hills and that day was over, it was a wonderful day."[33] To casually describe a visit to Hitler's home as "a wonderful day," as if it were, indeed, an outing to Coney Island, insisted, moreover, on Stein's fearlessness. What had once been a symbol of the Führer's terrifying power was

AFTERLIFE OF HITLER'S HOMES

Fig. 69. Troop Carrier Command, photograph of Gertrude Stein and G.I.'s doing "Hitler's pose on Hitler's balcony at Berchtesgaden," *Life*, August 6, 1945, 56.

now, in her eyes, nothing more than a victor's playground, both pleasurable and banal.

By 1947, occupied Berchtesgaden was being touted in the press as "one of the finest recreation areas in the world." Victor Jones reported in the *Daily Boston Globe* that "from all over Europe, Army and War Department civilian personnel come here for from three to seven-day visits." The 150-square-mile area of the Berchtesgaden command now offered "14 hotels with a total of 750 beds and few of them are ever empty." The sprawling resort, which catered to 150,000 visitors in 1947, was managed by twenty officers, an equal number of Women's Army Corps members, and one hundred enlisted men, "with the help of virtually the whole native population." The demand was unsurprising given the generous and inexpensive offerings: "Your G.I., the civilians and their dependents here can get for a couple of bucks a day the kind of luxurious resort living which before the war only titled Englishmen and American millionaires could afford." A room in any of the hotels cost only one dollar per night, meals were free for soldiers, and drinks cost just thirty cents. Additionally, one could sign up for a plethora of free activities, including ski lessons with "the best instructors in Europe" and hunting with a guide for elk and deer. Other entertainments were also at hand: "Every hotel has an orchestra at meal times and a night club complete with floor shows and plenty of Bavarian partners are available every evening." Further evoking the victor's sexual spoils, Jones reported that "the G.I. can even have his breakfast in bed. It's served to him by a fraulein, I'm told, and they have learned to make the soldier reach for the tray instead of setting it down, and to depart while the guest's hands are still engaged in holding the tray."[34]

Despite competing attractions, tours of the ruined houses of Hitler and his neighbors remained popular among American and Allied visitors. The desire to collect souvenirs also continued unabated, even in the face of an ever-diminishing supply. Indeed, once its contents had vanished, the Berghof itself began to disappear as souvenir-hunters carried away pieces of the structure itself. Pilgrims in the early 1930s had taken pieces of Hitler's wooden fence. In the postwar period, chunks of the marble fireplace in the Great Hall were particularly desirable, as were Hitler's green bathroom tiles. Guides did a brisk business selling the stones and tiles for one dollar each. When all the tiles had been stripped from Hitler's bathroom, "a smart local businessman manufactured thousands of new tiles for sale to tourists."[35]

A sanctioned souvenir trade also grew up locally in the sale of postcards and other mementoes, including handcrafted photographic albums that have since found their way into numerous archival collections.[36] Titled "Souvenir of Berchtesgaden" or "Souvenir of the Eagle's Nest," the small albums appear to have been created by a photographic studio in Berchtesgaden and, although not identical, follow a similar format: black-and-white photographs are pasted onto the thick paper and labeled in English using white ink and Gothic-style handwriting.[37] The albums begin with and give pride of place to the exterior and interiors of Hitler's house, both in its Wachenfeld and Berghof iterations. Other buildings on the Obersalzberg, namely the Platterhof Hotel, SS barracks, and Bormann's and Göring's houses, are also included, along with multiple views of and from the Kehlstein. In this way, the albums, while presenting an overview of the Nazis' Alpine retreat, focused their attention on the two buildings most closely associated with Hitler and where tourists usually lingered: the Berghof and Eagle's Nest.

More interesting than the images, however, is their presentation. The composer of the albums juxtaposed images from the Nazis' heyday on the Obersalzberg (using either actual or reproductions of Nazi postcards, particularly those of Heinrich Hoffmann) with views after the Allied attack in 1945. The "before," or pre-bombing, images appear first in the albums, followed by the "after," or postwar, images toward the end. Thus, Hoffmann's famous photograph of the large window in the Great Hall majestically framing the Untersberg found a twisted echo in an image of Hitler's ruined Berghof glimpsed through the charred and dangling roof beams of Bormann's bombed house (fig. 70).[38] Similarly, the newly expanded Berghof pictured in a pristine winter Alpine landscape appeared later from a similar angle as an exploded shell on a devastated hillside, and the sharp rectilinear forms of the intact SS barracks transformed on the next page into cows grazing in their ruins.[39] Most of the photographs, however, showed the Nazi buildings and Obersalzberg landscape as they had once been.

Through this selection and arrangement of images—coupled with the old-fashioned handwriting as well as the albums' intimate format and crafty, homemade feel, which evoked a personal or familial object—the books strongly cultivated a sense of nostalgia. That these keepsakes of the lost Nazi mountain were produced by the defeated for the victors reinforces their strangeness. Nonetheless, the number of such albums in American collections suggests that they appealed to American soldiers and officials touring the sites they had helped to destroy. One wonders whether an American reader would have felt the sentimental pull fostered by the German maker, or whether he or she would have read the book and its before-and-after narrative differently—as a tale of morality and proof of justice delivered. In any case, the albums constructed a hermetic view of the rise and fall of the regime that once again ignored its victims. Indeed, it was purely an architectural story, leaving out people altogether, who were nowhere to be seen in the photographs.

By the early 1950s, German nostalgia for the Obersalzberg's Nazi past had become a political and public problem. For four years after the war's end, the Nazi ruins had been off-limits to Germans unless they were accompanied by an American host. Official tours were conducted only in English, and for Allied or approved foreign visitors. That began to change in May 1949, when the U.S. Army took the first steps to lift restrictions to the site, a decision that sparked concerns about the landscape's moral toxicity.[40] An Associated Press article from December 1949 asked, "Is Hitler's

Fig. 70. Page from "Souvenir of Berchtesgaden," a souvenir album sold in Berchtesgaden in the postwar period.

former mountain retreat likely to become a Nazi shrine?" It cited efforts undertaken by Colonel Stanley Grogan, commander of the Berchtesgaden military post and former U.S. Army public relations director, to avoid such an outcome, which included changing place-names associated with the Nazis as well as removing "the bust of Hitler which used to be on display in the Eagle's nest" and storing it in the basement.[41] When problems did arise, however, they derived less from material objects than from their interpreters. By 1951, twenty freelance German guides offered tours of the Obersalzberg, and some did not hide their National Socialist sympathies. To the contrary, they delivered eulogies on the "unfortunate" end of the Nazi regime and even spoke of the "resurrection from the ruins." Others compensated for their lack of knowledge about the site with ghoulish details. One guide enjoyed revealing Hitler's torture chamber, a room that did not actually exist in the Berghof (although the Gestapo torture chambers elsewhere were real enough). As the number of daily visitors soared into the thousands, fears grew that once-"harmless" visits impelled by historic curiosity were tipping into sensationalism and pilgrimage.[42]

This period also saw the rise of neo-Nazi groups in Germany, and as apprehensions spread that democracy was faltering once again in Europe, the press was quick to pick up on rumors that fascism had returned to the Obersalzberg.[43] In the summer of 1951, the *Münchner Illustrierte* (Munich Illustrated) sent its senior journalist, Jürgen Neven-du Mont, on an undercover investigation of the German-language tours. Among the guides was Göring's former house manager, Herr Zychski, who nostalgically showed off his own destroyed apartment in Göring's bombed-out chalet. Standing on the Berghof terrace, Zychski reminisced about the Führer's fondness for German children and the parties he had hosted for them "here, where the red umbrellas once stood." Inside, Neven-du Mont heard another guide praising the modesty of the furnishings, and his impressed listeners commenting admiringly on what "a truly beautiful and yet simple house" it had been and bemoaning its destruction as "a crying shame." The guide added that the Führer had lived more simply than the politicians in Bonn, a comment met with approving murmurs. In the Berghof's main hall, Neven-du Mont described "how the guides point out in particular a block of red stone in the 'Führer's fireplace, which is getting smaller day by day, since pieces are constantly being taken as souvenirs. 'Many want to take home some of the Führer's fire,' explained the guides." Neven-du Mont considered their narrative approach a cross between propaganda and a "Here-you-see-Hitler's-toothbrush" type of sensational tourism.[44]

While some listeners reacted with disgust to the guides' National Socialist sympathies, including foreign visitors who understood German, others were emboldened. An older German man, mistakenly believing the undercover reporter to be a like-minded compatriot, agreed to be photographed taking a piece of the Berghof ruin as a memento, explaining that "I have remained loyal to my Führer. We will never again experience an age of such beauty and greatness." Neven-du Mont later saw him at one of the many souvenir kiosks buying photographs and a drawing of "The Obersalzberg, Then and Now." The reporter further noted that tourists were being sold tickets to the off-limits bunkers, the walls of which were inscribed not only with the names of people from around the world, but also with swastikas, SS runes, and messages, such as "Long live the SS!" and "Hail to our Great Führer," that left no doubt as to the scribblers' political leanings. Finally, the article included a photograph of a handkerchief decorated with an image of the Berghof and flowers, the kind of kitschy merchandise that even Goebbels had tried to ban. Neven-du Mont thus concluded that the

Obersalzberg's burgeoning Hitler tourism represented a multifaceted danger: proselytizing by guides and visitors to a younger and impressionable generation, encouraging nationalist pilgrims, sentimentalizing terror, and damaging Bavaria's international reputation and tourist industry. He urged the authorities to intervene and asked "whether this particular sort of tourism is healthy for the state of Bavaria."[45]

Neven-du Mont's story, which was also carried by the influential *Süddeutsche Zeitung,* infuriated Social Democratic politicians, many of whom had spent time in concentration camps or been forced into exile under the Nazi regime. After reading the article, Social Democrat Wilhelm Hoegner, Bavaria's minister of the interior, wrote a letter, dated July 12, to the district administrator in Berchtesgaden asking for verification of National Socialist activities on the Obersalzberg and stating that if Neven-du Mont's account proved to be true, "it would be advisable to cordon off the entire area and leave it to the chamois and ibex."[46] Satisfying as the thought may have been, replacing unrepentant Nazis with wild goats clearly was not a permanent solution. Sealing off the ruins, while making them inaccessible to pilgrims, would also preserve them, effectively freezing the site in 1945.[47] For the time being, however, local authorities ordered the bunkers on the Obersalzberg to be walled up, the road to the Kehlsteinhaus closed to cars, the eviction of tour guides from the ruins, and the confiscation of souvenirs.[48] On August 2, Hoegner and a group of Bavarian cabinet ministers toured the site and later met with delegates from the area to discuss the next steps.[49] The majority of the visiting statesmen favored obliterating the entire architectural presence of the Nazis on the Obersalzberg, including the Kehlstein. The local spokesmen focused their efforts on making a case for preserving the Eagle's Nest, which some considered an essentially blameless building (barely visited by Hitler and distinct from his residential compound), and hoped that experiencing the stunning views from the pavilion as well as realizing the enormous technical difficulties posed by its dismantling and removal would help to shift the cabinet members' opinion.[50]

The day after the politicians' visit, the *Berchtesgadener Anzeiger* (Berchtesgaden Advertiser), a conservative local paper owned by a former National Socialist Party member, surveyed its readers on the "dictatorial" handling of the Obersalzberg's future, which it felt should be decided by those who would be most affected—the area's residents. It printed what it claimed was a representative sample of the three hundred replies it received, most of which opposed clearing away the Nazi ruins or razing extant build-

AFTERLIFE OF HITLER'S HOMES

ings. A respondent described as "A Housewife" asked: "Is this what democracy looks like—a couple of gentlemen decree, like in 1933?" A man identified as "A Clerk" considered such measures an economic waste in a region of few resources and suggested reusing materials from the ruins for local housing. Wrecking the Kehlsteinhaus, he added, was "completely absurd," and if the intention was to avoid memorializing the Nazi regime through its structures, then, by extension, the government should dig up the Autobahns. "A Precision Engineer" asserted that the war had destroyed enough, and that the money intended for demolition would be better spent repairing salvageable buildings to help ease postwar overcrowding. Another reader wondered why keeping the Berghof ruins should be objectionable when other countries had preserved the monuments of history's "greatest political criminals," a group that in his mind included Napoleon, the emperor Nero in Italy, and the Turkic conqueror, Timur. Similarly, "An Employee" remarked that Joachim von Ribbentrop's summer residence near Salzburg had been converted by the Austrian government into a palatial hotel that attracted high-class foreign guests and brought the state needed foreign currency, thus transforming a legacy of the former regime into a positive benefit for the people. "A Catechist" proposed sealing the Berghof to visitors and hanging a banner across the void of its great window proclaiming "*Sic transit gloria mundi*" (Thus passes the glory of the world), as a reminder to politicians of the transience of their preaching and plans. He also warned that if the Obersalzberg were to avoid becoming a fascist pilgrimage site, the removal of the ruins had to be accompanied by the creation of jobs and housing for the dispossessed Germans who had arrived in Berchtesgaden from former parts of the Reich, and that eradicating the remains of a disastrous past without creating new life would be meaningless. Another reader suggested that the endless stories about Hitler and his cronies in the tabloids did more to promote fascism than any ruin.[51]

Because the Obersalzberg was still a U.S. military post in 1951, German officials consulted with George Shuster, U.S. land commissioner to Bavaria, on the site's development. On August 6, Waldemar von Knoeringen, chairman of the Bavarian Social Democratic Party, announced the Cabinet's decision to demolish the Berghof and surrounding ruins and replant the area with trees and grass. Knoeringen explained that the vast geographies of ruins within Germany sufficiently testified to the legacy of the National Socialist regime, and that there was no reason to foster neo-Nazism by preserving the ruins on the Obersalzberg as a memorial.[52] Nonetheless,

Shuster confirmed that the Eagle's Nest would be saved as a reminder to posterity of the social irresponsibility of the Nazi regime, which had built castles in the sky while depriving its own people.[53] In November, in light of the opposition from Berchtesgaden residents, the U.S. High Commissioner formally reinforced the demolition initiative by making it a condition for returning the Obersalzberg properties (Bormann's house, Göring's house, SS barracks, and the Berghof) to the Bavarian state: namely, that "the buildings be razed completely and all structural evidences of their location be erased."[54] The American authorities thus passed on a responsibility that they themselves had neglected for years. Ironically, when the U.S. Army had tried to demolish the ruins in 1947, in part because of fears of their structural instability, they had been stopped from doing so by the U.S. Special Services, who were making a hefty profit charging admission to the site.[55]

For months following the August announcement, the *Anzeiger* actively campaigned against the proposed demolition. It gave various reasons to preserve the ruins, but above all emphasized their value as an attraction for the local tourist trade and their ability to bring in foreign currency. The numbers seemed to support its claim: from July to October 1951, 136,560 people toured the Obersalzberg ruins, 80 percent of whom were non-Germans. But while the Social Democrats argued that it was the beauty of nature that brought visitors to the mountain, the *Anzeiger* insisted that they came for the ruins, and it looked to the American media for proof. It quoted at length, for example, from an article in the *Denver Post* that described the Berghof ruins as Berchtesgaden's main point of attraction for foreign travelers. In mid-August, it also cited a recent media story of a "well known American hotelier" who had offered to buy the ruins of Hitler's Berghof with the intention of transporting and reconstructing them at one of his hotels in the Rocky Mountains. The paper implied that if a successful capitalist recognized the Berghof ruins as a tourist goldmine and proposed setting up a Hitler theme park in the American West, then Bavarians would be foolish to miss out on the economic opportunity presented to them by the original sites of their own history.[56]

Meanwhile, a rival newspaper, the *Südost-Kurier* (Southeast Courier)—based in the nearby town of Bad Reichenhall and led by a Social Democrat, Josef Felder—fought just as vigorously and just as long for the eradication of the Nazi ruins on the Obersalzberg.[57] Felder, "an old Dachau alumnus," antagonized conservatives in the region with his insistence on confronting its

Nazi past and resurgent fascist sympathies.[58] To contest the *Anzeiger's* claim that all local residents wanted to preserve the ruins, he gave demolition proponents a voice. Felder also agreed with his party in treating the ruins as an essentially political, rather than economic, issue.[59] A November editorial by Sepp Kiene, a Social Democratic delegate to the Bavarian parliament from neighboring Traunstein, pointed out that the decision to eradicate the ruins had been taken by democratically elected representatives, whose understanding of the public good extended beyond the self-interests of a kiosk owner on the Obersalzberg. As West Germany tried to legitimize itself in the world's eyes, larger issues were at stake, he argued, than the profits of local merchants.[60]

For many West Germans, the search for some form of normalcy after the war involved developing selective memories of the Third Reich. As historians have amply documented, although a few localities erected memorials to victims before 1950, a broader desire for an honest confrontation with the nation's crimes took decades to develop. In 1968, a young generation rebelled against the lingering amnesia and pushed for greater openness in exploring National Socialism's legacy, and, particularly, their parents' complicity in the Holocaust, which would be fully realized, however, only in the period after the Cold War ended in 1989.[61] In the context of this long national aversion to atoning for and commemorating victims' suffering, the Obersalzberg stands out by virtue of how early it confronted, as a community, the preservation of National Socialism's physical remains. But whether this can be construed as a true reckoning with the past is doubtful. The mountain sites were associated with the regime's perpetrators, not its victims, and pro-preservation forces considered them to be largely innocuous—a gangsters' vacation colony. Among this faction, the ruins' proposed removal stirred little self-critical awareness with regard to profiting from a genocidal regime, but rather fostered a sense of victimhood in the perceived loss of economic freedom at the hands of remote state politicians and American occupiers. Pro-demolition advocates, by contrast, viewed the mountain as a place of almost cultic power, as seen in the dangerous magnetism of Hitler's house. But while seeking to stamp out fascist "cells" drawn to it, they were equally concerned with protecting Bavaria's image as a reformed, democratic state. Perhaps as a result, they gingerly avoided the thorny question of just how widespread sympathy for Hitler remained in the area—which did not, however, stop the pro-preservation camp from asserting that the vocal attention brought to a few bad apples had effectively smeared the entire local population.[62] Thus, discussions about what to do with the ruins revolved less around respecting the memory of past victims or standing accountable for past sins than around defending current interests. Both sides had much at stake in their opposing interpretations of the site, for which there seemed to be no room for compromise.

Within weeks of Knoeringen's announcement, the issue had become so emotionally fraught that the debate between the *Anzeiger* and the *Kurier* about the "Obersalzberg question" spilled off their pages and into the area's beer halls. The escalating tensions and rhetoric attracted international media attention, reminding some a little too closely of beer-hall agitations in Bavaria thirty years earlier. In an article for *Harper's Magazine*, American writer Paul Moor recounted how the newspaper exchanges devolved into shouting matches: "A seven-column editorial on the front page of the *Anzeiger's* September 7 issue categorically denied the existence of neo-Nazism in Berchtesgaden. At a public meeting the following day, Herr Felder of the rival *Kurier*, took the *Anzeiger* to task for this statement; late in the evening a cry of 'The real and only culprits are the Jews!' rent the air, and things disintegrated into tumultuous disorder." Later that month, the Social Democrats held a meeting to rally pro-demolition forces, but hundreds of vocal opponents turned up, and the evening again ended badly.[63]

By October, Moor continued, the Social Democrats were worried enough to organize a debate between Knoeringen and Heinz Erich Krause. Better known under his nom de plume, Hek Rau, Krause was a young man from Austria who wrote and edited a clandestine Nazi monthly, *Deutschland Brief* (Letter from Germany), and who had been a chief instigator of trouble at the local meetings. On October 26, the packed restaurant in the Berchtesgaden train station (a monumental Third Reich structure) heard Knoeringen, a seasoned politician and one of the party's finest orators, appeal to the crowd to rise above hatred in objectively assessing the issues at hand. Taking the podium, Krause adopted a different approach, insulting and goading those present; he asked Knoeringen, for example, why he bad-mouthed Hitler when he owed him his current position. (As a young man, Knoeringen had been so effective a speaker against Hitler that he had been forced to flee for his life in 1933 and spent the next twelve years in exile, working for the resistance.[64]) At the end of the night, Krause was escorted out of the room under police protection. As Moor reported, such gatherings "provided the first open proof that there might be something in what the Social Democrats were saying about a Nazi renaissance here." While opponents of the demolition had hoped protests would strengthen their cause, the unwanted media attention they drew to the region cemented the cabinet members' resolution, prompting them to give the go-ahead to begin dismantling the ruins in mid-November.[65]

Göring's and Bormann's houses, pulverized by Allied bombs, were among the first to go.[66] Visiting the Obersalzberg in the winter of 1951, Moor noticed some trucks by the ruins, into which men were shoveling the rubble. "It somehow seemed an anticlimactic way to raze anything with so flamboyant a history," he wrote, "but the truth is that most of the ruins were too unstable to require any blasting. It was mainly a matter of pushing them over, picking them up, and carting them off." In the debates preceding the demolition, neither side had raised the cost to taxpayers of preserving the ruins—only of what it would cost to take them down. But given the perilous condition of the structures, the government would have had to expend considerable public funds to make them safe for visitors. It is hard to imagine a newly democratic nation, struggling to overcome a disastrous world war and the lingering wounds of fascism, agreeing to literally prop up the houses of Hitler and his cronies. In any case, the ruins were so deteriorated that some questioned the possibility of keeping them at all. Everett Schoening, the State Department's resident officer, told Moor that "the ruins *had* to come down . . . it wasn't safe having all those thousands of people climbing on them—what that air raid didn't blow up was left pretty shaky."[67]

To spare taxpayers the expense of clearing the site, the Bavarian government sold salvage rights to a local construction firm on the strict condition that none of the materials be resold as souvenirs.[68] In addition to handling the ruins, the company agreed to remove a number of intact buildings associated with the Nazi regime, including the Kampfhäusl where Hitler had written the second volume of *Mein Kampf.*[69] All of this was to be accomplished by the end of May 1952; the reforestation of the site would come later, at a cost to the state of some 100,000 Deutsche Marks. Fearing neo-Nazi protests, Hoegner posted thirty policemen to the demolition site "to protect democracy."[70] Work stopped over the winter months and resumed the following spring. By the end of April, the demolition crews had almost finished dismantling the Berghof. The last thing to go was the facade that had once held the great picture window that looked out at the Untersberg—without doubt, the most symbolic part of the house. On April 30, on the seventh anniversary and almost to the hour of Hitler's

Fig. 71. "The Fall of
the House of Hitler,"
photographs from
the article "Blowup at
Berchtesgaden," *Life,*
June 2, 1952, 42.

THE FALL OF THE HOUSE OF HITLER

HITLER'S ERA AND END were shared by the Berghof. Here, resting from
the war in 1944, Hitler brooded over his estate. One year later the Führer was
dead, and six-ton bombs in a 350-plane British raid had gutted the structure.

THE BERGHOF, whitewashed and flag-decked, flaunted the Nazi swastika in
1937. But a direct bomb hit, fire and years of looting by GIs and tourists left
only this blackened ruin where curious sightseers prowled Hitler's balcony.

HOUSE GUESTS in 1937 were bride and groom when Duke of Windsor was
in Germany studying labor. Uninvited postwar guests roamed about, hunting
souvenirs, undaunted by signs saying weakened shell was dangerous to enter.

THE VIEW through this 10- by 25-foot picture window framed the Bavarian
mountains and furnished a majestic backdrop for this conference chamber
with its long table and vase of roses. Long afterward only the view remained.

suicide, the remaining walls were dynamited. The *Berchtesgadener Anzeiger,* which recorded the event in detail, complained that the announcement was made at 3:00 P.M., only two hours before the blast was due to occur. Rushing to the site, its reporter found a small group of American officers and Bavarian government representatives gathered to watch the explosion. Evoking a state execution, he gave a minute-by-minute account of the house's final moments, leading to the detonation at 5:05 P.M., after which "a brown cloud of dust covered the site of the explosion for a few minutes." The site was then inspected by the American and German authorities in attendance.[71] Images of the exploding facade were published worldwide and must have been cathartic for many viewers: as *Life* magazine acknowledged, "Hitler's era and end were shared by the Berghof." To mark the event, *Life* published a before-and-after photographic narrative of the house, recalling its heyday and demise (fig. 71).[72] The *New York Times,* which itself had once lavished attention on the house, now noted that "the restless ghost of Hitler will have to look for another place to haunt."[73]

But if Hitler's ghost moved on after the demolition, the tourists did not. To the delight of local merchants, the numbers of visitors steadily increased in the decades following the contested removal of the Obersalzberg ruins. Despite the stipulation in the American transfer agreement that all traces of the Nazi buildings be removed, the construction firm had left foundations and other underground structures, including Hitler's garage. These remnants, along with the vast bunker system and the Kehlsteinhaus, which reopened as a restaurant, continued to draw the historically curious to the area. Indeed, the traffic on the Obersalzberg was so great that it interfered with the effort to grow grass over the cleared sites to obscure the Nazis' architectural footprints. Even after the disappearance of most of the house, the Berghof remained the largest unadvertised tourist attraction in Germany, attracting hundreds of thousands of visitors.[74] In 1962, Peter Brügge, a correspondent for *Der Spiegel* (The Mirror), likened the buses unloading their passengers and the crowds milling about the foundations to similar scenes in Pompeii.[75]

After the demolition, press reports about the Obersalzberg diminished significantly, but the occasional story in the German or foreign media over the next four decades served as a reminder that the issue of memory and monuments had not died with the blasting of the Berghof. Not only tourists, but also Nazi sympathizers found their way to the site and left behind reminders of their stubborn presence. And as neo-Nazism increasingly became recognized as a global phenomenon, these pilgrims could no longer be assumed to be German. Brügge described how shortly after arriving on the Obersalzberg, he entered Hitler's garage and was informed by a scrawled English text on the wall that "Hitler was right," a comment presumably put there by a foreign traveler who had come prepared with a can of paint.[76]

But Brügge was more interested in what was happening aboveground on the Obersalzberg, particularly the continuing absence of a critical context in which to understand the Nazis' presence on the mountain and its physical remains. The lack of serious histories about the Obersalzberg's Nazi period, combined with the natural beauty of the landscape, left the past open to reinvention. Visitors drinking Hofbräu beer on the Kehlsteinhaus terrace, glorying in the blue skies and mountain scenery, were prone to spontaneous outbursts praising Hitler's sense of beauty.[77] It was all so pleasant that it made it hard to remember the human suffering on which the place had been built, and such reminders were, in any case, conspicuously absent.

What remained of the Obersalzberg ruins was similarly devoid of official markers other than rusted "keep out" signs, and since the government insisted that there was nothing left to see, there were also no official tours. Nonetheless, freelance guides continued to give tours based on what they thought their listeners wanted to hear. Brügge interviewed a tour guide who claimed that he neither praised nor criticized Hitler, but simply stuck to the facts: "My tours have to be objective," he insisted. "I can't say, 'over there lived that bastard Hitler.' People don't want to hear that." A similar attitude informed the offerings on hand at area souvenir shops, which included locally produced books that sanitized the mountain's National Socialist history.[78] Taking their cue from propaganda of the 1930s, and reusing period photographs, these publications represented the Nazis' Obersalzberg activities as wholesome, recreational, and largely nonpolitical. Their pages revealed Hitler relaxing on the Berghof terrace, Göring curling on his frozen pool, and Eva Braun sunning herself, among other scenes of domestic innocence.[79] Souvenir stands also sold postcards and color slides of the Obersalzberg before 1945 and before the demolition. In 1986, Peter Kurz, a local Social Democratic representative in the Bavarian state parliament, caused a stir by complaining about the nostalgic tone of such souvenirs.[80] When more explicitly political material was made available for sale, it was presented in a thoroughly decontextualized manner. A travel writer visiting the Obersalzberg in 1978 was surprised to find shopkeepers displaying records of speeches by Hitler and Goebbels alongside albums by Pink Floyd and Plastic Bertrand.[81]

While government authorities would occasionally remove more offensive souvenirs, a laissez-faire attitude generally prevailed on the Obersalzberg. Therese Partner, owner of the Türken Inn, took advantage of the laxity to offer access to the Berghof's underground bunker. Partner, the daughter of Karl Schuster, was among the very few former Obersalzberg residents to successfully petition to have property seized by Bormann restored after the war.[82] All entrances to the bunker system had been sealed by the American occupiers and again by the Bavarian authorities in the early 1950s. Partner claimed that in 1954, a dream guided her to a blocked door underneath the inn. When it was opened, she discovered a long tunnel leading to Hitler and Eva Braun's private bunker rooms beneath the adjacent Berghof. She began to admit visitors and soon was making a fortune from the fifty thousand people who toured the bunker annually. Its walls, which she would occasionally whitewash, became an international canvas on which to express pro- and anti-Nazi sentiments.[83] In 1966, responding to complaints "that Berchtesgaden was cashing in on Hitler's memory," the Bavarian finance minister ordered the Berghof bunker sealed, a rare act of intervention that made the headlines of major American newspapers.[84] Nonetheless, the Schuster family continued to sell tickets to the tunnel and underground rooms still accessible from their inn.[85]

In 1995, when the U.S. Army announced the closure of the Armed Forces Recreation Center in Berchtesgaden, the problem of the mountain's half-remembered history could no longer be ignored. Despite the legal transfer of the Nazi properties on the Obersalzberg to the state of Bavaria decades earlier, the Americans had retained the exclusive use of a large part of the mountain for their recreation center, which had grown to encompass several lodges, a hotel, a ski resort, and a golf course. Now this land and the former Nazi buildings on it, including the once-luxurious Platterhof Hotel (renamed the General Walker Hotel) and Martin Bormann's experimental farm, would be accessible to all. German officials, who had long believed that the American presence on the Obersalzberg had discouraged neo-Nazi activities, expressed their concern about what would fill the vacuum after they left.[86] Neo-Nazi pilgrims were already becoming more brazen, erecting makeshifts altars to Hitler in the now heavily wooded area of the Berghof ruins. The American departure, Stephen Kinzer wrote in the *New York Times,* "will leave Berchtesgaden alone with its ghosts."[87]

Subsequent debates about what to do with the Obersalzberg took place in the context of the end of the Cold War and the reunification of Germany, a period that often saw the desire to confront the nation's bloody past pitted against the investments needed to revive its economy.[88] Yet clearly both were needed to combat the sharp rise in neo-Nazi activity after 1989, when a lack of education about the Third Reich combined with shrinking prospects for employment and social advancement drew young people from former East Germany into the arms of extremist groups. Moreover, in the galloping pursuit of new markets, historical sensitivities sometimes fell by the wayside. In 1991, the construction of a shopping center on a cobblestone road paved by slave labor just outside Ravensbrück, a women's concentration camp in a former East German town near Berlin, created an international furor that embarrassed the German government and halted the project.[89] Seeking a compromise, Kurt Faltlhauser, the Bavarian finance minister, decided on a "two-column model" for the Obersalzberg's redevelopment: the creation of a luxury resort alongside a documentation center that would inform hotel guests and other visitors of the mountain's National Socialist history.[90] Faltlhauser presented these two pillars as a balanced and integrated unit, but his critics argued the plan was contradictory, commemorating with the one hand and erasing with the other.

While a small group of Berchtesgaden residents had lobbied for some form of memorial, others feared that bringing attention to the town's "brown" past would forever sully it with evil. "We don't want another Dachau here," Berchtesgaden mayor Rudolf Schaupp said. "Nothing terrible happened here. This was only a place where the bandits came for vacation."[91] Martin Seidl, a Berchtesgaden councilor, claimed that "in principle, I have nothing against the idea, but such a center belongs in Berlin or Munich, not here."[92] But the leader of Berlin's Jewish community, Andreas Nachama, who served as an advisor on the project, reinforced the need for greater on-site awareness, saying that on an earlier visit to the area, he had been "strongly angered that there was no information—only souvenirs."[93]

When it opened in October 1999, on the foundations of a former Nazi guesthouse, the Obersalzberg Documentation Center effectively refuted any lingering assertions that the mountain had been no more than a holiday destination for Hitler. The carefully researched exhibits revealed the Obersalzberg to have been a central hub of Nazi power and a place where its leaders had discussed and planned their crimes. This curatorial viewpoint necessitated moving beyond a narrow focus on the daily lives of the mountain's elite residents to include a panorama of the events that unfolded throughout Europe.[94] Displays also explored how publicity about the Obersalzberg fed the personality cult around Hitler that had helped to consolidate his regime. Finally, and in contrast to the Türken Inn's unregulated access, the center offered a curated experience of the underground bunker spaces, entered at the end of the exhibits.[95] Rather than damaging tourism, as its critics had once feared, the Documentation Center became a considerable attraction in itself, and in May 2007 surpassed the one million visitor mark.[96]

Having paid its dues to historical memory, the Bavarian government then turned its attention to the business of forgetting, building the five-star InterContinental Berchtesgaden Resort on the former site of Göring's residence. The spa hotel, with its slogan "Time-Out in the Mountains," offered an array of wellness services to a wealthy clientele seeking to relax and leave their cares behind. Unlike the Documentation Center, which conspicuously integrated Nazi architectural remains into its design, the InterContinental Resort just as conspicuously asserted its break with the past through its modernist facades and curvilinear forms. Jonathan Margolis, in a travel review for the *Independent,* compared it to "a software company's Colorado HQ."[97] In designing the building, Herbert Kochta, an established Munich architect, sought "an expression of human confidence in the face of some of the most stunning natural beauty on earth." His original plan for the 138-room hotel featured two parallel wings sweeping gently outward and joined in the middle by a central corridor. But, as historian Timothy Ryback reported, "when the model was complete, it became clear that from an airplane or an adjacent peak the hotel would look like a giant 'H' branded on the landscape, an uncomfortable reminder of the mountain's most infamous former resident." Kochta modified the design by turning the wings inward and connecting them at their northern ends, thereby arriving at the present horseshoe shape. Modernism, as the design process revealed, was by no means a simple antidote to Nazi architecture or its perceived "aesthetic pollution" of the landscape.[98]

By the time the hotel opened on March 1, 2005, it had already been deluged with negative press.[99] While much of it originated in Germany, the English media had also been highly critical, provoked by the involvement of the London-based Six Continents, which owned InterContinental and other hotel brands. In September 2002, in its typically provocative fashion, the British tabloid the *Sun* dubbed it the "Hitler Hilton."[100] Mitchell Symons, writing shortly afterward in the *Daily Express,* argued that "there's nothing wrong with people visiting sites of sensitive historical significance but they shouldn't take holidays there and you shouldn't make money out of it." He demanded of Six Continents' directors, "Why not stop being coy and open a chain? The Warsaw Ghetto Crowne Plaza, the Auschwitz Holiday Inn, the Treblinka Intercontinental—you get the picture."[101] Faltlhauser, Bavaria's finance minister, admitted the hotel stood on highly sensitive ground, but maintained that the Obersalzberg should be allowed to return to being a tourist resort, as it had been long before Hitler's arrival.[102] Yet was normalcy possible anymore in such a setting? For the many journalists who poured into Berchtesgaden to review the hotel, this was the question foremost in their minds. Reflecting on his visit, writer and *Guardian* contributor Ian Buruma mused, "sitting back in your comfortable chair at the wellness hotel, enjoying Hitler's view with a glass of fine wine, is a kind of sacrilege. Or is it?"[103]

The hotel's management was abundantly aware of the difficult position it had to navigate and was alert to potential insensitivities or dangers. The international staff had all undergone police background checks and signed a declaration of support for Germany's democratic ideals. They had also been instructed on the area's Nazi history and on how to respond to inquiries, directing guests to the nearby Documentation Center.[104] Moreover, in each room, the bedside table contained not only a Gideon Bible, but also a copy of the Documentation Center's eight-hundred-page, "no-holds-barred" exhibition catalogue, *The Deadly Utopia* (*Die tödliche Utopie*). On a visit to the hotel in March 2005, journalist Max Davidson took a break from the spa to read the book in his room: "I sip a beer from the mini-bar and study black-and-white photographs of Auschwitz. It is an uncomfortable half hour."[105] (Other guests likewise found the books to make for disturbing holiday reading, and they were eventually removed to the hotel's library.[106]) Beyond such measures, the hotel defended against "the dread possibility of a neo-Nazi group managing to book it for a convention" by pricing itself out of the "unemployed and disgruntled youth" market.[107] As an extra precaution, in its first year of operation, the hotel refused all reservations for April 20, Hitler's birthday, at a loss of 10,000 Euros in revenue.[108] It was able to do so because the Bavarian government had funded and managed the project through the Bavarian State Bank, with the InterContinental chain providing no more than its name and booking system.[109] While this arrangement gave the hotel considerable freedom, it also made Bavarian

AFTERLIFE OF HITLER'S HOMES

taxpayers liable, obliging them to absorb its considerable losses when it proved unable to fill its rooms.[110] Fiscal irresponsibility thus joined the list of criticisms lobbed at the Bavarian government for its Obersalzberg redevelopment plan.

But above all, it was the loss of historic sites and landscapes that proved to be the most controversial. Between 1995 and 2008, in the process of reinventing the Obersalzberg as a tourist recreation center, state authorities dismantled the mountain. The hill on which Göring's house had once stood, known officially during the Third Reich as Adolf Hitler Hill, and where, on May 5, 1945, members of the Third U.S. Infantry Division had raised the Stars and Stripes, was removed to create more level ground for the hotel, leading to accusations that the Bavarian government was engaging in an "abuse of nature" reminiscent of the Nazis.[111] Contractors also razed almost all the remaining visible historic traces of the National Socialist regime on the mountain, leaving only the Kehlsteinhaus and a few other buildings. This wholesale destruction of structures that the state itself had declared to be historic provoked angry protests within and beyond Germany. Ryback, present at the demolition of the basement of the Modellhaus, a building near the Berghof where Hitler had kept his architectural models, described how the excavator rammed into the walls with little concern for the historic objects they contained.[112] Michel Friedman, vice president of the Central Council of Jews in Germany, decried the replacement of historical fabric with new structures, which obscured what had actually taken place on the mountain.[113] The former Platterhof Hotel, for example, became a parking lot, and the remnants of the SS barracks gave way to a Segway track for hotel guests to practice their riding skills. Josef Dürr, head of the Bavarian Green Party, argued that these historic traces were important to democracy, and accused the conservative Bavarian government of wanting "to reduce the Nazi past to a minimum."[114] Others pointed out that as the last of the Nazi-era generation passed away, the buildings remained as the only physical link to that history.[115]

As part of the toxic cleanup of the mountain's Nazi past, and at considerable expense to the state, Hitler's garage and the terrace above it were dug up and removed in 1995. Having a neo-Nazi pilgrimage site so close to the planned Documentation Center posed potential hazards in terms of physical damage (the center was smeared with Nazi graffiti while under construction) and of international public relations. In 1999, the chance discovery of a warren of underground rooms led to further excavations and the partial removal of the Berghof's basement. Orders were given to destroy the material and remove all debris from the site.[116] Today, a retaining wall and small traces of the foundation are all that remain visible of the house. Yet despite such efforts, the site continues to attract Hitler's faithful, although notably fewer since the Documentation Center opened.[117] With the garage now gone, they signal their presence by carving SS runes into the towering trees planted after the 1952 demolition. When these markings are discovered, the tree's bark is either removed or the tree itself felled. Ryback and Florian Beierl, a local historian, have argued that the wooded location, with its moss-covered rubble, lends itself to romanticization, and that the best way to demystify the site would be to expose it to public view: "Historicizing the ruins will help leach them of the current cultish aura that surrounds the property."[118] In 2008, for the first time since Allied soldiers arrived at the Berghof in 1945 and triumphantly staked their claim, a sign was posted that identifies the former location of Hitler's house. In English and German, it gives a brief history that challenges a simple view of its domestic function: "Hitler spent more than a third of his time in power here. Important political discussions and negotiations were conducted here and incisive decisions were made, which led to the catastrophes of the Second World War and the Holocaust, causing the death of millions." Those interested in learning more are directed with an arrow to the nearby Documentation Center. On the German side of the sign, the word "Holocaust" has been freshly repainted after having been scratched out.[119]

If state authorities believed that such actions would contain the toxicity of the Berghof site, they were rudely surprised when its traces reappeared in an unexpected and embarrassing location. In 2010, Richard Nemec, the spokesperson for the Bavarian Monument Protection Agency, which was already under fire for the destruction of historic structures on the mountain, revealed that red marble flagstones removed from the Berghof's terrace in 1995 had been used to pave the floor of the Wegmacher Chapel, a small roadside Catholic chapel erected in 1997 near Bad Reichenhall. This recycling of materials had occurred despite government orders to obliterate all remaining vestiges of the site. Yet tourists, local residents, and those clearing the site had surreptitiously taken materials and souvenirs. Matthias Ferwagner, the chapel's architect and head of the state building authority in nearby Traunstein, which was responsible for the removal work at the Berghof in 1995 and later for building the chapel, admitted that he had saved some of the flagstones, which he was reluctant to destroy, given their

AFTERLIFE OF HITLER'S HOMES

fine craftsmanship and material value. The stones were loaded onto a truck and sent to the authority's building yard; two years later, when it came time to lay the floor of the chapel, the stones were both convenient and free.[120]

Soon after Nemec's announcement, historians Ryback and Beierl published the story of the reused flagstones in the *New York Times* and the *International Herald Tribune*. As they reported:

> In defense, the chapel's architect, Matthias Ferwagner, said that his design explicitly addressed the use of the Hitler-era masonry. Ferwagner said he arranged the flagstones in the shape of a cross on the assumption that they had been quarried by Jewish slave laborers and would be "redeemed" through this symbol of suffering and salvation. He also installed a glass ceiling designed to "float" over the stones like the Holy Ghost. "The idea was that the stones somehow needed to be cleansed, blessed," Ferwagner said. He said he envisioned the roadside chapel as a place where people with "evil intentions" could stop and purge their minds.[121]

In a subsequent interview, Ferwagner pointed out that materials from the Berghof had found their way into many local buildings, both private and public, saying, "You can hardly find a mason in the region who isn't storing columns and stone blocks from Obersalzberg."[122]

Ryback and Beierl's revelations, appearing in two international newspapers, aroused yet more media criticism of the Bavarian government's mismanagement of the Obersalzberg. But some of the debate also centered on Ryback and Beierl's actions in speaking up, which, in the opinion of some commentators, provided fodder for another nuisance scandal. *Der Spiegel*, by contrast, argued for taking "the fight over Hitler's flagstones" seriously, citing the stones' highly symbolic value. On this well-known stage, the Führer had been photographed playing with children and entertaining party officials, such as Himmler and Goebbels.[123] Some local residents called for the chapel to be demolished and complained that "a number of shaven-headed, leather jacket-wearing 'pilgrims' leave behind notes of praise to Hitler and candles burning in his memory." A small carved swastika also appeared on one of the wooden roof beams.[124] Ferwagner later stated that the stones might have come from the Platterhof rather than the Berghof, although he could no longer be sure.[125] Whatever the facts, the controversy over the recycling of "polluted" materials made clear that the lack of transparency among the state agencies charged with banishing Hitler's ghost from the area was actually keeping it alive. Although Nemec's disclosure about the stones alerted the media to the chapel's possibly tainted foundations and increased pressure on his agency to better protect the few remaining historic sites on the Obersalzberg, including what is left of the Berghof, Ryback and Beierl commended him for having taken the first step toward greater public accountability.[126]

In light of the Berghof's turbulent postwar history, involving beer hall brawls, police cordons, dynamiting, reforestation, neo-Nazis, and political scandals, the quietude surrounding Hitler's Munich apartment on Prince Regent Square seems almost anticlimactic. Until 1946, the apartment building was occupied by American armed forces. That year, the Bavarian State Office for Asset Administration and Restitution—charged with managing Third Reich property that had been seized by the Allies and returned to German authorities as well as processing the claims of Nazi victims—took over the premises. It was superseded in 1969 by the Traffic Violations Bureau, and since 1998, the entire building has been occupied by a police station.[127] The police presence ensures the building's security and discourages neo-Nazi pilgrims, souvenir hunters, and sensation-seekers. Only the reception rooms on the ground floor, which once housed Hitler's SS guards, are normally open to the public. Those who enter encounter the flowing, curvilinear Jugendstil decoration of the original interior, dating from the turn of the twentieth century. Visitors without police business are not encouraged to linger: this is a working police station, not a museum. Requests to see Hitler's apartment are politely but firmly denied.

There is no question, however, that the apartment remains a historically and architecturally important site. As one enters the bright, open foyer and sees the starkness of Gerdy Troost's renovations, one understands how modern the apartment must have seemed—indeed, still seems—in comparison to the older units in the building. It makes one realize that Lee Miller's published photographs constructed a sense of stodgy, cramped spaces that avoided capturing the light or space experienced in person. In short, like the physical experience of any architectural space, it leads to adjustments to perceptions derived from objects removed from their context, written texts, and even photographs. Despite the disappearance of the original furnishings and postwar alterations to some of the rooms, the apartment remains surprisingly intact. Still-preserved decorative features of the Troost renovation include parquet floors, doors, wainscoting and other woodwork, marble mantelpieces, and some built-in furniture, most strikingly the dark oak shelves that fill Hitler's library. Hitler's living room, where he met with Neville Chamberlain to discuss the Munich Accord in 1938, is used for

AFTERLIFE OF HITLER'S HOMES

conference meetings. The shelves in the library hold the trophies won by the police soccer team, named after the neighborhood, the Bogenhauser Cops (plate 12). The rooms once occupied by Geli Raubal and the Winters are offices; they have retained their elegant decorative ceilings and some built-in furniture. Hitler's bedroom, on the other end of the apartment, is a locker room, where police officers change into their uniforms (plate 13).

From outward appearances, the apartment seems a rather empty, functional space. But for a historian of the Third Reich, steeped in images of the crimes committed by its former resident, a visit is a disturbing and surreal experience. One stands in the room where Hitler slept warm and sheltered and imagines his starving, shivering victims; one looks at the nook where Chamberlain sat and thinks how things might have turned out differently, if only. For Police Chief Inspector Harald Freundorfer, who has worked in the building for years, 16 Prince Regent Square holds no such demons. It is only space contained by four walls, the place to which he and his staff of one hundred go to work every morning—even if there is a fully preserved luxury bunker in the backyard. Freundorfer would like people to forget the building's association with Hitler, and he discourages publicity for fear it will attract neo-Nazis and endanger the neighborhood.[128] While one sympathizes with his concerns, one wonders about the continuing feasibility of hiding in plain sight.

Admittedly, the virtual occupation of the building since 1949 has successfully prevented the troublesome activities that have plagued the Obersalzberg. The fact that Hitler's Munich residence did not function as a center of power and was not publicized during the Third Reich has also helped to maintain the building's low visibility. Also unlike the Berghof, few political events took place here, apart from visits by Chamberlain and Mussolini. Before 1933, Hitler also used his apartment as a party office, and would be visited regularly there by top Nazi leaders, such as Goebbels and Himmler.[129] From the point of view of the police, there is no reason to give the public access, since this was nothing more than a residence. Nonetheless, the historic draw for most people is precisely that, from 1929 to 1945, Hitler called this place home. Its state of preservation also adds to the appeal, especially as other sites associated with Hitler have decayed or disappeared. Once abundant in Munich, the Nazi birthplace and "capital of the movement," such sites have been systematically effaced since the war's end in the city's broader efforts to remove National Socialism's traces from the urban landscape and, with them, memories of a shameful past.[130] Yet the more such historic locations vanish, the greater the pressure grows on those that remain. In recent years, as a greater historical consciousness about place has emerged, increasing requests from journalists, scholars, and filmmakers to document the spaces of Hitler's Munich residence are making it more difficult to keep it out of the realm of public awareness. But what, if any, alternatives exist to the current defensive strategy remains unclear. Could 16 Prince Regent Square be something other than a police station? No one has yet openly broached the question, and the state of Bavaria seems in no hurry to have the discussion.

The troublesome afterlife of Hitler's homes has not only played out on the ground in Germany. It has also rippled through auction houses and museums in other countries, where objects looted from Hitler's residences at the war's end have made an unsettling reappearance. Nazi memorabilia may be sold legally in the United States and the United Kingdom, but the practice is outlawed or restricted in Germany, Austria, France, and Hungary. Hitler's domestic objects are particularly sought after by collectors and garner high prices; forgeries are common. Items auctioned in recent years from 16 Prince Regent Square and the Berghof have included silverware, china, tablecloths, napkins, monogrammed bed linen, a lamp, desk, globe, and marble paperweight, among others. Most Third Reich memorabilia trades hands quietly, through a dealer or antiques store, and the transactions are almost impossible to trace. By contrast, the visibility of auctions often attracts media attention as well as protests, the latter primarily from Jewish groups and survivors, who argue that these sales glamorize Hitler and profit from the deaths of Holocaust victims.[131] The motives of those who choose to live with the dictator's bed sheets and fish knives are as complex as their backgrounds, which range from sympathizers to history buffs to Jews whose own families were murdered. As one Jewish collector of Nazi militaria explained to the *New York Times,* there can be a sense of triumph in possession: "You may have killed my relatives," he said, "but I own you now."[132]

The objects of Hitler's domesticity are rarely seen outside the world of private collectors. While many museums have such items in their collections, they are almost never exhibited. In 2010, the German Historical Museum in Berlin opened a groundbreaking exhibition, *Hitler and the Germans: Nation and Crime,* which explored the reasons for the regime's widespread acceptance by German society. It was the first major exhibition on Hitler to be held in Germany since the end of the Third Reich, and the curators were understandably concerned about reviving admiration for the dictator. They refused to include any of Hitler's personal effects for fear that these "relics" still harbored a dangerous magnetism. Indeed, any object from the period deemed too alluring was visually obscured to prevent the viewer from the potential seduction of unmediated vision. For example, a vast sideboard designed by Albert Speer, which had stood in Hitler's New Chancellery office, was isolated in a corner, mounted on a tilt, and veiled with a thin, black mesh screen. This approach, the curatorial equivalent of a hazardous materials suit, functioned by frustrating the viewer's desire to see, enforcing disengagement from the object.[133]

In January 2012, the New-York Historical Society announced an upcoming exhibition of its silver collection, including a monogrammed fork and knife that had once belonged to Hitler. The flatware, part of a dinner service made to celebrate the dictator's fiftieth birthday in 1939, had been taken from the Berghof by an American soldier and given to the society in 1946. According to Margaret Hofer, the society's curator of decorative arts, the fork and knife had never been exhibited because there had not been "an appropriate context in which to do it." The show, which featured 150 of the "most aesthetically and historically compelling pieces" of the society's collection, took a broad cultural view, as suggested by its title, *Stories in Sterling: Four Centuries of Silver in New York*. For Hofer, whose Jewish relatives had fled Nazi Germany, the flatware represented a symbol of the Americans' triumph over tyranny, which is also how Hitler's silverware had been presented when it was displayed on a Victory Loan train in 1945 and by returning veterans who proudly showed off their war trophies.[134]

But sixty-six years after the war's end, and largely in the absence of the generation who had fought the war, the interpretation of those spoils had changed. Debórah Dwork, a professor of Holocaust history, called the inclusion of the silverware in the exhibition "totally tasteless" and intended "solely for sensational purposes." Dwork argued that the knife and fork "trivialize the evil that Hitler and his allies perpetrated."[135] In fact, historians of the Third Reich have long argued that aesthetics, from mass spectacles to everyday objects, played a crucial role in the regime's popular appeal.[136] Hitler's fork and knife do, indeed, have a "story in sterling" to tell that links together design, power, and violence. Nonetheless, Dwork's comments reveal that the society failed to tell the right story—or, rather, to make the political context of the objects relevant to New York. Hitler's flatware was exhibited in a section called "Elegant Dining" devoted mostly to

American dining customs. It was an incongruous setting, and the catalogue text, which focused on the design of the silver service and its discovery by American soldiers, did not help to make the connection between dining in Berchtesgaden and dining in New York.[137] A more compelling story might have discussed the allure of Hitler's home life for prewar American audiences, which contributed to their fascination with the domestic remnants that soldiers brought back. The contemporary puff pieces that appeared in the *New York Times* (among other respectable publications) about life at the Berghof, which charmed readers with details about the Führer's gracious living and love of gooseberry pie, provide one such possibility to explore the relationship between the objects in the glass display case and the image of the dictator once cultivated for an American audience.[138] Yet while Hitler's fork and knife have emerged out of storage, the story linking them to American celebrity journalism has remained buried.

An article in the *Guardian* published in November 2003 exposed the reluctance of the British media to investigate its own complicity in burnishing Hitler's prewar reputation through flattering portrayals of his domestic life. As *Guardian* journalist Simon Waldman recalled, one evening earlier that spring, his father-in-law had proudly taken out a family heirloom, a November 1938 edition of *Homes and Gardens,* to show him a feature about a modernist bungalow designed by his father. Flipping through the magazine, Waldman discovered "Hitler's Mountain Home," the account published by "Ignatius Phayre" of his visit to Haus Wachenfeld. Amazed that a British interiors magazine would treat Hitler like a fashionable design consultant, Waldman scanned the pages and posted them on his personal website. When, to Waldman's surprise, the Hitler pages attracted tens of thousands of readers worldwide, he wrote to the editor of the magazine, Isobel McKenzie-Price, to ask if she could shed more light on the sixty-five-year-old article. Claiming that Waldman had infringed the magazine's copyright of the text and images, she compelled him to remove the scans.[139]

But in their place, he posted their correspondence, which generated even more interest. In the resulting online discussions, Phayre was identified as William George Fitz-Gerald, but no other biographical information emerged. That he had been sympathetic to Hitler's beliefs and likely had never been to Haus Wachenfeld, but had instead assembled his fawning narrative from Nazi sources, remained unknown. A historian in Louisiana, however, told Waldman that the images used for the article had, in fact, come from Hitler's own photographer, Heinrich Hoffmann, and were not owned by *Homes and Gardens*. Waldman then reposted the images, but not the text. The story of the suppressed Hitler article was picked up by major news outlets and received further international coverage from the David S. Wyman Institute for Holocaust Studies, based in Washington, D.C., which organized a petition signed by seventy Holocaust scholars and educators demanding that the company that owned *Homes and Gardens,* IPC Media, Britain's largest media conglomerate, "face up to its past" and make the article publicly available. The publisher relented in so far as it agreed that it could not verify copyright ownership and would not contest reproduction of the article. Unsatisfied, the Wyman Institute insisted that IPC Media acknowledge its moral responsibility for having cast Hitler in a positive light, depicting him "as a gardener and a gourmet," at a time when his country openly and violently persecuted Jews. Following discussions with the Wyman Institute, IPC Media issued a statement in which it confessed to being "appalled" that *Homes and Gardens* had been "taken in by the Nazi propaganda of the 1930s." It also pointed out, however, that "much of the world's media" had been similarly duped.[140]

The international debate sparked by Waldman focused on journalism's accountability, but little was said about the audience. The abundance of prewar features on the domestic Hitler published outside Germany reflects not only the foreign media's willingness to disseminate flattering stories about the dictator, but also the existence of an eager audience. That Fitz-Gerald, who essentially published Nazi propaganda, was able to sell his work to so many outlets, ranging from a journal of contemporary world affairs to a popular dog magazine, testifies to the strength and breadth of this market. While the role of the foreign press in laundering Hitler's image thus must be examined, it is important not to overlook the magazine and newspaper readers around the world who wanted to believe the sanitized version. Indeed, the tens of thousands of readers who visited Waldman's Hitler pages and their subsequent reposting on websites around the globe reveal that there is still tremendous interest in such accounts, and not all of it is critical. Since being rediscovered, the *Homes and Gardens* article routinely is cited on websites as a reliable, firsthand account of Hitler's mountain retreat. Ironically, a young generation is again learning about the "Squire of Wachenfeld" from the same pseudo-journalist who misled readers in 1938. More than seventy-five years later, the distorting mirror of Hitler at home continues to deceive.

NOTES

INTRODUCTION

1. Sions, "Berchtesgaden," 4; Miller, "Hitleriana," 72.
2. Bullock, *Hitler*, 7. On the history of Hitler biographies, see Rosenbaum, *Explaining Hitler;* and Lukacs, *Hitler of History.*
3. Notable exceptions include Dahm et al., eds., *Tödliche Utopie*, 52–187; Herz, *Hoffmann und Hitler*, 242–59; and Günther, *Design der Macht.*
4. Speer, *Inside the Third Reich*, 85. On Speer, see Sereny, *Albert Speer.*
5. Entry for July 14, 1944, Goebbels, *Tagebücher*, pt. 2, vol. 13, 116.
6. Sontag, "Fascinating Fascism," 23–30; Pamela E. Swett, Corey Ross, and Fabrice d'Almeida, "Pleasure and Power in Nazi Germany: An Introduction," in Swett, Ross, and d'Almeida, eds., *Pleasure and Power*, 1–15; Hans Dieter Schäfer, "Das gespaltene Bewußtsein: Alltagskultur im Dritten Reich," in Schäfer, *Das gespaltene Bewußtsein*, 9–87; Baranowski, *Strength through Joy*, 1–10; Ogan and Weiss, eds., *Faszination und Gewalt.*

1. HITLER SETS UP HOUSE

1. Stachura, "Political Strategy," 261–88. For an overview of Hitler's rise to power and the Nazi state, see Burleigh, *Third Reich;* from a historiographical perspective, see Kershaw, *Nazi Dictatorship.*
2. Adolf Hitler's completed questionnaire for apartment seekers, September 13, 1929, Zim 117, Stadtarchiv München; police registration record for Jakob Ernst Reichert, PMB R80, Stadtarchiv München; Hanfstaengl, *Hitler*, 47.
3. Bullock, *Hitler*, 75.
4. Hanfstaengl, *Hitler*, 47.
5. Hale, "Adolf Hitler: Taxpayer," 833.
6. Joachimsthaler, *Hitlers Liste*, 288–89.
7. Trevor-Roper, ed., *Hitler's Table Talk*, 161–68; Feiber, "Filiale von Berlin," 60–63. For

an analysis of *Mein Kampf*, see Gregor, *How to Read Hitler;* and Jäckel, *Hitler's World View.*
8. Trevor-Roper, *Hitler's Table Talk*, 165, 554; Feiber, "Filiale von Berlin," 62; Joachimsthaler, *Hitlers Liste*, 271–76; *Prager Tageblatt*, "Hitlers Stiefschwester."
9. Joachimsthaler, *Hitlers Liste*, 287–90; Hale, "Adolf Hitler: Taxpayer," 830–42.
10. Anheier and Neidhardt, "Soziographische Entwicklung der NSDAP," 179–86.
11. *Scotsman*, "Police Trace Organisation."
12. See power of attorney and rental documents for 16 Prince Regent Square, Zim 117, Stadtarchiv München. The names and professions of the building's occupants are listed under the entry for Prinzregentenplatz 16 in the *Adressbuch der Stadt München und Umgebung* (Munich: Adressbuchverlag der Industrie-und Handelskammer München, 1929), Stadtarchiv München. On the Bruckmanns and their relationship to Hitler, see Martynkewicz, *Salon Deutschland;* and Käfer, "Hitlers frühe Förderer," 52–79. For an overview of National Socialism in Munich, see Large, *Where Ghosts Walked;* and Bauer et al., eds., *München.*
13. Rental contract between Hugo Schühle and Adolf Hitler, approved by the Municipal Housing Authority on September 18, 1929, Zim 117, Stadtarchiv München. The building plans are located at the Lokalbaukommission München.
14. Martynkewicz, *Salon Deutschland*, 76–77, 409.
15. Ottomeyer and Ziffer, *Möbel des Neoklassizismus*, 88–89; Barkow, Gross, and Lenarz, eds., *Novemberpogrom 1938*, 482–83.
16. Hermann Historica Catalogue (III), auction 45, October 17–18, 2003, lot 6558; Hermann Historica Catalogue, auction 46, May 7–8, 2004, lot 5575; Hermann Historica Catalogue, auction 59, April 15–16, 2010, lot 7272; *Birmingham (UK) Post*, "Hitler's Desk and Chair."
17. *Berliner Volkszeitung*, "Hitler braucht

9-Zimmer-Wohnung"; *New York Times,* "German Fascist Chief Prospers."

18. Police report dated September 28, 1931, MInn 72443, Bayerisches Hauptstaatsarchiv, Munich; Rosenbaum, *Explaining Hitler,* 99–134.

19. Schirach, *Ich glaubte an Hitler,* 109.

20. Grimm, "Selbstmord in Hitlers Wohnung."

21. Joachimsthaler, *Hitlers Liste,* 324; *Die Fanfare,* "Geliebte Hitlers verübt Selbstmord."

22. *Münchener Post,* "Rätselhafte Affäre," September 21, 1931; Rosenbaum, *Explaining Hitler,* 108.

23. *Münchener Post,* "Rätselhafte Affäre," September 22, 1931.

24. *Die Fanfare,* "Geliebte Hitlers verübt Selbstmord"; Rosenbaum, *Explaining Hitler,* 16–48, 109–17.

25. Rosenbaum, *Explaining Hitler,* 108.

26. Frank, *Im Angesicht des Galgens,* 90–91.

27. Rosenbaum, *Explaining Hitler,* 39.

2. HOW THE CHANCELLOR LIVES

1. Hitler, "Reichskanzlei," 277. According to Birgit Schwarz, despite Hitler's complaints about the bad quality of the state-loaned art, many of the paintings at the Chancellery borrowed from Berlin museums were rehung after its renovation. Schwarz, *Geniewahn,* 140.

2. Hitler, "Reichskanzlei," 277.

3. Ibid. I have borrowed from the translation in Speer, *Inside the Third Reich,* 29.

4. Speer, *Inside the Third Reich,* 29. In their memoirs, both Christa Schroeder and Traudl Junge repeat an anecdote that Hitler told them about the day he visited Hindenburg at the Chancellery to be sworn in as chancellor. As he entered the Congress Hall, where the ceremony was to be performed, he claims that Hindenburg warned him: "Keep to the walls, Herr Hitler, the floor won't last much longer." It is important to keep in mind that the source for this story is Hitler, who was committed to the narrative of decay. See Schroeder, *He Was My Chief,* 19; and Junge, *Until the Final Hour,* 149.

5. Pünder, ed., *Geschichte des Reichskanzlerpalais,* 67–72.

6. Hitler is often credited (as in the Schroeder and Junge memoirs; see note 4) with having rescued the historic Congress Hall by ordering the replacement of its rotted timber floor

with a new steel-girder construction. Dietmar Arnold convincingly argues, on the basis of archival records, that the work was done to allow the removal of a weight-bearing wall in the Reception Hall and four columns in the foyer directly below the Congress Hall. Arnold, *Neue Reichskanzlei,* 55–56, 172n36. On the 1926 renovations, see also Demps, *Berlin-Wilhelmstrasse,* 147, 150.

7. Gerdy Troost to Albert Speer, 28 November 1934, in German Captured Documents, Gerdy and Paul Troost Papers, Library of Congress, Washington, D.C., microfilm reel 452 (container 768). (After being microfilmed, the originals of the Gerdy and Paul Troost papers in the German Captured Documents collection were turned over to the Bayerische Staatsbibliothek, Munich.) The construction site manager was Josef Schatz, a Munich builder hired by Paul Troost. See Gerdy Troost, "Zur Frage Albert Speer" ("On the Albert Speer Question"), unpublished manuscript, n.d., Gerdy Troost Personal Papers, Ana 325, Bayerische Staatsbibliothek. The collection identified here and in subsequent endnotes as "Gerdy Troost Personal Papers" is the portion of her papers at the Bayerische Staatsbibliothek that is closed to scholars until 2019. It is uncatalogued and has been given a preliminary call number of Ana 325.

8. Gerdy Troost, interview by John Toland, November 5, 1971, transcript for tape C-50, John Toland Papers, Franklin D. Roosevelt Library, Hyde Park, N.Y.

9. List of renovation expenditures and payments, January 29, 1935; Reich Finance Ministry to Atelier Troost, 27 March 1934; and Atelier Troost to Reich Finance Ministry, 4 April 1934, all in German Captured Documents, Gerdy and Paul Troost Papers, microfilm reel 452 (container 768).

10. Schönberger, *Neue Reichskanzlei,* 21.

11. Wilderotter, *Alltag der Macht,* 74.

12. Gerdy Troost, "Adolf Hitler: Erste Begegnung—'Braunes Haus' (Umbau Palais Barlow)" ("Adolf Hitler: First Encounter—'Brown House' [Barlow Palace Renovation]"), undated manuscript, private collection.

13. Ibid.; Nüsslein, *Paul Ludwig Troost,* 68–69, 71–72.

14. Nüsslein, *Paul Ludwig Troost,* 86.

15. Ibid., 238–39.

16. Frank, *Im Angesicht des Galgens,* 122.

17. Arnold, *Neue Reichskanzlei,* 47. Arnold

mistakenly states that the apartment was located on the fifth floor (German fourth floor) of the Siedler building. In fact, it was on the fourth floor (German third floor).

18. Nüsslein, *Paul Ludwig Troost,* 67–68.

19. Speer, *Inside the Third Reich,* 50.

20. On the number of employees in the Atelier Troost, see Gerdy Troost's denazification registration form, May 6, 1946, SpkA K 1844: Troost, Gerdy, Staatsarchiv München.

21. Seckendorff, "Monumentalität und Gemütlichkeit," 120.

22. Werner, "Führer," 27.

23. See the mention of a furniture cost estimate from August 1933 in the invoice from Vereinigte Werkstätten für Kunst im Handwerk to Atelier Troost, March 15, 1934, in German Captured Documents, Gerdy and Paul Troost Papers, microfilm reel 452 (container 768).

24. NSDAP-Baupläne 11210, Bayerisches Hauptstaatsarchiv, Munich. See also Nüsslein, *Paul Ludwig Troost,* 132–34, 236–38. Gerdy Troost also credited Paul Troost with the design of Hitler's study. Gerdy Troost, "Zur Privat-Veröffentlichung von Dr. Sonja Günther: 'Innenräume des 3. Reiches'" ("On Dr. Sonja Günther's private publication, 'Interiors of the Third Reich'"), undated manuscript (commentary), Gerdy Troost Personal Papers, Ana 325.

25. Hitler, "Reichskanzlei," 277.

26. Pünder, *Geschichte des Reichskanzlerpalais,* 70, 74.

27. For the Atelier Troost's floor plans of the Old Chancellery (c. 1934–40), see NSDAP-Baupläne 11243, 11244, 11370, 11372, 11373, Bayerisches Hauptstaatsarchiv. The areas of the Old Chancellery renovated by Speer are sometimes indicated on these plans, but little is known about the work. Photographs of the Chancellery's public rooms were published in *die neue linie,* "Tradition und Gegenwart," 14–16, 48.

28. "Rede Hitlers zum Richtfest der Neuen Reichskanzlei in der Deutschlandhalle am 2.8.1938," in Schönberger, *Neue Reichskanzlei,* 178.

29. Ibid.

30. The Prints and Photographs Division of the Library of Congress in Washington, D.C., holds the Atelier Troost's photographs of the renovated spaces of the Old Chancellery, some of which are reproduced in this chapter. The full collection of images ("Interior Views of

the Chancellery, 1935–1945") is available in the online catalogue of the Print and Photographs Division (http://www.loc.gov/pictures/) under the call number LOT 3940 (H) [P&P].

31. Pünder, *Geschichte des Reichskanzlerpalais,* 74; Wilderotter, *Alltag der Macht,* 299.

32. See note 6.

33. Wagner and Cooper, *Heritage of Fire,* 120. Hitler told a more diplomatic version to British journalist George Ward Price, claiming that the carpet "was originally ordered for the new headquarters of the League of Nations at Geneva, but could not be completed in time and was bought by the German government." Ward Price, *I Know These Dictators,* 31. On Hitler's decision to withdraw from the League of Nations, see Kershaw, *Hitler: Hubris,* 490–95.

34. On the role of tapestries in National Socialist interiors, see Prölss-Kammerer, *Tapisserie im Nationalsozialismus.*

35. Ward Price, *I Know These Dictators,* 29–32. See also the description of the party and the renovated Reich Chancellery rooms in Tennant, *True Account,* 184–87.

36. Speer, *Inside the Third Reich,* 129; Wagner and Cooper, *Heritage of Fire,* 122.

37. Günther, *Design der Macht,* 21. Compare this to the pre-renovation foyer depicted in Pünder, *Geschichte des Reichskanzlerpalais,* 10.

38. Günther, *Design der Macht,* 21–22, 24.

39. Pünder, *Geschichte des Reichskanzlerpalais,* 73–74; Wildcrotter, *Alltag der Macht,* 115–22; Günther, *Design der Macht,* 23; hearing, Traunstein Denazification Tribunal, January 21, 1947, Gerdy Troost Personal Papers, Ana 325.

40. Schwarz, *Geniewahn,* 137–38; Zimmermanns, *Friedrich August von Kaulbach,* 193, 282.

41. Speer, *Inside the Third Reich,* 119–21.

42. Ibid., 119.

43. Dietrich, *Hitler I Knew,* 199.

44. Spitzy, *So haben wir das Reich verspielt,* 125.

45. Günther, *Design der Macht,* 27.

46. Speer, *Inside the Third Reich,* 118.

47. Rauschning, *Voice of Destruction,* 61. On Hitler's daily routine at the Chancellery, see Kershaw, *Hitler: Nemesis,* 32–33.

48. Schwarz, *Geniewahn,* 118ff.

49. Ryback, *Hitler's Private Library.*

50. Günther, *Design der Macht,* 24–26. A 1943 letter from Gerdy Troost to Martin Bormann discussing which of the Old Chancellery

furnishings to place in protective storage mentions books in the library and in Hitler's study. Gerdy Troost to Martin Bormann, 1 September 1943, Troost, Gerhardine, Prof., RKK 2401, Box 257, File 8, microfilm G-0087/92, frame 1848, National Archives, College Park, Md. (originals in the Bundesarchiv Berlin-Lichterfelde).

51. Wagner and Cooper, *Heritage of Fire*, 122.

52. Ibid.

53. Speer dates this renovation, which is visible in fig. 4, to 1939. Speer, *Inside the Third Reich*, 130. Speer designed the furniture for her. Günther, *Design der Macht*, 70–72.

54. Seckendorff, "Monumentalität und Gemütlichkeit," 120.

55. NSDAP-Baupläne 11316, Bayerisches Hauptstaatsarchiv. For a photograph showing the state of the room in 1928, see Pünder, *Geschichte des Reichskanzlerpalais*, 14.

56. Viktor Hannemann, invoice, March 13, 1934; Gobelin Manufaktur A. Barfuss and Vikt. Hannemann to Atelier Troost, invoice, July 20, 1934; Mü. Gobelin Manufaktur to Atelier Troost, invoice, August 9, 1934; Max Schwarzer to Atelier Troost, invoice, September 3, 1934; all in German Captured Documents, Gerdy and Paul Troost Papers, microfilm reel 452 (container 768).

57. Günther, *Design der Macht*, 29–30; Dietrich, *Hitler I Knew*, 196; Kershaw, *Hitler*, 135.

58. 1935 invoices, Captured German Documents, Gerdy and Paul Troost Papers, microfilm reel 452 (container 768).

59. Troost, "Privat-Veröffentlichung."

60. Wilderotter, *Alltag der Macht*, 149–50.

61. Günther, *Design der Macht*, 31–33; Schwarz, *Geniewahn*, 133–35, 141–42; Schroeder, *He Was My Chief*, 37.

62. 1935–36 invoices, German Captured Documents, Gerdy and Paul Troost Papers, microfilm reel 452 (container 768).

63. NSDAP-Baupläne 11373, Bayerisches Hauptstaatsarchiv; *Silberspiegel*, "Neuen Räume," 524–26.

64. Schönberger, *Neue Reichskanzlei*, 34.

65. Arnold, *Neue Reichskanzlei*, 126–27.

66. Hitler, "Reichskanzlei," 280; Schönberger, *Neue Reichskanzlei*, 37ff; Arnold, *Neue Reichskanzlei*, 62ff. On the role of buildings in Hitler's vision of empire, see Thies, *Hitler's Plans for Global Domination*.

67. Günther, *Design der Macht*, 33; Schroeder, *He Was My Chief*, 38.

68. Kellerhoff, *Mythos Führerbunker*, 69–71.

69. Junge, *Until the Final Hour*, 148, 150.

3. CULTIVATED INTERIORS

1. Bathrick, "Cinematic Remaskings of Hitler," 152–55.

2. See receipts for payments totaling 120,000 Reichsmarks from the Eher Verlag to the Atelier Troost, dated March 27, 1935, May 10, 1935, May 15, 1935, and June 12, 1935; all in German Captured Documents, Gerdy and Paul Troost Papers, Library of Congress, Washington, D.C., microfilm reel 451 (container 767). The average taxable income of a doctor in Germany in 1935 was 11,608 Reichsmarks. Wuttke-Groneberg, *Medizin im Nationalsozialismus*, 347.

3. Police registration record for Jakob Ernst Reichert, PMB R80, Stadtarchiv München; SpkA 1393: Reichert, Ernst (8.10.1881), Staatsarchiv München. In the police investigation concerning Geli Raubal's death, Ernst Reichert is identified as a "*Bürovorsteher*," meaning head clerk or office manager. Police report dated September 28, 1931, MInn 72443, Bayerisches Hauptstaatsarchiv, Munich.

4. Adolf Hitler, completed questionnaire for apartment seekers, September 13, 1929, Zim 117, Stadtarchiv München.

5. In a postwar interview with the journalist Nerin E. Gun, Anni Winter mentioned that in 1931, when Geli Raubal died, she and her husband had their own apartment to which they returned at the end of the workday. In a 1948 interrogation, however, she indicated that the couple moved in with Hitler on October 1, 1929, and acquired their own "wing" during the subsequent renovation. Georg Winter is listed in the 1931 Munich address book as living in Hitler's apartment. Gun, *Eva Braun*, 8; Anni Winter, interrogation by Michael Musmanno, March 30, 1948, 1, Musmanno Collection, Duquesne University Archives, Pittsburgh, Pa.; entry for Prinzregentenplatz 16, *Adressbuch für München und Umgebung 1931*, microfilm, Stadtarchiv München.

6. Testimony of Georg Winter, May 25, 1948; and Ernst Hermann Sund to the Enforcement Division of the Internees' Hospital Garmisch-Partenkirchen, 29 January 1948, both in SpkA K 1985: Winter, Georg, Staatsarchiv München; Schirach, *Frauen um Hitler*, 44.

7. Ernst Hermann Sund to the Enforcement Division of the Internees' Hospital Garmisch-Partenkirchen, 21 January 1948; testimony

of Georg Winter, May 25, 1948; testimony of Julius Schaub, February 16, 1948; and verdict justification, August 13, 1948, all in SpkA K 1985: Winter, Georg, Staatsarchiv München.

8. Winter, Musmanno interrogation, March 30, 1948, 1, Musmanno Collection; Gerdy Troost to Frau v. Kardorf, n.d. [c. 1978], carbon copy, Gerdy Troost Personal Papers, Ana 325, Bayerische Staatsbibliothek, Munich; Nüsslein, *Paul Ludwig Troost,* 68–69; Seckendorff, "Monumentalität und Gemütlichkeit," 119. In 1978, Gerdy Troost recalled that although Elsa Bruckmann had taken Hitler to the United Workshops for Art in Handicraft to outfit his Munich apartment, he had found their prices too high and had not made additional purchases (although he did own a previously acquired Paul Troost desk). See Gerdy Troost to Frau v. Kardorf, n.d. [c. 1978], carbon copy, Gerdy Troost Personal Papers, Ana 325.

9. Winter, Musmanno interrogation, March 30, 1948, 12, and Winter, Musmanno interrogation, April 28, 1948, both in the Musmanno Collection; Schirach, *Frauen um Hitler,* 68, 73–75.

10. Junge, *Until the Final Hour,* 100.

11. Police report dated September 28, 1931, MInn 72443, Bayerisches Hauptstaatsarchiv.

12. Gerdy Troost, questionnaire, n.d., Karen Kuykendall Papers, MS 243, Special Collections, University of Arizona, Tucson.

13. Miller, "Hitleriana," 72–73. Only a small number of the photographs Lee Miller took at the apartment were published in this issue. The originals are held by the Lee Miller Archives, Farley Farm House, Muddles Green, Chiddingly, East Sussex, UK.

14. Reich Minister for Public Enlightenment and Propaganda [Joseph Goebbels] to State Secretary and Reich Chancellery Chief [Hans Lammers], 18 August 1935, R43 II/1065, Bundesarchiv Berlin-Lichterfelde. For the published photographs, see *die neue linie,* "Tradition und Gegenwart," 14–16, 48.

15. Plan of the apartment with proposed architectural modifications, January 1935, building file for 16 Prince Regent Square, number 169265, Lokalbaukommission München.

16. M. Rosenmüller to Atelier Troost, invoice for cleaners working from April 15–20, 1935, May 27, 1935, German Captured Documents, Gerdy and Paul Troost Papers, microfilm reel 451 (container 767). On April 27, 1935, Joseph

Goebbels visited the apartment and enthused: "His new apartment has turned out very gemütlich." Entry for April 27, 1935, Goebbels, *Tagebücher,* pt. 1, vol. 3 (book I), 223.

17. Bruppacher, *Adolf Hitler,* vol. 1, 405. On support for Hitler among Germany's aristocrats, see Petropoulos, *Royals and the Reich.*

18. Winter, Musmanno interrogation, March 30, 1948, 4, 14, Musmanno Collection.

19. Schirach, *Frauen um Hitler,* 46; Junge, *Until the Final Hour,* 100.

20. Invoice J. and F. Diepold, September 4, 1935, German Captured Documents, Gerdy and Paul Troost Papers, microfilm reel 451 (container 767).

21. Rasp, "Bauten und Bauplanung," 297; Nüsslein, *Paul Ludwig Troost,* 238–39.

22. Albert Speer to Karen Kuykendall, 19 February 1972, Karen Kuykendall Papers; Speer, *Inside the Third Reich,* 39.

23. Ward Price, *I Know These Dictators,* 27; Kershaw, *Making Friends with Hitler,* 51.

24. Max Färber Carpet Manufactory to Atelier Troost, invoice, June 3, 1935 (duplicate from April 24, 1935); Max Färber to Gerdy Troost, 20 April 1935; Max Färber to Gerdy Troost, 18 April 1935, all in German Captured Documents, Gerdy and Paul Troost Papers, microfilm reel 451 (container 767).

25. Jones, *Diary with Letters,* 197–98.

26. Craig, *Germany,* 692.

27. Northedge, *Troubled Giant,* 389; quoted in Hall, "Foreign Policy-Making Process," 477–99. For further reading on British-German naval relations, see Maiolo, *Royal Navy and Nazi Germany.*

28. Peterborough, "Baroque," *Daily Telegraph; New York Times,* "Hitler's Taste Shows Wagnerian Influence."

29. Stankiewitz, *Prachtstrassen in München,* 89–91.

30. Koss, *Modernism after Wagner,* 131–36; Seidel, ed., *Prinzregenten-Theater,* 20–21, 25–26, 28; Schläder and Braunmüller, *Tradition mit Zukunft,* 108, 115; Köhler, *Wagner's Hitler,* 262–63.

31. Stankiewitz, *Prachtstrassen in München,* 152. Another nearby musical reference, although to a different composer, is found in Grillparzer Street, which Hitler's apartment faced on its eastern side. The street was named after Franz Grillparzer, an Austrian poet who wrote a libretto as well as the funeral oration for Ludwig van Beethoven, also a

Hitler favorite.

32. Schwarz, *Geniewahn,* 110–11; Schirach, *Frauen um Hitler,* 46.

33. Danzker, ed., *Villa Stuck,* 296.

34. Spotts, *Hitler and the Power of Aesthetics,* 124; Schnöller, "Malerfürsten im 19. Jahrhundert," 195–217; Orosz, "Der Makart-Stil," 116–24; Jooss, "'Bauernsohn,'" 196–228; Muthesius, *Poetic Home,* 116. On conceptions of the artist's home more broadly, see Gribenski, Meyer, and Vernois, eds., *La Maison de l'artiste.*

35. Schwarz, *Geniewahn,* 70–75, 271–72.

36. Wichmann, *Neue Sammlung,* 25, 44, 46.

37. Aynsley, *Designing Modern Germany,* 117–18, 133–36.

38. Nüsslein, *Paul Ludwig Troost,* 250–51.

39. Götz, *Friedensengel,* 9, 12.

40. Nerdinger, ed., *Ort und Erinnerung,* 122.

41. Donath, *Architektur in München,* 38–39.

42. Letter to Dr. Schels of the Local Building Authority from the Munich Employment Office, dated 25 November 1939, building file for 16 Prince Regent Square, number 169265, Lokalbaukommission München.

43. Property tax registry (Grundsteuer-Kataster) 12994, Staatsarchiv München.

44. Jones, *Diary with Letters,* 198; Ward Price, *I Know These Dictators,* 27; Junge, *Until the Final Hour,* 99.

45. Bruppacher, *Adolf Hitler,* vol. 1, 509; Bruppacher, *Adolf Hitler,* vol. 2, 66; Winter, Musmanno interrogation, March 30, 1948, 4, Musmanno Collection.

46. Faber, *Munich, 1938,* 414–16.

47. Two similar bronze busts used to stand on the sideboard behind Hitler's desk in his formal office in the Old Chancellery; see "Large credenza in the study, over which hangs a large Renaissance painting, Reichs Chancellery, Berlin, Germany," in the online catalogue of the Print and Photographs Division of the Library of Congress, http://www.loc.gov/pictures/, under the call number LOT 3940 (H) [P&P]. These had been loaned to Hitler by Gerdy Troost and were identified in a 1935 inventory as two bronze heads by Luca della Robbia (list of antiques and bronzes owned by Gerdy Troost, March 22, 1935, R 43 I/1609, Bundesarchiv Berlin-Lichterfelde). One of the heads from the Chancellery office very closely resembles that seen in Hoffmann's photograph of Hitler's Munich apartment, where it may have been moved. Two bronze busts identical to those in the Old Chancellery were in

Troost's possession upon her death, when they were sold to private collectors. On the art collection in Hitler's Munich apartment, see Schwarz, *Geniewahn,* 105–15.

48. Faber, *Munich, 1938,* 415.

49. Carbon copy of letter to Franz Steigerwalds Neffe, 19 May 1942, German Captured Documents, Gerdy and Paul Troost Papers, microfilm reel 457 (container 774).

50. *New York Times,* "Capture of Kerch Claimed in Berlin"; Harris, "Today and Yesterday."

51. Invoices ranging from February 12, 1943, to July 13, 1943, Troost, Gerhardine, Prof., RKK 2401, Box 257, File 8, microfilm G087, frames 2562–2582, BDC Series 2401, A3339-RKK, National Archives, College Park, Md.

52. Fischer, *Hitler and America,* 199–225.

4. FROM HAUS WACHENFELD TO THE BERGHOF

1. Josef Neumaier, plan for building a garage and annex on the property of Frau "Councilor of Commerce" Winter, Obersalzberg, September 8, 1932, BLP Berchtesgaden 1933/27, Staatsarchiv München. The 1916 plans are reproduced in Joachimsthaler, *Hitlers Liste,* 278–79. Contemporary photographs also show that the front door was moved to the northeast side of the house and the kitchen expanded, but these do not appear on Neumaier's plan.

2. Dietrich, *With Hitler,* 44; Joachimsthaler, *Hitlers Liste,* 298.

3. Trevor-Roper, *Hitler's Table Talk,* 166; Joachimsthaler, *Hitlers Liste,* 294–96, 299; Chaussy and Püschner, *Nachbar Hitler,* 81; Schöner and Irlinger, *Alte Obersalzberg,* 16; Feiber, "Filiale von Berlin," 69.

4. Tolischus, "Where Hitler Dreams," 1.

5. Linge, *With Hitler to the End,* 22.

6. Various invoices from 1933 for domestic goods and plants sent to the Obersalzberg, NS-10 120, Bundesarchiv Berlin-Lichterfelde. This file also contains purchases made for Hitler's Munich apartment in the same period.

7. Speer, *Inside the Third Reich,* 85–86. On Speer's relationship to Hitler, see Sereny, *Albert Speer.*

8. Hans Friederich to the chairman, Miesbach Denazification Tribunal, 28 April 1948; and Baurat (building councilor) Adlmüller, declaration, May 19, 1948, both in SpkA K

262: Degano, Alois, Staatsarchiv München. For the 1936 Berghof building plans and elevations approved by the Berchtesgaden municipal authorities, see the collection BPL Berchtesgaden 1936-14 at the Staatsarchiv München.

9. Adolf Wagner to Hans Lammers, 25 September 1936, R43/4326, 10–11, Bundesarchiv Berlin-Lichterfelde.

10. Speer, *Inside the Third Reich,* facing 167; Pogge, "Berghof," 20; Chaussy and Püschner, *Nachbar Hitler,* 110.

11. On farmhouses in southeastern Upper Bavaria, see Gebhard and Keim, eds., *Oberbayern.*

12. L. Werner München to Adolf Hitler, invoices from 1933 and 1934, NS 10/120, Bundesarchiv Berlin-Lichterfelde. On March 20, 1934, Hitler purchased Klaus Thiede, *Deutsche Bauernhäuser* (Königstein im Taunus: Langewiesche, 1934).

13. *Innen-Dekoration,* "Berghof," 51; St[einlein], "Berghof Wachenfeld auf Obersalzberg," 457; Berndt, "Berghof," 769.

14. Speer, *Inside the Third Reich,* 46.

15. Mitchell, *Hitler's Mountain,* 44.

16. Speer, *Inside the Third Reich,* 86.

17. Trevor-Roper, *Hitler's Table Talk,* 184.

18. Alt's painting is reproduced in Gleis, ed., *Makart,* 27; Werckmeister, "Hitler the Artist," 270–97; Spotts, *Hitler and the Power of Aesthetics,* 43–94; Michaud, *Cult of Art,* 1–73; Schroeder, *He Was My Chief,* 164; drawing of the table, Berghof portfolio of drawings, Gerdy Troost Professional Papers, Ana 325.A.V.4, #2, Bayerische Staatsbibliothek, Munich. Most of the documentation pertaining to the Atelier Troost's projects held by the Bayerische Staatsbibliothek is open to researchers (under the call numbers Ana 325.A and Ana325.B). I have identified this material here and in subsequent endnotes as the "Gerdy Troost Professional Papers" to distinguish it from the sealed "Gerdy Troost Personal Papers." Nonetheless, the collections overlap somewhat with regard to the personal and professional nature of their contents.

19. "Umbau Berghof" ("Berghof renovation"), B1081, negatives 5–7, and B1084, negatives 1–7, 22–33, album 15, Heinrich Hoffmann Photograph Collection, Record Group 242-HLB, National Archives, College Park, Md.

20. Unity Mitford to Diana Mitford, 18 July 1938, in Mosley, *Mitfords,* 127.

21. Gerdy Troost, questionnaire, n.d.; Gerdy Troost to Karen Kuykendall, 15 January 1975, both in Karen Kuykendall Papers, MS 243, Special Collections, University of Arizona, Tucson. Troost also felt that the gabled front of the Berghof was too narrow for the structure as a whole.

22. Jones, *Diary with Letters,* 249.

23. Sylvester, *Real Lloyd George,* 235.

24. Lloyd George, "I Talked to Hitler." On Lloyd George's visit to the Berghof, see Lentin, *Lloyd George and Lost Peace,* 89–105.

25. Kirkpatrick, *Inner Circle,* 96–97. On Halifax's visit to Germany, see Faber, *Munich, 1938,* 9–45.

26. Stadler, "Hitler's Rooms," 64, 66; drawing of the sofa, January 10, 1936, Berghof portfolio of drawings, Gerdy Troost Professional Papers, Ana 325.A.V.4, #65.

27. Kirkpatrick, *Inner Circle,* 97.

28. Jones, *Diary with Letters,* 244. On the couches, see also Schroeder, *He Was My Chief,* 164.

29. Speer, *Inside the Third Reich,* 90, 86. On the visuality of the Great Hall, see also Koepnick, *Framing Attention,* 163–99.

30. For a list of prominent foreign visitors to the Berghof, see Feiber, "Filiale von Berlin," 133–34.

31. Jones, *Diary with Letters,* 249.

32. Undated pencil drawing of the marble mantel for the Great Hall fireplace, Berghof portfolio of drawings, Gerdy Troost Professional Papers, Ana 325.A.V.4, #8.

33. *Innen-Dekoration,* "Innenräume des Berghofes," 60; Speer, *Inside the Third Reich,* 90; drawing of the cupboard, December 5, 1935, Berghof portfolio of drawings, Gerdy Troost Professional Papers, Ana 325.A.V.4, #77.

34. Gerdy Troost to Karen Kuykendall, 15 January 1975, Karen Kuykendall Papers.

35. Seckendorff, "Monumentalität und Gemütlichkeit," 131; Schaffing, *Obersalzberg,* 95.

36. *Innen-Dekoration,* "Innenräume des Berghofes," 59.

37. Gerdy Troost to Karen Kuykendall, 15 January 1975, Karen Kuykendall Papers.

38. Heinrich Kreisel, report, September 12, 1936, German Captured Documents, Gerdy and Paul Troost Papers, Library of Congress, Washington, D.C., microfilm reel 449 (container 765). Gerdy Troost's use of colors

in the Great Hall is described at length in *Innen-Dekoration,* "Innenräume des Berghofes," 59–60.

39. Fabric sample book for the Berghof, Gerdy Troost Professional Papers, Ana325.A.V.4, #137.

40. Gerdy Troost to Karen Kuykendall, 27 November 1973, Karen Kuykendall Papers. See also Gerdy Troost to Winifred Wagner, 30 April 1975, carbon copy, Gerdy Troost Personal Papers, Ana 325.

41. Gerdy Troost, questionnaire, Karen Kuykendall Papers.

42. Toland, *Adolf Hitler,* 220.

43. Feiber, "Filiale von Berlin," 70.

44. *Innen-Dekoration,* "Berghof," 51, 53; *Innen-Dekoration,* "Innenräume des Berghofes," 57, 59.

45. Speer, *Inside the Third Reich,* 86.

46. Erlanger, "Hitler Loved Money."

47. Gerdy Troost to E. Fritzsche, 8 July 1936, German Captured Documents, Gerdy and Paul Troost Papers, microfilm reel 449 (container 765); Gerdy Troost, interview by John Toland, November 5, 1971, interview transcript for tape C-50, John Toland Papers, Franklin D. Roosevelt Library, Hyde Park, N.Y.; Silverman, *Hitler's Economy,* 171.

48. D'Almeida, *High Society,* 132–33; Speer, *Inside the Third Reich,* 90; drawing of the sideboard, Berghof portfolio of drawings, Gerdy Troost Professional Papers, Ana 325.A.V.4, #41 and #43.

49. Alois Degano to Julius Schaub, 27 November 1936, and Ludwig Zerzog to Adolf Hitler, 4 November 1936, both in NS-10 117, Bundesarchiv Berlin-Lichterfelde.

50. *Hitlers Berghof,* 54–55, 60–61.

51. Jones, *Diary with Letters,* 248.

52. Carroll, "Editorial Notes," 5; *Anglo-German Review* 2, no. 10 (September 1938): cover. On Chamberlain's visit to Berchtesgaden, see Faber, *Munich, 1938,* 272–96.

53. Schroeder, *He Was My Chief,* 155; Gerdy Troost, questionnaire, n.d., Karen Kuykendall Papers; Speer, *Inside the Third Reich,* 88.

54. Schwarz, *Geniewahn,* 124–27.

55. Storey, "Novel Decorations."

56. *Innen-Dekoration,* "Innenräume des Berghofes," 60–61, 63.

57. Machtan, "Hitler, Röhm," 17; Fromm, *Blood and Banquets,* 92.

58. Schwarz, *Geniewahn,* 159–64.

59. Junge, *Until the Final Hour,* 59–60.

60. Linge, *With Hitler to the End,* 24; "Der

Führer beim Kegeln. Berghof" ("The Führer bowling at the Berghof"), album 19, page B 1379, negatives 28–30, Heinrich Hoffmann Photograph Collection, Record Group 242-HLB.

61. Junge, *Until the Final Hour,* 58.

62. Speer, *Inside the Third Reich,* 86.

63. Junge, *Until the Final Hour,* 60–61; Schroeder, *He Was My Chief,* 149–50.

64. Martin Bormann, circular, October 5, 1938, NS 6/231, Bundesarchiv Berlin-Lichterfelde.

65. Schroeder, *He Was My Chief,* 141–42.

66. Linge, "I Was Hitler's Valet"; Görtemaker, *Eva Braun,* 164–66, 209.

67. Gerdy Troost, questionnaire, n.d., Karen Kuykendall Papers.

68. Eva Braun's Photo Albums, album 12, 242-EB-12–12A, Record Group 242-EB, National Archives, College Park, Md. A rare color photograph of this same room shows the color of the bird-motif fabric as blue rather than terra-cotta. Either Troost (or Braun) opted for a different color from the swatch in the sample book, or the color printed in the photograph was altered. See Capelle and Bovenkamp, *Berghof,* 44.

69. Gun, *Eva Braun,* 112–13; Sigmund, *Frauen der Nazis,* 263.

70. Schaub, *In Hitlers Schatten,* 278.

71. Linge, "Valet Upsets Love Scene." See also Schroeder, *He Was My Chief,* 143.

72. Berghof third- (attic-) story floor plan, BPL Berchtesgaden 1936-14-B116, Staatsarchiv München. This apartment also matches the description of Braun's rooms given by Sergeant Harry Sions when he visited the Berghof at the war's end (see Chapter 10). Sions, "Berchtesgaden," 4.

73. Schmölders, *Hitler's Face,* 72–73.

74. Eva Braun's Photo Albums, album 12, page 13, Record Group 242-EB.

75. Guerin, *Through Amateur Eyes,* 217–86; Lambert, *Eva Braun,* 161–74; McCrum and Downing, "Hitler Home Movies," 25.

76. Eva Braun's Photo Albums, album 6, 242-EB-6–26, 242-EB-6–30a, and 242-EB-6–34, Record Group 242-EB; Linge, *With Hitler to the End,* 70; Gun, *Eva Braun,* 160–61.

77. List of guests, security personnel, and domestic staff on the Obersalzberg dated May 10, 1939, NS-10 124, Bundesarchiv Berlin-Lichterfelde. A higher number of fifty domestic employees at the Berghof is given in

Remme, "Life with Hitler."

78. Neul, *Hitler und der Obersalzberg,* 85.
79. OBB KuPL 5441, 5450–5476, Bayerisches Hauptstaatsarchiv, Munich.
80. OBB KuPL 5441, 5471, Bayerisches Hauptstaatsarchiv.
81. OBB KuPL 5454, Bayerisches Hauptstaatsarchiv.
82. OBB KuPL 5456–5459, Bayerisches Hauptstaatsarchiv.
83. Habel, *Festspielhaus und Wahnfried,* 536–37.
84. OBB KuPL 5468, Bayerisches Hauptstaatsarchiv.
85. OBB KuPL 5462–5463, 5465–5467, Bayerisches Hauptstaatsarchiv.
86. Trevor-Roper, *Hitler's Table Talk,* 161.
87. Chaussy and Püschner, *Nachbar Hitler,* 111.
88. Feiber, "Filiale von Berlin," 176.
89. Trevor-Roper, *Hitler's Table Talk,* 162.
90. Trevor-Roper, ed., *Bormann Letters,* 171.

5. GERDY TROOST

1. The news of Hitler's death was broadcast on German radio at 10:30 P.M. on May 1, 1945. Gerdy Troost, 1945 datebook, Gerdy Troost Personal Papers, Ana 325, Bayerische Staatsbibliothek, Munich.
2. On women's architectural education, see Stratigakos, "I Myself Want to Build," 727–56. On women architects in Germany generally, see Stratigakos, *Women's Berlin.*
3. Gerdy Troost, curriculum vitae, n.d. [c. 1947], Gerdy Troost Personal Papers, Ana 325; Nüsslein, *Paul Ludwig Troost,* 56–57; Gerdy Troost letters to Maria Nachtigal, Gerdy Troost Personal Papers, Ana 325.
4. Nüsslein, *Paul Ludwig Troost,* 51, 52, 174ff. Gerdy Troost to Jessy Schroeder, 11 December 1934, quoted in ibid., 52. Gerdy Troost made a similar, if less personal, statement about her work with her husband in Rützow, "Betreuerin eines Vermächtnisses."
5. Gerdy Troost, "Adolf Hitler: Erste Begegnung—'Braunes Haus' (Umbau Palais Barlow)" ("Adolf Hitler: First Encounter—'Brown House' [Barlow Palace Renovation]"), undated manuscript, private collection.
6. Ibid.
7. Gerdy Troost to Maria Andresen, 25 November 1930, quoted in Schad, *Sie liebten den Führer,* 152.

8. Troost, "Adolf Hitler: Erste Begegnung." Gerdy Troost's postwar account suggesting that the couple shared concerns about Hitler's politics is contradicted by Paul Troost's entry into the National Socialist Party nearly two months before he met Hitler. His biographer, Timo Nüsslein, postulates, however, that Troost's membership card was backdated by the party, and that Troost joined the party with his wife in 1932. See Nüsslein, *Paul Ludwig Troost,* 68.
9. Nüsslein, *Paul Ludwig Troost,* 61–63, 66.
10. Ibid., 175–76; Albert Speer, *Inside the Third Reich,* 39; Schaub, *In Hitlers Schatten,* 138.
11. Hearing, Traunstein Denazification Tribunal, January 21, 1947, Gerdy Troost Personal Papers, Ana 325; Nüsslein, *Paul Ludwig Troost,* 66–67; Schaub, *In Hitlers Schatten,* 137; hearing, Munich I Denazification Tribunal, February 13, 1948, Gerdy Troost Personal Papers, Ana 325.
12. Gerdy Troost to Alice Hess, 14 April 1933, Gerdy Troost Personal Papers, Ana 325.
13. Ibid.
14. Brandt, "Hitler's Legion of Ladies."
15. Hearing, Traunstein Denazification Tribunal, January 21, 1947, Gerdy Troost Personal Papers, Ana 325.
16. Schwarz, *Geniewahn,* 84; Nüsslein, *Paul Ludwig Troost,* 75.
17. Adolf Hitler to Gerdy Troost, 21 January 1944, Gerdy Troost Personal Papers, Ana 325. The letter (abridged) is reprinted in Picker, *Hitlers Tischgespräche,* 204.
18. Hearing, Traunstein Denazification Tribunal, January 21, 1947, Gerdy Troost Personal Papers, Ana 325; Schaub, *In Hitlers Schatten,* 140.
19. Gerdy Troost to Karen Kuykendall, 12 February 1973, Karen Kuykendall Papers, MS 243, Special Collections, University of Arizona, Tucson; Jellonnek, *Homosexuelle unter dem Hakenkreuz,* 26.
20. Schaub, *In Hitlers Schatten,* 140.
21. August Wagner, Vereinigte Werkstätten für Mosaik und Glasmalerei to Vereinigte Süddeutsche Werkstätten für Mosaik und Glassmalerei, 1 June 1935; Vereinigte Süddeutsche Werkstätten to August Wagner, 5 June 1935; August Wagner to Gerdy Troost, 21 June 1935; Vereinigte Süddeutsche Werkstätten to August Wagner, 9 March 1936; Vereinigte Süddeutsche Werkstätten to August Wagner, 15 August 1936; August Wagner to "Nau," 28 September 1935;

Vereinigte Süddeutsche Werkstätten to August Wagner, 31 August 1936; Vereinigte Süddeutsche Werkstätten to August Wagner, 8 January 1937; and Atelier Troost to August Wagner, 18 February 1937, all in the Puhl and Wagner Collection, Berlinische Galerie, Berlin.

22. Dietrich, *Hitler I Knew,* 156; Gillessen, *Auf verlorenem Posten,* 457–502; entry for May 7, 1943, Goebbels, *Tagebücher,* pt. 2, vol. 8, 223; entry for June 17, 1943, ibid., 487.

23. Speer, *Inside the Third Reich,* 50–51. See also Schlenker, *Hitler's Salon,* 141–42; and Schad, *Sie liebten den Führer,* 164–65.

24. Wagner and Cooper, *Heritage of Fire,* 157.

25. Ibid.; Schultze-Naumburg, *Kunst und Rasse;* Schultze-Naumburg, *Gesicht des Deutschen Hauses;* Michaud, *Cult of Art,* 127–34; Borrmann, *Paul Schultze-Naumburg,* 208–9; Schad, *Sie liebten den Führer,* 164–65; Nüsslein, *Paul Ludwig Troost,* 76–77.

26. Winifred Wagner to Gerdy Troost, 7 July 1962; Gerdy Troost to Winifred Wagner, 14 July 1962; and Winifred Wagner to Gerdy Troost, 17 July 1962, all in Gerdy Troost Personal Papers, Ana 325. Emphasis in the original.

27. Schad, *Sie liebten den Führer,* 164–65; Günther, *Mein Eindruck,* 89–91. Günther's views are quoted and supported by Schultze-Naumburg's biographer; see Borrmann, *Paul Schultze-Naumburg,* 208–9.

28. Troost, ed., *Das Bauen im Neuen Reich,* 5–10.

29. Ibid., 10ff.

30. Kurt Trampler to Gerdy Troost, 4 January 1938, Troost Papers, NL Troost 16, Bayerisches Hauptstaatsarchiv, Munich. For additional letters between Trampler and Troost, see NL Troost 32, Bayerisches Hauptstaatsarchiv.

31. Publishing contract between Gauverlag Bayreuth, Gerdy Troost, and Kurt Trampler, June 23, 1944, Gerdy Troost Professional Papers, Ana 325.B, Bayerische Staatsbibliothek.

32. Preliminary overview of the conception and organization of the building and decorative arts exhibition planned for the House of German Art, October 6, 1937, German Captured Documents, Gerdy and Paul Troost Papers, Library of Congress, Washington, D.C., microfilm reel 461 (container no. 778).

33. *1. Deutsche Architektur und Kunsthandwerkausstellung.* See also images of the exhibition in "Im Kampf um das Dritte Reich," presentation album for Adolf Wagner, January 1938, LOT 2970–8, Prints and Photographs Division, Library of Congress, Washington, D.C.

34. Schad, *Sie liebten den Führer,* 163; Gerdy Troost, interview by John Toland, November 5, 1971, interview transcript for tape C-50, John Toland Papers, Franklin D. Roosevelt Library, Hyde Park, N.Y.; Albert Speer to Gerdy Troost, 2 August 1944, German Captured Documents, Gerdy and Paul Troost Papers, microfilm reel 458 (container no. 775).

35. This is evident in the 1970s correspondence of Karen Kuykendall with various members of Hitler's inner circle, including Speer. See Karen Kuykendall Papers.

36. Gerdy Troost, interview by John Toland, November 5, 1971, interview transcripts for tapes C-37 and tape C-50, John Toland Papers.

37. Gerdy Troost, "Zur Frage Albert Speer," unpublished manuscript, n.d., Gerdy Troost Personal Papers, Ana 325; Toland, *Adolf Hitler,* 414–15.

38. Gerdy Troost, notes on a telephone conversation with historian Matthias Schmidt of Berlin, October 27, 1981, Gerdy Troost Personal Papers, Ana 325.

39. Speer, *Inside the Third Reich,* 39–43, 49–51.

40. Feuchtmayr, *Prinz Carl-Palais,* 87; Walther and Gelberg, "Nationalsozialistische Aussenpolitik," 379.

41. Various 1937 invoices for Persian carpets purchased for the Prince Carl Palace, German Captured Documents, Gerdy and Paul Troost Papers, microfilm reel 459 (container 776).

42. Feuchtmayr, *Prinz Carl-Palais,* 82–90; Walther and Gelberg, "Nationalsozialistische Aussenpolitik," 379; Gerhard Stinglwagner, *Von Mönchen, Prinzen und Ministern,* 86–92.

43. Guenther, *Nazi Chic?,* 234–35. On the Four-Year Plan, see Tooze, *Wages of Destruction,* 203–84.

44. Leo Killy to Walter Köhler, 5 December 1936, Troost, Gerhardine, Prof., RKK 2401, Box 257, File 8, microfilm G087, frame 1732, BDC Series 2401, A3339-RKK, National Archives, College Park, Md. (originals in the Bundesarchiv Berlin-Lichterfelde).

45. Heinrich Ruelberg to Franz Willuhn, 20 March 1937, R43 II/375, Bundesarchiv Berlin-Lichterfelde.

46. Jaskot, *Architecture of Oppression,* 80–113.

47. Petropoulos, *Faustian Bargain,* 137.

48. Heinrich Doehle to Colonel Keil, 16 July 1940, microfilm reel 452 (container 768);

Recruiting District Headquarters Munich I to Atelier Troost, 20 March 1941, microfilm reel 450 (container 766); Recruiting District Headquarters Munich I to Gerdy Troost, 24 April 1941, microfilm reel 450 (container 766); and Ernst Heigenmooser to Gerdy Troost, 18 December 1943, microfilm reel 458 (container 775), all in German Captured Documents, Gerdy and Paul Troost Papers.

49. Wilhelm Corsten to the chairman, Traunstein Denazification Tribunal, May 27, 1947, SpkA K 1844: Troost, Gerdy, Staatsarchiv München; Nüsslein, *Paul Ludwig Troost,* 187–88.

50. Nüsslein, "Gerdy Troost," 128–36.

51. Gerdy Troost to Willy Wiegand, 8 August 1940, German Captured Documents, Gerdy and Paul Troost Papers, microfilm reel 450 (container 766). See also the memo specifying the tasks and responsibilities of each member of the artistic team (including Troost) involved in the design and making of the certificate and presentation folder for the awarding of Reich Marshal Hermann Göring's Grand Cross, December 19, 1941, German Captured Documents, Gerdy and Paul Troost Papers, microfilm reel 461 (container 778).

52. Kiener, "Ritterkreuzurkunden," 247–55.

53. Gerdy Troost to Heinrich Doehle, 9 November 1940, German Captured Documents, Gerdy and Paul Troost Papers, microfilm reel 452 (container 768).

54. Nüsslein, *Paul Ludwig Troost,* 188.

55. Carl Wildbrett to Ministerial Advisor Dr. v. Schröder, 25 April 1944; and Lüdke to Atelier Troost, 30 April 1944, both in German Captured Documents, Gerdy and Paul Troost Papers, microfilm reel 458 (container 775).

56. Wandinger to the Jean Wunderlich Firm, 25 February 1943, German Captured Documents, Gerdy and Paul Troost Papers, microfilm reel 461 (container 778); and F. H. Wandinger to the Reich Office for Precious Metals, 7 June 1943; Helmut von Hummel to the Reich Office for Precious Metals, 8 June 1943; Gerdy Troost to Otto Meissner, 28 July 1943; F. H. Wandinger, invoice, October 8, 1943; and authorization certificate (to import jewels) for Jean Wunderlich from F. H. Wandinger, n.d., all in German Captured Documents, Gerdy and Paul Troost Papers, microfilm reel 458 (container 775).

57. *Der Spiegel,* "Kriegsorden," 34.

58. Gerdy Troost to Willy Wiegand, 8 August 1940, German Captured Documents, Gerdy and Paul Troost Papers, microfilm reel 450 (container 766).

59. Schaub, *In Hitlers Schatten,* 140.

60. Hearing, Traunstein Denazification Tribunal, January 21, 1947, Gerdy Troost Personal Papers, Ana 325.

61. Ferdinand Mößmer to Gerdy Troost, 22 February 1934, German Captured Documents, Gerdy and Paul Troost Papers, microfilm reel 449 (container 765).

62. Wilhelm Corsten to the chairman, Traunstein Denazification Tribunal, 22 April 1947; and Gerdy Troost to C. Sachs, 15 May 1950, both in SpkA K 1844: Troost, Gerdy, Staatsarchiv München; M.-M., jr., "Frau Troost."

63. Julius Schaub to Hans Lammers, 8 January 1940; Julius Schaub to Hans Lammers, 2 March 1942; and Julius Schaub to Hans Lammers, 10 February 1943, all in R43II/1242, Bundesarchiv Berlin-Lichterfelde.

64. Petropoulos, *Art as Politics,* 277.

65. Proceedings of the Hauptkammer München, February 23, 1950; and Therese Lang, sworn declaration, May 30, 1949, both in SpkA K 1844: Troost, Gerdy, Staatsarchiv München.

66. *Völkischer Beobachter,* "Deutsche Künstler"; Academy of the Fine Arts to the Ministry of Education and Culture, 1 June 1937, MK 40901, Bayerisches Hauptstaatsarchiv; *Bauwelt,* "Persönliches," 670; Bachmann to Gerdy Troost, 9 April 1943, Troost, Gerhardine, Prof., RKK 2401, Box 257, File 8, microfilm G087, frame 1888, BDC Series 2401, A3339-RKK, National Archives.

67. 1939 Party Survey, NSDAP chancellery correspondence, Troost, Gerdy, H., VBS 1, 1180015252, Bundesarchiv Berlin-Lichterfelde.

68. Gerda [*sic*] Troost to Adolf Hitler, 31 January 1943, carbon copy, SpkA K 1844: Troost, Gerdy, Staatsarchiv München.

69. Hearing, Traunstein Denazification Tribunal, January 21, 1947, Gerdy Troost Personal Papers, Ana 325.

70. Rützow, "Betreuerin eines Vermächtnisses"; *Welt-Spiegel,* "Führer im Haus der Deutschen Kunst," cover page; I. v. W., "Aus der Arbeit von Frau Prof. Troost."

71. Werner, "Führer und seine Architekten," 27.

72. Lochner, "Hitler Looks to Aides"; Dickson, "Europe's Man of Mystery!"

73. Nüsslein, *Paul Ludwig Troost,* 178.

74. Dora Herrmann to Gerdy Troost, 12 July 1938, German Captured Documents, Gerdy and Paul Troost Papers, microfilm reel 450 (container 766); Hans Rose to Gerdy Troost, 1 October 1938; Leo Perlstein to Gerdy Troost, 12 November 1938; and Theresia Lisch-Hasenforther to Gerdy Troost, 2 November 1941, all in German Captured Documents, Gerdy and Paul Troost Papers, reel 462 (container 779).

75. "[Na?]chspiel zur Fernfahrt des kgl. Italienischen Automobilklubs von Mailand nach Stolp," *Die Wochenschau,* April 21, 1928, 3, newspaper clipping, private collection; "Schweres Autounglück am Dorfner Berg," *Wolfratshauser Wochenblatt,* April 21, 1928, newspaper clipping, private collection; Gerdy Troost to Adolf Hitler, 8 September 1942, and Gerdy Troost to Ernst Haiger, 9 November 1942, both in German Captured Documents, Gerdy and Paul Troost Papers, reel 457 (container 774); Gerdy Troost's medical records, German Captured Documents, Gerdy and Paul Troost Papers, microfilm reel 451 (container 767). Gerdy Troost also discussed Zabel's diet with Hitler: see Gerdy Troost to Werner Zabel, 10 July 1943, SpkA K 1844: Troost, Gerdy, Staatsarchiv München.

76. Ragnar Berg to Gerdy Troost, n.d. [December 1942]; Lammers to Ragnar Berg, 30 November 1942, photocopy; and Gerdy Troost to Ragnar Berg, 23 December 1942, carbon copy, all in Gerdy Troost Personal Papers, Ana 325.

77. Burleigh and Wipperman, *Racial State,* 77–112; Burleigh, *Third Reich,* 281–342; Karl Wessely, sworn declaration, December 2, 1946, carbon copy; and Maria Nachtigal, sworn declaration, December 11, 1946, carbon copy, both in SpkA K 1844: Troost, Gerdy, Staatsarchiv München; Friedel, "Karl Wessely," 25–30, 109–16, 143–44.

78. Maria Nachtigall, sworn declaration, December 11, 1946, carbon copy, SpkA K 1844: Troost, Gerdy, Staatsarchiv München.

79. Selig, *"Arisierung" in München,* 809; Nüsslein, *Paul Ludwig Troost,* 177–78; Löhr, *Braune Haus der Kunst,* 56, 117, 129. For a broader European perspective, see Dean, *Robbing the Jews.*

80. Gerdy Troost to Karen Kuykendall, 12 February 1973, Karen Kuykendall Papers; Gerdy Troost to Hans Lammers, 21 August 1936; Hans Lammers to Gerdy Troost, 28 August 1936; Gerdy Troost to Hans Lammers, 3 September 1936; and Gerdy Troost to Hans Lammers, 12 October 1936, all in German Captured Documents, Gerdy and Paul Troost Papers, microfilm reel 449 (container 765); Gerdy Troost to Alwin-Broder Albrecht, 9 November 1943, German Captured Documents, Gerdy and Paul Troost Papers, microfilm reel 458 (container 775). Albert Speer claimed that this "silver work of high artistic merit" was carried out according to Gerdy Troost's sketches and under her supervision. Albert Speer to Karen Kuykendall, 19 February 1972, Karen Kuykendall Papers.

81. Schlenker, *Hitler's Salon,* 140–41.

82. Albert Stenzel, expert opinion, October 24, 1946, SpkA K 1844: Troost, Gerdy, Staatsarchiv München.

83. Brantl, *Haus der Kunst,* 81–84; Toland interview with Troost, transcript for tape C-50, John Toland Papers. On the *Degenerate Art* exhibition, see Barron et al., *"Degenerate Art";* and Peters, ed., *Degenerate Art.*

84. Brantl, *Haus der Kunst,* 83–84; Toland, *Adolf Hitler,* 415; Toland interview with Troost, transcript for tape C-50 (quotes slightly amended), John Toland Papers; entry for June 6, 1937, Goebbels, *Tagebücher,* pt. 1, vol. 4, 170.

85. Westheim, "Die janze Richtung"; Gerdy Troost to Karen Kuykendall, 29 September 1977, Karen Kuykendall Papers.

86. Hearing, Traunstein Denazification Tribunal, January 21, 1947, Gerdy Troost Personal Papers, Ana 325.

87. Toland interview with Troost, transcript for tape C-50, John Toland Papers. Hearing, Traunstein Denazification Tribunal, January 21, 1947; and hearing, Munich I Denazification Tribunal, February 13, 1948, both in Gerdy Troost Personal Papers, Ana 325.

88. Gerdy Troost to Karen Kuykendall, 25 September 1978, Karen Kuykendall Papers; Toland interview with Troost, transcript for tape C-50, John Toland Papers.

89. Entry for January 21, 1936, Goebbels, *Tagebücher,* pt. 1, vol. 3 (book I), 366. See also entry for March 24, 1934, ibid., pt. 1, vol. 2 (book III), 390; entry for January 23, 1938, ibid., pt. 1, vol. 5, 112; and entry for June 27, 1943, ibid., pt. 2, vol. 8, 552.

90. "Grosse Halle, Geiselgasteig—Filmwerkstätten" ("Soundstage, Geiselgasteig Film Studios"), photocopy of text prepared for Martha Schad, n.d.; and hearing, Traunstein

Denazification Tribunal, January 21, 1947, both Gerdy Troost Personal Papers, Ana 325; entry for February 17, 1938, Goebbels, *Tagebücher,* pt. 1, vol. 5, 160.

91. Entry for June 22, 1938, Goebbels, *Tagebücher,* pt. 1, vol. 5, 355. In a later diary entry, however, he seems convinced that he had transformed her into an ally for his film plans. Entry for February 26, 1939, ibid., pt. 1, vol. 6, 269. Hellmut Keil, who knew Troost from the Bavaria Filmkunst board, claimed that she did resist Goebbels's influence. Hellmut Keil, sworn declaration, March 29, 1949, SpkA K 1844: Troost, Gerdy, Staatsarchiv München.

92. Entry for November 21, 1940, Goebbels, *Tagebücher,* pt. 1, vol. 8, 429.

93. Copies of both films are in the Bundesarchiv-Filmarchiv, Berlin. An undated list of films (pre-1945), noting thirty-two titles and the storage of the negatives with Kinokop in Berlin, is among Gerdy Troost Personal Papers, Ana 325.

94. Hanni Umlauf, appendix to curriculum vitae, n.d. (postwar), Gerdy Troost Personal Papers, Ana 325.

95. Hanni Umlauf to Gerdy Troost, 1 March 1951, Gerdy Troost Personal Papers, Ana 325; Johanna Umlauf, police registration record, Stadtarchiv München; Dieter Umlauf, in discussion with the author, November 2010.

96. Winifred Wagner to Gerdy Troost, 31 December 1965; Winifred Wagner to Gerdy Troost, 6 September 1965; and Gerdy Troost to Winifred Wagner, 21 November 1966, all in Gerdy Troost Personal Papers, Ana 325.

97. Schoppmann, *Zeit der Maskierung,* 15.

98. Hearing, Traunstein Denazification Tribunal, January 21, 1947, Gerdy Troost Personal Papers, Ana 325; Paul Capellmann, sworn declaration, June 25, 1947, carbon copy, SpkA K 1844: Troost, Gerdy, Staatsarchiv München.

99. L. Werner München, invoice, September 9, 1939, NL Troost 24, Bayerisches Hauptstaatsarchiv.

100. Schad, *Sie liebten den Führer,* 177; Junge, *Until the Final Hour,* 137–38; Martin Bormann to Gerdy Troost, 18 April 1943; and Martin Bormann to Gerdy Troost, 8 May 1943, both in German Captured Documents, Gerdy and Paul Troost Papers, microfilm reel 458 (container 775).

101. Schad, *Sie liebten den Führer,* 177; hearing, Traunstein Denazification Tribunal, January 21, 1947, Gerdy Troost Personal Papers, Ana 325.

102. Hearing, Traunstein Denazification Tribunal, January 21, 1947, Gerdy Troost Personal Papers, Ana 325; Gerdy Troost to Paul Giesler, 17 August 1944, SpkA K 1844: Troost, Gerdy, Staatsarchiv München.

103. Attestation from Police Station 4 (16 Emil Riedel Street, Munich) confirming the date when Gerdy Troost fled Munich, April 23, 1948, SpkA K 1844: Troost, Gerdy, Staatsarchiv München.

104. Gerdy Troost to Winifred Wagner, 18 March 1947, Gerdy Troost Personal Papers, Ana 325.

105. Hauptkammer München, proceedings (continuation) of the public hearing on February 23, 1950, SpkA K 1844: Troost, Gerdy, Staatsarchiv München.

106. Hanni Umlauf, denazification registration form, May 5, 1946, SpkA K 2616: Umlauf, Hanni, Staatsarchiv München; Hanni Umlauf, appendix to curriculum vitae, n.d. (postwar), Gerdy Troost Personal Papers, Ana 325; Werner Zabel, medical report, February 21, 1950, SpkA K 1844: Troost, Gerdy, Staatsarchiv München; *Die Abendzeitung,* "Gerhardine Troost."

107. Schad, *Sie liebten den Führer,* 178. Troost, then in her mid-nineties, told Schad that she had been placed under house arrest for six years, but there is no evidence to support this claim. To the contrary, in an application submitted by Wilhelm Corsten, Troost's financial advisor, to the military government on November 12, 1946, he stated that Gerdy Troost had never been arrested. Wilhelm Corsten, application for a special license to engage in a transaction, submitted to the Military Government Finance Section, November 12, 1946, Gerdy Troost Personal Papers, Ana 325.

108. "Auszug aus dem Bericht: Chieming 11. Juli 1945: Frau Professor Troost" ("Excerpt from the report: Chieming, July 11, 1945: Frau Professor Troost"), SpkA K 1844: Troost, Gerdy, Staatsarchiv München. This is an excerpt of a fuller report on Troost that apparently went missing. Mayor of Chieming Municipality, "Beurteilung der Frau Gerhardine Troost" ("Assessment of Gerhardine Troost"), August 11, 1946, SpkA K 1844: Troost, Gerdy, Staatsarchiv München.

109. Emphasis in the original. Wilhelm Corsten to Gerdy Troost, 16 January 1947, Gerdy Troost Personal Papers, Ana 325.

110. Hearing, Traunstein Denazification

Tribunal, January 21, 1947; hearing, Munich I Denazification Tribunal, February 13, 1948; and court transcript, denazification hearings on February 23–24, 1950, before the Hauptkammer München, all in Gerdy Troost Personal Papers, Ana 325.

111. Curt von Stackelberg, defense brief, October 27, 1947, SpkA K 1844: Troost, Gerdy, Staatsarchiv München; W. Schmitz-Bäumer to Gerdy Troost, 30 January 1956, Gerdy Troost Personal Papers, Ana 325.

112. Hearing, Traunstein Denazification Tribunal, January 21, 1947, Gerdy Troost Personal Papers, Ana 325.

113. Hearing, Munich I Denazification Tribunal, February 13, 1948, Gerdy Troost Personal Papers, Ana 325.

114. Curt von Stackelberg, defense brief, October 27, 1947, SpkA K 1844: Troost, Gerdy, Staatsarchiv München.

115. M.-M., jr., "Frau Troost."

116. Albert Stenzel, expert opinion, September 4, 1948; and chairman of the Hauptkammer München to Dr. Lutz, 27 January 1949, both in SpkA K 482: Gall, Leonhard, Staatsarchiv München.

117. Reichel, *Schöne Schein des Dritten Reiches;* Spotts, *Hitler and the Power of Aesthetics;* Rentschler, *Ministry of Illusion.*

118. Hearing, Munich I Denazification Tribunal, February 13, 1948, Gerdy Troost Personal Papers, Ana 325.

119. Report on Gerdy Troost's trial addressed to State Secretary C. Sachs, Bavarian State Ministry for Special Affairs, February 24, 1950, SpkA K 1844: Troost, Gerdy, Staatsarchiv München.

120. Verdict, March 2, 1950, in ibid.

121. Ibid. The *Süddeutsche Zeitung* incorrectly reported that Troost was forbidden to work for ten years (in fact, it was two). Lb, "Frau Troost."

122. Denazification verdict, December 21, 1948; proceedings of the public hearing on December 21, 1948; and Professor Peter Birkenholz testimonial, November 20, 1945, all in SpkA K 482: Gall, Leonhard, Staatsarchiv München; verdict, March 2, 1950, SpkA K 1844: Troost, Gerdy, Staatsarchiv München.

123. Gerdy Troost to C. Sachs, 15 May 1950; and resolution, Minister for Political Liberation in Bavaria, August 7, 1950, both in SpkA K 1844: Troost, Gerdy, Staatsarchiv München; Leonhard Gall, petition for a reduction in fees,

March 22, 1949; and Prosecutor, Hauptkammer München to Leonhard Gall, 4 April 1949, both in SpkA K 482: Gall, Leonhard, Staatsarchiv München. On fines in denazification trials, see Petropoulos, "Postwar Justice," 325–38.

124. Wilhelm Corsten to Tax Office for Munich North, 14 May 1946, carbon copy, Gerdy Troost Personal Papers, Ana 325.

125. Tax Office for Munich North, certified copy of the notice of income tax assessment, carbon copy, August 22, 1946, Gerdy Troost Personal Papers, Ana 325.

126. *Bayerisches Gesetz-u. Verordnungsblatt,* "Gesetz zum Abschluss." The law became effective on September 1, 1950; A. Templer to Hauptkammer München, 17 October 1950; and Hauptkammer München, certificate, October 30, 1950, both in SpkA K 1844: Troost, Gerdy, Staatsarchiv München.

127. Gerdy Troost to Arfmann and Festerling, 1 August 1954; 1955 income statement; Deutsche Holzkunstwerkstätten, list of commissions paid to Gerdy Troost from October 1, 1955, to December 31, 1955, n.d.; Deutsche Holzkunstwerkstätten to Heinrich Arfmann, 20 March 1956; and Deutsche Holzkunstwerkstätten, list of commissions paid to Gerdy Troost from January 1, 1956, to March 31, 1956, April 25, 1956, all in Gerdy Troost Personal Papers, Ana 325.

128. Gerdy Troost to Dr. Mulzer, 29 September 1962, carbon copy; Gerdy Troost to Dr. Mulzer, 5 July 1962, carbon copy; and Gerdy Troost to Dr. Mulzer, 5 April 1962, carbon copy, all in Gerdy Troost Personal Papers, Ana 325.

129. Troost to Dr. Mulzer, 29 September 1962, carbon copy; Gerdy Troost to Heinrich Arfmann, 23 March 1959, carbon copy; and Gerdy Troost to Bavarian State Bank, 20 April 1966, all in Gerdy Troost Personal Papers, Ana 325. On postwar design in West Germany, see Betts, *Authority of Everyday Objects.*

130. Gerdy Troost to Karen Kuykendall, 25 September 1978, Karen Kuykendall Papers.

131. Hanni Umlauf, appendix to curriculum vitae, n.d. (postwar), Gerdy Troost Personal Papers, Ana 325.

132. Umlauf, *Zwischen Rhein und Ruhr.*

133. Gerdy Troost to Winifred Wagner, 14 August 1970, carbon copy, Gerdy Troost Personal Papers.

134. Winifred Wagner to Gerdy Troost, 6

September 1962, Gerdy Troost Personal Papers, Ana 325.

135. Winifred Wagner to Gerdy Troost and Hanni Umlauf, 1 October 1969; and Gerdy Troost to Winifred Wagner, 14 October 1968, carbon copy, both in Gerdy Troost Personal Papers, Ana 325.

136. Lotte Pfeiffer-Bechstein to Winifred Wagner, 15 July 1975, letter enclosed with Winifred Wagner to Gerdy Troost, 16 July 1975, Gerdy Troost Personal Papers, Ana 325. In her book on Winifred Wagner, Brigitte Hamann misidentifies the artwork that Troost hoped to sell as a bust of Hitler. Hamann, *Winifred Wagner,* 502. On the Bechsteins, see Joachimsthaler, *Hitlers Liste,* 63–102.

137. "Eugen Henke" folder, Gerdy Troost Personal Papers, Ana 325; "BND: 'Die Welt ist voller Wunder,'" *Der Spiegel,* December 11, 1978, 20–21.

138. Photocopies of the letters are among Gerdy Troost Personal Papers, Ana 325.

139. Johnson, "Nazi Feminists," 55–62; Gordon, "Review Essay: Nazi Feminists?," 97–105.

140. Emphasis in the original. Hanna Löv to Gerdy Troost, 14 June 1939; Gerdy Troost to Hanna Löv, 28 June 1939; and Hanna Löv to Gerdy Troost, 9 December 1939, all in German Captured Documents, Gerdy and Paul Troost Papers, microfilm reel 455 (container 772); Gerdy Troost to Karen Kuykendall, 12 February 1973, Karen Kuykendall Papers. On Löv, see Aicher and Drepper, eds., *Robert Vorhoelzer.*

141. Braveheart, "Remember Gerdy Troost."

142. Williamson, *Knight's Cross,* 7.

6. CAMPAIGN POLITICS AND THE INVENTION OF THE PRIVATE HITLER

1. Toland, *Adolf Hitler,* 263.

2. Herz, *Hoffmann und Hitler,* 194, 243. My discussion of this critical shift in National Socialist propaganda is indebted to Rudolf Herz's study of Heinrich Hoffmann's broad role in the creation of the Führer myth.

3. Kershaw, *Hitler: Hubris,* 363.

4. Herz, *Hoffmann und Hitler,* 190–94, 242–48; Kershaw, *"Hitler Myth,"* 41–42; Goltz, *Hindenburg,* 156.

5. Herz, *Hoffmann und Hitler,* 194, 197.

6. Hoffman, ed., *Hitler wie ihn keiner kennt,* 40.

7. Baldur von Schirach, "Zum Geleit," in Hoffmann, *Hitler wie ihn keiner kennt,*

x–xi. Capitals in the original.

8. Ibid., xiii. Capitals in the original.

9. Hoffmann, *Hitler wie ihn keiner kennt,* 69.

10. Schirach, "Zum Geleit," xiii–xiv.

11. Hoffmann, *Hitler wie ihn keiner kennt,* 61.

12. Schirach, "Zum Geleit," xiv.

13. Hoffmann, *Hitler wie ihn keiner kennt,* 88.

14. Ibid., 14–15.

15. Reinhold, "Unwiderstehliche," 839.

16. Hoffmann, *Hitler wie ihn keiner kennt,* 74, 38–39.

17. Ibid., 75, 77.

18. Goebbels, "Adolf Hitler als Mensch."

19. *Vorwärts,* "Vielgeknipste."

20. Schirach, "Zum Geleit," xi–xiii.

21. Friedrich, *Hitler's Berlin,* 217.

22. Reinhold, "Unwiderstehliche," 837–40.

23. Herz, *Hoffmann und Hitler,* 244, 372.

24. *Life,* "Speaking of Pictures," 6–7, 9.

25. McDaniel, "Hitler Myth?," 46–53. On American views of the Nazi regime, see also Moore, *Know Your Enemy.*

26. Ploch, "Bild als Ware," 8, 12.

7. AN ALPINE SEDUCTION

1. Schuster-Winkelhof, *Adolf Hitlers Wahlheimat.*

2. Walter Schmidkunz, "Begleitworte," in ibid., 2.

3. Chaussy and Püschner, *Nachbar Hitler,* 69–70.

4. Schmidkunz, "Begleitworte," 4.

5. Schuster, *Weisse Berge, Schwarze Zelte.* The following year, he began to publish under the name Schuster-Winkelhof.

6. Speer, *Inside the Third Reich,* 48.

7. Schmidkunz, "Begleitworte," 15. The Obersalzberg was part of the Salzberg municipality, which should not be confused with the nearby Austrian city of Salzburg.

8. Schmidkunz, "Begleitworte," 15.

9. Ibid., 1.

10. Ibid., 10; Herfried Münkler, *Deutschen und ihre Mythen,* 36–68; Uhlir, ed., *Schattenreich des Untersberges,* 43–46, 73–75.

11. Schmidkunz, "Begleitworte," 14–15. On the shaping of the public image of Hitler's domesticity in 1932, see Chapter 6.

12. Ibid., 15, 9.

13. Sontag, "Fascinating Fascism," 23–30.

14. *Deutschland-Bericht der Sopade* 1, no. 2 (May–June 1934), reprinted in *Deutschland-Berichte,* 101.

15. Chaussy and Püschner, *Nachbar Hitler,* 72–73.

16. Ibid., 73–80. In a later, officially sanctioned

publication about the Berghof, the history of the Türken Inn was cynically rewritten to erase the memory of the Schuster family's presence and replace it with that of another. See Hamm, *Obersalzberg,* 14–18.

17. Evans, *Third Reich in Power,* 81.

18. Chaussy and Püschner, *Nachbar Hitler,* 94–107, 116–20. For details on the sale of the Obersalzberg properties, see Schöner and Irlinger, *Alte Obersalzberg.*

19. Baldur von Schirach, "Zum Geleit," in Hoffmann, ed., *Hitler in seinen Bergen,* n.p.

20. See, for example, Hoffmann, ed., *Hitler Abseits vom Alltag.*

21. Schirach, "Zum Geleit."

22. Hoffmann, ed., *Jugend um Hitler,* n.p.

23. Schirach, "Zum Geleit."

24. Knopp and Staehler, "Familie Hitler," 39–43.

25. *Adolf Hitler an seine Jugend,* n.p. Further reinforcing the connection, Hitler's Nuremberg words were used as a caption for two photographs of Hitler posing with children in *Jugend um Hitler* and repeated in the foreword by Baldur von Schirach.

26. Herz, *Hoffmann und Hitler,* 248–52.

27. *Life,* "Speaking of Pictures," 6–7, 9.

28. See Pine, *Nazi Family Policy;* Pine, *Education in Nazi Germany;* and Kater, *Hitler Youth.*

29. *Münchner Illustrierte Presse* 13, no. 3 (1936): 412.

30. Ploch, "Bild als Ware," 8.

31. Richard F. Reiter, e-mail message to the author, August 13, 2012. See also Knox and Obee, "Uncle Wolf and Me."

32. Chaussy and Püschner, *Nachbar Hitler,* 152, 238n15.

33. Dietrich, *Road to Power,* 43.

34. Trevor-Roper, *Hitler's Table Talk,* 128.

35. Schirach, "Zum Geleit."

36. Ozturk, "Interlude," 77–97; Rosenblum, *Modern Painting,* 10–40; Schwarz, *Geniewahn,* 34.

37. Rentschler, *Ministry of Illusion,* 27–51; Hake, *German National Cinema,* 45–46.

38. In later wartime newsreels, Hitler did appear near the window, but in carefully staged dramatic and dynamic contexts. See Chapter 9.

39. *Deutschland Erwacht,* 141. On the Nazi domination of nature in the east, see Blackbourn, *Conquest of Nature,* 251–309.

40. Hoffmann, *Hitler in seinen Bergen,* n.p.

41. H. E., "'Führer' hinter Stacheldraht."

42. *Pariser Tageszeitung,* "Hitlers Bergfestung in Berchtesgaden."

43. Jacobs, "Zwischen Intuition und Experiment," 171.

44. *Adolf Hitler: Bilder;* Herz, *Hoffmann und Hitler,* 372.

45. Koonz, *Nazi Conscience,* 77.

46. Steinberg, *Nazi-Kitsch,* 5–6, 80–81.

47. *New York Times,* "Reich Exhibits"; *Deutscher Reichsanzeiger,* "Entscheidungen"; *Deutsche Handels-Wacht,* "Pleite, die uns freut," 198.

48. For an extensive collection of newspaper and journal articles on the campaign against kitsch, see Bundesarchiv Berlin-Lichterfelde (BArch) NS 5 VI/19127, NS 5 VI/19128, and NS 15/157. On the German Werkbund, see Campbell, *German Werkbund;* Schwartz, *Werkbund;* and Stratigakos, "Women and the Werkbund," 490–511.

49. Hopmann, "Fort mit dem nationalen Kitsch," 255; *Niedersachsen-Stürmer,* "Wasserkopf als Salzstreuer," 7; Dr. M. V., "Typen des Kitsches," 21–23; *New York Times,* "Reich Exhibits"; *Boston Sunday Globe,* "Bad Taste, Says Hitler." See also Betts, *Authority of Everyday Objects,* 31–34.

50. Kolbrand, "Kampf dem Kitsch," 14. See also van Dyke, "Kunst, Propaganda und Kitsch," 250–57.

51. Steinberg, *Nazi-Kitsch,* 81.

52. Ornamental plates that depicted the large swastika flag that hung outside the house were also forbidden. Feiber, "Filiale von Berlin," 68–69.

53. Ibid., 69.

54. Steinberg, *Nazi-Kitsch,* 81.

55. Feiber, "Filiale von Berlin," 69.

56. *Innen-Dekoration,* "Berghof," 50–53; *Innen-Dekoration,* "Innenräume des Berghofes," 54–64; Pogge, "Berghof," 18–26, 52.

57. *Innen-Dekoration,* "Berghof," 51, 53.

58. *Innen-Dekoration,* "Innenräume des Berghofes," 55, 59–61.

59. *Innen-Dekoration,* "Berghof," 53. On the problematic position of modern design in the Third Reich, see Betts, *Authority of Everyday Objects,* 23–72; Nerdinger, ed., *Bauhaus-Moderne;* Lane, *Architecture and Politics;* and Heskett, "Modernism and Archaism," 110–27.

60. Wilson, *Livable Modernism;* Buckley, *Designing Modern Britain,* 83–123; Battersby, *Decorative Thirties.*

61. Brantl, *Haus der Kunst,* 96–99, 107–8.

See also Schlenker, *Hitler's Salon*, 88–92; and Günther, *Das Deutsche Heim*, 118–23. The Prints and Photographs Division of the Library of Congress in Washington, D.C., has two photographic collections of the 1938 and 1939 Architecture and Applied Arts exhibitions at the House of German Art, which are among Bavarian Gauleiter Adolf Wagner's albums, "Im Kampf um das Dritte Reich" (LOT 2970: vol. 8, January 1938; and vol. 15, Nov.–Dec. 1938). Additionally, they have an album of Hitler's purchases from the first show (LOT 11362).

62. Kükelhaus and Hirzel, eds., *Deutsche Warenkunde*; see also Betts, *Authority of Everyday Objects*, 63.

63. Petsch, "Möbeldesign im Dritten Reich," 43, 46; Godau, "Anti-Moderne?," 77–79, 82.

64. *Innen-Dekoration*, "Deutsche Architektur," 160. The article credited Gerdy Troost with a guiding role in the arrangement of the room exhibits and display cases, in collaboration with the Bavarian Arts and Crafts Association, which was responsible for the planning and direction of the applied arts section of the 1938 exhibition.

65. *1. Deutsche Architektur und Kunsthandwerkausstellung*, 17–21, 86–89, 91.

66. *Hitlers Berghof*, 54–55.

67. *Innen-Dekoration*, "Deutsche Architektur," 166.

68. Baldur von Schirach, epigraph, Hoffmann, ed., *Hitler wie ihn keiner kennt*.

69. Fritz Bäuml, sworn declaration, October 10, 1947, SpkA K 1844: Troost, Gerdy, Staatsarchiv München; Ziffer, *Nymphenburger Moderne*, 9, 69, 277, 290–93, 314–15, 338–40.

70. Bäuml, sworn declaration, October 10, 1947, SpkA K 1844: Troost, Gerdy, Staatsarchiv München. On Mittelbau-Dora, see Wagner, *Produktion des Todes*.

71. Steinweis, *Kristallnacht*, 46, 61ff, 127–34.

8. THE SQUIRE OF BERCHTESGADEN

1. Phayre, "Man of Peru"; Phayre, "Italy's Military Problems"; Phayre, "Japan's 'World-War.'" For a brief biographical note on Fitz-Gerald's world travels, see *North American Review*, "By Way of Introduction."

2. See, for example, the positive reviews of Fitz-Gerald's first book, *America's Day* (1918), in *Saturday Review*, "America of To-Day," 1132–33; and *New Age*, "America's Day," 282.

3. Phayre, "Hitler as a Countryman"; Phayre, "Holiday *with* Hitler"; Fitz-Gerald, "Summer Chalet"; Phayre, "Hitler at Home"; Phayre, "With Herr Hitler"; Phayre, "Dogs Are Real Friends"; Phayre, "Hitler's Mountain Home."

4. [Fitz-Gerald], "Dictator at Home"; Phayre, "'Squire' Among His Dogs."

5. Phayre, "Race-Hatred." Despite his contempt for such violence, Fitz-Gerald's own racism, which I discuss below, is apparent throughout the article.

6. Phayre, "Slave-Trade To-Day," 55–65.

7. FitzGerald, *All in a Life*, 4, 7–10; *American Forests and Forest Life*, "Who's Who," 128; Murphy, "FitzGerald," 820–24.

8. Fitz-Gerald, *Voice of Ireland*.

9. Brannigan, *Race*, 22–23.

10. Phayre, "Japan's 'World-War,'" 1.

11. Phayre, *Can America Last?*, 38–39.

12. Phayre, "League's 'Black Baby,'" 237.

13. Phayre, *Can America Last?*, ix.

14. Ibid., 308. FitzGerald explicitly evoked the racial meaning of the word "master," claiming that "even the Southern negroes now favour a more despotic sway." Ibid., 308–9.

15. Phayre, "Man of Peru," 567, 565. Fitz-Gerald, according to his nephew, "offered his services as a public relations officer to various South American governments, apparently with some success" (FitzGerald, *All in a Life*, 4.) The article on Leguía thus may have been a paid endorsement. Nonetheless, the sentiments expressed accord with the broader ideological stream of Fitz-Gerald's writings.

16. Phayre, "Holiday *with* Hitler," 50–51. All italics in the original.

17. Ibid., 51.

18. Phayre, "Hitler as a Countryman," 322, 324. For a broader discussion of the prewar British newspaper coverage of Hitler, see Kershaw, *Making Friends*, 25–64.

19. Phayre, "Holiday *with* Hitler," 51; Fitz-Gerald, "Summer Chalet," 10.

20. [Fitz-Gerald], "Dictator at Home."

21. Peterson and Kellogg, eds., *Greenwood Encyclopedia of Clothing*, vol. 1, 267; Phayre, "Hitler as a Countryman," 324; [Fitz-Gerald], "Dictator at Home."

22. Phayre, "Hitler as a Countryman," 322.

23. Ibid., 324.

24. Phayre, "Hitler's Mountain Home," 194.

25. Ibid., 195. The picture was originally published in Hoffmann, ed., *Hitler wie ihn keiner kennt*, 37.

26. Phayre, "Hitler as a Countryman," 324.
27. Ibid., 323.
28. Phayre, "Dogs Are Real Friends," 6.
29. Phayre, "Holiday *with* Hitler," 58.
30. Ibid., 54. See also Phayre, "Hitler as a Countryman," 324; and Phayre, "With Herr Hitler," 46–47.
31. For more on the ideal attributes and history of the country squire, see Ditchfield, *Old English Country Squire.*
32. Phayre, "Holiday *with* Hitler," 53–54.
33. Phayre, "Hitler's Mountain Home," 195.
34. Phayre, "Hitler as a Countryman," 324.
35. Phayre, "Hitler's Mountain Home," 194–95. Italics in the original.
36. It is hard to imagine that Hitler's Bavarian chef counted pressed duck, an elaborate French dish requiring special equipment, in his cooking repertoire. Nor was the vegetarian Hitler likely to approve the serving of such a bloody dish at his table. Fitz-Gerald no doubt invented this detail in order to create an aura of sophistication around the Hitler household.
37. Fitz-Gerald, "Summer Chalet," 29.
38. Phayre, "Hitler's Mountain Home," 194.
39. Phayre, "Hitler at Home," 362.
40. Phayre, "Holiday *with* Hitler," 54; see also Fitz-Gerald, "Summer Chalet," 27.
41. Fitz-Gerald, "Summer Chalet," 27; Phayre, "Hitler's Mountain Home," 195. Fitz-Gerald based his comments on the size and nature of Hitler's library on the description given by Baldur von Schirach in his foreword to Hoffmann, *Hitler wie ihn keiner kennt,* xiv. Schirach was referring, however, to the library in Hitler's Munich apartment. See Walter Schmidkunz, afterword, Schuster-Winkelhof, *Adolf Hitlers Wahlheimat,* 15.
42. Phayre, "Hitler's Mountain Home," 194.
43. Phayre, "Holiday *with* Hitler," 52–53. See also Phayre, "Hitler as a Countryman," 324.
44. Phayre, "Holiday *with* Hitler," 54. See also Phayre, "Hitler at Home," 362; and Fitz-Gerald, "Summer Chalet," 11.
45. Phayre, "Hitler's Mountain Home," 195.
46. Phayre, "Hitler as a Countryman," 322; Phayre, "Hitler's Mountain Home," 193–94; Phayre, "Holiday *with* Hitler," 52.
47. Phayre, "Hitler's Mountain Home," 194.
48. Phayre, "Hitler as a Countryman," 324.
49. Phayre, "Holiday *with* Hitler," 52; Phayre, "Hitler's Mountain Home," 195.
50. The closest airport to the Obersalzberg was at Ainring, near Freilassing. It opened in 1934 for government business. Train travel, however, was the far more common form of transportation to Berchtesgaden. On the Ainring airport, see Rolinek, Lehner, and Strasser, *Im Schatten der Mozartkugel,* 252–55.
51. Phayre, "Dogs Are Real Friends," 5.
52. As Martin Bormann discovered when he established an unviable farming complex on the Obersalzberg in 1938. See Feiber, "Filiale von Berlin," 77.
53. On the expulsion of the Obersalzberg's inhabitants, see Chaussy and Püschner, *Nachbar Hitler,* 94–107.
54. Conradi, *Hitler's Piano Player,* 182.
55. See, for example, Henry Haskell's 1935 article, which noted that Hanfstaengl "has slipped from the charmed circle and no longer plays the piano to lull the Fuehrer to sleep." Haskell, "Germany's 1000 Dictators"; *Chicago Daily Tribune,* "Hitler's Bosom Pal."
56. Compare the story about Ignatz Westenkirchner in Phayre, "With Herr Hitler," 36–37, with *Time,* "Adolf and Ignatz," 13–14, and "Bless Me Natzi!," 21.
57. Peterborough, "Baroque," *Daily Telegraph.* Compare to Phayre, "Hitler as a Countryman," 322.
58. Hoffmann, ed., *Hitler in seinen Bergen.*
59. *Observer,* "Hitler at Home."
60. Hoffmann, *Hitler in seinen Bergen,* n.p.
61. Phayre, "Holiday *with* Hitler," 55. In the version he recounts in *Windsor Magazine,* he attributes the information about Hitler's autographs funding charities to Joseph Goebbels and Alfred Rosenberg. Phayre, "With Herr Hitler," 48.
62. Phayre, "Holiday *with* Hitler," 53. Compare to Hoffmann, *Hitler in seinen Bergen,* n.p.
63. *Times Literary Supplement,* "Can America Last?," 245.
64. FitzGerald, *All in a Life,* 4.
65. Ibid. Even as a novelist, Fitz-Gerald had been criticized for romantic excess; see *Saturday Review,* "The Shrine of Sebekh," 118.
66. Historicus, "England's Sore Need," 560–61. On Lady Houston and the *Saturday Review,* see McKie, *Bright Particular Stars,* 271–90.
67. Nor is this the only instance of a foreign journalist publishing a suspicious pro-Hitler account of a visit to his house. In 1938, Australian newspapers carried stories by an Australian writer who claimed to have had tea with Hitler. Like Fitz-Gerald's articles, her narrative

is marked by plagiarized content. See Merrill, "Hitler's Life at Berchtesgaden"; Merrill du Cane, "Tea with Hitler."

68. Griffiths, *Fellow Travellers,* 191–244.

69. Henderson, "Media and Celebrity Culture," 52.

70. *Daily Express,* "Hitler's Sister."

71. Bronner, "Beautiful Wife."

72. Tange, *Architectural Identities;* Silverman, *Art Nouveau,* 75–106; Clark, *American Family Home.*

73. Henderson, "Barnum to 'Bling Bling,'" 44. See also Barbas, *First Lady of Hollywood.*

74. Abrams, *Hollywood Bohemians,* 113, 119–20, 122.

75. *Newsweek,* "Hitler at Bavarian Retreat."

76. Coleman, *Historic House Museums,* 18.

77. Woolf, "Great Men's Houses," 23.

78. *Vogue* (U.S.), "Mussolini, Hitler, and Eden," 70.

79. Ibid., 70–71.

80. Ibid.

81. On the 1936 Olympics, see Large, *Nazi Games.*

82. *New York Times Magazine,* "Hitler His Own Architect," 15. Large portions of this text reappear almost verbatim in the articles that Fitz-Gerald published on Hitler's home the following year. These similarities and the lack of a byline raise the question of his authorship. Fitz-Gerald did contribute to the *New York Times* under the pseudonym of Ignatius Phayre in the 1920s. However, given the numerous instances of plagiarism evident in his reports on Hitler, as noted previously, I am inclined to believe that he copied rather than wrote this article.

83. Tolischus, "Where Hitler Dreams," 1.

84. Ibid.

85. Ibid., 1–2.

86. Ibid.

87. Ibid., 2, 16.

88. Ibid., 16.

89. Ibid.

90. Simpson, "Home in the Clouds," 5, 22.

91. Ibid., 5.

92. Ibid., 5, 22.

93. Ibid., 22.

94. *New York Times,* "War Moves Go On," "Pontiff," "Coup Fear," and "Developments in Europe."

9. WAR AND THE ENGLISH-LANGUAGE MEDIA'S REAPPRAISAL OF THE DOMESTIC HITLER

1. Doberer, "New Reich Weapon."

2. *Life,* "Paintings by Adolf Hitler," 52–58.

3. Ibid., 52–53.

4. Ibid., 52, 55.

5. Ibid., 52.

6. Ibid., 56.

7. For contemporary views on Hitler's sober temperament, see Tolischus, "Hitler," 2, 21; and Ferguson, "Dictators Don't Drink," 103–5.

8. *Life,* "Paintings by Adolf Hitler," 56–58.

9. *Life,* "Letters to the Editors," 2, 4.

10. Ibid.

11. *Life,* "Paintings by Adolf Hitler," 58.

12. Tolischus, "Where Hitler Dreams," 1–2, 16.

13. Peters, "In Hitler's Chalet," 9, 21.

14. Ibid., 9.

15. Dietrich, *Hitler in die Macht,* 121–27.

16. Peters, "In Hitler's Chalet," 9, 21.

17. See, for example, Dickson, "Europe's Man of Mystery!"

18. Simpson, "Home in the Clouds," 5, 22.

19. On the dangers faced by foreign correspondents in Germany, see Voss, *Reporting the War.*

20. Peters, "In Hitler's Chalet," 9.

21. Wagnon, "Churchill Devotes."

22. Wagnon, "Britain's Hopes."

23. Grover, "Life of Wakeful Spartan." On the Nazi "Law on Animal Protection," see Sax, *Animals in the Third Reich,* 179–83.

24. Grover, "Warlord Hitler."

25. Ibid.

26. Ernest Howard Shepard, "The White Paper Hanger," *Punch,* April 10, 1940, 391. The Karen Kuykendall Papers (MS 243) held by the University of Arizona's Special Collections in Tucson contain numerous political cartoons depicting Hitler as a paperhanger.

27. *New York Times,* "Our Role Abroad."

28. George Butterworth, "Inferior Decoration," *Daily Dispatch,* August 6, 1941.

29. *Manchester (UK) Guardian,* "Pervasive Madness," and "Bavaria's Fascists"; *Fitchburg (Mass.) Sentinel,* "Bavaria Leads"; Gierasch, "Bavarian Menace," 226; Jordan, "Ex-Chief Facing Trial."

30. Hitler, *Mein Kampf,* 24, 40–42. On historians' dismissal of Hitler's claims, see, for example, Hamann, *Hitler's Vienna,* 142–44; and Kershaw, *Hitler: Hubris,* 53.

31. *New York Times,* "Says Hitler's Father Changed Name." Hitler's father's birth name was Alois Schicklgruber. It was misspelled in the article. On the name change, see Hamann, *Hitler's Vienna,* 43–44.

32. On Brecht, see Hermand, "More than a House-Painter?"

33. *Daily Boston Globe,* "Cardinal Mundelein Scores Nazis."

34. Schultz, "Nazis Angered"; *Time,* "Peeved Paperhangers," 15; *New York Times,* "Links to Hitler Enrage."

35. "The Paper Hanger Returns," editorial cartoon, *Los Angeles Times,* March 3, 1938. The cartoon was originally published in the *New York Times.*

36. See the cartoons published in the *Louisville Courier-Journal* and the *Houston Post* in the Karen Kuykendall Papers.

37. *Daily Boston Globe,* "Hitler Couldn't Hang Paper." Nussbaum's account seems unlikely, given that Hitler never used the name Schicklgruber.

38. *New York Times,* "Effigies of Hitler."

39. Shirer, "Germans Blame Hitler." See also *Observer,* "R.A.F. Destroying Civilian Morale"; and Axelsson, "Cynical German Humor."

40. Cartoon dated February 1944 (source not given), Karen Kuykendall Papers.

41. Low, *Years of Wrath,* 251.

42. Both cartoons are in the Karen Kuykendall Papers.

43. Brown, "Hitler's Real 'Kampf,'" 5, 33.

44. Matthews, "Fliers Punish Berchtesgaden"; *Los Angeles Times,* "Dynamite Parcel 'Sent'"; *New York Times,* "One Year."

45. Seerwald, *Gipfel der Macht?,* 13, 55, 5, 47. See also Beierl, *Geschichte des Kehlsteins.*

46. Barnes, "Hitler Builds Hideaway."

47. *Living Age,* "German Scene," 32; Lochner, "Der Fuehrer's Thoughts"; Panton, "Hitler's New Hide-Away."

48. *New York Times,* "Hitler Eyrie."

49. Associated Press, "Hitler's 'Eagle Nest.'"

50. Oechsner, "Hitler Fantasies."

51. *Los Angeles Times,* "Hitler Gets His Hideout Prepared," based on a dispatch from the *Daily Mail.*

52. As evidence of the confusion, see, for example, Fodor, "Conqueror's Manual." Fodor believed that the Kehlsteinhaus was Hitler's new residence and that it was connected to the Berghof by an elevator.

53. *New York Times,* "Hour of Suspense."

54. See, for example, Hoffmann, ed., *Hitler in Polen, Mit Hitler im Westen,* and *Für Hitler bis Narvik.* See also Herz, *Hoffmann und Hitler,* 300–327.

55. Hoffmann, "Propagandistic," 133–42; *Baltimore Sun,* "Hitler Receives Leader"; *Deutsche Wochenschau* 519, released on August 16, 1940; *Deutsche Wochenschau* 547, released on February 26, 1941; *Deutsche Wochenschau* 548, released on March 5, 1941; *Deutsche Wochenschau* 562, released on June 11, 1941; *Deutsche Wochenschau* 609, released on May 6, 1942. The films are available in the Bundesarchiv-Filmarchiv, Berlin.

56. Châteaubriant, foreword, *Chef et son Peuple*; Fiss, *Grand Illusion,* 9–44, 191–218; Duroselle, *France and the Nazi Threat,* 158; Weber, *Hollow Years,* 130. On the French experience under the occupation, see Vinen, *Unfree French.*

57. Châteaubriant, *Chef et son Peuple,* 3. On Châteaubriant, see Chadwick, *Alphonse de Châteaubriant.*

58. Châteaubriant, *Chef et son Peuple,* 5.

59. Ibid., n.p.

10. SECRETS IN THE CELLAR

1. *Los Angeles Times,* "Allies Destroy Nazi Planes"; *New York Times,* "Luftwaffe Is 'Out.'"

2. Huston, *American Airpower,* 166.

3. Mitchell, *Hitler's Mountain,* 51–54.

4. Matthews, "Fliers Who Hit Berchtesgaden"; Gowran, "Hurl Rockets"; *Daily Boston Globe,* "Hitler's Berchtesgaden Lair Lashed"; *Life,* "Berchtesgaden," 34.

5. Robert C. Powell, letter to the editor, *Washington Post,* March 1, 1945.

6. Domarus, ed., *Hitler: Speeches and Proclamations,* vol. 4, 3018.

7. Johanna Stangassinger quoted in Chaussy and Püschner, *Nachbar Hitler,* 183.

8. Royal Air Force Operations Record Books, National Archives, Kew, UK: AIR 27/169/8; AIR 27/483A/8; AIR 27/798/8; AIR 27/804/8; AIR 27/817/8; AIR 27/828/8; AIR 27/1013/16; AIR 27/1029/32; AIR 27/1089/57; AIR 27/1097/8; AIR 27/1236/16; AIR 27/1410/28; AIR 27/1658/37; AIR 27/1679/50; AIR 27/1701/32; AIR 27/1790/7; AIR 27/1882/28; AIR 27/1910/8; AIR 27/2037/36; AIR 27/2047/34; AIR 27/2111/32; AIR 27/2128/42; AIR 27/2131/46; AIR 27/2143/38; AIR 27/2145/36; AIR 27/2152/36; AIR 27/2155/28.

The logged times in these reports are based on Greenwich Mean Time. I have adjusted them to indicate the time the bombings occurred on the Obersalzberg.

9. Chamberlain, "6-Ton Bomb"; *Daily Mirror*, "RAF Score"; Gruson, "RAF 6-Ton Bombs"; Mitchell, *Hitler's Mountain*, 116; Beierl, *Hitlers Berg*, 123, 128, 134; Hartmann, *Verwandlung eines Berges*, 100.

10. Chamberlain, "6-Ton Bomb"; Frank, *Rettung von Berchtesgaden*, 99.

11. Haller, "Destroying Hitler's Berghof," 13–14.

12. Chamberlain, "6-Ton Bomb."

13. Middlebrook and Everitt, *Bomber Command War Diaries*, 701.

14. Operations Record Books, National Archives: AIR 27/1236/16; AIR 27/1410/28; AIR 27/2128/42; AIR 27/2152/36.

15. Operations Record Book, no. 617 Squadron, National Archives: AIR/27/2128/42.

16. Richard F. Reiter, e-mail messages to author, August 15, 2012, February 19, 2013, and March 2, 2013. Reiter, a courier delivering documents to Hermann Göring's house that morning (see below), estimates that he saw the Berghof less than an hour after the bombing had ended. He may have been the first on the scene, as he arrived before the all-clear had sounded and did not see anyone else there, either guards or civilians. Other eyewitnesses do not mention a fire, but it may have gone out by the time they emerged from the bomb shelters. According to Christa Schroeder, Hitler's secretary, the all-clear did not sound until about 2:30 P.M. (local time), three and a half hours after the raid ended. See Beierl, *Hitlers Berg*, 127–128.

17. Schroeder, *He Was My Chief*, 187–88.

18. Beierl, *Hitlers Berg*, 128. For a description of the condition of the house after the Allied troops arrived, see Johnston, "Hitler's House Completely Ruined." Johnson wrongly attributed all the damage he saw to the aerial bombing on April 25, ignoring the fires set by the SS.

19. Geiss, *Obersalzberg*, 94; Haller, "Destroying Hitler's Berghof," 14–15; and Mitchell, *Hitler's Mountain*, 116, 129, 132–33. While Mitchell cites compelling firsthand accounts that the Berghof was not as badly damaged as was formerly believed, his assertion that "the building had suffered no damage from the April 25 bombing" (129) contradicts other evidence, including aerial photographs.

20. Chamberlain, "6-Ton Bomb."

21. Ibid.; Eisenhower, *Crusade in Europe*, 433–34, 456–58. On the myth of the National Redoubt, see Mitchell, *Hitler's Mountain*, 67–82.

22. Chamberlain, "6-Ton Bomb."

23. Williams, "Allied Armies Intent."

24. John W. Snyder, interview by Jerry N. Hess, March 12, 1968, transcript, 455–89, Harry S. Truman Library and Museum, Independence, Mo.

25. McKinstry, *Lancaster*, 481–82; Operations Record Books, National Archives: AIR 27/1236/16; AIR 27/1410/28; AIR 27/2145/36.

26. Eisenhower, *Crusade in Europe*, 458.

27. Haller, "Destroying Hitler's Berghof," 6; Neillands, *Bomber War*, 367–73.

28. Chamberlain, "6-Ton Bomb"; Gruson, "RAF 6-Ton Bombs"; *Daily Mirror*, "RAF Score."

29. Miller, "Hitleriana," 37.

30. Mitchell, *Hitler's Mountain*, 120–36; McManus, *American Courage*, 525–29.

31. Miller, "Hitleriana," 37, 72.

32. Richard F. Reiter, e-mail messages to author, August 15, 2012, January 28, 2013, March 2, 2013, and March 12, 2014. Reiter reports that, after the war, he gave the Persian plate and knife as gifts to U.S. officials who had helped him. He kept the folio of art prints, which had been produced by the Franz Hanfstaengl Art Publishing House. Some of the prints were subsequently published in a two-part feature on Reiter's experiences in the *Times Colonist* (Victoria, B.C.): "Art from Hitler's Lair," and Knox and Obee, "Uncle Wolf and Me." After American soldiers arrived on the Obersalzberg, more exploded objects from Göring's house—along with two bodies—were found in the pool. See Alford, *Nazi Plunder*, 70–71.

33. Beierl, *Hitlers Berg*, 139.

34. Schroeder, *He Was My Chief*, 190.

35. Beierl, *Hitlers Berg*, 132; Feiber, "Lange Schatten Adolf Hitlers," 711–12; Hartmann, *Verwandlung eines Berges*, 104.

36. Webster, "We Drank Hitler's Champagne," 25, 135.

37. Ibid., 136–37.

38. Sions, "Berchtesgaden," 3–4. Both at the Berghof and in Hitler's Munich apartment, the sealed house safes contained only signed copies of *Mein Kampf*—perhaps the author's idea of a

final joke. On the Munich safe's contents, see Lochner, "Faces of Hopeful GI's."

39. Sions, "Berchtesgaden," 4.

40. Anni Winter, interrogation by Michael Musmanno, March 30, 1948, 2, Musmanno Collection, Duquesne University Archives, Pittsburgh, Pa.

41. Lee Miller to Audrey Withers, undated service message, reprinted in Penrose, ed., *Lee Miller's War*, 188.

42. Miller, "Hitleriana," 72–73.

43. Ibid., 73. On Miller in Hitler's bathtub, see Kaplan, *Landscapes of Holocaust Postmemory*, 71–98; Monahan, "Waste Management," 98–119; Zox-Weaver, *Women Modernists and Fascism*, 150–91; and Burke, "Lee Miller in Hitler's Bathtub," 148–57.

44. Miller to Withers, undated service message, reprinted in Penrose, *Lee Miller's War*, 189.

45. Miller, "Hitleriana," 74; Penrose, *Lee Miller's War*, 191–203.

46. Sions, "Berchtesgaden," 4.

47. Webster, "We Drank Hitler's Champagne," 137.

48. Sions, "Berchtesgaden," 4.

49. Webster, "We Drank Hitler's Champagne," 137; Nicholas, *Rape of Europa*, 354–57; Wales, "Yanks' Looting in Reich."

50. *Pampa (Tex.) Daily News*, "Hitler's Silverware."

51. Alford, *Nazi Plunder*, 67–69.

52. *Morning Herald* (Hagerstown, Md.), "She Has Hitler's Silverware"; *Carbondale (Ill.) Free Press*, "Wife Receives Hitler's Silver."

53. *New York Times*, "15,000 on Train See Surrender Papers"; *Hartford (Conn.) Courant*, "Loan Train Exhibit."

54. Ransom, "Secret Weapons on Display."

55. *Big Spring (Tex.) Daily Herald*, "Hitler's Silverware on 'Victory Loan.'"

56. Bernard, "Press Representatives Eat Meal." Bernard states that the silverware came from Hitler's headquarters in Munich, but other accounts give the source as his Munich dwelling.

57. *Manchester (UK) Guardian*, "Nazi Looting in Poland."

58. *Daily Boston Globe*, "Engineers Blast into 'Gold Room'"; Bradsher, "Nazi Gold," 11–12. Valuable artworks from the state museums in Berlin had also been stored in the mine.

59. Lochner, "Hitler's Chalet." For a report similar to that of Lochner, see Fleischer,

"Hitler's Eagle Nest."

60. Lochner, "Fuehrer's Thoughts in Clouds."

61. Lochner, "Nazis' Hideouts Ready"; Lochner, "Der Fuehrer's Thoughts"; Lochner, "Hitler's Retreat."

62. Lochner, "Faces of Hopeful GI's"; [Lochner], "Hitler's Safe." For another account of the Munich homes of Hitler and Braun, see Schultz, "Hitler's Two Love Nests."

63. Lochner, "Faces of Hopeful GI's"; [Lochner], "Hitler's Safe."

64. *Los Angeles Times*, "Goering's Looted Art Treasure"; *New York Times*, "Tenants Purchase Apartment House: Property at Park Avenue and 58th," December 4, 1945.

65. Yeide, *Beyond the Dreams of Avarice*, 16.

66. *New York Times*, "'Liberated' Nazi Loot"; *Baltimore Sun*, "Goering's Art Booty."

67. Rapport and Northwood, *Rendezvous with Destiny*, 748–49; Thalhofer, *Company A!*, 228–38.

68. Johnston, "Vast Art Collection Found." Nancy Yeide disputes this claim, pointing out that the contents of the collection do not support the widely held view of Göring's exceptional ability to spot a masterpiece. Yeide, *Beyond the Dreams of Avarice*, 17.

69. *Baltimore Sun*, "Goering's Art Booty"; *New York Times*, "'Liberated' Nazi Loot"; Johnston, "Goering's Private Art Collection"; *Newsday (Long Island, N.Y.)*, "Goering 'Bought' Treasure Trove"; *Los Angeles Times*, "Vast Goering Loot Operations"; Johnston, "Vast Art Collection Found"; *Chicago Daily Tribune*, "Art Collectors." On the Nazis' practices of art collecting and looting, see Nicholas, *Rape of Europa*; and Petropoulos, *Art as Politics*.

70. *Washington Post*, "Yanks Uncover 5 Billions"; *Chicago Daily Tribune*, "Yank Who Found Nazi Gold"; Bradsher, "Nazi Gold," 17.

71. *Chicago Daily Tribune*, "Gold Piled Up Like Cordwood"; Barden, "Nazis Made Piker."

72. *Chicago Daily Tribune*, "Gold Piled Up Like Cordwood."

11. "ADOLF DOESN'T LIVE HERE ANYMORE"

1. Stead, "Hitler's Berchtesgaden."

2. Ziemke, *U.S. Army in the Occupation*, 332–33.

3. Stead, "Hitler's Berchtesgaden."

4. See, for example, Stead, "Germans Clear Debris"; and Stead, "Nuremberg: Grim

Housing Shortage."
5. Stead, "Hitler's Berchtesgaden."
6. Ibid.
7. Taylor, "Berchtesgaden."
8. Day, "Berchtesgaden Chalet."
9. Stead, "Hitler's Berchtesgaden."
10. Ibid.
11. Day, "Berchtesgaden Chalet."
12. Richard F. Reiter, e-mail messages to author, August 15, 2012, and August 21, 2012.
13. Such Nazi propaganda is discussed in Chapter 7.
14. Day, "Berchtesgaden Chalet."
15. Stead, "Hitler's Berchtesgaden."
16. Hamburger, "Letter from Berchtesgaden," 46.
17. *Christian Science Monitor*, "Hitler's Berchtesgaden Retreat."
18. Day, "Berchtesgaden Chalet."
19. Taylor, "Berchtesgaden."
20. Day, "Berchtesgaden Chalet."
21. For an analysis of Gertrude Stein's preoccupation with authoritarian male figures and her visit to Berchtesgaden in the context of literary modernism, see Zox-Weaver, *Women Modernists and Fascism*, 59–107.
22. Stein, "Now We Are Back in Paris," 59.
23. Malcolm, *Two Lives*, 6, 48–53, 97–99; Will, *Unlikely Collaboration*.
24. Joan Retallack, "Introduction," in Retallack, ed., *Gertrude Stein: Selections*, 55–70; Sawyer-Lauçanno, *Continual Pilgrimage*, 46–66.
25. *Life*, "Liberation of Gertrude Stein," 83–84.
26. Stein, "Off We All Went," 56.
27. *Life*, "Paintings by Adolf Hitler," 56; Stein, "Off We All Went," 58.
28. Stein, "Off We All Went," 56–57.
29. Whittier-Ferguson, "Liberation of Gertrude Stein," 417.
30. Corn and Latimer, *Seeing Gertrude Stein*, 61–117.
31. Retallack, "Introduction," 60, 68.
32. Malcolm, *Two Lives*, 24, 93–94, 106, 190.
33. Stein, "Off We All Went," 57; Zox-Weaver, *Women Modernists and Fascism*, 106.
34. Jones, "Globe Man in Berchtesgaden"; Mitchell, *Hitler's Mountain*, 170.
35. *Washington Post*, "Hitler's 'Love Nest' Razed"; Muhlen, *Return of Germany*, 31.
36. "Souvenir of Berchtesgaden," NL Ehard 781, Bayerisches Hauptstaatsarchiv, Munich; "Souvenir of the Eagle's Nest," catalogued

as "Pictures of Hitler's House and Eagle's Nest," LOT 9704 (F), Print and Photographs Division, Library of Congress, Washington, D.C. Brett Ashley Kaplan examines three similar "Souvenir of Berchtesgaden" albums in collections in California, Indiana, and Illinois in her book, *Landscapes of Holocaust Postmemory*, 48–56. On American-sanctioned sales of memorabilia in Berchtesgaden, see Feiber, "Lange Schatten Adolf Hitlers," 679–80.
37. The copy of "Souvenir of the Eagle's Nest" owned by the Library of Congress bears a stamp at the back identifying the album maker as Photo-Haus Hugo Babnigg in Berchtesgaden. Whether the "Souvenir of Berchtesgaden" albums in other collections were also made by this photography studio is uncertain. The quality of "Souvenir of the Eagle's Nest" is not as high as the other "Souvenir of Berchtesgaden" albums. Nonetheless, given the similarities, it seems either that all of the albums were produced by Hugo Babnigg's studio (but perhaps by different hands) or this album closely imitated another's model.
38. "Souvenir of Berchtesgaden," NL Ehard 781, Bayerisches Hauptstaatsarchiv.
39. Ibid.; "Souvenir of the Eagle's Nest," Library of Congress.
40. Schöner, *Berchtesgadener Land*, 374.
41. *Mansfield (Ohio) News-Journal*, "Hitler's Former Mountain Retreat."
42. Neven-du Mont, "Propagandazelle Obersalzberg," 31; Geiss, *Obersalzberg*, 96–97.
43. Tauber, *Beyond Eagle and Swastika*, vol. 1, 82–83.
44. Neven-du Mont, "Propagandazelle Obersalzberg"; Neven du Mont, "Kleine Geschäfte."
45. Ibid.
46. Quoted in Kuby, "Wahrheit über den Obersalzberg."
47. Ibid.
48. *Berchtesgadener-Kurier*, "Am Obersalzberg wird zugegriffen," and "Ministerrat besichtigt Obersalzberg"; Theodor Jacob to Wilhelm Hoegner, 17 July 1951, StK 14105, Bayerisches Hauptstaatsarchiv.
49. *Berchtesgadener-Kurier*, "Der Ministerbesuch"; *Südost-Kurier*, "Problem Obersalzberg."
50. *Berchtesgadener Anzeiger*, "Das Kehlsteinhaus bleibt erhalten," and "Obersalzberg-Problem in Berchtesgadener Sicht."
51. *Berchtesgadener Anzeiger*, "Bitte an alle Leser," "Nicht Befragten," and "Nicht

Befragten: II"; Moor, "Old Order," 58.

52. *Berchtesgadener Anzeiger,* "Berghof wird dem Erdboden gleichgemacht."

53. *Berchtesgadener-Kurier,* "Um Obersalzberg und Kehlstein."

54. George Shuster to Hans Ehard, November 1951, StK 14105, Bayerisches Hauptstaatsarchiv. The Platterhof Hotel had originally been included in this list, but was later omitted because of restitution proceedings. Hans Ehard to Charles W. Thayer, 6 November 1952, StK 14105, Bayerisches Hauptstaatsarchiv.

55. Moor, "Old Order," 65.

56. *Der Spiegel,* "Obersalzberg," 12; *Berchtesgadener Anzeiger,* "Hitlers Berghof," and "Berghof Hauptanziehungspunkt."

57. Frei, *Amerikanische Lizenzpolitik,* 162.

58. Moor, "Old Order," 58; Frei, *Amerikanische Lizenzpolitik,* 163.

59. *Berchtesgadener-Kurier,* "Entschlossene Haltung der SPD." The *Berchtesgadener-Kurier* was the local edition of the *Südost-Kurier.*

60. Kiene, "Offener Brief." See also *Berchtesgadener-Kurier,* "Nochmals das Thema."

61. On the problematic history of postwar memorialization in Germany, see Niven and Paver, eds., *Memorialization in Germany;* Rosenfeld and Jaskot, eds., *Beyond Berlin;* Rosenfeld, *Munich and Memory;* Neumann, *Shifting Memories;* Meng, *Shattered Spaces;* and Moeller, *War Stories.*

62. Hilpoltsteiner, "Neofaschismus in Berchtesgaden?"

63. Moor, "Old Order," 60.

64. Ibid., 59–60; see Mehringer, *Waldemar von Knoeringen.*

65. Moor, "Old Order," 59–60; Hilpoltsteiner, "Neofaschismus in Berchtesgaden?"; *Berchtesgadener-Kurier,* "Neofaschisten schädigen Berchtesgadener Land!"; Frei, *Amerikanische Lizenzpolitik,* 164. On Heinz Erich Krause, see Tauber, *Beyond Eagle and Swastika,* vol. 2, 1074–1075n177.

66. *Chicago Daily Tribune,* "Goering's Villa Being Razed"; Feiber, "Lange Schatten Adolf Hitlers," 700.

67. Moor, "Old Order," 64–65.

68. *Life,* "Blowup at Berchtesgaden," 41.

69. *Berchtesgadener-Kurier,* "Bagger auf dem Obersalzberg."

70. *Der Spiegel,* "Obersalzberg," 10–11.

71. [H]ilpoltsteiner, "Der 'Berghof' wurde gesprengt."

72. *Life,* "Blowup at Berchtesgaden," 42.

73. *New York Times,* "House that Hitler Built."

74. Neuerbourg, "Kilroy's Been at Hitler's Aerie."

75. Brügge, "In Hitlers Bunker," 42–43.

76. Ibid., 42.

77. Ibid., 42–43.

78. Ibid., 42, 44

79. Fabritius, *Obersalzberg.*

80. *Jerusalem Post,* "Row over Souvenirs."

81. Anderson, "Bavarian Stronghold."

82. On the protracted property struggles of former Obersalzberg residents, see Feiber, "Lange Schatten Adolf Hitlers," 685–94.

83. Brügge, "In Hitlers Bunker," 44–45.

84. *Los Angeles Times,* "Bavaria Seals 'Eagle's Nest'"; *New York Times,* "Hitler Bunker Shut."

85. *New York Times,* "Hitler's Alpine Hideaway."

86. Miller, "Nazi Symbol to Return"; *Der Spiegel,* "Nazi-Erbe," 94.

87. Kinzer, "Unspoiled Alpine View."

88. Jordan, *Structures of Memory,* 92–133.

89. Tagliabues, "Construction at Nazi Death Camp"; Fisher, "Market at Nazi Camp Site"; *Globe and Mail,* "Germans Scrap Market."

90. Bernstein, "Where Hitler Played."

91. Kinzer, "Unspoiled Alpine View."

92. Leidig, "Outrage at Third Reich Museum."

93. Losch, "New Exhibit"; Dahm, "Dokumentationsstätte," 327.

94. Dahm, "Obersalzberg als historischer Ort," 20–21.

95. Finger, "Nie wieder Schnörkel."

96. Dahm, "Obersalzberg als historischer Ort," 24; Huber, "Geleitwort," 11.

97. Margolis, "Night on Evil Mountain."

98. Ryback, "Hitler Shrine," 131; Kaplan, *Landscapes of Holocaust Postmemory,* 57.

99. Peter Roos, reporting for *Die Zeit,* cited five thousand articles published globally about the opening. Peter Roos, "Hitlerconti."

100. Harvey, "Hitler Hilton."

101. Symons, "Hitler Hotel."

102. Connolly, "British to Revive"; Eisinger, "Hitler's Villa Site."

103. Buruma, "Tainted Ground." See also Bernstein, "Where Hitler Played."

104. Margolis, "Night on Evil Mountain."

105. Davidson, "World of Evil and Hope."

106. *Calgary Herald,* "Haunted by Ghost of Hitler."

107. Margolis, "Night on Evil Mountain";

Williams, "Resort Bids to Balance."

108. Roos, "Hitlerconti."

109. *Welt Kompakt,* "Millionengrab auf dem Obersalzberg."

110. Stumberger, "Luft wird dünner"; Förster, "Problemberg."

111. Zekri, "Berge versetzen"; Beierl, *Hitlers Berg,* 151–52.

112. Ryback, "Hitler Shrine," 131, 133–34.

113. Connolly, "British to Revive."

114. Bernstein, "Where Hitler Played"; Eisinger, "Hitler's Villa Site."

115. Boyes, "Luxury Spa at Hitler's Lair."

116. Neumann, "Adolfs Platten," 50.

117. Feiber, "Lange Schatten Adolf Hitlers," 721.

118. Ryback, "Hitler Shrine," 131, 134; Ryback and Beierl, "Damnation of Memory."

119. Förster, "Problemberg."

120. Neumann, "Adolfs Platten"; Ryback and Beierl, "Damnation of Memory."

121. Ryback and Beierl, "Damnation of Memory."

122. Neumann, "Adolfs Platten," 51.

123. Ibid., 50.

124. Hall, "Chapel 'Becomes Nazi Shrine.'"

125. D. M., "Gerüchte aus Marmor."

126. Ryback and Beierl, "Damnation of Memory."

127. Nüsslein, *Paul Ludwig Troost,* 245; Pröse, "Daheim bei Hitler," 124.

128. Harald Freundorfer (police chief inspector, Police Station 22, Munich), in discussion with the author, November 11, 2010.

129. Anni Winter, interrogation by Michael Musmanno, March 30, 1948, 9, Musmanno Collection, Duquesne University Archives, Pittsburgh, Pa.

130. Beginning in 1945 and continuing into the 1990s, Munich purged its urban landscape of National Socialism's physical remains, either through removal or the normalizing reuse of Nazi structures. It has also been reluctant to create memorials, preferring to leave that function to nearby Dachau. Munich's evasion (to use Gavriel Rosenfeld's term) of its Nazi past became a particularly contentious issue after 1989, when memorialization movements arose in other German cities. See Rosenfeld, "Memory and the Museum," 163–84; Rosenfeld, *Munich and Memory;* Large, *Where Ghosts Walked,* 347–61; and Winifried Nerdinger, "Ort und Erinnerung," in Nerdinger, ed., *Ort und Erinnerung,* 7–9.

131. See, for example, Hendrick, "Hitler Sale Tasteless"; and Wagner, "Yad Vashem."

132. Sturz, "Evil for Sale," 70–72.

133. Ottomeyer, "Vorwort," 14.

134. Barron, "Plan to Display Silver."

135. Ibid.

136. See, for example, Spotts, *Hitler and the Power of Aesthetics;* Reichel, *Schöne Schein des Dritten Reiches;* and Ogan and Weiss, *Faszination und Gewalt.*

137. Hofer et al., *Stories in Sterling,* 282–83.

138. See, for example, Simpson, "Home in the Clouds," 5, 22. The American media's coverage of Hitler's domestic life is discussed at length in chapters 8 and 9.

139. Waldman, "At Home with the Führer."

140. Ibid.; Glenn, "Hitler at Home"; *U.S. Newswire,* "Publication of Article Was 'Appalling.'" The press release "Statement Regarding Homes and Gardens, November 1938," originally posted on IPC Media's website, has since been removed.

WORKS CITED

1. Deutsche Architektur-und Kunsthandwerk-ausstellung im Haus der Deutschen Kunst zu München, 22. Januar bis 27. März 1938: Offizieller Ausstellungskatalog. Munich: Knorr and Hirth, 1938.

Abrams, Brett L. *Hollywood Bohemians: Transgressive Sexuality and the Selling of the Movieland Dream.* Jefferson, N.C.: McFarland, 2008.

Adolf Hitler an seine Jugend. Berlin: Eher, 1937.

Adolf Hitler: Bilder aus dem Leben des Führers. Altona-Bahrenfeld: Cigaretten-Bilderdienst, 1936.

Aicher, Florian, and Uwe Drepper, eds. *Robert Vorhoelzer: Ein Architektenleben: Die klassische Moderne der Post.* Munich: Callwey, 1990.

Alford, Kenneth D. *Nazi Plunder: Great Treasure Stories of World War II.* Cambridge, Mass.: Da Capo, 2001.

American Forests and Forest Life. "Who's Who among the Authors in This Issue." February 1929, 128.

Anderson, Susan. "Bavarian Stronghold: Hitler Still Draws a Crowd." *Globe and Mail,* September 9, 1978.

Anheier, Helmut K., and Friedhelm Neidhardt. "Soziographische Entwicklung der NSDAP in München 1925 bis 1930." In *München: "Hauptstadt der Bewegung, "* edited by Richard Bauer, Hans Günther Hockerts, Brigitte Schütz, et al., 179–86. Munich: Münchner Stadtmuseum, 2002.

Arnold, Dietmar, with Reiner Janick. *Neue Reichskanzlei und "Führerbunker": Legenden und Wirklichkeit.* Berlin: Links, 2009.

Associated Press. "Hitler's 'Eagle Nest' Gave Envoy the Creeps." *Lewiston (Maine) Daily Sun,* December 22, 1939.

Axelsson, George. "Cynical German Humor Turns against Nazis." *New York Times,* January 23, 1944.

Aynsley, Jeremy. *Designing Modern Germany.* London: Reaktion, 2009.

Baltimore Sun. "Hitler Receives Leader of New Croat Kingdom." June 7, 1941.

———. "Yank Soldiers View Goering's Art Booty." May 21, 1945.

Baranowski, Shelley. *Strength through Joy: Consumerism and Mass Tourism in the Third Reich.* Cambridge: Cambridge University Press, 2004.

Barbas, Samantha. *First Lady of Hollywood: A Biography of Louella Parsons.* Berkeley: University of California Press, 2005.

Barden, Judy. "Nazis Made Piker Out of Ali Baba." *Hartford (Conn.) Courant,* November 4, 1945.

Barkow, Ben, Raphael Gross, and Michael Lenarz, eds. *Novemberpogrom 1938: Die Augenzeugenberichte der Wiener Library, London.* Frankfurt am Main: Jüdischer/ Suhrkamp, 2008.

Barnes, Ralph W. "Hitler Builds Hideaway on Mountain Peak." *Washington Post,* January 15, 1939.

Barron, James. "A Plan to Display Silver with a Dark History." *New York Times,* January 26, 2012.

Barron, Stephanie, et al. *"Degenerate Art": The Fate of the Avant-Garde in Nazi Germany.* New York: Abrams; Los Angeles: Los Angeles County Museum of Art, 1991.

Bathrick, David. "Cinematic Remaskings of Hitler: From Riefenstahl to Chaplin." In *Unmasking Hitler: Cultural Representations of Hitler from the Weimar Republic to the Present,* edited by Klaus L. Berghahn and Jost Hermand, 147–69. Oxford: Peter Lang, 2005.

Battersby, Martin. *The Decorative Thirties.* Revised and edited by Philippe Garner. New York: Whitney Library of Design, 1988.

Bauer, Richard, Hans Günther Hockerts, Brigitte Schütz, et al., eds. *München: "Hauptstadt der Bewegung. "* Munich: Münchner Stadtmuseum, 2002.

Bauwelt. "Persönliches." 28, no. 29 (1937): 670.

Bayerisches Gesetz- u. Verordnungsblatt. "Gesetz zum Abschluss der politischen Befreiung vom 27. Juli 1950." No. 17 (1950): 107–8.

Beierl, Florian M. *Geschichte des Kehlsteins: Ein Berg verändert sein Gesicht.* Berchtesgaden: Plenk, 2004.

———. *Hitlers Berg: Licht ins Dunkel der Geschichte.* 3rd rev. ed. Berchtesgaden: Beierl, 2010.

Berchtesgadener Anzeiger. "Berghof Hauptan-ziehungspunkt für Fremde." November 3–4, 1951.

———. "Berghof wird dem Erdboden gleich-gemacht." August 8–9, 1951.

———. "Das Kehlsteinhaus bleibt erhalten." August 6–7, 1951.

———. "Die nicht Befragten haben eine andere Meinung." August 10–11, 1951.

———. "Die nicht Befragten haben eine an-dere Meinung: II. Teil." August 14–15, 1951.

———. "Eine Bitte an alle Leser." August 3–4, 1951.

———. "Hitlers Berghof in den Rocky Mountains." August 22–23, 1951.

———. "Obersalzberg-Problem in Berchtes-gadener Sicht." August 3–4, 1951.

Berchtesgadener-Kurier. "Ab heute Bagger auf dem Obersalzberg." November 13, 1951.

———. "Am Obersalzberg wird zugegriffen." July 11, 1951.

———. "Der Ministerbesuch." August 3, 1951.

———. "Entschlossene Haltung der SPD in der Obersalzbergfrage!" November 6, 1951.

———. "Ministerrat besichtigt Obersalzberg." July 27, 1951.

———. "Neofaschisten schädigen Berchtes-gadener Land!" October 30, 1951.

———. "Nochmals das Thema: Obersalz-berg." November 23, 1951.

———. "Um Obersalzberg und Kehlstein." August 3, 1951.

Berghahn, Klaus, and Jost Hermand. *Unmask-ing Hitler: Cultural Representations of Hitler from the Weimar Republic to the Present.* Vol. 44 of *German Life and Civilization,* edited by Jost Hermand. Oxford: Peter Lang, 2005.

Berliner Volkszeitung. "Hitler braucht 9-Zim-mer-Wohnung: Auch ohne Diener geht es nicht." October 14, 1929.

Bernard, William C. "Press Representatives Eat Meal with Hitler's Silver." *Big Spring (Tex.) Daily Herald,* November 27, 1945.

Berndt, Alfred Ingemar. "Der Berghof: Das Haus des Führers auf dem Obersalzberg." *Silberspiegel,* August 3, 1937, 766–69, 796.

Bernstein, Richard. "Where Hitler Played,

Should the Rich Do Likewise?" *New York Times,* October 21, 2004.

Betts, Paul. *The Authority of Everyday Objects.* Berkeley: University of California Press, 2004.

Big Spring (Tex.) Daily Herald. "Hitler's Silver-ware on 'Victory Loan.'" November 15, 1945.

Birmingham (UK) Post. "Hitler's Desk and Chair Could Fetch $1 Million." September 5, 2006.

Blackbourn, David. *The Conquest of Nature: Water, Landscape, and the Making of Modern Germany.* New York: Norton, 2006.

Borrmann, Norbert. *Paul Schultze-Naumburg, 1869–1949.* Essen: Bacht, 1989.

Boston Sunday Globe. "Bad Taste, Says Hitler." February 17, 1935.

Boyes, Roger. "Luxury Spa at Hitler's Lair." *The Times,* October 25, 2004.

Bradsher, Greg. "Nazi Gold: The Merkers Mine Treasure." *Prologue: Quarterly of the National Archives and Records Administration* 31, no. 1 (1999): 6–21.

Brandt, Karl. "Hitler's Legion of Ladies Ranged from Scullery Help to Chatelaines." *Washington Post,* January 19, 1947.

Brannigan, John. *Race in Modern Irish Liter-ature and Culture.* Edinburgh: Edinburgh University Press, 2009.

Brantl, Sabine. *Haus der Kunst, München: Ein Ort und seine Geschichte im Nationalsozialis-mus.* Munich: Allitera, 2007.

Braveheart. "Remember Gerdy Troost, R. I. P." Stormfront.org, http://www.stormfront.org/forum/t57468.

Bronner, Milton. "Beautiful Wife of Propagan-da Minister Is Germany's Woman of Power." *The Lowell (Mass.) Sun,* June 11, 1934.

Brown, Walter. "Hitler's Real 'Kampf.'" *New York Times Magazine,* June 14, 1942, 5, 33.

Brügge, Peter. "In Hitlers Bunker stand ein Altar." *Der Spiegel,* June 27, 1962, 42–45.

Bruppacher, Paul. *Adolf Hitler und die Geschichte der NSDAP, 1889–1937.* Vol. 1, 2nd ed. Norderstedt: Books on Demand, 2009.

———. *Adolf Hitler und die Geschichte der NSDAP, 1938–1945.* Vol. 2. Norderstedt: Books on Demand, 2008.

Buckley, Cheryl. *Designing Modern Britain.* London: Reaktion, 2007.

Bullock, Alan. *Hitler: A Study in Tyranny.* London: Odhams, 1952.

Burke, Carolyn. "Lee Miller in Hitler's Bath-tub." *Heat* 12 (1999): 148–57.

Burleigh, Michael. *The Third Reich: A New History.* New York: Hill and Wang, 2000.

Burleigh, Michael, and Wolfgang Wipperman. *The Racial State: Germany, 1933–1945.* Cambridge: Cambridge University Press, 1991.

Buruma, Ian. "Tainted Ground: In a Landscape Scarred by History, Is Fresh Paint an Appropriate Memorial?" *Guardian,* October 15, 2005.

Calgary Herald. "German Town Haunted by Ghost of Hitler." September 17, 2011.

Campbell, Joan. *The German Werkbund: The Politics of Reform in the Applied Arts.* Princeton, N.J.: Princeton University Press, 1978.

Capelle, H. van, and A. P. Bovenkamp. *Der Berghof: Adlerhorst: Hitlers verborgenes Machtzentrum.* Translated by Geertrui Visser and Ludger Gausepohl. Vienna: Tosa, 2007.

Carbondale (Ill.) Free Press. "Wife of Illinois Officer Receives Hitler's Silver." June 27, 1945.

Carroll, C. E. "Editorial Notes." *Anglo-German Review* 1, no. 1 (November 1936): 5.

Chadwick, Kay. *Alphonse de Châteaubriant: Catholic Collaborator.* Vol. 14 of *Modern French Identities.* Oxford: Lang, 2002.

Chamberlain, Charles. "6-Ton Bomb Puts End to Berghof." *Atlanta Constitution,* April 26, 1945.

Châteaubriant, Alphonse de. Foreword to *Un Chef et son Peuple: Un Homme parmi les Autres,* by H. Hess and Heinrich Hoffmann, 3–8. 3 Épis, 1941.

Chaussy, Ulrich, and Christoph Püschner. *Nachbar Hitler: Führerkult und Heimatzerstörung am Obersalzberg.* 6th ed. Berlin: Links, 2007.

Chicago Daily Tribune. "Art Collectors." May 25, 1945.

———. "Goering's Villa Being Razed." November 18, 1951.

———. "Gold Piled Up Like Cordwood in Nazi Hoard." July 14, 1945.

———. "Hitler's Bosom Pal Dodges One Way Plane 'Ride': 'Putzi' Hanfstaengl Tells Nazi Plot to Kill Him." August 12, 1937.

———. "Yank Who Found Nazi Gold Hoard Is Home with 15c." May 26, 1945.

Christian Science Monitor. "Hitler's Berchtesgaden Retreat Chosen for Tourist Attraction." August 10, 1946.

Clark, Clifford Edward, Jr. *The American Family Home, 1800–1960.* Chapel Hill: University of North Carolina Press, 1986.

Coleman, Laurence Vail. *Historic House Museums.* Washington, D.C.: American Association of Museums, 1933.

Connolly, Kate. "British to Revive Hitler's Favourite Holiday Spot." *Observer,* August 5, 2001.

Conradi, Peter. *Hitler's Piano Player.* London: Duckworth Overlook, 2006.

Corn, Wanda M., and Tirza True Latimer. *Seeing Gertrude Stein: Five Stories.* Berkeley: University of California Press, 2011.

Craig, Gordon Alexander. *Germany, 1866–1945.* New York: Oxford University Press, 1978.

Dahm, Volker. "Der Obersalzberg als historischer Ort und als Stätte historisch-politischer Bildung." In *Die tödliche Utopie: Bilder, Texte, Dokumente, Daten zum Dritten Reich,* edited by Volker Dahm, Albert A. Feiber, Harmut Mehring, and Horst Möller, 17–27. 5th ed. Munich: Institut für Zeitgeschichte, 2008.

———. "Dokumentationsstätte am Obersalzberg bei Berchtesgaden." *Vierteljahrshefte für Zeitgeschichte* 46, no. 2 (1998): 327–29.

Dahm, Volker, Albert A. Feiber, Harmut Mehring, and Horst Möller, eds. *Die tödliche Utopie: Bilder, Texte, Dokumente, Daten zum Dritten Reich.* 5th ed. Munich: Institut für Zeitgeschichte, 2008.

Daily Boston Globe. "Cardinal Mundelein Scores Nazis, Refers to 'Austrian Paperhanger.'" May 19, 1937.

———. "Hitler Couldn't Hang Paper Straight, Says Ex-Union Brother." February 19, 1942.

———. "Hitler's Berchtesgaden Lair Lashed by U.S. Rocket-Firing Planes." February 22, 1945.

———. "U. S. Engineers Blast Way into Hitler's 'Gold Room.'" April 9, 1945.

Daily Express. "Hitler's Sister, Aged 50, Marries." February 26, 1936.

Daily Mirror. "RAF Score 6-Ton Hits on Hitler's Hide-Out." April 26, 1945.

D'Almeida, Fabrice. *High Society in the Third Reich.* Translated by Steven Rendall. Cambridge: Polity, 2008.

Danzker, Jo-Anne Birnie, ed. *Villa Stuck.* Ostfildern: Hatje Cantz, 2006.

Davidson, Max. "A World of Evil and Hope amid the Dark Pine Trees." *Observer,* March 13, 2005.

Day, Price. "Berchtesgaden Chalet Is Center for GI Tourists." *Baltimore Sun,* June 7, 1945.

Dean, Martin. *Robbing the Jews: The Confiscation of Jewish Property in the Holocaust, 1933–1945.*

Cambridge: Cambridge University Press, 2008.

Demps, Laurenz. *Berlin-Wilhelmstrasse: Eine Topographie preussisch-deutscher Macht.* 4th rev. ed. Berlin: Links, 2010.

Der Spiegel. "Kriegsorden: Ritterkreuze: Mit jüdischen Brillanten." November 5, 1958, 34.

———. "Obersalzberg: Verzehr bedingt." December 5, 1951, 10–12.

———. "Nazi-Erbe: Tarnname Wolf." December 12, 1994, 89–94.

Deutsche Handels-Wacht. "Eine Pleite, die uns freut." July 28, 1933, 198.

Deutscher Reichsanzeiger. "Entscheidungen auf Grund der §§ 2 und 4 des Gesetzes zum Schutze der nationalen Symbole." July 7, 1937.

Deutschland-Berichte der Sozialdemokratischen Partei Deutschlands (Sopade) 1934–1940. Salzhausen: Nettelbeck, 1980.

Deutschland Erwacht: Werden, Kampf und Sieg der NSDAP. Hamburg-Bahrenfeld: Cigaretten-Bilderdienst, 1933.

Dickson, John [Sigrid Schultz]. "Europe's Man of Mystery! His Daily Life Revealed." *Chicago Daily Tribune,* August 6, 1939.

Die Abendzeitung: Unabhängiges Münchener Nachrichtenblatt. "Gerhardine Troost: Verhandlung vertagt." March 31, 1949.

Die Fanfare. "Geliebte Hitlers verübt Selbstmord; Jungsellen und Homosexuelle als Naziführer." October 31, 1931.

die neue linie. "Tradition und Gegenwart: Die Reichskanzlei." January 1936, 14–16, 48.

Dietrich, Otto. *The Hitler I Knew.* Introduction by Roger Moorhouse. New York: Skyhorse, 2010.

———. *Mit Hitler in die Macht.* Munich: Eher, 1934.

———. *With Hitler on the Road to Power.* London: Lucas, 1934.

Ditchfield, P. H. *The Old English Country Squire.* London: Methuen, 1912.

Doberer, Kurt. "New Reich Weapon May Be Dust Bomb." *New York Times,* October 15, 1939.

Domarus, Max, ed. *Hitler: Speeches and Proclamations, 1932–1945.* 4 vols. Wauconda, Ill.: Bolchazy-Carducci, 2004.

Donath, Matthias. *Architektur in München, 1933–1945: Ein Stadtführer.* Berlin: Lukas, 2007.

Duroselle, Jean-Baptist. *France and the Nazi Threat: The Collapse of French Diplomacy,* 1932–1939. Translated by Catherine E. Dop and Robert L. Miller. New York: Enigma, 2004.

Dyke, James van. "Über die Beziehungen zwischen Kunst, Propaganda und Kitsch in Deutschland 1933 bis 1945." In *Kunst und Propaganda im Streit der Nationen 1930–1945,* edited by Hans-Jörg Czech and Nikola Doll, 250–57. Dresden: Sandstein, 2007.

E., H. "Ein 'Führer' hinter Stacheldraht." *Neuer Vorwärts,* April 4, 1937, suppl.

Eisenhower, Dwight D. *Crusade in Europe.* London: Heinemann, 1948.

Eisinger, Oliver. "Hitler's Villa Site to Become Resort." *Globe and Mail,* July 7, 2001.

Erlanger, Steven. "Hitler, It Seems, Loved Money and Died Rich." *New York Times,* August 8, 2002.

Evans, Richard J. *The Third Reich in Power, 1933–1939.* London: Lane, 2005.

Faber, David. *Munich, 1938: Appeasement and World War II.* New York: Simon and Schuster, 2008.

Fabritius, Erwin. *Obersalzberg: Vor und Nach der Zerstörung.* Berchtesgaden: Berchtesgadener Anzeiger, n.d.

Feiber, Albert A. "Der lange Schatten Adolf Hitlers: Der Obersalzberg, 1945–2005." In *Die tödliche Utopie: Bilder, Texte, Dokumente, Daten zum Dritten Reich,* edited by Volker Dahm, Albert A. Feiber, Harmut Mehring, and Horst Möller, 670–729. 5th ed. Munich: Institut für Zeitgeschichte, 2008.

———. "'Filiale von Berlin': Der Obersalzberg im Dritten Reich." In *Die tödliche Utopie: Bilder, Texte, Dokumente, Daten zum Dritten Reich,* edited by Volker Dahm, Albert A. Feiber, Harmut Mehring, and Horst Möller, 53–187. 5th ed. Munich: Institut für Zeitgeschichte, 2008.

Ferguson, Charles W. "Dictators Don't Drink." *Harper's Magazine,* June 1937, 103–5.

Feuchtmayr, Inge. *Das Prinz Carl-Palais in München.* Munich: Süddeutscher, 1966.

Finger, Evelyn. "Nie wieder Schnörkel." *Die Zeit,* March 3, 2005.

Fischer, Klaus P. *Hitler and America.* Philadelphia: University of Pennsylvania Press, 2011.

Fisher, Marc. "Market at Nazi Camp Site Brings Worldwide Outcry." *Los Angeles Times,* July 19, 1991.

Fiss, Karen. *Grand Illusion: The Third Reich, the Paris Exposition, and the Cultural Seduction of France.* Chicago: University of Chicago

Press, 2009.

Fitchburg (Mass.) Sentinel. "Bavaria Leads German States for Monarchism." September 29, 1923.

FitzGerald, Garret. *All in a Life.* London: Macmillan London, 1992.

[Fitz-Gerald, W. G.]. "A Dictator at Home: Herr Hitler as Host and Village Squire." *Launceston Examiner* (Tasmania), May 30, 1936. Reprinted from the *Sunday Pictorial.*

Fitz-Gerald, W. G. "On Holiday with Hitler in His Summer Chalet." *National Home Monthly,* November 1936, 10–11, 27, 29, 45.

———. *The Voice of Ireland: A Survey of the Race and Nation from All Angles.* Dublin: Virtue, 1923.

Fleischer, Jack. "Hitler's Eagle Nest." *Indian Journal* (Eufaula, Okla.), June 14, 1945.

Fodor, M. W. "Conqueror's Manual." *Washington Post,* August 11, 1940.

Förster, Andreas. "Der Problemberg." *Berliner Zeitung,* July 23, 2009.

Frank, Bernhard. *Die Rettung von Berchtesgaden und der Fall Göring.* Berchtesgaden: Plenk, 1984.

Frank, Hans. *Im Angesicht des Galgens.* Neuhaus bei Schliersee: Frank, 1955.

Frei, Norbert. *Amerikanische Lizenzpolitik und deutsche Pressetradition: Die Geschichte der Nachkriegszeitung Südost-Kurier.* Munich: Oldenbourg, 1986.

Friedel, Thomas. "Karl Wessely: Sein Leben, sein Wirken und sein Einfluß auf die Augenheilkunde in Deutschland und in der Welt." PhD diss., Universität Würzburg, 2008.

Friedrich, Thomas. *Hitler's Berlin. Abused City.* Translated by Stewart Spencer. New Haven, Conn.: Yale University Press, 2012.

Fromm, Bella. *Blood and Banquets: A Berlin Social Diary.* New York: Kensington, 2002.

Gebhard, Helmut, Bayerisches Staatsministerium für Ernährung, Landwirtschaft und Forsten, and Bayerischer Landesverein für Heimatpflege e.V., et al., eds. *Bauernhäuser in Bayern: Dokumentation.* 7 vols. Munich: Hugendubel, 1994–99.

Gebhard, Helmut, and Helmut Keim, eds. *Oberbayern.* Vol. 6, pt. 2, of *Bauernhäuser in Bayern: Dokumentation.* Munich: Hugendubel, 1998.

Geiss, Josef. *Obersalzberg: Die Geschichte eines Berges.* Berchtesgaden: Geiss, 1952.

Gierasch, Paul. "The Bavarian Menace to German Unity." *Current History* 19, no. 2 (1923): 221–29.

Gillessen, Günther. *Auf verlorenem Posten: Die Frankfurter Zeitung im Dritten Reich.* Berlin: Siedler, 1986.

Gleis, Ralph, ed. *Makart: Ein Künstler regiert die Stadt.* Munich: Prestel; Vienna: Wien Museum, 2011.

Glenn, Joshua. "Hitler at Home." *Boston Globe,* November 2, 2003.

Globe and Mail. "Germans Scrap Market: Protest Ends Project at Death Camp Site." July 23, 1991.

Godau, Marion. "Anti-Moderne?" In *Design in Deutschland 1933–45: Ästhetik und Organisation des Deutschen Werkbundes im "Dritten Reich,"* edited by Sabine Weissler, 74–87. Giessen: Anabas, 1990.

Goebbels, Joseph. "Adolf Hitler als Mensch." *Der Angriff,* April 4, 1932, suppl.

———. *Die Tagebücher von Joseph Goebbels.* Edited by Elke Fröhlich. 32 vols. Saur: Munich, 1993–2008.

Goltz, Anna von der. *Hindenburg: Power, Myth, and the Rise of the Nazis.* Oxford: Oxford University Press, 2009.

Gordon, Linda. "Review Essay: Nazi Feminists?" *Feminist Review,* no. 27 (1987): 97–105.

Görtemaker, Heike B. *Eva Braun: Life With Hitler.* New York: Knopf, 2011.

Götz, Norbert. *Friedensengel: Bausteine zum Verständnis eines Denkmals der Prinzregentenzeit.* Munich: Münchner Stadtmuseum, 1999.

Gowran, Clay. "Hurl Rockets at Town near Hitler Hideout." *Chicago Daily Tribune,* February 22, 1945.

Gregor, Neil. *How to Read Hitler.* London: Granta, 2005.

Gribenski, Jean, Véronique Meyer, and Solange Vernois, eds. *La Maison de l'artiste: Construction d'un espace de représentations entre réalité et imaginaire (XVIIe–XXe siècles).* Rennes: Presses Universitaires de Rennes, 2007.

Griffiths, Richard. *Fellow Travellers of the Right: British Enthusiasts for Nazi Germany, 1933–39.* London: Constable, 1980.

Grimm, Melchior. "Der Selbstmord in Hitlers Wohnung: Die Tragödie in München-Bogenhausen." *Regensburger Echo,* September 25, 1931.

Grover, Preston. "Hitler Leads Life of Wakeful Spartan." *Washington Post,* January 1, 1941.

———. "Warlord Hitler Designs Table Silver in Spare Time." *Washington Post,* January 2, 1941.

Gruson, Sydney. "RAF 6-Ton Bombs Score Hits

on Hitler's Mountain Chalet." *New York Times,* April 26, 1945.

Guenther, Irene. *Nazi Chic? Fashioning Women in the Third Reich.* Oxford: Berg, 2004.

Guerin, Frances. *Through Amateur Eyes: Film and Photography in Nazi Germany.* Minneapolis: University of Minnesota Press, 2012.

Gun, Nerin E. *Eva Braun: Hitler's Mistress.* New York: Meredith, 1968.

Günther, Hans F. K. *Mein Eindruck von Adolf Hitler.* Pähl: Bebenburg, 1969.

Günther, Sonja. *Das Deutsche Heim: Luxusinterieurs und Arbeitermöbel von der Gründerzeit bis zum "Dritten Reich."* Vol. 12, *Werkbund-Archiv.* Giessen: Anabas, 1984.

———. *Design der Macht: Möbel für Repräsentanten des "Dritten Reiches."* Stuttgart: Deutsche, 1992.

Habel, Heinrich. *Festspielhaus und Wahnfried.* Munich: Prestel, 1985.

Hake, Sabine. *German National Cinema.* 2nd ed. London: Routledge, 2008.

Hale, Oron James. "Adolf Hitler: Taxpayer." *American Historical Review* 60, no. 4 (1955): 830–42.

Hall, Allan. "Chapel Built with Remains of Hitler's Luxury Retreat 'Becomes Nazi Shrine.'" *Telegraph,* April 1, 2010.

Hall, Hines H. "The Foreign Policy-Making Process in Britain, 1934–1935, and the Origins of the Anglo-German Agreement." *The Historical Journal* 19, no. 2 (1976): 477–99.

Haller, Oliver. "Destroying Hitler's Berghof: The Bomber Command Raid of 25 April 1945." *Canadian Military History* 20, no. 1 (2011): 5–20.

Hamann, Brigitte. *Hitler's Vienna: A Portrait of the Tyrant as a Young Man.* London: Tauris Parke, 2010.

———. *Winifred Wagner: A Life at the Heart of Hitler's Bayreuth.* Translated by Alan Bance. Orlando, Fla.: Harcourt, 2005.

Hamburger, Philip. "Letter from Berchtesgaden." *New Yorker,* June 9, 1945, 46–49.

Hamm, Florentine. *Obersalzberg: Wanderungen zwischen Gestern und Heute.* Munich: Eher, 1937.

Hanfstaengl, Ernst. *Hitler: The Memoir of a Nazi Insider Who Turned against the Führer.* Arcade: New York, 2011.

Harris, John G. "Today and Yesterday: On the War Fronts." *Daily Boston Globe,* May 24, 1942.

Hartford (Conn.) Courant. "Loan Train to Exhibit War Items: Heroes, Weapons, Trophies." October 31, 1945.

Hartmann, Max. *Die Verwandlung eines Berges unter Martin Bormann, 1936–1945.* Berchtesgaden: Plenk, 1989.

Harvey, Oliver. "Welcome to the Hitler Hilton." *Sun,* September 3, 2002.

Haskell, Henry J. "Germany's 1000 Dictators." *Daily Boston Globe,* September 7, 1935.

Henderson, Amy. "From Barnum to 'Bling Bling': The Changing Face of Celebrity Culture." *Hedgehog Review* 7, no. 1 (2005): 37–46.

———. "Media and the Rise of Celebrity Culture." *OAH Magazine of History* 6, no. 4 (1992): 49–54.

Hendrick, Bill. "Hitler Sale Tasteless, Jews Say." *Atlanta Constitution,* November 19, 1999.

Hermand, Jost. "More than a House-Painter? Brecht's Hitler." In *Unmasking Hitler: Cultural Representations of Hitler from the Weimar Republic to the Present,* edited by Klaus L. Berghahn and Jost Hermand, 171–92. Oxford: Peter Lang, 2005.

Herz, Rudolf. *Hoffmann und Hitler: Fotografie als Medium des Führer-Mythos.* Munich: Fotomuseum im Münchner Stadtmuseum, 1994.

Heskett, John. "Modernism and Archaism in Design in the Third Reich." In *The Nazification of Art: Art, Design, Music, Architecture and Film in the Third Reich,* edited by Brandon Taylor and Wilfried van der Will, 110–27. Winchester, Hampshire, UK: Winchester, 1990.

[H]ilpoltsteiner, [F]ranz. "Der 'Berghof' wurde gesprengt. *Berchtesgadener Anzeiger,* May 5–6, 1952.

Hilpoltsteiner, Franz. "Neofaschismus in Berchtesgaden?" *Berchtesgadener Anzeiger,* September 7–8, 1951.

Historicus. "England's Sore Need—A Benevolent Dictator." *Saturday Review,* May 2, 1936, 560–61.

Hitler, Adolf. "Die Reichskanzlei." *Die Kunst im Dritten Reich* 3, no. 7 (1939): 277–80.

———. *Mein Kampf.* Munich: Eher, 1933.

Hitlers Berghof, 1928–1945. Kiel: Arndt, 2000.

Hofer, Margaret K., et al. *Stories in Sterling: Four Centuries of Silver in New York.* New York: New-York Historical Society; London: D. Giles, 2011.

Hoffmann, Heinrich, ed. *Für Hitler bis Narvik.*

Munich: Hoffmann, 1941.

———, ed. *Hitler abseits vom Alltag.* Berlin: Zeitgeschichte, 1937.

———, ed. *Hitler in Polen.* Munich: Hoffmann, 1939.

———, ed. *Hitler in seinen Bergen.* Berlin: Zeitgeschichte, 1935.

———, ed. *Hitler wie ihn keiner kennt.* Berlin: Zeitgeschichte, 1932.

———, ed. *Jugend um Hitler.* Berlin: Zeitgeschichte, 1934.

———, ed. *Mit Hitler im Westen.* Berlin: Zeitgeschichte, 1940.

Hoffmann, Kay. "Propagandistic Problems of German Newsreels in World War II." *Historical Journal of Film, Radio and Television* 24, no. 1 (2004): 133–42.

Hopmann, Ernst. "Fort mit dem nationalen Kitsch." *Die Form* 8, no. 8 (August 1933): 255.

Huber, Erwin. "Geleitwort." In *Die tödliche Utopie: Bilder, Texte, Dokumente, Daten zum Dritten Reich,* edited by Volker Dahm, Albert A. Feiber, Harmut Mehring, and Horst Möller, 11–12. 5th ed. Munich: Institut für Zeitgeschichte, 2008.

Huston, John W., ed. *American Airpower Comes of Age: General Henry H. "Hap" Arnold's World War II Diaries.* 2 vols. Maxwell Air Force Base, Ala.: Air University Press, 2002.

Hüttinger, Eduard. ed., *Künstlerhäuser von der Renaissance bis zur Gegenwart.* Zurich: Waser, 1985.

Innen-Dekoration. "Der Berghof." February 1938, 50–53.

———. "Deutsche Architektur- und Kunsthandwerk-Ausstellung." May 1938, 158–67.

———. "Die Innenräume des Berghofes." February 1938, 54–64.

Ireton, Sean, and Caroline Schaumann, eds. *Heights of Reflection: Mountains in the German Imagination from the Middle Ages to the Twenty-First Century.* Rochester, N.Y.: Camden House, 2012.

Jäckel, Eberhard. *Hitler's World View: A Blueprint for Power.* Translated by Herbert Arnold. Cambridge, Mass.: Harvard University Press, 1981.

Jacobs, Tino. "Zwischen Intuition und Experiment: Hans Domizlaff und der Aufstieg Reemtsmas, 1921 bis 1932." In *Marketinggeschichte: Die Genese einer modernen Sozialtechnik,* edited by Hartmut Berghoff,

148–76. Frankfurt am Main: Campus, 2007.

Jaskot, Paul B. *The Architecture of Oppression: The SS, Forced Labor and the Nazi Monumental Building Economy.* London: Routledge, 2000.

Jellonnek, Burkhard. *Homosexuelle unter dem Hakenkreuz: Die Verfolgung von Homosexuellen im Dritten Reich.* Paderborn: Schöningh, 1990.

Jerusalem Post. "Row over Souvenirs at Hitler's 'Eagle's Nest.'" October 2, 1986.

Joachimsthaler, Anton. *Hitlers Liste.* Munich: Herbig, 2003.

Johnson, Richard L. "Nazi Feminists: A Contradiction in Terms." *Frontiers: A Journal of Women's Studies* 1, no. 3 (1976): 55–62.

Johnston, Richard J. H. "Goering's Private Art Collection, Put at $200,000,000, Is on Show." *New York Times,* May 21, 1945.

———. "Hitler's House Completely Ruined as a Result of RAF Bomber Attack." *New York Times,* May 8, 1945.

———. "Vast Art Collection Stolen by Nazis Found." *New York Times,* May 14, 1945.

Jones, Thomas. *A Diary with Letters, 1931–1950.* London: Oxford University Press, 1954.

Jones, Victor O. "Globe Man in Berchtesgaden: G.I.'s Served Free Meals in Bed by Frauleins." *Daily Boston Globe,* February 4, 1947.

Jooss, Birgit. "'Bauernsohn, der zum Fürsten der Kunst gedieh': Die Inszenierungsstrategien der Künstlerfürsten im Historismus." *Plurale* 5 (2005): 196–228.

Jordan, Jennifer A. *Structures of Memory: Understanding Urban Change in Berlin and Beyond.* Stanford, Calif.: Stanford University Press, 2006.

Jordan, M. Arthur. "Ex-Chief of German Army Facing Trial." *Ireton (Iowa) Ledger,* February 28, 1924.

Junge, Traudl. *Until the Final Hour.* Edited by Melissa Müller. Translated by Anthea Bell. New York: Arcade, 2004.

Käfer, Miriam. "Hitlers frühe Förderer aus dem Münchner Großbürgertum—das Verlegerehepaar Elsa und Hugo Bruckmann." In *Rechte Karrieren in München: Von der Weimarer Zeit bis in die Nachkriegsjahre,* edited by Marita Krauss, 52–79. Munich: Volk, 2010.

Kaplan, Brett Ashley. *Landscapes of Holocaust Postmemory.* New York: Routledge, 2011.

Kater, Michael H. *Hitler Youth.* Cambridge, Mass.: Harvard University Press, 2004.

Kellerhoff, Sven Felix. *Mythos Führerbunker:*

Hitlers letzter Unterschlupf. Rev. ed. Berlin: Berlin Story, 2012.

Kershaw, Ian. *Hitler.* London: Longman, 1991.

———. *Hitler, 1889–1936: Hubris.* New York: Norton, 1999.

———. *Hitler, 1936–1945: Nemesis.* New York: Norton, 2000.

———. *The "Hitler Myth": Image and Reality in the Third Reich.* Oxford: Oxford University Press, 1987.

———. *Making Friends with Hitler: Lord Londonderry, the Nazis, and the Road to War.* New York: Penguin, 2004.

———. *The Nazi Dictatorship: Problems and Perspectives of Interpretation.* 4th ed. London: Bloomsbury Academic, 2000.

Kiene, Sepp. "Offener Brief an den 'Berchtesgadener Anzeiger.'" *Berchtesgadener-Kurier,* November 9, 1951.

Kiener, Hans. "Die Ritterkreuzurkunden." *Die Kunst im Deutschen Reich* 6, no. 10 (1942): 247–55.

Kinzer, Stephen. "An Unspoiled Alpine View, a Legacy of Demons." *New York Times,* September 13, 1995.

Kirkpatrick, Ivone. *The Inner Circle: Memoirs of Ivone Kirkpatrick.* London: MacMillan; New York: St. Martin's, 1959.

Knopp, Guido, and Thomas Staehler. "Familie Hitler." In *Geheimnisse des "Dritten Reichs,"* edited by Guido Knopp, 15–74. Munich: btb, 2012.

Knox, Jack, and Dave Obee. "Uncle Wolf and Me." *Times-Colonist* (Victoria, B.C.), August 7, 2005.

Koepnick, Lutz. *Framing Attention: Windows on Modern German Culture.* Baltimore. Johns Hopkins University Press, 2007.

Köhler, Joachim. *Wagner's Hitler: The Prophet and His Disciple.* Translated by Ronald Taylor. Cambridge: Polity, 2000.

Kolbrand, Franz. "Im Kriege Kampf dem Kitsch." *Die innere Front,* November 14, 1939, 14.

Koonz, Claudia. *The Nazi Conscience.* Cambridge, Mass.: Harvard University Press, 2003.

Koss, Juliet. *Modernism after Wagner.* Minneapolis: University of Minnesota Press, 2010.

Krauss, Marita, ed. *Rechte Karrieren in München: Von der Weimarer Zeit bis in die Nachkriegsjahre.* Munich: Volk, 2010.

Kuby, Erich. "Die Wahrheit über den Obersalzberg." *Süddeutsche Zeitung,* February 7–8, 1953.

Kükelhaus, Hugo, and Stefan Hirzel, eds. *Deutsche Warenkunde.* Berlin: Metzner, 1939.

Lambert, Angela. *The Lost Life of Eva Braun.* New York: St. Martin's, 2008.

Lane, Barbara Miller. *Architecture and Politics in Germany, 1918–1945.* Cambridge, Mass.: Harvard University Press, 1985.

Large, David Clay. *Nazi Games: The Olympics of 1936.* New York: Norton, 2007.

———. *Where Ghosts Walked: Munich's Road to the Third Reich.* New York: Norton, 1997.

Lauterbach, Iris, Julian Rosefeldt, and Piero Steinle, eds. *Bürokratie und Kult: Das Parteizentrum der NSDAP am Königsplatz in München.* Munich: Deutscher Kunstverlag, 1995.

Lb. "Frau Troost wurde Minderbelastete." *Süddeutsche Zeitung,* March 3, 1950.

Leidig, Michael. "Outrage at Third Reich Museum." *Sunday Telegraph,* October 24, 1999.

Lentin, Antony. *Lloyd George and the Lost Peace: From Versailles to Hitler, 1919–1940.* New York: Palgrave Macmillan, 2001.

Life. "Berchtesgaden: U.S. Fighter Bombers Pay a Visit to Adolf Hitler's Mountain Home." March 19, 1945, 34.

———. "Blowup at Berchtesgaden." June 2, 1952, 41–42.

———. "Letters to the Editors." November 20, 1939, 2, 4.

———. "The Liberation of Gertrude Stein." October 2, 1944, 83–84.

———. "Paintings by Adolf Hitler: The Statesman Longs to Be an Artist and Helps Design His Mountain Home." October 30, 1939, 52–58.

———. "Speaking of Pictures: Jugend um Hitler." December 6, 1937, 6–7, 9.

Linge, Heinz. "I Was Hitler's Valet—VIII: Hitler Hoped to Retire and Marry Eva." *Daily Boston Globe,* November 6, 1955.

———. "Valet Upsets Love Scene between Hitler and Eva." *Los Angeles Times,* November 6, 1955.

———. *With Hitler to the End.* Translated by Geoffrey Brooks. London: Frontline; New York: Skyhorse, 2009.

Living Age. "The German Scene: I. Hitler's Palace in the Clouds." Translated from the *Telegraaf* (Amsterdam). March 1939, 32–33.

Lloyd George, David. "I Talked to Hitler." *Daily Express,* September 17, 1936.

[Lochner, Louis P.]. "Hitler's Safe Holds Only 'Mein Kampfs.'" *New York Times,*

May 12, 1945.

Lochner, Louis P. "Adolf Hitler's Retreat Symbolizes His Entire Work—It Is a Wreck." *Emporia Gazette* (Kansas), May 7, 1945.

———. "Der Fuehrer's Thoughts Now up in the Clouds." *Hartford (Conn.) Courant,* March 19, 1939.

———. "Faces of Hopeful GI's Fall as Hitler's Safe Is Opened." *Milwaukee Journal,* May 11, 1945.

———. "Hitler Looks to Aides Not in Public Eye: Widows Troost and Wagner Help Der Führer Woo the Muses." *Baltimore Sun,* September 4, 1938.

———. "Hitler's Chalet Was Like Lavish Castle." *Big Spring (Tex.) Daily Herald,* May 10, 1945.

———. "Nazis' Hideouts Ready in Mountains: Wild Terrain, Loyal Guards Could Delay War Criminals' Doom." *Washington Post,* February 25, 1945.

Löhr, Hanns Christian. *Das Braune Haus der Kunst und der "Sonderauftrag Linz."* Berlin: Akademie, 2005.

Los Angeles Times. "Allies Destroy 905 Nazi Planes." April 17, 1945.

———. "Bavaria Seals Hitler's 'Eagle's Nest' Bunkers." August 28, 1966.

———. "Dynamite Parcel 'Sent' to Hitler." September 13, 1943.

———. "Goering's Looted Art Treasure on Exhibit." May 21, 1945.

———. "Hitler Gets His Hideout Prepared." June 30, 1944.

———. "Yanks Uncover Vast Goering Loot Operations." May 14, 1945.

Losch, Roland. "New Exhibit Details Hitler's Mountain Retreat." *Atlanta Constitution,* October 21, 1999.

Low, David. *Years of Wrath: A Cartoon History, 1932–1945.* London: Gollancz, 1949.

Lukacs, John. *The Hitler of History.* New York: Knopf, 1997.

M., D. "Gerüchte aus Marmor." *Berchtesgadener Anzeiger,* March 6–7, 2010.

M. -M., jr. "Frau Troost und Balthasar Neumann." *Süddeutsche Zeitung,* February 25–26, 1950.

Machtan, Lothar. "Hitler, Röhm and the Night of the Long Knives." *History Today* 51, no. 11 (2001): 5–17.

Maiolo, Joseph A. *The Royal Navy and Nazi Germany, 1933–39: A Study in Appeasement and the Origins of the Second World War.* Basingstoke, UK: Macmillan, 1998.

Malcolm, Janet. *Two Lives: Gertrude and Alice.* New Haven, Conn.: Yale University Press, 2007.

Manchester (UK) Guardian. "Bavaria's Fascists." February 8, 1923.

———. "Nazi Looting in Poland." March 2, 1940.

———. "Pervasive Madness." January 30, 1923.

Mansfield (Ohio) News-Journal. "Hitler's Former Mountain Retreat Still Center of Attention." December 25, 1949.

Margolis, Jonathan. "My Night on Evil Mountain." *Independent,* March 9, 2005.

Martynkewicz, Wolfgang. *Salon Deutschland: Geist und Macht 1900–1945.* Berlin: Aufbau, 2009.

Matthews, Herbert. "Fliers Who Hit Berchtesgaden Didn't Know Hitler Lives There." *New York Times,* February 23, 1945.

———. "P-47 Fliers Punish Berchtesgaden; Rip Traffic at Hitler's Hideaway." *New York Times,* February 22, 1945.

McCrum, Robert, and Taylor Downing. "The Hitler Home Movies." *Observer Magazine,* January 27, 2013, 20–25.

McDaniel, Toni. "A 'Hitler Myth'? American Perception of Adolf Hitler, 1933–1938." *Journalism History* 17, no. 3 (1990): 46–53.

McKie, David. *Bright Particular Stars: A Gallery of Glorious British Eccentrics.* London: Atlantic, 2011.

McKinstry, Leo. *Lancaster: The Second World War's Greatest Bomber.* London: Murray, 2009.

McManus, John C. *American Courage, American Carnage: 7th Infantry Chronicles.* New York: Forge, 2009.

Mehringer, Hartmut. *Waldemar von Knoeringen: Eine politische Biographie.* Munich: Saur, 1989.

Meng, Michael. *Shattered Spaces: Encountering Jewish Ruins in Postwar Germany and Poland.* Cambridge, Mass.: Harvard University Press, 2011.

Merrill, Jean. "Hitler's Life at Berchtesgaden: Australian Has Tea with the Fuhrer, Writes Impressions." *Advertiser* (Adelaide), September 17, 1938.

Merrill du Cane, Jean. "Tea with Hitler: His Bavarian Mountain Home." *Nambour Chronicle,* July 8, 1938.

Michaud, Eric. *The Cult of Art in Nazi Germany.* Stanford, Calif.: Stanford University Press, 2004.

Middlebrook, Martin, and Chris Everitt. *The Bomber Command War Diaries*. Rev. ed. Leicester: Midland, 1996.

Miller, Lee. "Hitleriana." *Vogue* (UK), July 1945, 37, 72–74.

Miller, Marjorie. "Nazi Symbol to Return to German Hands." *Los Angeles Times,* February 3, 1995.

Mitchell, Arthur H. *Hitler's Mountain: The Führer, Obersalzberg and the American Occupation of Berchtesgaden.* Jefferson, N.C.: McFarland, 2007.

Moeller, Robert G. *War Stories: The Search for a Usable Past in the Federal Republic of Germany.* Berkeley: University of California Press, 2001.

Monahan, Laurie. "Waste Management: Hitler's Bathtub." *Journal of Surrealism and the Americas* 5, nos. 1–2 (2011): 98–119.

Moor, Paul. "The Old Order: Berchtesgaden Seven Years After." *Harper's Magazine,* December 1952, 57–67.

Moore, Michaela Hoenicke. *Know Your Enemy: The American Debate on Nazism, 1933–1945.* New York: Cambridge, 2010.

Morning Herald (Hagerstown, Md.). "She Has Hitler's Silverware." July 17, 1945.

Mosley, Charlotte, ed. *The Mitfords: Letters between Six Sisters.* New York: Harper, 2007.

Muhlen, Norbert. *The Return of Germany: A Tale of Two Countries.* Chicago: Regnery, 1953.

Münchner Post. "Eine rätselhafte Affäre: Selbstmord der Nichte Hitlers." September 21, 1931.

Münchner Post. "Eine rätselhafte Affäre: Selbstmord der Nichte Hitlers." September 22, 1931.

Münkler, Herfried. *Die Deutschen und ihre Mythen.* Berlin: Rowohlt, 2009.

Murphy, William. "FitzGerald, (Thomas Joseph) Desmond." *Dictionary of Irish Biography: From the Earliest Times to the Year 2002,* edited by James McGuire and James Quinn, 820–24. Vol. 3. Cambridge: Cambridge University Press and Royal Irish Academy, 2009.

Muthesius, Stefan. *The Poetic Home: Designing the 19th-Century Domestic Interior.* New York: Thames and Hudson, 2009.

Neillands, Robin. *The Bomber War: Arthur Harris and the Allied Bomber Offensive, 1939–1945.* London: Murray, 2001.

Nerdinger, Winfried, ed. *Bauhaus-Moderne im Nationalsozialismus: Zwischen Anbiederung und Verfolgung.* Munich: Prestel, 1993.

———, ed. *Ort und Erinnerung: Nationalsozialismus in München.* Salzburg: Pustet, 2006.

Neuerbourg, Hanns. "Kilroy's Been at Hitler's Aerie." *Washington Post,* July 31, 1966.

Neul, Josef. *Adolf Hitler und der Obersalzberg.* Rosenheim: Deutsche, 1997.

Neumann, Conny. "Nazi-Bauten: Adolfs Platten." *Der Spiegel,* March 31, 2010, 50–51.

Neumann, Klaus. *Shifting Memories: The Nazi Past in the New Germany.* Ann Arbor: University of Michigan Press, 2000.

Neven-du Mont, Jürgen. "Kleine Geschäfte mit verblichenem Glanz." *Süddeutsche Zeitung,* July 11, 1951.

———. "Propagandazelle Obersalzberg." *Münchner Illustrierte,* no. 28 (1951): 31.

New Age. "America's Day." February 27, 1919, 282.

Newsday (Long Island, N.Y.). "Claims Goering 'Bought' Treasure Trove." May 21, 1945.

Newsweek. "Hitler at Bavarian Retreat." March 2, 1935, 12–13.

New York Times. "15,000 on Train See Surrender Papers." November 6, 1945.

———. "Capture of Kerch Claimed in Berlin." May 17, 1942.

———. "Coup Fear Takes Halifax to London." August 20, 1939.

———. "The Developments in Europe." August 20, 1939.

———. "Effigies of Hitler Hung in Yorkville." October 16, 1942.

———. "German Fascist Chief Prospers." November 3, 1929.

———. "Hitler Bunker Shut to Bar Profiting." August 28, 1966.

———. "Hitler Eyrie Held Mentality Symbol." December 24, 1939.

———. "Hitler's Alpine Hideaway Is a Tourist Town's Gold Mine." August 24, 1980.

———. "Hitler's Taste Shows Wagnerian Influence." May 19, 1935.

———. "The Hour of Suspense." March 30, 1944.

———. "House That Hitler Built." August 9, 1951.

———. "'Liberated' Nazi Loot." June 10, 1945.

———. "Links to Hitler Enrage Unions of Paperhangers." May 27, 1937.

———. "Luftwaffe Is 'Out.'" April 17, 1945.

———. "One Year—: Where Britain and Germany Give Blow for Blow." September 1, 1940.

———. "Our Role Abroad: A German Report

Is Contradicted." March 31, 1940.

———. "Pontiff Still Sees a Chance for Peace." August 20, 1939.

———. "Reich Exhibits Articles Banned for Bad Taste." June 8, 1935.

———. "Says Hitler's Father Changed Name from Schuecklgruber." April 9, 1932.

———. "War Moves Go On." August 20, 1939.

New York Times Magazine. "Hitler His Own Architect: He Practices His Art on a Simple Chalet." October 13, 1935, 15.

Nicholas, Lynn H. *The Rape of Europa.* New York: Vintage, 1995.

Niedersachsen-Stürmer. "Der Wasserkopf als Salzstreuer: Eine bemerkenswerte Säuberungsaktion der Reichskunstkammer." October 31, 1936, 7.

Niven, Bill, and Chloe Paver, eds. *Memorialization in Germany since 1945.* Basingstoke, UK: Palgrave Macmillan, 2010.

North American Review. "By Way of Introduction." 225, no. 5 (1928): n.p.

Northedge, F. S. *The Troubled Giant: Britain among the Great Powers, 1916–1939.* New York: Praeger, 1966.

Nüsslein, Timo. "Gerdy Troost: Urkunden und kunsthandwerkliche Arbeiten, 1937–1945." *Militaria,* no. 4 (2011): 128–36.

———. *Paul Ludwig Troost, 1878–1934.* Vienna: Böhlau, 2012.

Observer. "Hitler at Home: A Country Gentleman." December 15, 1935.

———. "R. A. F. Destroying Civilian Morale in Germany." January 16, 1944.

Oechsner, Frederick C. "Hitler Fantasies Foster His Legend." *New York Times,* June 9, 1942.

Ogan, Bernd, and Wolfgang W. Weiss, eds. *Faszination und Gewalt: Zur politischen Ästhetik des Nationalsozialismus.* Nurnberg: Tümmels, 1992.

Orosz, Eva-Maria. "Der Makart-Stil: Ein Atelier als Vorbild für das Wiener Interieur." In *Makart: Ein Künstler regiert die Stadt,* edited by Ralph Gleis, 116–25. Munich: Prestel; Vienna: Wien Museum, 2011.

Ottomeyer, Hans. "Vorwort." In *Hitler und die Deutschen: Volksgemeinschaft und Verbrechen,* edited by Hans-Ulrich Thamer and Simone Erpel, 13–14. Berlin: Deutsches Historisches Museum; Dresden: Sandstein, 2010.

Ottomeyer, Hans, and Alfred Ziffer. *Möbel des Neoklassizismus und der Neuen Sachlichkeit.* Munich: Prestel, 1993.

Ozturk, Anthony. "Interlude: Geo-Poetics: The Alpine Sublime in Art and Literature, 1779–1860." In *Heights of Reflection: Mountains in the German Imagination from the Middle Ages to the Twenty-First Century,* edited by Sean Ireton and Caroline Schaumann, 77–97. Rochester, N.Y.: Camden House, 2012.

Pampa (Tex.) Daily News. "Austin Family to Use Hitler's Silverware." August 2, 1945.

Panton, Silkirk. "Hitler's New Hide-Away." *Current History* 50, nos. 71–72 (1939): 51–52.

Pariser Tageszeitung. "Hitlers Bergfestung in Berchtesgaden." June 21, 1937.

Penrose, Antony, ed. *Lee Miller's War.* London: Thames and Hudson, 2005.

Peterborough. "Baroque." *Daily Telegraph,* April 25, 1935.

Peters, C. Brooks. "In Hitler's Chalet." *New York Times Magazine,* March 16, 1941, 9, 21.

Peters, Olaf, ed. *Degenerate Art: The Attack on Modern Art in Nazi Germany, 1937.* New York: Neue Galerie; Munich: Prestel, 2014.

Peterson, Amy T., and Ann Kellogg, eds. *The Greenwood Encyclopedia of Clothing through American History 1900 to the Present.* 2 vols. Westport, Conn.: Greenwood, 2008.

Petropoulos, Jonathan. *Art as Politics in the Third Reich.* Chapel Hill: University of North Carolina Press, 1996.

———. *The Faustian Bargain: The Art World in Nazi Germany.* New York: Oxford, 2000.

———. "Postwar Justice and the Treatment of Nazi Assets." In *Gray Zones: Ambiguity and Compromise in the Holocaust and Its Aftermath,* edited by Jonathan Petropoulos and John K. Roth, 325–38. New York: Berghahn, 2006.

———. *Royals and the Reich: The Princes von Hessen in Nazi Germany.* New York: Oxford University Press, 2006.

Petropoulos, Jonathan, and John K. Roth, eds. *Gray Zones: Ambiguity and Compromise in the Holocaust and Its Aftermath.* New York: Berghahn, 2006.

Petsch, Joachim. "Möbeldesign im Dritten Reich und die Erneuerung des Tischler-Gewerbes seit dem ausgehenden 19. Jahrundert." In *Design in Deutschland 1933–45: Ästhetik und Organisation des Deutschen Werkbundes im "Dritten Reich,"* edited by Sabine Weissler, 42–55. Giessen: Anabas, 1990.

Phayre, Ignatius [W. G. Fitz-Gerald]. *Can America Last?* London: Murray, 1933.

———. "Hitler as a Countryman: The 'Squire' of Wachenfeld." *Country Life,* March 8, 1936, 322–24.

———. "Hitler at Home." *Saturday Review,* March 21, 1936, 362–63.

———. "Hitler at Home: 'Squire' among His Dogs." *West Australian* (Perth), August 7, 1937.

———. "Hitler Says His Dogs Are Real Friends." *American Kennel Gazette,* January 1, 1937, 5–7, 164.

———. "Hitler's Mountain Home: A Visit to 'Haus Wachenfeld,' in the Bavarian Alps." *Homes and Gardens,* November 1938, 193–95.

———. "Holiday *with* Hitler: A Personal Friend Tells of a Personal Visit with Der Führer—with a Minimum of Personal Bias." *Current History* 44, no. 4 (1936): 50–58.

———. "Italy's Military Problems in Abyssinia." *English Review* 61 (1935): 270–81.

———. "Japan's 'World-War' in Trade." *Quarterly Review* 264, no. 523 (1935): 1–21.

———. "The League's 'Black Baby.'" *North American Review* 238, no. 3 (1934): 237.

———. "The Man of Peru." *North American Review* 225, no. 843 (1928): 564–68.

———. "Race-Hatred in the United States." *Observer,* August 3, 1919.

———. "The Slave-Trade To-Day." *English Review* 60 (1935): 55–65.

———. "With Herr Hitler in His Holiday Home." *Windsor Magazine,* June–November 1936, 35–51.

Picker, Henry. *Hitlers Tischgespräche im Führerhauptquartier.* Berlin: Ullstein, 1997.

Pine, Lisa. *Education in Nazi Germany.* Oxford: Berg, 2010.

———. *Nazi Family Policy, 1933–1945.* Oxford: Berg, 1997.

Ploch, Arthur. "Das Bild als Ware." *Deutsche Presse* 24, no. 17 (1934): 8–12.

Pogge, Ernst. "Der Berghof: Das Heim des Führers." *Elegante Welt,* April 14, 1939, 18–26, 52.

Prager Tageblatt. "Hitlers Stiefschwester und die rituelle Küche." September 27, 1931.

Prölss-Kammerer, Anja. *Die Tapisserie im Nationalsozialismus: Propaganda, Repräsentation und Produktion.* Hildesheim: Olms, 2000.

Pröse, Tim. "Daheim bei Hitler." *Focus,* May 7, 2007, 122–27.

Pünder, Hermann [Staatssekretär der Reichskanzlei], ed. *Zur Geschichte des Reichskanzlerpalais und der Reichskanzlei.* Berlin: Zentralverlag, 1928.

Ransom, Tina. "Secret Weapons to Go on Display in Victory Loan Special on Nov. 21." *Atlanta Constitution,* November 9, 1945.

Rapport, Leonard, and Arthur Northwood, Jr. *Rendezvous with Destiny: A History of the 101st Airborne Division.* Washington, D.C.: Infantry Journal, 1948.

Rasp, Hans-Peter. "Bauten und Bauplanung für die 'Hauptstadt der Bewegung.'" In *München: "Hauptstadt der Bewegung,"* edited by Richard Bauer, Hans Günther Hockerts, Brigitte Schütz, et al., 294–99. Munich: Münchner Stadtmuseum, 2002.

Rauschning, Hermann. *The Voice of Destruction.* New York: Putnam, 1940.

Reichel, Peter. *Der schöne Schein des Dritten Reiches.* Hamburg: Eilert and Richter, 2006.

Reinhold, Kurt. "Der Unwiderstehliche." *Das Tagebuch,* May 28, 1932, 837–40.

Remme, Tilman. "Life with Hitler and His Mistress." *Daily Telegraph,* September 27, 1997.

Rentschler, Eric. *The Ministry of Illusion: Nazi Cinema and Its Afterlife.* Cambridge, Mass.: Harvard University Press, 1996.

Retallack, Joan, ed. *Gertrude Stein: Selections.* Berkeley: University of California Press, 2008.

———. "Introduction." In *Gertrude Stein: Selections,* edited by Joan Retallack, 3–84. Berkeley: University of California Press, 2008.

Rolinek, Susanne, Gerald Lehner, and Christian Strasser. *Im Schatten der Mozartkugel: Reiseführer durch die braune Topografie von Salzburg.* Vienna: Czernin, 2009.

Roos, Peter. "Hitlerconti: Im Luxushotel auf dem Obersalzberg am 20. April." *Die Zeit,* April 28, 2005.

Rosenbaum, Ron. *Explaining Hitler.* New York: Random House, 1998.

Rosenblum, Robert. *Modern Painting and the Northern Romantic Tradition: Friedrich to Rothko.* New York: Harper and Row, 1975.

Rosenfeld, Gavriel D. "Memory and the Museum: Munich's Struggle to Create a Documentation Center for the History of National Socialism." In *Beyond Berlin: Twelve German Cities Confront the Nazi Past,* edited by Gavriel D. Rosenfeld and Paul B. Jaskot, 163–84. Ann Arbor: University of Michigan Press, 2008.

———. *Munich and Memory: Architecture,*

Monuments, and the Legacy of the Third Reich. Berkeley: University of California Press, 2000.

Rosenfeld, Gavriel D., and Paul B. Jaskot, eds. *Beyond Berlin: Twelve German Cities Confront the Nazi Past.* Ann Arbor: University of Michigan Press, 2008.

Rützow, Sophie. "Betreuerin eines Vermächtnisses: Gerdy Troost und Ihr Wirken." *Münchner Neueste Nachrichten,* July 25, 1937.

Ryback, Timothy W. "The Hitler Shrine." *Atlantic Monthly,* April 2005, 131–34.

———. *Hitler's Private Library.* New York: Vintage, 2008.

Ryback, Timothy, and Florian M. Beierl. "A Damnation of Memory." *New York Times,* February 12, 2010, and *International Herald Tribune,* February 13, 2010.

Saturday Review. "America of To-Day." December 7, 1918, 1132–33.

———. "The Shrine of Sebekh." January 27, 1912, 118.

Sawyer-Lauçanno, Christopher. *The Continual Pilgrimage: American Writers in Paris, 1944–1960.* New York: Grove, 1992.

Sax, Boria. *Animals in the Third Reich.* Providence: Yogh and Thorn, 2013.

Schad, Martha. *Sie liebten den Führer: Wie Frauen Hitler verehrten.* Munich: Herbig, 2009.

Schäfer, Hans Dieter. *Das gespaltene Bewußtsein: Vom Dritten Reich bis zu den langen Fünfziger Jahren.* Göttingen: Wallstein, 2009.

Schaffing, Ferdinand. *Der Obersalzberg: Brennpunkt der Zeitgeschichte.* Munich: Langen and Müller, 1985.

Schaub, Julius. *In Hitlers Schatten: Erinnerungen und Aufzeichnungen des Chefadjutanten, 1925–1945.* Edited by Olaf Rose. 2nd ed. Stegen am Ammersee: Druffel and Vowinckel, 2010.

Schirach, Baldur von. *Ich glaubte an Hitler.* Hamburg: Mosaik, 1967.

Schirach, Henriette von. *Frauen um Hitler.* Munich: Herbig, 1983.

Schläder, Jürgen, and Robert Braunmüller. *Tradition mit Zukunft: 100 Jahre Prinzregententheater München.* Feldkirchen bei München: Ricordi, 1996.

Schlenker, Ines. *Hitler's Salon: The Grosse Deutsche Kunstausstellung at the Haus der Kunst in Munich, 1937–1944.* Oxford: Peter Lang, 2007.

Schmölders, Claudia. *Hitler's Face: The Biography of an Image.* Translated by Adrian Daub. Philadelphia: University of Pennsylvania Press, 2006.

Schnöller, Martin. "Malerfürsten im 19. Jahrhundert: Hans Makarts Atelier in Wien, die Villen von Franz Lenbach und Franz Stuck in München." In *Künstlerhäuser von der Renaissance bis zur Gegenwart,* edited by Eduard Hüttinger, 195–218. Zurich: Waser, 1985.

Schönberger, Angela. *Die Neue Reichskanzlei von Albert Speer.* Berlin: Gebr. Mann, 1981.

Schöner, Hellmut, ed. *Das Berchtesgadener Land im Wandel der Zeit: Ergänzungsband I zu dem 1929 erschienenen Werk von A. Helm.* Berchtesgaden: Verein für Heimatkunde des Berchtesgadener Landes, 1982.

Schöner, Hellmut, and Rosl Irlinger. *Der alte Obersalzberg bis 1937: Dokumentation über die durch Zwangsaufkauf und Abbruch zerstörte ursprüngliche Besiedlung.* Berchtesgaden: Berchtesgadener Anzeiger, 1989.

Schoppmann, Claudia. *Zeit der Maskierung: Lebensgeschichten lesbischer Frauen im "Dritten Reich."* Berlin: Orlanda: 1993.

Schroeder, Christa. *He Was My Chief.* Translated by Geoffrey Brooks. London: Frontline, 2009.

Schultz, Sigrid. "Nazis Angered by Mundelein's Blow at Hitler." *Chicago Daily Tribune,* May 20, 1937.

———. "Tribune Writer Visits Hitler's Two Love Nests." *Chicago Daily Tribune,* May 10, 1945.

Schultze-Naumburg, Paul. *Das Gesicht des Deutschen Hauses.* Munich: Callwey, 1929.

———. *Kunst und Rasse.* Munich: Lehmanns, 1928.

Schuster, Karl. *Weisse Berge, Schwarze Zelte. Eine Persienfahrt.* Munich: Gesellschaft Alpiner Bücherfreunde, 1932.

Schuster-Winkelhof, Karl. *Adolf Hitlers Wahlheimat.* Munich: Münchner, 1933.

Schwarz, Birgit. *Geniewahn: Hitler und die Kunst.* Vienna: Böhlau, 2009.

Schwartz, Frederic. *The Werkbund: Design Theory and Mass Culture before the First World War.* New Haven, Conn.: Yale University Press, 1996.

Scotsman. "Police Trace Organisation of Bomb-Throwers: Ringleaders Caught." September 12, 1929.

Seckendorff, Eva von. "Monumentalität und

Gemütlichkeit: Die Interieurs der NSDAP-Bauten am Königsplatz." In *Bürokratie und Kult: Das Parteizentrum der NSDAP am Königsplatz in München,* edited by Iris Lauterbach, Julian Rosefeldt, and Piero Steinle, 119–46. Munich: Deutscher Kunstverlag, 1995.

Seerwald, Michael E. *Gipfel der Macht? Hitlers Teehaus am Kehlsteinhaus.* Berchtesgaden: Beierl, 2007.

Seidel, Klaus Jürgen, ed. *Das Prinzregenten-Theater in München.* Nuremberg: Schoierer, 1984.

Selig, Wolfram. *"Arisierung" in München: Die Vernichtung jüdischer Existenz 1937–1939.* Berlin: Metropol, 2004.

Sereny, Gitta. *Albert Speer: His Battle with Truth.* New York: Random, 1996.

Shirer, William. "Shirer Says Germans Blame Hitler for Russian Disaster." *Daily Boston Globe,* January 2, 1944.

Sigmund, Anna Maria. *Die Frauen der Nazis.* Munich: Heyne, 2005.

Silberspiegel. "Die Neuen Räume der Reichskanzlei." May 25, 1937, 524–26.

Silverman, Dan P. *Hitler's Economy: Nazi Work Creation Programs, 1933–1936.* Cambridge, Mass.: Harvard University Press, 1998.

Silverman, Debra. *Art Nouveau in Fin-de-Siècle France: Politics, Psychology and Style.* Berkeley: University of California Press, 1989.

Simpson, Hedwig Mauer. "Herr Hitler at Home in the Clouds." *New York Times Magazine,* August 20, 1939, 5, 22.

Sions, Harry. "Berchtesgaden." *Yank: The Army Weekly,* June 22, 1945, 2–4.

Sontag, Susan. "Fascinating Fascism." *New York Review of Books,* February 6, 1975, 23–30.

Speer, Albert. *Inside the Third Reich.* Translated by Richard and Clara Winston. New York: Touchstone, 1997.

Spitzy, Reinhard. *So haben wir das Reich verspielt: Bekenntnisse eines Illegalen.* Munich: Langen Müller, 1986.

Spotts, Frederic. *Hitler and the Power of Aesthetics.* Woodstock, N.Y.: Overlook, 2002.

St[einlein], G. "Berghof Wachenfeld auf Obersalzberg, das Heim unseres Führers." *Bauzeitung* 34, no. 33 (1937): 457–61.

Stachura, Peter D. "The Political Strategy of the Nazi Party, 1919–1933." *German Studies Review* 3, no. 2 (1980): 261–88.

Stadler, Matthew. "Hitler's Rooms." *Nest: A Magazine of Interiors,* Fall 2003, 62–81.

Stankiewitz, Karl. *Prachtstrassen in München: Brienner und Prinzregentenstrasse.* Dachau: Bayerland, 2009.

Stead, Ronald. "Germans Clear Debris." *Christian Science Monitor,* June 28, 1945.

———. "Hitler's Berchtesgaden Turns into 'Coney Island.'" *Christian Science Monitor,* July 5, 1945.

———. "Nuremberg: Grim Housing Shortage." *Christian Science Monitor,* July 2, 1945.

Stein, Gertrude. "Now We Are Back in Paris." *Compass: Current Reading* (December 1945): 56–60.

———. "Off We All Went to See Germany." *Life,* August 6, 1945, 54–58.

Steinberg, Rolf. *Nazi-Kitsch.* Darmstadt: Melzer, 1975.

Steinweis, Alan E. *Kristallnacht 1938.* Cambridge, Mass.: Harvard University Press, 2009.

Stinglwagner, Gerhard. *Von Mönchen, Prinzen und Ministern: Das Gebäude des Landwirtschaftsministeriums und seine Nachbarschaft.* Munich: Bayerisches Staatsministerium für Ernährung, Landwirtschaft und Forsten, 1991.

Storey, Walter Rendell. "Novel Decorations for a Great Liner: The Europa's Color Scheme and Furnishings Are Subdued Modernism." *New York Times,* April 6, 1930.

Stratigakos, Despina. "'I Myself Want to Build': Women, Architectural Education and the Integration of Germany's Technical Colleges." *Paedagogica Historica* 43, no. 6 (2007): 727–56.

———. "Women and the Werkbund: Gender Politics and German Design Reform, 1907–14." *Journal of the Society of Architectural Historians* 62, no. 4 (2003): 490–511.

———. *A Women's Berlin: Building the Modern City.* Minneapolis: University of Minnesota Press, 2008.

Stumberger, Rudolf. "Die Luft wird dünner." *Welt am Sonntag,* July 12, 2009.

Sturz, James. "Evil for Sale: The Market for Nazi Memorabilia Is Thriving." *New York Times Magazine,* November 28, 1993, 70–72.

Südost-Kurier. "Problem Obersalzberg und Kehlstein vor der Lösung." August 4, 1951.

Swett, Pamela E., Corey Ross, and Fabrice d'Almeida, eds. *Pleasure and Power in Nazi Germany.* Houndmills, UK: Palgrave Macmillan, 2011.

WORKS CITED

Sylvester, Albert James. *The Real Lloyd George.* London: Cassell, 1947.

Symons, Mitchell. "The Hitler Hotel Has No Room for a Sense of Shame." *Daily Express,* September 6, 2002.

Tagliabues, John. "Construction at Nazi Death Camp Site Stirs Protest." *New York Times,* July 21, 1991.

Tange, Andrea Kaston. *Architectural Identities: Domesticity, Literature, and the Victorian Middle Classes.* Toronto: University of Toronto Press, 2010.

Tauber, Kurt P. *Beyond Eagle and Swastika: German Nationalism since 1945.* 2 vols. Middletown, Conn.: Wesleyan University Press, 1967.

Taylor, Henry J. "Berchtesgaden." *Los Angeles Times,* May 22, 1945.

Tennant, Ernest William Dalrymple. *True Account.* London: Parish, 1957.

Thalhofer, Robert L. *Company A! Combat Engineers Remember World War II.* Bloomington, Ind.: Xlibris, 2010.

Thamer, Hans-Ulrich, and Simone Erpel, eds. *Hitler und die Deutschen: Volksgemeinschaft und Verbrechen.* Berlin: Deutsches Historisches Museum; Dresden: Sandstein, 2010.

Thiede, Klaus. *Deutsche Bauernhäuser.* Königstein im Taunus: Langewiesche, 1934.

Thies, Jochen. *Hitler's Plans for Global Domination: Nazi Architecture and Ultimate War Aims.* Translated by Ian Cooke and Mary-Beth Friedrich. New York: Berghahn, 2012.

Time. "Adolf and Ignatz." January 1, 1934, 13–14.

———. "Bless Me Natzi!" January 8, 1934, 21.

———. "Peeved Paperhangers." June 7, 1937, 15.

Times-Colonist (Victoria, B.C.). "Art from Hitler's Lair." August 7, 2005.

Times Literary Supplement. "Can America Last?" April 5, 1934, 245.

Toland, John. *Adolf Hitler.* New York: Anchor, 1992.

Tolischus, Otto. "Hitler." *New York Times Magazine,* March 11, 1934, 2, 21.

———. "Where Hitler Dreams and Plans." *New York Times Magazine,* May 30, 1937, 1–2, 16.

Tooze, Adam. *The Wages of Destruction.* New York: Penguin, 2008.

Trevor-Roper, H. R., ed. *The Bormann Letters.* London: Weidenfeld and Nicolson, 1954.

———. *Hitler's Table Talk, 1941–1944: His Private Conversations.* Translated by Norman Cameron and R. H. Stevens. New York: Enigma, 2008.

Troost, Gerdy, ed. *Das Bauen im Neuen Reich.* 2 vols. Bayreuth: Gauverlag Bayerische Ostmark, 1939 and 1943.

Uhlir, Christian F., ed. *Im Schattenreich des Untersberges: Von Kaisern, Zwergen, Riesen und Wildfrauen.* Norderstedt: Books on Demand, 2004.

Umlauf, Hanni. *Zwischen Rhein und Ruhr.* Miesbach: Mayr, 1952.

U.S. Newswire. "'Homes and Gardens' Admits Publication of 1938 Pro-Hitler Article Was 'Appalling,' Drops Effort to Suppress Reprints." November 5, 2003.

V., Dr. M. "Typen des Kitsches erprobt in einem Wettbewerb des guten Geschmacks." *Deutsches Handwerk* 7, no. 2 (1938): 21–23.

Vinen, Richard. *The Unfree French: Life under the Occupation.* New Haven, Conn.: Yale University Press, 2006.

Vogue (U.S.). "Mussolini, Hitler, and Eden—In Retreat." August 15, 1936, 70–71.

Völkischer Beobachter. "Deutsche Künstler vom Führer ausgezeichnet." April 21, 1937.

Vorwärts. "Der Vielgeknipste: Adolf in allen Lebenslagen." March 19, 1932.

Voss, Frederick S. *Reporting the War: The Journalistic Coverage of World War II.* Washington, D.C.: Smithsonian Institution, 1994.

W., I. v. "Aus der Arbeit von Frau Prof. Troost." *Völkischer Beobachter,* July 15, 1937.

Wagner, Friedelind, and Page Cooper. *Heritage of Fire: The Story of Richard Wagner's Granddaughter.* New York: Harper, 1945.

Wagner, Jens-Christian. *Produktion des Todes: Das KZ Mittelbau-Dora.* Göttingen: Wallstein, 2001.

Wagner, Thomas. "Yad Vashem, Simon Wiesenthal Center Blast English Auction House's Sale of Hitler Paintings." *Jerusalem Post,* September 28, 2006.

Wagnon, Hugh. "Britain's Hopes for Future Personified in Churchill." *Washington Post,* December 31, 1940.

———. "Churchill Devotes 17 Hours a Day to His Only Hobby—War." *Washington Post,* December 30, 1940.

Waldman, Simon. "At Home with the Führer." *Guardian,* November 3, 2003.

Wales, Henry. "Yanks' Looting in Reich Called Major Problem." *Chicago Daily Tribune,*

May 14, 1945.

Walther, Christoph, and Karl-Ulrich Gelberg. "Nationalsozialistische Aussenpolitik in München und das Münchner Abkommen." In *München: "Hauptstadt der Bewegung,"* edited by Richard Bauer, Hans Günther Hockerts, Brigitte Schütz, et al., 378–91. Munich: Münchner Stadtmuseum, 2002.

Ward Price, George. *I Know These Dictators.* London: Harrap, 1937.

Washington Post. "Hitler's 'Love Nest' to Be Razed." November 4, 1951.

———. "Yanks Uncover 5 Billions in Nazi Treasure." June 20, 1945.

Weber, Eugen. *The Hollow Years: France in the 1930s.* New York: Norton, 1994.

Webster, David Kenyon. "We Drank Hitler's Champagne." *Saturday Evening Post,* May 3, 1952, 25, 135–38.

Weissler, Sabine. *Design in Deutschland 1933–45: Ästhetik und Organisation des Deutschen Werkbundes im "Dritten Reich."* Giessen: Anabas, 1990.

Welt Kompakt. "Millionengrab auf dem Obersalzberg." May 26, 2009.

Welt-Spiegel (Sunday supplement of the *Berliner Tageblatt*). "Der Führer im Haus der Deutschen Kunst." July 18, 1937, cover page.

Werckmeister, O. K. "Hitler the Artist." *Critical Inquiry* 23, no. 2 (1997): 270–97.

Werner, Bruno E. "Der Führer und seine Architekten." *die neue linie,* April 1939, 25–32.

Westheim, Paul. "Die janze Richtung passt ihm nicht: Hitler 'säubert' das 'Haus der Kunst.'" *Pariser Tageszeitung,* July 17, 1937.

Whittier-Ferguson, John. "The Liberation of Gertrude Stein: War and Writing." *Modernism/Modernity* 8, no. 3 (2001): 405–28.

Wichmann, Hans. *Die Neue Sammlung: Ein neuer Museumstyp des 20. Jahrhunderts.* Munich: Prestel, 1985.

Wilderotter, Hans. *Alltag der Macht: Berlin Wilhelmstrasse.* Berlin: Jovis, 1998.

Will, Barbara. *Unlikely Collaboration: Gertrude Stein, Bernard Faÿ, and the Vichy Dilemma.* New York: Columbia University Press, 2011.

Williams, Carol J. "Resort Bids to Balance Past, Future." *Los Angeles Times,* July 29, 2001.

Williams, J. Emlyn. "Allied Armies Intent upon Dealing Quickly with Nazi Redoubt." *Christian Science Monitor,* April 26, 1945.

Williamson, Gordon. *Knight's Cross and Oak-Leaves Recipients, 1941–45.* Oxford: Osprey, 2005.

Wilson, Kristina. *Livable Modernism.* New Haven, Conn.: Yale University Press, 2004.

Woolf, Virginia. "Great Men's Houses." 1932. Reprinted in Virginia Woolf. *The London Scene: Five Essays,* 23–29. New York: Hallman, 1975.

Wuttke-Groneberg, Walter. *Medizin im Nationalsozialismus.* Rottenburg: Schwäbische, 1982.

Yeide, Nancy H. *Beyond the Dreams of Avarice: The Herman Goering Collection.* Dallas: Laurel, 2009.

Zekri, Sonja. "Berge versetzen: Natur als Machtinstrument." *Süddeutsche Zeitung,* May 19, 2010.

Ziemke, Earl F. *The U.S. Army in the Occupation of Germany, 1944–1946.* Washington, D.C.: Center of Military History, U.S. Army, 1975.

Ziffer, Alfred. *Nymphenburger Moderne.* Eurasburg: Minerva, 1997.

Zimmermanns, Klaus. *Friedrich August von Kaulbach, 1850–1920.* Munich: Prestel, 1980.

Zox-Weaver, Annalisa. *Women Modernists and Fascism.* New York: Cambridge University Press, 2011.

ARCHIVAL SOURCES

Bayerische Staatsbibliothek, Munich
Bayerisches Hauptstaatsarchiv, Munich
Berlinische Galerie, Berlin
Bundesarchiv Berlin-Lichterfelde
Bundesarchiv-Filmarchiv, Berlin
Deutsches Historisches Museum, Berlin
Duquesne University Archives, Pittsburgh, Pa.
Franklin D. Roosevelt Library, Hyde Park, N.Y.
Harry S. Truman Library and Museum, Independence, Mo.
Institut für Zeitgeschichte, Munich
Lee Miller Archives, Farley Farm House, Muddles Green, Chiddingly, East Sussex, UK
Library of Congress, Washington, D.C.
Lokalbaukommission München
National Archives, College Park, Md.
National Archives, Kew, Richmond, Surrey, UK
Staatsarchiv München
Stadtarchiv München
University of Arizona, Special Collections, Tucson
Vereinigte Werkstätten für Kunst im Handwerk, Amira Verwaltungs AG, Munich
The Wolfsonian–Florida International University, Miami Beach

INDEX

renovation of, 35–38; dining room, 38–41,
37, 41, 98; financing of renovation, 27; floor
plans, *32–33, 36–37,* 320n27; furnishings
of, 31, 32–33, 34, 35, 39, 40, 42, 43, 44, 45,
46; Hitler's deterioration claims about, 23,
24–27, 30, 31, 319n4; Hitler's objectives in
renovation of, 30–31; imperial and Weimar
renovations to, 26–27, 31, 36–37; library,
34, 35, 41–42; office, *44,* 45; Paul Troost's
design for, 28, 29, 30, 38–39, *41,* 42, *43,* 44,
45, 98, 111; Persian carpet in, 32–33, 320n33;
private apartment in, 30, *33, 35,* 41–43,
42; Reception Building extension, 45–46;
Reception Hall renovation, 31–34, *36, 38,*
46; Smoking Room, *40,* 41, 87; study, 41,
42; Waiting Room (foyer), 34–35, *39;* Winter
Garden, 40, 45
Olympic Games of 1936, 47, 196, 212
Operation Barbarossa, 86
Ōshima, Hiroshi, 242

Pariser Tageszeitung, 184
Parsifal, 61
Partner, Therese, 305
Paul, Bruno, 18
Pavelić, Ante, 242
People's Theater (Prince Regent Theater),
Munich, 61
Persian carpets, 32–33, 58, 121, 320n33
Pesne, Antoine, 92
Peters, C. Brooks, 226–227
Pfeiffer-Bechstein, Lotte, 144–145
Phayre, Ignatius. *See* Fitz-Gerald, William
George
Photography: of Braun, 96, 97, 99;
Hoffmann's collector albums, 185;
Hoffmann's images of pilgrimages, 169, 173–
174, *175,* 176, *183,* 218; Hoffmann's postcards,
156, *159,* 182, 183, 185, *247–249, 254, 256,* 293;
souvenir albums, 292–293, *294,* 340n37
Pilgrimages to Obersalzberg: encounters
with Hitler, 169–171, 173–174, 176, 237;
Hoffmann's photographs of, 173–174, *175,*
183, 218; national unity manifested by, 176;
neo-Nazi, 303–304, 305, 309, 310; problems
caused by, 171; as promised land, 160,
182–184
Pius XII, Pope, 219
Platterhof Hotel, 72, 292, 305, 309, 311, 341n54
Poland: invasion of, 64, 136, 220, 231, 240;
plunder of valuables from, 277–278, 283
Popp, Franz, 15, *16,* 50
Postcards, of Hitler's domestic life, 156, *159,*
160, 183, *247–249, 254, 256,* 293

Press, English-language, 2; on artistic
ambitions/tastes of Hitler, 221–225, *222;*
audience for Hitler's domesticity stories,
2, 194–195, 197, 198, 201, 207–208, 317;
on Berghof bombing raid, 260–263; on
Berghof design, 216, 218, 223–224, 226; on
Berghof wartime isolation and estrangement,
235–239, *237, 238;* comparison of Hitler/
Churchill personality and character, 227–
230; comparison of Hitler/Eden/Mussolini
domestic spaces, 209, *210–211,* 212–213; on
domestic tastes and pursuits of Hitler, 197–
198, 200–202, 229–231, 316; on Gerdy Troost,
113, 128, 130; Hoffmann's photographs of
Hitler's domesticity in, 156, 159, 316; idyllic
views of Hitler's domestic life in, 194–220,
199, 210, 214, 316–317; inaccurate/plagiarized
content in, 203–207, 335–336n67; on
InterContinental Berchtesgaden Resort,
307–308; on Kehlsteinhaus (Eagle's Nest),
239–242; on Nazi plunder, 277–278,
282–283; neutral tone about Hitler in, 159,
225, 227; paperhanger cartoons of Hitler in,
231–232, *232, 233,* 234–235, *236;* on postwar
demolition of Obersalzberg ruins, 300, 301,
302, 303; postwar search of Hitler's houses,
267–276, *269, 272, 273,* 278–280; on Prince
Regent Square apartment, 58, 60–61; shift
from positive assessments of Hitler, 225, 231,
236–239
Press, German: on Berghof's interior design,
187–189; critique of private Hitler myth,
155–156, 184–185; on early life of Hitler,
233–234; in exile, 133, 184; on Gerdy Troost,
127–128, *129,* 133, 138, 146, 187–188; on Hitler
in private life, 19–21, 154–155, 159–160,
178, 184–185; on postwar demolition of
Obersalzberg ruins, 296–297, 298–299, 300,
303; on postwar Hitler tourism, 295–296,
298–299; suppression of *Frankfurter Zeitung,*
114–115
Prince Carl Palace, Munich, 61, 63, 121–122, *123*
Prince Regent Square apartment, Munich, *16,*
204; artworks in, 59, 60, 62, 66; bedrooms,
49, 55, *272,* 280, 313; British press coverage
of, 58, 60; building purchased by Hitler,
65; bunker at, 65, 279–280, 313; cost of
renovations, 48, 58; cultural refinement
conveyed by, *56,* 60–61, 66; elevation
drawing of *52–53, 54–55,* floor plan of, 15,
16–17, 50–51, 54; furniture/fittings of, 15, 18,
49, 56–58, 59, 312; Geli Raubal's room at, 49,
57, 313; Geli Raubal's suicide at, 11, 19–21,
280; household members at, 20, 48–49, 54,

White Mountains, Black Tents (Schuster-
    Winkelhof), 162
White, Willard, 276
Wide World, 206
Wiener Sonn-und-Montags-Zeitung, 233–234
Wiener Werkstätte, 40
Windsor, Duke and Duchess of, 265
Windsor Magazine, 194
Winter, Anni, 48, 49, 54, 56, 57, 270, 313, 321n5
Winter, Georg, 48–49, 54, 56, 57, 313, 321n5
Winter, Otto, 13
Winter Garden, Old Chancellery, 40, 45
Winter-Wachenfeld, Margarete, 13, 69
Withers, Audrey, 271–272
Wolf's Lair, 3, 103, 137
Woolf, Virginia, 209
World War II: Berghof as military
    headquarters in, 3, 103; bombing raid on
    Obersalzberg, 258–266, *263, 264, 270;* forced
    labor during, 123, 125, 192, 193; Hitler's
    redecorating projects during, 66–67;
    invasion of Poland, 64, 136, 220, 231, 240;
    invasion of Soviet Union, 66–67, 86, 234,
    235; military exemptions, 124; occupation of
    France, 243–244, 288–289, 290; Operation
    Barbarossa, 86; outbreak of, 136–137, 219,
    220, 227, 231; plunder of occupied countries,
    125, 277–278, 282–283
Wyman (David S.) Institute for Holocaust
    Studies, 317

Yank magazine, 1, 268
Youth around Hitler (Hoffmann), 156, 174, *175,*
    177–178

Zabel, Werner, 130
Ziegler, Adolf, 144, 223
Zychski (Göring's house manager), 295

ILLUSTRATION CREDITS

The photographers and the sources of visual material other than the owners indicated in the captions are as follows. Every effort has been made to supply complete and correct credits; if there are errors or omissions, please contact Yale University Press so that corrections can be made in any subsequent edition.

Fig. 2. NSDAP-Baupläne 8395, Bayerisches Hauptstaatsarchiv, Munich

Fig. 4. NSDAP-Baupläne 11244, Bayerisches Hauptstaatsarchiv, Munich

Fig. 5. 146–1991–078–19A, Digital Picture Archive, Bundesarchiv

Figs. 6, 8–14. LOT 3940 (H) [P&P], Library of Congress, Washington, D.C., Prints and Photographs Division

Fig. 7. NSDAP-Baupläne 11243, Bayerisches Hauptstaatsarchiv, Munich

Fig. 15. NSDAP-Baupläne 6132, Bayerisches Hauptstaatsarchiv, Munich

Fig. 16. Author

Fig. 17. NSDAP-Baupläne 8374, Bayerisches Hauptstaatsarchiv, Munich

Fig. 18. NSDAP-Baupläne 6134, Bayerisches Hauptstaatsarchiv, Munich

Fig. 19. Image Collection, Bayerisches Hauptstaatsarchiv, Munich

Fig. 20. Heinrich Hoffmann and Albert Burckhard Müller, *Tag der Deutschen Kunst* (Diessen am Ammersee: Raumbild, 1937)

Figs. 21–24. BPL Berchtesgaden, Staatsarchiv München

Fig. 25. 146–1991–077–31, Digital Picture Archive, Bundesarchiv

Fig. 26. 242-HB, Album 15, B1082, Heinrich Hoffmann Collection, National Archives, College Park, Maryland

Fig. 27. TD 1991.223.15, Paul Troost Papers, The Mitchell Wolfson, Jr. Collection, The Wolfsonian–Florida International University, Miami Beach

Fig. 28. TD 1991.222.25, Paul Troost Papers, The Mitchell Wolfson, Jr. Collection, The Wolfsonian–Florida International University, Miami Beach

Fig. 29. Courtesy of Hoover Institution Library and Archives, Stanford University, California

Fig. 30. TD 1991.223.24, Paul Troost Papers, The Mitchell Wolfson, Jr. Collection, The Wolfsonian–Florida International University, Miami Beach

Fig. 31. 242-EB-12–2, Eva Braun Photographic Albums, National Archives, College Park, Maryland

Fig. 32. 242-EB-6–26, Eva Braun Photographic Albums, National Archives, College Park, Maryland

Fig. 33. OBB KuPl 5465, Bayerisches Hauptstaatsarchiv, Munich

Fig. 34. OBB KuPL 5454, Bayerisches Hauptstaatsarchiv, Munich

Fig. 35. OBB KuPL 5458, Bayerisches Hauptstaatsarchiv, Munich

Figs. 36, 38. Private collection

Fig. 37. LOT 8625 (G) [P&P], Library of Congress, Washington, D.C.

Fig. 39. 242-HK-685, National Archives, College Park, Maryland

Fig. 43. Deutsches Historisches Museum, Berlin

Fig. 53. *Innen-Dekoration* 49, no. 5 (1938): 168

Figs. 58–60. MS 243, series 5, volume 2, Karen Kuykendall Papers, Special Collections, University of Arizona, Tucson

Fig. 61. MS 243, series 5, volume 4, Karen Kuykendall Papers, Special Collections, University of Arizona, Tucson

Fig. 62. MS 243, series 5, volume 3, Karen Kuykendall Papers, Special Collections, University of Arizona, Tucson

Figs. 63, 67, 68. © Lee Miller Archives, England, 2014. All rights reserved.

Fig. 64. 239-PA-8–76–2, National Archives, College Park, Maryland

Fig. 65. David Kenyon Webster, "We Drank
   Hitler's Champagne," *Saturday Evening Post,*
   May 3, 1952, 25. Courtesy U.S. Army.
Fig. 66. Courtesy Dean Rodina
Fig. 70. NL Ehard 781, Bayerisches
   Hauptstaatsarchiv, Munich

Plate 1. Image Collection, Bayerisches
   Hauptstaatsarchiv, Munich
Plates 2–4, 9. Private collection
Plate 5. 68881, Heinrich Hoffmann
   Photographic Archive, Bayerische
   Staatsbibliothek, Munich
Plates 6–8. Gerdy Troost Papers, Ana 325
   A.V.4, Bayerische Staatsbibliothek, Munich
Plate 10. 26211, Heinrich Hoffmann
   Photographic Archive, Bayerische
   Staatsbibliothek, Munich
Plate 11. 260-NSA-37, National Archives,
   College Park, Maryland
Plates 12, 13. Courtesy of *FOCUS Magazin,*
   Munich